DOCUMENTS OF
American Catholic History

DOCUMENTS OF
American Catholic History

EDITED BY
John Tracy Ellis

VOLUME 2
1866 to 1966

MICHAEL GLAZIER
Wilmington Delaware

About the Editor

John Tracy Ellis is Professorial Lecturer in Church History in the Catholic University of America. He is a member of the American Catholic Historical Association and the American Society of Church History. Throughout his career he has received many honors. In 1978 he was honored with the Laetare Medal of the University of Notre Dame—an award presented to the outstanding contributor to the life of the Church in the United States. Monsignor Ellis has written seventeen books over the course of his career and he is best known for *The Life of James Cardinal Gibbons, Archbishop of Baltimore, 1834-1921* (2 volumes); and *American Catholicism.*

Published in 1987 by Michael Glazier, Inc., 1935 West Fourth Street, Wilmington, Delaware 19805 ● ©Copyright 1987 by John Tracy Ellis ● All rights reserved

Library of Congress Cataloging-in-Publication Data

Documents of American Catholic History
Volumes 1-2 are reprints   Originally published:
Chicago : H. Regnery Co., 1967.   Vol. 3 is a new work.

   Includes bibliographies and index.
   Contents: v.1. 1493-1865 — v. 2. 1866-1966 —
v. 3. 1966-1986.
   1. Catholic Church—United States—History—
Sources.
2. United States—Church history—Sources I. Ellis,
John Tracy, 1905-
BX1405.D63 1987   282'.73   86-80801
ISBN 0-89453-611-7 (vol. 1)
       0-89453-612-5 (vol. 2)
       0-89453-588-9 (vol. 3)

Printed in the United States of America.

Contents

93804

viii   *Contents*

114. The Bishops and the Catholic Press, October 21, 1866

FROM the birth of the Catholic Press in 1822 (see document no. 69) it had been in good measure a private lay enterprise, although a number of priests and a few bishops were also involved. At times the espousal by the lay editors of various European political causes, to say nothing of domestic issues, caused a certain uneasiness in clerical circles lest the Church be identified with positions which were essentially those of the lay editors alone. In this connection, John Hughes, Archbishop of New York, was especially strong-minded as is exemplified in the pastoral letter he composed and which was published (October 8, 1854) at the close of the First Provincial Council of New York. Hughes was at pains to warn the faithful against the supposition that

> every paper which advocates, or professes to advocate, the Catholic re-ligion. . . . is, as a matter of course, under the direction of the priests and bishops in the locality where it is published, and consequently author-ized to speak for and in the name of the Catholic Church. [John R. G. Hassard, *Life of the Most Reverend John Hughes, First Archbishop of New York* (New York: D. Appleton and Co., 1966), pp. 368-369.]

It was not surprising that the seven archbishops and thirty-eight bishops who attended the Second Plenary Council of Baltimore should have devoted a section of their pastoral letter to what they termed, "On Books and News-papers—The Press." In this instance, however, there was a more positive note with an attempt to show appreciation of what those working in the press had done for the Church and the handicaps under which they had labored. The hope that the bishops entertained for the Catholic Publication Society founded the previous year by the superior of the Paulist Fathers was never realized, nor was the relationship between bishops and editors notably improved in the years after the council. This was one of the principal reasons why the Catholic newspapers of the United States were more and more absorbed by the ordinaries of most dioceses which, in turn, led to the largely "official" press which exists today. Source: Peter Guilday (ed.), *The National Pastorals of the American Hierarchy, 1792-1919* (Washington: National Catholic Welfare Conference, 1923), pp. 213-214.

The Council of Trent requires that all books which treat of Religion should be submitted before publication to the Ordinary of the Diocese in which they are to be published for the purpose of obtaining his sanction, so as to assure the faithful that they contain nothing contrary to faith or morals. This law is still of force; and in the former Plenary Council (1852) its observance was urged, and the Bishops were exhorted to approve of no book which had not been previously examined by themselves, or by clergymen appointed by them for that purpose, and to confine such approbation to works published in their respective dioceses. The faithful should be aware that such approbation is rather of a negative than a positive character; that it by no means imparts to the statements or sentiments such works may contain any episcopal sanction; but merely guarantees them as free from errors in faith or morals.

In many of our dioceses there are also published Catholic papers, mostly of a religious character; and many of such papers bear upon them the statement that they are the "organs" of the Bishop of the diocese in which they are published, and sometimes of other Bishops in whose dioceses they circulate. We cheerfully acknowledge the services the Catholic Press has rendered to Religion, as also the disinterestedness with which, in most instances, it has been conducted, although yielding to publishers and editors a very insufficient return for their labors. We exhort the Catholic community to extend to these publications a more liberal support, in order that they may be enabled to become more worthy of the great cause they advocate.

We remind them that the power of the press is one of the most striking features of modern society; and that it is our duty to avail ourselves of this mode of making known the truths of our Religion, and removing the misapprehensions which so generally prevail in regard to them. If many of these papers are not all that we would wish them to be, it will be frequently found, that the real cause of their shortcomings is the insufficient support they receive from the Catholic public. Supply and demand act and react on each other; and if in many instances the former produces the latter, in regard at least to Catholic publications, demand must precede supply. We also wish to guard against the misapprehension, which frequently arises from the Bishop's name being connected with such papers, insofar as they are recognized as "organs," that is, as mediums through which the Ordinary communicates with his diocesans. This circumstance gives no sanction to the articles which appear in such papers, other than that which they may derive from the name of the writer when given: still less does it identify the Bishop with the paper, so as to justify the conclusion that whatever appears in it has his sanction and authority. It merely designates the paper as one in which the Bishop will cause to be inserted such official documents as he, from time to time, may have to publish, and in regard to which it is obviously desirable that there should be some regular mode of communication.

In connection with this matter we earnestly recommend to the Faithful of our charge the Catholic Publication Society, lately established in the City of New York by a zealous and devoted clergyman (Isaac T. Hecker, C.S.P.). Besides the issuing of short tracts, with which this Society has begun, and which may be so usefully employed to arrest the attention of many whom neither inclination nor leisure will allow to read larger works, this Society contemplates the publication of Catholic books, according as circumstances may permit, and the interests of Religion appear to require. From the judgment and good taste evinced in the composition and selection of such tracts and books as have already been issued by this Society, we are encouraged to hope that it will be eminently effective in making known the truths of our Holy Religion, and dispelling the prejudices which are mainly owing to want of information on the part of so many of our fellow-citizens. For this, it is necessary that a generous co-operation be given, both by clergy and laity, to the undertaking, which is second to none in importance, among the subsidiary aids which the inventions of modern times supply to our Ministry for the diffusion of Catholic Truth.

115. Bishop McQuaid Describes the Vatican Council, April 24, 1870

DURING the Vatican Council which was in session from December 8, 1869, to July 18, 1870, forty-six Americans — six archbishops, thirty-nine bishops, and one abbot — were numbered among the nearly 700 prelates from every part of the world who at one time or another were in attendance at this first ecumenical council of the Church since that of Trent over 300 years before. On the great issue of defining papal infallibility the Americans were as divided as the hierarchies of other nations, and on January 15, 1870, twenty-one bishops from the United States joined with about 120 bishops from other countries in signing a petition against the definition. Among the most persistent members of the minority party was Bernard J. McQuaid (1823–1909) who had been consecrated on July 12, 1868, as first ordinary of the new See of Rochester. During the council McQuaid wrote a number of lengthy letters to the Reverend James M. Early, vicar-general and rector of St. Patrick's Cathedral, Rochester, in which he discoursed on council business, as well as on affairs of his diocese. He arrived in Rome on November 26, 1869, and five days later he remarked to Early:

Since coming to Europe I have heard much on the question of the infallibility of the Pope, which with us in America was scarcely talked of. The feeling is very strong, *pro* and *con*. It seems that the Jesuits have

been at the bottom of it, and have been preparing the public mind for
it for the past two years. They have not made friends for themselves by
the course they have followed, and if in any way the harmony of the
Council is disturbed it will be by the introduction of this most unnecessary
question (December 1, 1869).

McQuaid remained opposed to the definition to the very end and the day
before he left Rome he told Early:

Tomorrow the public session will be held in which the final voting on
the Infallibility will take place. They have ended by making the definition as absolute and strict as it was possible to make it. As a consequence
a large *non-placet* vote will be recorded against it. What will be the consequence in some· of these European countries God only knows (July
17, 1870).

The bishop's prediction of the *non-placet* vote on July 18 proved to be
wide of the mark, only two of the 535 bishops present voting against the
definition. Although he had received permission on July 16 to return home,
McQuaid was still in Rome on the day of the final session but he absented
himself on that occasion. Shortly after his arrival in Rochester, however, he
delivered a sermon on August 28, 1870, in his cathedral in which he made a
public proclamation of his faith in the newly defined dogma. Source:
McQuaid to Early, Rome, April 24, 1870, Henry J. Browne (Ed.), "The
Letters of Bishop McQuaid from the Vatican Council," *Catholic Historical
Review*, XLI (January, 1956), 423–427.

Rome, April 24, 1870

Dear Father Early:

I have just returned from the first public session of the Council,[1]
and having some spare time I thought I would send you a few lines.

You will doubtless have read all that we have done in the papers
before this letter reaches you. The matter consists of an introductory
chapter, & four chapters with canons attached. Chap. I. is on God,
the Creator of all things: Chap. II. is on Revelation: Chap. III. on
Faith: Chap. IV. on Faith and Reason.

There are some obstruse metaphysical points which few can fathom
and certainly will never trouble the brains of any but a German
Philosopher for whose especial benefit they seem to have been made.
The rest is quite simple Theology. Yet it was wonderful the care
that was needed and the pains taken to make every thing just as it
ought to be.

The Decrees and Canons were passed unanimously. I know of only
one Bishop who, having objections to some points and not wishing

---

[1] Strictly speaking, the public session held on April 24, 1870, was the third,
not the first of the council, but it was the first at which decrees were passed. The
first public session took place on December 8, 1869, with Pope Pius IX in
attendance.

to break the unanimity of the voting, remained away and did not attend. The sight in the Council Hall was very beautiful. It was the first time that the Bishops appeared in red copes. The rich bright color contrasting with the simple white mitres had a charming effect. There was no great crowd compared with the crowds of Holy Week and Easter Sunday. On the last named day the crowd in the piazza of St. Peter's numbered from 100 to 150 thousand people. It is only in Rome that such mixed crowds can be gathered, and it is only in Rome that such orderly, quiet, pleasant and *gentlemanly* crowds can be found. What I have seen in this regard has filled me with amazement, not only at religious ceremonies but at public gatherings for festivities.

There will be a great exodus from Rome after today. The ceremonies, illuminations, and now the first promulgation of decrees are over, the visitors of all kinds and classes will leave us.[2] Several American Bishops leave this week, although some will not go home directly. I stay to fight the great battle if it should come up. We ourselves know little of what we shall have to do next. We may take up the second part of the first *Schema de Fide,* and we may pass at once to the *Schema de Ecclesia,* taking the question of the Infallibility first of all and out of its place. Some Bishops are urging the Holy Father to have this done; on the other hand, the difficulties in the way of such a definition are so many and so serious that there is some hesitation. Opposed to the definition are so many Bishops of unquestionable devotion to the Holy See, who will vote a *non-placet* if it should come before them that men stop to think. Besides the governments of Europe are alarmed.[3] They remember that Popes in the past absolved subjects from their allegiance and in many ways interfered with governments. Even in our country there will arise more or less difficulty on this head. At least politicians will try to use the difficulty against us.

Yet with all these reasons weighing against the definition I am

---

[2] McQuaid alluded here to the ceremonies of Easter Week which ended that year on Low Sunday, April 24. The bishops wore red copes because the Mass on Low Sunday was in honor of the Holy Spirit.

[3] The threat of intervention in the council by the governments of Bavaria, Great Britain, and France seemed very real at the time that McQuaid was writing. The spearhead of the attack was Comte Napoléon Daru, Minister of Foreign Affairs of France and a Catholic. Oddly enough, the tension was broken by the Protestant premier, Emile Ollivier, who took over the portfolio of foreign affairs after Daru had resigned for other reasons. Ollivier was sympathetic to the Church and the council and at once reversed Daru's policy of intervention. Cf. Cuthbert Butler, *The Vatican Council* (London, 1930), II, 16–25.

inclined to think that it will pass in some modified form. The Holy Father wishes it, and lets every one see that he does, the Jesuits are as busy as bees of late and the French Bishops of that way of thinking are as enthusiastic and excitable over the subject as they well can be.

My hope is that in the definition the Pope will in some [way] be connected with the Church. I cannot conceive of a living head without a body. However, I must not enter into the vexed question, which has been such a disturbance to my mind since I came to Rome that once it is disposed of one way or another I will never want to hear of its controversy again.

Should the discussion begin this coming week the cable will have informed you of it before this reaches you.

Monday, the 25th.

I resume my letter this morning. Since writing the above I learn as certain that the next point for discussion is to be the old one of the "little Catechism." Some are opposed to a uniform little Catechism for one reason, others for another. It is not a question that troubles me much, as the Catechism itself can be reconstructed as often as they find it expedient until they get one that will be satisfactory. The reason alleged for a general one is that uniformity may be obtained. But whilst saying this, they at the same time contradict themselves, as each Bishop will still be allowed to have larger ones for his own Diocese and according to its peculiar needs. Hence we at once get back to our old condition. So long as the same faith is taught, the less interference in such matters, the better is my judgment. The rumor has it that the Infallibility question will follow next.

I have been amused at reading in the Freeman's Journal what he [James A. McMaster, the editor] has to say about the Council. He draws all his facts or supposed facts from the London Tablet and Vatican.[4] Many of those *facts* amuse us at the power of invention, if not of malice, they display.

No one here has been able to discover the representative of "Jus."[5]

---

[4] *The Tablet* of London had been acquired in November, 1868, by Herbert Vaughan (1832–1903), the future cardinal, who shared the infallibilist views of his superior, Henry Edward Manning (1808–1892), Archbishop of Westminster. By "Vatican" McQuaid was referring to a series of special supplements brought out by the *Tablet* under the title of *The Vatican: A Weekly Record of the Council* which contained documents and reports from Rome but never printed any letters on the side of the inopportunists or opponents of the definition of papal infallibility.

[5] "Jus" was one of several anonymous writers of the New York *Freeman's Journal* whom McMaster had as fairly regular correspondents. "Jus" was the Reverend Eugene M. O'Callaghan (d. 1901) who held a number of pastorates

We can only laugh at the tone of the Freeman. It is probable that when his agitation dies out that Bishops themselves will take up the matter and see what can be done, in justice to the interests of religion as well as of Priests. The matter only once came up in a meeting of the American Bishops and on that occasion the only difficulty in the way of giving it examination was McMaster's agitation. . . .

Bp. Purcell leaves for home in a few days; worried almost to death by the trouble of the Infallibility question;[6] Bp. Bayley[7] leaves today; he is only too glad to get away from the fight. In fact, some of the strongest opponents of the Infallibility are leaving.[8] The Americans, of course, cannot return should the question come up, whilst the Europeans will be back in time.

After many an effort I obtained the receipt for the money given to the Holy Father by the Diocese. On the 18th. of March I received a letter in reply to the address of the Priests. I will forward the letter and the receipt by Father Hecker[9] who leaves Rome on Wednesday.

---

in the Diocese of Cleveland during these years. In 1869 he was pastor of St. Columba's Church, Youngstown, and by 1870 was listed as the pastor of Ashtabula, Ohio. O'Callaghan had trouble with Amadeus Rappe (1801–1877), first Bishop of Cleveland, and was one of the leading agitators for canonical legislation that would regulate the relations between bishops and their priests.

[6] John B. Purcell (1800–1883) was consecrated in October, 1833, as second Bishop of Cincinnati and became first archbishop of that see in July, 1850. Purcell was one of the strongest inopportunists among the American delegation to the council, and was opposed to the definition of the doctrine of infallibility itself until it was clearly stated what was meant. At a reception which was given for him in Mozart Hall, Cincinnati, on August 21, 1870, a few days after his return from Rome, he publicly read the definition and professed his faith in it; he likewise wrote a letter to Pius IX on December 5, 1870, signifying his acceptance of the decree.

[7] James Roosevelt Bayley (1814–1877) was first Bishop of Newark, 1853–1872, and eighth Archbishop of Baltimore, 1872–1877. Actually Bayley returned to Rome after a visit to Paris and left the Eternal City only on July 18 in company with McQuaid.

[8] Seven American prelates, including McQuaid, registered a *non-placet* in the crucial trial vote of the general congregation on July 13. At the final vote on July 18 all but two of these absented themselves, namely, William G. McCloskey (1823–1909), Bishop of Louisville, who voted *placet* and Edward Fitzgerald (1833–1907), Bishop of Little Rock, who voted *non-placet*. Fitzgerald and Bishop Luigi Riccio of Cajazzo in the former Kingdom of Naples were the only two among the 535 prelates voting who returned a *non-placet*. Fitzgerald made his profession of faith in the newly defined dogma, however, to Pius IX personally immediately after the close of the public session on July 18.

[9] Isaac T. Hecker, C.S.P. (1819–1888), founder of the Paulists, was theologian to Archbishop Martin J. Spalding of Baltimore during the council. He also acted as a liaison between the American bishops and the Germans, and he was especially close to Friedrich Cardinal Schwarzenberg (1809–1885), Archbishop of Prague, who was one of the most vigorous leaders of the minority which had opposed the definition of the infallibility of the pope.

You can, if you please, have the letter translated and published. It comes so long after date, and so long after others presented at the same time, that I feel by no means pleased. . . .

Direct your letters to the American College as I call there every day and I am no longer at the Minerva, having left the hotel last week. I have taken the rooms occupied by Father Quinn.[10] They are large and pleasantly situated. The family are kind, obliging and not obtrusive. I pay but 6 francs a day for three rooms. At the Hotel I paid 4½ for one small bed room in the fourth story, here called the third. My breakfast is served to me in my room, and I go to a restaurant for my dinner, at about 3 o'clock & at a cost of from 2 to 4 francs, according to my appetite or my extravagance.

Father De Regge[11] ought to be back with you about the time you receive this letter. There is an Italian I intend to send to you. I am undecided whether I shall send him at once or keep him until I go myself. It is probable that I shall send him in a few days.

You are aware that Father O'Hara[12] passed his examination and obtained his degree of D.D. Dr. O'Hara! henceforth, if you please. Unfortunately just after all his hard study, on his return from Naples to which he went for a few days, he was taken down with the Roman fever. He has been very sick, but is at the present out of danger and recovering rapidly. He had a great start out of that piece of waggery in the papers appointing a Bishop to Syracuse.[13] As the story was told to him he was not able to see that it was a joke and attached importance to it.

Dr. Anderson[14] of New York has also been quite ill — is getting better. Father Healey [sic][15] late of Troy Seminary, was at death's door for days — he is now well. He was confined to bed for nearly a month. They tell us that such a winter has not been known in the memory of that famous individual, to be found here as well as in

---

[10] An effort to identify Quinn was unsuccessful.

[11] Hippolyte de Regge was pastor of Our Lady of Victory Church, Rochester, a French congregation, in 1869 and was named chancellor of the diocese in 1870.

[12] This would seem to have been James O'Hara, pastor of St. Mary's Church in Syracuse.

[13] The Diocese of Syracuse was not erected until November 22, 1886.

[14] William Henry Anderson (1799–1875), professor of astronomy in Columbia College, New York, had been converted to Catholicism in 1849.

[15] Alexander Sherwood Healy (1836–1875) acted as theologian to Bishop John J. Williams of Boston during the council. He was later rector of the Cathedral of the Holy Cross, and when his brother, James A. Healy (1830–1900), was named second Bishop of Portland in February, 1875, he succeeded him in the pastorate of St. James Church, Boston, but died a few months thereafter.

America — "the oldest inhabitant." Bp. Ryan[16] has kept very well — seems to fatten up a little.

I see the papers have published the rescript of the Holy Father permitting the use of the Holy Oils of last year. I did not send it to you because I thought it just as well to get supplied with fresh oil and be done with the matter for this year.

A good word for me to all my good friends in the Diocese. Indeed it has been a good thing for me to be absent so long as it has caused me to think so much more of home and all my friends, priests and people in it. I thought a great deal of you during Holy Week, whilst I had such an easy time here.

Very sincerely your friend in Xt.,

B. J. McQuaid

116. Grant's Proposal and Blaine's Amendment to Prevent Public Funds for Religious Schools, September 29 – December 14, 1875

EVER since Bishop Hughes' New York school controversy of the 1840's the issue of public aid for private religious schools has been more or less a perennial one in American history. In 1875 the Republican Party found itself on the defensive by reason of the widespread corruption during the two terms of Ulysses S. Grant (1822–1885). In spite of that fact, however, Grant wanted a third term, and in an effort to head off the reform element in his own party, and likewise to distract the voters from the Democrats who were then staging a comeback, he chose to inject the highly controversial question of public funds to private schools into the campaign. In a speech to a reunion of the Army of the Tennessee at Des Moines on September 29, 1875, he raised the issue, following it up on December 7 with a proposal for an amendment to the Constitution that would forbid all public funds for religious schools. Grant's proposal was framed into a joint resolution of both houses of Congress by James G. Blaine (1830–1893), a representative from Maine, who on December 14, 1875, introduced what came to be called the Blaine Amendment. Catholics were aroused, and with the *Kulturkampf* then in full swing against the Church in Germany, James O'Connor declared the move "eminently Bismarckian" ("Anti-Catholic Prejudice," *American Catholic Quarterly Review,* I [January, 1875], 17). The Blaine resolution passed the House without serious trouble in August, 1876. In the Senate a substitute amendment was framed which contained an additional clause permitting the reading of the Bible in the public schools, but here the resolution failed to gain the necessary two-thirds ma-

---

[16] Stephen V. Ryan, C.M. (1826–1896), was consecrated in November, 1868, as second Bishop of Buffalo.

jority. Both parties mentioned the subject in their national platforms, the Republicans coming out for an amendment while the Democrats hedged by proclaiming their support of public education but leaving it to the states to regulate. Sources: Frank A. Burr, *A New, Original and Authentic Record of the Life and Deeds of General U. S. Grant* (St. Paul: Empyreal Publishing House, 1885), pp. 871–872; *Congressional Record*, 44th Congress, 1st Session (Washington, 1876), IV, 175, 205.

Grant's Speech to the Army of the Tennessee, Des Moines, September 29, 1875.

. . . In this centennial year of our national existence, I believe it is a good time to begin the work of strengthening the foundation of the house commenced by our patriotic forefathers one hundred years ago at Concord and Lexington. Let us all labor to add all needful guarantees for the more perfect security of free thought, free speech and free press, pure morals, unfettered religious sentiments, and of equal rights and privileges to all men irrespective of nationality, color or religion. Encourage free schools, and resolve that not one dollar of money appropriated to their support, no matter how raised, shall be appropriated to the support of any sectarian school. Resolve that neither the state or nation, nor both combined, shall support institutions of learning other than those sufficient to afford every child growing up in the land the opportunity of a good common-school education, unmixed with sectarian, pagan or atheistical dogmas. Leave the matter of religion to the family altar, the church and the private school supported entirely by private contribution. Keep the church and state forever separate. With these safeguards I believe the battles which created the Army of the Tennessee will not have been fought in vain. . . .

Grant's Message to Congress, December 7, 1875.

As we are now about to enter upon our second centennial — commencing our manhood as a nation — it is well to look back upon the past and study what will be best to preserve and advance our future greatness. From the fall of Adam for his transgression to the present day, no nation has even been free from threatened danger to its prosperity and happiness. We should look to the dangers threatening us, and remedy them so far as lies in our power. We are a republic whereof one man is as good as another before the law. Under such a form of government it is of the greatest importance that all should be possessed of education and intelligence enough to cast a vote with the right understanding of its meaning. A large association of ignorant men cannot, for any considerable period, oppose a successful resistance to tyranny and oppression from the educated few, but will inevitably sink into acquiescence to the will of intelligence, whether directed by the demagogue or by priestcraft. Hence the education of the masses becomes of the first necessity for the preservation of our institutions. They are worth preserving, because they have secured the greatest good to the greatest proportion of the population of any form of government yet devised. All other forms of government approach it just in proportion to the general diffusion of education and independence of thought and action. As the primary step, therefore, to our advancement in all that has marked our progress in the past century, I suggest for your earnest consideration — and most earnestly recommend it — that a constitutional amendment be submitted to the Legislatures of the several States for ratification making it the duty of the several States to establish and forever maintain free public schools adequate to the education of all the children in the rudimentary branches within their respective limits, irrespective of sex, color, birthplace, or religions; forbidding the teaching in said schools of religious, atheistic, or pagan tenets; and prohibiting the granting of any school funds, or school taxes, or any part thereof, either by the legislative, municipal, or other authority, for the benefit or in aid, directly or indirectly, of any religious sect or denomination, or in aid for the benefit of any other object of any nature or kind whatever.[1]

Blaine's Proposed Amendment, December 14, 1875.

Resolved by the Senate and House of Representatives, That the following be proposed to the several States of the Union as an amendment to the Constitution:

Article XVI

No State shall make any law respecting an establishment of religion or prohibiting the free exercise thereof; and no money raised by taxation in any State for the support of public schools, or derived from any public fund therefor, nor any public lands devoted thereto, shall ever be under the control of any religious sect, nor shall any money so raised or lands so devoted be divided between religious sects or denominations.

---

[1] Grant's message to Congress also contained the following proposal: "I would suggest the taxation of all property equally, whether church or corporation, exempting only the last resting-place of the dead, and possibly, with proper restrictions, church edifices" (*ibid.*). The New York League for the Separation of Church and State, founded in 1938, carried on its letterhead a picture of Grant and a phrase from his Des Moines speech as its slogan.

117. The Catholic Church Is Awarded the Pious Fund of the Californias, November 11, 1875

LATE in the seventeenth century the Jesuit missionaries received a number of private benefactions to help finance their difficult missions in Lower California. The fund grew to large proportions and when the Jesuits were expelled by Spain in 1767 it was taken over by the government and its income assigned to the Franciscans and Dominicans who had replaced the Jesuits in the missions. In 1821 Mexico revolted from Spain, secularized the California missions in the 1830's, and petitioned the Holy See for the establishment of a bishopric in California. In April, 1840, the Diocese of California was erected and the income from the Pious Fund was assigned to it as the heir to the missions. But due to a revolution in Mexico and the war with the United States no support was forthcoming. In an effort to adjust a number of disputed claims of Americans versus Mexicans and vice versa, the two governments signed a convention in 1868 which created a commission for their adjudication. Attempts of the commissioners to reach agreement on the Pious Fund failed and the case was then given over to an umpire, Sir Edward Thornton, British Ambassador to Washington. In 1875 Thornton decided in favor of the Church's claims. Mexico paid the award but refused to pay the accumulated interest. The dispute dragged on until 1902 when the two parties agreed to submit their differences to the new Permanent Court of International Arbitration at The Hague. In the first decision of the international tribunal on October 14, 1902, the justices ruled that Mexico should pay $1,420,682.67 in interest accumulated between 1869–1902, and an annual sum of $43,050 in perpetuity to begin in 1903. The Mexican government paid the interest and made the annual payment up to and including 1913, but no further payments have been made since that time, although the Department of State has more than once called attention to the matter. Source: James Brown Scott (Ed.), *The Hague Court Reports* (New York: Oxford University Press, 1916), pp. 48–53.

This case having been referred to the umpire for his decision upon a difference in opinion between the commissioners, the umpire rendered the following decision:

In the case of "Thaddeus Amat,[1] Bishop of Monterey, and Joseph S. Alemany,[2] Archbishop of San Francisco *vs.* Mexico" No. 493, it will be impossible for the umpire to discuss the various arguments which have been put forward on each side.

He will be able only to state the conclusions which he has arrived

---

[1] Thaddeus Amat, C.M. (1811–1878), of Spanish birth, was named second Bishop of Monterey on July 29, 1853.

[2] Joseph S. Alemany, O.P. (1814–1888), born in Spain, was consecrated Bishop of Monterey on June 30, 1850, and promoted to be first Archbishop of San Francisco on July 29, 1853.

at after a careful and lengthened study of all the documents which have been submitted to him.

He is about to give his decision with a profound sense of the importance of the case in accordance with what he considers to be just and equitable as far as he can rely upon his own judgment and conscience.

The first question to be considered is the citizenship of the claimants.

On this point the umpire is of opinion that the Roman Catholic Church of Upper California became a corporation of citizens of the United States on the 30th of May, 1848, the day of the exchange of ratifications of the Treaty of Guadalupe Hidalgo [ending the war between the United States and Mexico].

By the VIII Article of the treaty it was agreed that those Mexicans residing in the territories ceded by Mexico to the United States, who wished to retain the title and rights of Mexican citizens should be under the obligation to make their election within one year from the date of the exchange of the ratifications of the treaty; and that those who should remain in the said territories after the expiration of that year, without having declared their intention to retain the character of Mexicans, should be considered to have elected to have become citizens of the United States. It has not been shown that the Roman Catholic Church in Upper California had declared any intention of retaining its Mexican citizenship and it can not but be concluded that it had elected to assume the citizenship of the United States as soon as it was possible for it to do so, which in the opinion of the umpire was when Upper California was actually incorporated into the United States on the exchange of the ratifications of the Treaty of Guadalupe Hidalgo.

With regard to any claim which may have originated before that date the claimants could not have been entitled to appear before the mixed commission established by the Convention of July 4, 1868; but a claim arising after that date would come under the cognizance of the commission.

The claim now put forward is for interest upon the so-called "Pious Fund of the Californias." If this interest should have been paid to the Right Reverend Francisco Garcia Diego, the Bishop of California, before the separation of Upper California from the Republic of Mexico, it seems to the umpire that a fair proportion of it ought now and since the 30th of May, 1848, to be paid to the claimants, who in his opinion are the direct successors of that Bishop, as far as Upper California is concerned.

The "Pious Fund of the Californias" was the result of donations by various private persons for the purpose of establishing, supporting and maintaining Roman Catholic missions in California, and for converting to the Roman Catholic faith the heathens of that region. The disbursements of the proceeds of these donations was entrusted by the donors to the Society of Jesus. The object of the donors was without doubt principally the advancement of the Roman Catholic religion. The donations were made by private persons for particular and expressed objects and had nothing public, political or national in their character. Once permission was granted to the Jesuit fathers Salvatierra[3] and Kühu [sic][4] to establish missions in California, to take charge of the conversion to Christianity of the heathens, and to solicit alms for that purpose, it does not seem that the Spanish Government assisted them with any considerable sums, if any at all, and certainly with not so much as almost any Government would have considered itself bound to furnish for the benefit of a region over which it claimed dominion.

It can be easily understood that the Spanish Government was very glad to avail itself of the religious feelings of its subjects, and saw with great satisfaction that their donations would powerfully contribute to the political conquest of the Californias; but the object of the donors was the religious conquest alone, though they too might have felt some pride in the consciousness that they were at the same time contributing to the extension of the possessions of Spain.

The alms, however, solicited in the first instance by the Jesuit fathers, and the donations subsequently made by the piously disposed persons were neither political nor national; they were directed to the religious conquest of the Californias, and were the gifts of private persons for that particular object.

On the expulsion of the Jesuits from the Spanish Dominions, and the abolition of the Order, occurrences which the donors to the Pious Fund could not have foreseen, the Spanish Government naturally became the trustee and caretaker of that fund, but it took charge of it avowedly with all the duties and obligations attached to it. The missions were confided to the Franciscan Order, and subsequently they were divided between this Order and the Dominicans, but

---

[3] Juan Maria Salvatierra, S.J. (1648–1717), was one of the prime leaders in the evangelization of the Indian tribes of Lower California.

[4] Eusebius Kino, S.J. (1644–1711), was one of the greatest of all the Jesuit missionaries in colonial America. The principal scene of his labors was in northern Mexico and present-day Arizona. Kino's descriptions of his numerous and widespread explorations are of high scientific value.

although the Pious Fund was administered by the Spanish Government, its proceeds were applied to the maintenance of the missions belonging to both Orders.

When Mexico became independent she succeeded to the trust which had been held by the Spanish Government, and continued to apply the proceeds of the fund to the maintenance of the missions. In 1836 it was considered desirable to establish a Bishopric which was to comprise the two Californias.

An Act of Congress was passed for this purpose, and the same act entrusted to the Bishop, who was to be appointed, the administration and application of the Pious Fund in accordance with the wishes of its founders.

On the 8th of February, 1842, President Santa Anna[5] repealed the latter part of the Act of 1836 and assigned the administration and application of the fund to the Mexican Government, but the decree which he signed for this purpose also declared that the object of the donor was to be carried out by the civilization and conversion of the savages. On the 24th of October of the same year another decree was issued by the above-mentioned President to the effect that the real estate and other property of the Pious Fund were to be incorporated into the national treasury and were to be sold at a certain price, the treasury recognizing the total proceeds of these sales at an interest of six per cent and the preamble of this decree declaring that the assumption by the Government of the care and of administration of the Pious Fund was for the express purpose of scrupulously carrying out the objects proposed by the founders.

Neither by the Spanish nor by the Mexican Government was it ever pretended that the proceeds of the fund were not finally to find their way into the hands of the ecclesiastical authorities in the Californias, or that they were to be applied to any other objects than those pointed out by the donors. Subsequently to the decree of October 24, 1842, the Mexican Government admitted its indebtedness and the obligation it was under to remit the proceeds of the fund to the Bishop of California by issuing orders in his favor on the custom house at Guaymas.

This obligation is still further acknowledged by the Act of Congress of April 3, 1845, which restored to the Bishop of the Californias and to his successors all credits and other properties belonging to the Pious Fund which were still unsold, for the objects mentioned in

---

[5] Antonio López de Santa Anna (1795–1876), an anti-clerical revolutionary, was several times dictator and president of Mexico.

the law of September 29, 1836, without prejudice to what Congress might decide with regard to those properties which had already been alienated.

The above-mentioned credits must surely have included the indebtedness of the Government with regard to the unpaid interest upon the property sold, the proceeds of which had been incorporated into the national treasury. The umpire does not find that any further legislation has been effected upon the subject since the Decree of April 3, 1845.

Such then was the state of the Mexican laws with regard to the Pious Fund at the time of the cession of Upper California to the United States, and the umpire is clearly of the opinion that both the acts of the Mexican Government and its decrees above mentioned as well as the Act of Congress of 1845 are so many admissions that the Mexican Government was under the obligation to remit to the Bishop of California and his successors the interest on the proceeds of the property belonging to the Pious Fund which were held in trust by the Mexican Treasury, in order ·that the Bishop and his successors might carry out the wishes of the founders of that fund.

The umpire has already stated that he considers that as far as Upper California is concerned, the claimants are the direct successors of the Bishop of California, whose Diocese before the Treaty of Guadalupe Hidalgo, comprised both Upper and Lower California;[6] and they ought therefore to receive a fair share of the interest upon the proceeds of the Pious Fund, in order to devote it to the purposes for which it was founded, and which are of so decidedly a religious nature, that the ecclesiastical authorities must be the most proper persons to be employed in its application.

The beneficiaries of this share of the fund are the Roman Catholic Church in Upper California, and the heathens who are to be converted to Christianity; and indirectly all the inhabitants of the State of California, and even the whole population of the United States, are interested in the proper application of the portion which should be entrusted to the claimants, upon whom, considering the purposes to which the founders assigned their donations, the employment of the fund would most suitably devolve.

With regard to the proportion of the interest which should be paid to the claimants, the umpire is of opinion that nothing can be fairer

---

[6] The Bishop of Monterey continued to exercise jurisdiction over both Upper and Lower California until 1852 when, at his request, Lower California was detached from his see.

than that the whole of the interest for twenty-one years should be divided into two equal parts, of which one should be paid to the claimants.[7]

It has been argued that the award should be made in proportion to the populations respectively of Upper and Lower California.

The umpire is not of that opinion; for it seems to him that as the population and civilization increase, the number of conversions to be made diminish and there can be little doubt that Lower California needs the beneficial assistance of the Pious Fund as much and even more in proportion to its population than Upper California now does. The equal division of the interest seems to be the fairest award.

After a careful examination of the data furnished with regard to the yearly amount of the interest, the umpire is constrained to adopt the views of the commissioner of the United States. A larger sum is claimed on the part of the claimants; but even with regard to this larger sum the defense has not shown, except indirectly, that its amount was exaggerated.

There is no doubt that the Mexican Government must have in its possession all the accounts and documents relative to the sale of the real property belonging to the Pious Fund and proceeds thereof; yet these have not been produced; and the only inference that can be drawn from silence upon this subject is that the amount of the proceeds actually received into the treasury was at least not less than it is claimed to be.

The annual amount of interest therefore which should fall to the share of the Roman Catholic Church of Upper California is $43,080.99 and the aggregate sum for twenty-one years will be $904,700.79.[8]

---

[7] The counsel for the bishops, John T. Doyle, taking into account the amount of work actually done in Upper California, as compared to that in the barren peninsula of Lower California, had asked for a division of the funds in a proportion of nine to one or eight to one. It was the counsel's opinion that the umpire had been influenced in his decision on this point by the precedent applied in commercial cases, i.e., that in the absence of evidence to the contrary, the interests of partners should be considered equal. Cf. "Points Submitted by Messrs. Doyle & Doyle," *Senate Document No. 28, 57th Congress, 2nd Session* (Washington, 1902), pp. 278–279. The pertinent documents in this case are printed in this publication.

[8] The figure was arrived at as follows.

Total value of the Pious Fund as accepted by the American commissioner	$1,436,033.00
Interest at 6 per cent	86,161.98
One half, to which the claimants were entitled	43,080.99
Twenty-one installments from October 24, 1848, to February 1, 1869	904,700.79

It has been urged that interest should be paid upon each annual amount from the respective date at which it became due. The umpire is not of this opinion. It is true that the Archbishop of San Francisco states in his deposition that when in the City of Mexico in 1852, he demanded payment of the amounts, of property of the Pious Fund, and that receiving no answer to his demands he reiterated the same, and only after a long time was officially informed that the Government could not accede to them.

From a man of the position and character of the Archbishop there can be no doubt of the truth of this statement; but yet there is no documentary evidence of these facts, and the umpire therefore supposes that the demand and the refusal were both verbal.[9] Upon a matter of such serious importance the umpire does not think that a verbal refusal by a Government to make a certain payment can be taken as its final determination upon the subject. The refusal may even have been qualified by the inability of the Government to provide the necessary funds at the time of the demand. Of this in the absence of any writing upon the subject, no judgment can be found. The umpire further thinks that considering the troubles and difficulties to which Mexico and her Government have been subject for several years past it would not be generous nor even fair to punish them for their failure to pay interest upon a capital of the nature of the Pious Fund, so far as to insist upon the payment of interest upon that interest. As a matter therefore both of justice and equity the umpire thinks that this second interest ought not to be demanded.

The umpire consequently awards that there be paid by the Mexican Government on account of the above-mentioned claim the sum of nine hundred and four thousand, seven hundred Mexican gold dollars and seventy-nine cents ($904,700.79) without interest.

Washington, November 11, 1875.

"Opinion of Mr. Wadsworth, in the original Pious Fund Case before the United States and Mexican Claims Commission of 1868" (Scott, *op. cit.,* p. 20). William H. Wadsworth was the American representative on the commission. On October 24, 1876, Thornton amended the above figures by reason of an error in computing the amount of bad debts. The rectification reduced the over-all sum to be paid by Mexico to $904,070.79.

[9] In the hearing before the Hague Court in 1902 the counsel for the bishops presented a letter from the Mexican Department of Justice and of Church Affairs to Bishop Alemany, dated September 29, 1852, in which the bishop's request for a portion of the Pious Fund was refused by the Mexican government. This evidence had not been presented in 1875. Cf. "Deposition of Mr. John T. Doyle," *Senate Document No. 28,* pp. 405–406.

118. Instruction of the Congregation de Propaganda Fide Concerning Catholic Children Attending American Public Schools, November 24, 1875

IN SPITE of the legislation of the First and Second Plenary Councils of Baltimore in May, 1852, and October, 1866, on the necessity of Catholic children attending Catholic schools in order to safeguard their religious faith, large numbers of Catholic children continued to go to the public schools. A number of American bishops felt this as a heavy burden on their conscience and, therefore, solicited from the Holy See a directive to the hierarchy for the purpose of correcting the situation. As a consequence the Congregation de Propaganda Fide sent an instruction on the subject which was intended to emphasize the danger to Catholic children enrolling in the public schools and to strengthen the hands of the bishops with their priests and people in their efforts to provide more Catholic schools. The instruction came, as was clear from the previous document, at a time when the entire question was being hotly debated in the United States. Sources: Latin text in *Acta et decreta concilii plenarii Baltimorensis tertii* (Baltimore, 1886), pp. 279–282; English translation, *The Pastor,* IV (June, 1886), 232–237.

The Sacred Congregation of Propaganda has been many times assured that for the Catholic children of the United States of America evils of the gravest kind are likely to result from the so-called public schools.

The sad intelligence moved the Propaganda to propose to the illustrious prelates of that country a series of questions, with the object of ascertaining, first, why the faithful permit their children to attend non-catholic schools, and secondly, what may be the best means of keeping the young away from schools of this description. The answers, as drawn up by the several prelates, were submitted, owing to the nature of the subject, to the Supreme Congregation of the Holy Office. The decision reached by their Eminences, Wednesday, June 30, 1875, they saw fit to embody in the following *Instruction,* which the Holy Father graciously confirmed on Wednesday, November 24, of the same year.

1. The first point to come under consideration was the system of education itself, quite peculiar to those schools. Now, that system seemed to the S. Congregation most dangerous and very much opposed to Catholicity. For the children in those schools, the very principles of which exclude all religious instruction, can neither learn the rudiments of the faith nor be taught the precepts of the Church; hence,

they will lack that knowledge, of all else, necessary to man without which there is no leading a Christian life. For children are sent to these schools from their earliest years, almost from their cradle; at which age, it is admitted, the seeds sown of virtue or of vice take fast root. To allow this tender age to pass without religion is surely a great evil.

2. Again, these schools being under no control of the Church, the teachers are selected from every sect indiscriminately; and this, while no proper precaution is taken to prevent them injuring the children, so that there is nothing to stop them from infusing into the young minds the seeds of error and vice. Then evil results are certainly to be dreaded from the fact that in these schools, or at least in very many of them, children of both sexes must be in the same class and class-room and must sit side by side at the same desk. Every circumstance mentioned goes to show that the children are fearfully exposed to the danger of losing their faith and that their morals are not properly safeguarded.

3. Unless this danger of perversion can be rendered remote, instead of proximate, such schools cannot in conscience be used. This is the dictate of natural as well as of divine law. It was enunciated in unmistakable terms by the Sovereign Pontiff, in a letter addressed to a former Archbishop of Freiburg, July 14, 1864. He thus writes: "There can be no hesitation; wherever the purpose is afoot or carried out of shutting out the Church from all authority over the schools, there the children will be sadly exposed to loss of their faith. Consequently the Church should, in such circumstances, not only put forth every effort and spare no pains to get for the children the necessary Christian training and education, but would be further compelled to remind the faithful and publicly declare that schools hostile to Catholicity cannot in conscience be attended." These words only express a general principle of natural and divine law and are consequently of universal application wherever that most dangerous system of training youth has been unhappily introduced.

4. It only remains, then, for the prelates to use every means in their power to keep the flocks committed to their care from all contact with the public schools. All are agreed that there is nothing so needful to this end as the establishment of Catholic schools in every place, — and schools no whit inferior to the public ones. Every effort, then, must be directed towards starting Catholic schools where they are not, and, where they are, towards enlarging them and providing them with better accommodations and equipment until they have

nothing to suffer, as regards teachers or equipment, by comparison with the public schools. And to carry out so holy and necessary a work, the aid of religious brotherhoods and of sisterhoods will be found advantageous where the bishop sees fit to introduce them. In order that the faithful may the more freely contribute the necessary expenses, the bishops themselves should not fail to impress on them, at every suitable occasion, whether by pastoral letter, sermon or private conversation, that as bishops they would be recreant to their duty if they failed to do their very utmost to provide Catholic schools.[1] This point should be especially brought to the attention of the more wealthy and influential Catholics and members of the legislature.

5. In that country there is no law to prevent Catholics having their own schools and instructing and educating their youth in every branch of knowledge. It is therefore in the power of Catholics themselves to avert, with God's help, the dangers with which Catholicity is threatened from the public school system. Not to have religion and piety banished from the school-room is a matter of the very highest interest, not only to certain individuals and families, but to the entire country, — a country now so prosperous and of which the Church has had reason to conceive such high hopes.

6. However, the S. Congregation is not unaware that circumstances may be sometimes such as to permit parents conscientiously to send their children to the public schools. Of course they cannot do so without having sufficient cause. Whether there be sufficient cause in any particular case is to be left to the conscience and judgment of the bishop. Generally speaking, such cause will exist when there is no Catholic school in the place, or the one that is there cannot be considered suitable to the condition and circumstances in life of the pupils. But even in these cases, before the children can conscientiously attend the public school, the danger, greater or less, of perversion, which is inseparable from the system, must be rendered remote by proper precaution and safeguards. The first thing to see to, then, is whether the danger of perversion, as regards the school in question, is such as cannot possibly be rendered remote; as, for instance,

---

[1] That the American bishops had not been unmindful of their duty in this regard was evident from the decree passed in their First Plenary Council of Baltimore in May, 1852, which read: "We exhort the bishops, and in view of the very grave evils which usually result from the defective education of youth, we beseech them through the bowels of the mercy of God, to see that schools be established in connection with all the churches of their dioceses. . . ." (*Concilium plenarium totius Americae septentrionalis foederatae Baltimori habitum anno 1852* [Baltimore, 1853], p. 47).

whether the teaching there is such, or the doings of a nature so repugnant to Catholic belief and morals, that ear cannot be given to the one, nor part taken in the other without grievous sin. It is self-evident that danger of this character must be shunned at whatever cost, even life itself.

7. Further, before a child can be conscientiously placed at a public school, provision must be made for giving it the necessary Christian training and instruction, at least out of school hours. Hence parish priests and missionaries in the United States should take seriously to heart the earnest admonitions of the Council of Baltimore,[2] and spare no labor to give children thorough catechetical instructions, dwelling particularly on those truths of faith and morals which are called most in question by Protestants and unbelievers: children beset with so many dangers they should guard with tireless vigilance, induce them to frequent the sacraments, excite in them devotion to the Blessed Virgin and on all occasions animate them to hold firmly by their religion. The parents or guardians must look carefully after those children. They must examine them in their lessons, or if not able themselves, get others to do it. They must see what books they use and, if the books contain passages likely to injure the child's mind, explain the matter. They must keep them from freedom and familiarity with those of the other school children whose company might be dangerous to their faith or morals, and absolutely away from the corrupt.

8. Parents who neglect to give this necessary Christian training and instruction to their children, or who permit them to go to schools in which the ruin of their souls is inevitable, or finally, who send them to the public school without sufficient cause and without taking the necessary precautions to render the danger of perversion remote, and do so while there is a good and well-equipped Catholic school in the place, or the parents have the means to send them elsewhere to be educated, — that such parents, if obstinate, cannot be absolved, is evident from the moral teaching of the Church.

---

[2] The Second Plenary Council of Baltimore in October, 1866, went beyond the legislation of 1852 and devoted an entire chapter to the subject, "De scholis parochialibus ubique fundandis," *Concilii plenarii Baltimorensis II. . . . Acta et decreta* (Baltimore, 1868), pp. 218–225.

119. Building a Missionary School on the Colorado Frontier, June, 1876

THE thriving spiritual state of American Catholicism owes an incalculable debt to the religious congregations of women. From the time that Mother Seton founded her Sisters of Charity in 1808 thousands of self-sacrificing American women have devoted their lives to the religious education of youth and to every variety of works of charity, a force that now numbers 159,545 religious women in the United States. For the most part their striking contributions have gone unrecorded, but occasionally there comes to light the story of one or another of these heroic women, and of none can it be said that her career was more fruitful and dramatic than Sister Blandina Segale (1850–1941), whose family immigrated to Cincinnati from a small town near Genoa when she was four years old. Entering the Sisters of Charity of Cincinnati in 1866, she was sent — alone — to the rough cowboy town of Trinidad in Colorado Territory, where she arrived in December, 1872, after a series of incidents that would have tested the courage of a stouthearted man. She spent the next twenty-one years in the Southwest until recalled to Cincinnati, where in 1897 she and her sister, Sister Justina, set up the first aid center for Italian immigrants. For the following thirty-five years she labored relentlessly at the Santa Maria Institute in the city's slums and personally gave religious instruction to 80 per cent of the Italian population. The experiences of this diminutive religious during the 1870's in the wild Southwest included an encounter with the country's most famous desperado, Billy the Kid [Bonney] (1859–1881), whom she succeeded in bringing around to an offer of friendly assistance if ever she should need it, and the rescue of a prisoner from lynching by a mob. During her days in Colorado and New Mexico, Sister Blandina kept a journal in the form of reminiscences addressed to her sister back in Cincinnati. The following excerpt, concerning how she got a new school built, reveals the resourcefulness, energy, and personal magnetism of this amazing woman; it also affords insights into the crude frontier life of Colorado in the year it entered the union. Source: Sister Blandina Segale, *At the End of the Santa Fe Trail* (Milwaukee: The Bruce Publishing Co., 1948), pp. 62–65.

June, 1876.

Dear Sister Justina:

To-day I asked Sister Eulalia[1] if, in her opinion, we did not need a new school building, which would contain a hall and stage for all school purposes.[2] She said: "Just what we need, Sister. Do you want

---

[1] Sister Eulalia Whitty (d. 1917) had been among the three pioneer Sisters of Charity of Cincinnati who had come to Trinidad in February, 1870. After several years in Santa Fe she had returned to Trinidad and was at this time assistant teacher to Sister Blandina in the school.

[2] Land for the original school had been given by one of the founders of Trinidad, Don Felipe Baca, at the request of Bishop Machebeuf, and it had been opened on March 4, 1870.

to build it?" I answered, "Yes, I do." She added, "We have not enough cash to pay interest on our indebtedness. Have you a plan by which you can build without money? If so, I say build."

"Here is my plan, Sister. Borrow a crowbar, get on the roof of the schoolhouse and begin to detach the adobes. The first good Mexican who sees me will ask, "What are you doing, Sister?" I will answer, "Tumbling down this structure to rebuild it before the opening of the fall term of school."

You should have seen Sister Eulalia laugh! It did me good. After three days' pondering how to get rid of low ceilings, poor ventilation, acrobats from log-rafters introducing themselves without notice, and now here is an opportunity to carry out a test on the good in human nature, so I took it. I borrowed a crowbar and went on the roof, detached some adobes and began throwing them down. The school building is only one story high.

The first person who came towards the schoolhouse was Doña Juanita Simpson, wife of the noted hero of Simpson's Rest. When she saw me at work, she exclaimed, *"Por amor de Dios, Hermana, qué está Vd. haciendo?"* (For the love of God, Sister, what are you doing?)

I answered, "We need a schoolhouse that will a little resemble those we have in the United States, so I am demolishing this one in order to rebuild."

"How many men do you need, Sister?"

"We need not only men, but also straw, moulds, hods, shovels — everything it takes to build a house with a shingle roof. Our assets are good-will and energy."

Earnestly Mrs. Simpson said: "I go to get what you need."

The crowbar was kept at its work. In less than an hour, Mrs. Simpson returned with six men. One carried a mould, another straw, etc. The mould carrier informed me at once that women only know how to *encalar* (whitewash), the men had the trades and they would continue what I began. In a few days the old building was thrown down, the adobes made and sun-burnt. In two weeks all the rubbish was hauled away. The trouble began when we were ready for the foundation. Keep in mind it was only by condescension I was permitted to look on. At this juncture I remarked to the moulder:

"Of course, we will have a stone foundation."

"Oh, no!" he answered, "we use adobes laid in mud."

"Do you think if we laid a foundation with stone laid in mortar, the combination would resist the rainy season better than adobes laid in mud?"

"No, no, Sister we never use stone for any of our houses," he replied.

I was at the mercy of the good natives and my best move was to let them have their way. Moreover, I recalled the fact that in the Far East there are mud structures centuries old in a good state of preservation. No mistake would be made by not changing their mode of building in that one point. We got the necessary lumber, sashes and shingles from Chené's mill, sixty miles from Trinidad. Wagons hauled the material. As the Chené family has a daughter at our boarding school, there will be no difficulty in meeting our bill. Mr. Hermann's daughter is a resident student, and Mr. Hermann is a carpenter and will pay his bill by work.

When the schoolhouse was ready for roofing, a number of the town carpenters offered to help. The merchants gave nails, paints, brushes, lime, hair, etc.

But now came the big obstacle. There is but one man who calls himself a plasterer, and his method is to plaster with mud. It is impossible to get a smooth surface with mud. I remarked to the plasterer: "You will use lime, sand and hair to plaster the schoolrooms."

His look plainly said: "What do women know of men's work?" Yet he condescended to explain: "I am the plasterer of this part of the country; if I should use any material but mud, my reputation would be lost."

I said to him, "But if lime, sand and hair made a better job, your reputation would gain."

He made answer, "Sister, I'll make a bargain with you. I will do as you suggest, but I will tell my people I carried out your American idea of plastering."

We both agreed to this. Meanwhile, the other men had shouldered their implements and were on their way home. The plasterer had to mix the sand, lime and hair following my directions. All that was done satisfactorily to me, at least. But there was not a man to carry the mortar to the plasterer, so I got the bucket and supplied a man's place. The comedy follows:

Rev. Charles Pinto, S.J.,[3] pastor, took pleasure in telling his co-religionists that the study of human nature, combined with good will and tactfulness, were building a schoolhouse.

---

[3] Charles Pinto, S.J., had become pastor of Holy Trinity Church, Trinidad, in 1875.

On this day of my hod-carrying, the Rt. Rev. Bishop Machebeuf[4] of Denver, Colorado, arrived on his visitation. The first place to which he was taken was the schoolhouse being built without money. Bishop and Pastor had just turned the kitchen corner when the three of us came face to face. Both gentlemen stood amazed. I rested my hod-bucket. Father Pinto looked puzzled. The Bishop remarked:

"I see how you manage to build without money." I laughed and explained the situation.

They took the bucket, and the three of us went to where the plasterer was working. After the welcome to the Bishop, the plasterer said:

"Your Reverence, look at me, the only Mexican plasterer, and I am putting aside my knowledge to follow American ways of doing my trade; but I told Sister the failure will not be pointed at me." The Rt. Rev. Bishop analyzed the material at a glance, then said: "Juan, if this method of plastering is better than yours, come again to help Sister when she needs you. If it fails, report to me and between us we shall give her the biggest penance she ever received."

The schoolroom walls turned out smooth, the plaster adhesive, and the plasterer will now make a lucrative living at his American method of plastering. . . .[5]

120. Patrick C. Keely Receives the Laetare Medal, March 30, 1884

THE most prominent American Catholic architect of the nineteenth century was Patrick Charles Keely (c. 1816–1896). Born in Ireland, Keely emigrated in 1841 and settled in Brooklyn where his first church, that of SS. Peter and Paul, was dedicated in May, 1848. Previous to Keely's time the only Catholic Church building in this country that had followed the Gothic design was the chapel of St. Mary's Seminary, Baltimore, dedicated in June, 1808, of which Maximilien Godefroy (d. 1824) had been the archi-

---

4 Joseph P. Machebeuf (1812–1889), a French-born priest, had spent nearly thirty years as a missionary in the Diocese of Cincinnati and Santa Fe when he was consecrated in August, 1868, as first Vicar Apostolic of Colorado and Utah; he was named first Bishop of Denver on August 16, 1887.

5 That September Sister Blandina wrote in her journal: "The pupils and myself will have to be introduced daily to our schoolroom. It will take some time to wear off the novelty of entering a well-lighted, well-ventilated room, flowers in blossom on window sills, blackboard built into the walls, modern desks, and a stage for Friday exercises. I think one of my ambitions has been reached, viz.: to walk into my schoolroom and feel that it is 'up-to-date' and I, 'Mistress of all I survey,' particularly of the minds to be taught" (*ibid.*, p. 67).

tect. Keely may have been influenced by the Gothic revival in England, of which the convert architect, Augustus Welby Pugin (1812–1852), who had entered the Church in 1834, was a leader. In any case, most of the astonishing number of Catholic churches designed by Keely followed that pattern, and in this he was but a part of a current trend, for the Gothic and the contemporary Renaissance work in France were said to be "the two principal and almost exclusive influences at work in America in this period of a full generation from 1850 to 1880. . . ." (Thomas E. Tallmadge, *The Story of Architecture in America* [New York, 1936], p. 144). By the time he received the Laetare Medal in 1884 Keely had served as architect for a very large number of church edifices, among them the Cathedral of the Holy Cross, Boston, 1867–1875, and the Cathedral of the Holy Name, Chicago, 1874–1875. Source: *Catholic Review* (New York), April 5, 1884.

The *Laetare* Medal[1] of the University of Notre Dame was conferred last Sunday on the great Catholic architect, Mr. Patrick Charles Keely, of Brooklyn. No more honorable selection could have been made, nor one that would more certainly reflect back on the University conferring it an honor fully corresponding to that which it gave. All public testimonies of honor, such as this, ought to have a mutual and reciprocal effect. In this case it undoubtedly had. In material value and external ornament the *Laetare* Medal and its accompanying address, designed and wrought by skilful hands, are things of beauty, and coming from such a respectable, progressive and far-seeing Institution as Notre Dame are well worthy of acceptance by even so eminent a master as Mr. Keely. On the other hand, when the University of Notre Dame determined to mark out for its homage and distinction a man eminent in his science and a great master in his truly Christian art, it selected one, the glory of whose achievements and the lustre of whose life must reflect honorably on it and this great prize that it has established. The personal modesty of Mr. Keely's life will not permit us to say a single word in praise of himself, but everyone can infer what might be said when it is remembered to what Mr. Keely has devoted himself and his wonderful gifts. "The undevout astronomer is mad." Certainly it would be equally impossible for a Christian architect, who designs temples for the Eucharistic Sacrifice, to lack that enthusiasm for his faith which comes from the hourly expression in permanent forms of the most precious thoughts

---

[1] The *Laetare* Medal was instituted in 1883 when it was conferred for the first time on the noted lay historian of the American Church, John Gilmary Shea (1824–1892). Keely, the second recipient, received the medal in a ceremony on March 30, 1884.

of religion. That condition of the *Laetare* Medal may therefore be passed as entirely filled in this case. Of Mr. Keely's genius we need speak just as briefly. Already he has built *seven hundred churches*[2] in honor of the Christian name, not to speak of the numberless institutions that accompanied them. The number is wholly unprecedented in the history of any architect of ancient or modern times. It could have been reached only in the phenomenal period of Catholic history that the Church in America has known during the present half century. Mr. Keely was a Providential man, raised up to meet, in his particular line, this marvellous emergency. Nor must it be supposed that these are petty little structures, suitable for mission chapels in rural districts. Few of them are of that character. Numbers of them are works of the first class. Scores of them are cathedrals that in cost, size and structure recall the amazement of those who saw the Cathedral of Seville and believed its designers and builders mad to attempt such a gigantic task. Even a few of them would stamp Mr. Keely as a man of genius and make his reputation anywhere. His first great work was to carve out, with his own hands, the beautiful canopies of the altars in the old Cathedral of Brooklyn,[3] and the crown of all his works, though we trust not his last, will be the new Cathedral of Brooklyn.[4] That in size alone will be greater than any church yet planned on the American continent. Those who have been favored with a glimpse of the well nigh completed plans, are of opinion that its great size will be the very least of its claims to notice. Mr. Keely in his modesty never permits without protest its comparison with any other work. We will therefore simply say that it will be a most beautiful as well as a massive and impressive structure, leaving to the future to contrast it with anything that the piety of a succeeding generation may achieve. Among his other works, of which every newspaper reader must have heard, are the Jesuit churches in Montreal, Boston and New York, the cathedrals of Buffalo, Boston, Providence, Hartford, Chicago and Newark. That which he is building for Bishop

---

[2] The number of churches designed and built by Keely has been variously estimated from 500 to 700.

[3] St. James Church at Jay and Chapel Streets was dedicated in August, 1823. Keely was the architect for its enlargement which tripled the size and the newly refurnished building was blessed by Bishop John Hughes of New York in September, 1846. When the Diocese of Brooklyn was erected on July 29, 1853, it became St. James Pro-Cathedral.

[4] The cornerstone of the projected new Cathedral of the Immaculate Conception, Brooklyn, was laid in June, 1868, but only St. John's Chapel — from which Keely himself was buried in 1896 — was ever completed. In 1913 the chapel was closed and in 1931 the partly constructed walls of the new cathedral were razed.

Hendricken,[5] though not the largest, will be in every way one of the most complete and beautiful in the country. These facts may show that Notre Dame in selecting Mr. Keely as the medallist of this year, has chosen a man of great eminence, whose life and work will be a suggestion to the young men who are growing up in the fine atmosphere of Catholic public spirit that this Western University is creating within its sphere. . . .

121. Bishop Spalding on the Intellectual Weakness Among American Catholics, November 16, 1884

WITH the maturity of the Church in the twentieth century it has become increasingly evident that the principal weakness of American Catholicism lies in its lack of national influence and intellectual leadership. One of the keenest foreign observers of the Church in the United States has said, not without reason, that "in no modern Western society is the intellectual prestige of Catholicism lower than in the country where, in such respects as wealth, numbers, and strength of organization, it is so powerful" (D. W. Brogan, *U.S.A. An Outline of the Country, Its People and Institutions* [London, 1941], p. 65). No American Catholic spotted this weakness earlier, nor emphasized it more forcefully, than John Lancaster Spalding (1840–1916), first Bishop of Peoria. Spalding was easily the most intellectual American Catholic bishop of his lifetime, a man who had capitalized to the fullest extent on his training at the Catholic University of Louvain and his additional study at several German universities and in Rome. Over sixty years ago — when he was only forty-four — he made a powerful plea to the hierarchy for an American Catholic university that would be worthy of the name in a sermon preached during the Third Plenary Council of Baltimore. In that sermon Spalding showed his awareness of the need for quality rather than quantity in higher education, while at the same time the optimism of the Gilded Age in which he lived and the deep love he had for the United States. It was this sermon which, in a sense, launched the Catholic University of America. The bishop's contribution to American life was well summarized in the citation for the honorary degree of doctor of letters conferred on him by Columbia University on June 11, 1902, which read: "Descendant of a house honored among two peoples; Christian priest and prelate, man of letters, orator, educator and patriotic citizen." Spalding's analysis of 1884 still has pertinence for those who believe that the intellectual life has in no way won the esteem and support among the more than thirty million American Catholics that might have been hoped. Source: John Lancaster

---

[5] Thomas F. Hendricken (1827–1886) was consecrated as first Bishop of Providence on April 28, 1872. The cornerstone of the Cathedral of SS. Peter and Paul, Providence, was laid in November, 1878, and the building completed in 1889.

Spalding, *Means and Ends of Education* (Chicago: A. C. McClurg and Co., 1897), pp. 219–223.

. . . And now, when at length a fairer day has dawned for us in this new world, what can be more natural than our eager desire to move out from the valleys of darkness towards the hills and mountain tops that are bathed in sunlight? What more praiseworthy than the fixed resolve to prove that not our faith, but our misfortunes made and kept us inferior. And, since we live in the midst of millions who have indeed good will towards us, but who still bear the yoke of inherited prejudices, and who, because for three hundred years real cultivation of mind was denied to Catholics who spoke English, conclude that Protestantism is the source of enlightenment, and the Church the mother of ignorance, do not all generous impulses urge us to make this reproach henceforth meaningless? And in what way shall we best accomplish this task? Surely not by writing or speaking about what the influence of the Church is, or by pointing to what she has done in other ages, but by becoming what we claim her spirit tends to make us. Here, if anywhere, the proverb is applicable — *verba movent, exempla trahunt.* As the devotion of American Catholics to this country and its free institutions, as shown not on battlefields alone, but in our whole bearing and conduct, convinces all but the unreasonable of the depth and sincerity of our patriotism, so when our zeal for intellectual excellence shall have raised up men who will take place among the first writers and thinkers of their day their very presence will become the most persuasive of arguments to teach the world that no best gift is at war with the spirit of Catholic faith, and that, while the humblest mind may feel its force, the lofty genius of Augustine, of Dante, and of Bossuet is upborne and strengthened by the splendor of its truth. But if we are to be intellectually the equals of others, we must have with them equal advantages of education; and so long as we look rather to the multiplying of schools and seminaries than to the creation of a real university, our progress will be slow and uncertain, because a university is the great ordinary means to the best cultivation of mind. The fact that the growth of the Church here, like that of the country itself, is chiefly external, a growth in wealth and in numbers, makes it the more necessary that we bring the most strenuous efforts to improve the gifts of the soul. The whole tendency of our social life insures the increase of churches, convents, schools, hospitals, and asylums; our advance in population and in wealth will be counted from decade to decade by millions, and our worship will approach more and more to the pomp and splendor of the full ritual; but this very growth makes such demands upon our energies, that we are in danger of forgetting higher things, or at least of thinking them less urgent. Few men are at once thoughtful and active. The man of deeds dwells in the world around him; the thinker lives within his mind. . . .

But the Church needs both the men who act and the men who think; and since with us everything pushes to action, wisdom demands that we cultivate rather the powers of reflection. And this is the duty alike of true patriots and of faithful Catholics. All are working to develop our boundless material resources; let a few at least labor to develop man. The millions are building cities, reclaiming wildernesses, and bring forth from the earth its buried treasures; let at least a remnant cherish the ideal, cultivate the beautiful, and seek to inspire the love of moral and intellectual excellence. And since we believe that the Church which points to heaven is able also to lead the nations in the way of civilization and of progress, why should we not desire to see her become a beneficent and ennobling influence in the public life of our country? She can have no higher temporal mission than to be the friend of this great republic, which is God's best earthly gift to His children. . . . If we keep ourselves strong and pure, all the peoples of the earth shall yet be free; if we fulfil our providential mission, national hatred shall give place to the spirit of generous rivalry, the people shall become wiser and stronger, society shall grow more merciful and just, and the cry of distress shall be felt, like the throb of a brother's heart, to the ends of the world. Where is the man who does not feel a kind of religious gratitude as he looks upon the rise and progress of this nation? Above all, where is the Catholic whose heart is not enlarged by such contemplation? Here, almost for the first time in her history, the Church is really free. Her worldly position does not overshadow her spiritual office, and the State recognizes her autonomy. The monuments of her past glory, wrenched from her control, stand not here to point, like mocking fingers, to what she has lost. She renews her youth, and lifts her brow, as one who, not unmindful of the solemn mighty past, yet looks with undimmed eye and unfaltering heart to a still more glorious future. Who in such a presence, can abate hope, or give heed to despondent counsel, or send regretful thoughts to other days and lands? Whoever at any time, in any place, might have been sage, saint, or hero, may be so here and now; and though he had the heart of Francis, and the mind of Augustine, and the courage of Hildebrand, here is work for him to do. . . .

122. The Pastoral Letter of the Third Plenary Council of Baltimore on Forbidden Societies, December 7, 1884

FROM the first papal condemnation of Free Masonry by Clement XII in 1738 to the present time the problem of Catholic membership in societies forbidden by the Church has been a real one. As early as the Fourth Provincial Council of Baltimore in May, 1840, the American bishops expressed concern on this score and there were repeated warnings to the faithful thereafter. Many of the earlier societies had been of foreign birth, but in the last decades of the nineteenth century Americans "turned with furious zeal to the creation of secret societies cut to their own pattern" (Arthur Meier Schlesinger, *The Rise of the City, 1878–1898* [New York, 1933], p. 288). It was with this increased danger to the faith of Catholic men in mind that the bishops of the Third Plenary Council of Baltimore included in their pastoral letter — the most detailed to date — a lengthy section on the forbidden societies. Source: Peter Guilday (Ed.), *The National Pastorals of the American Hierarchy, 1792–1919* (Washington: National Catholic Welfare Conference, 1923), pp. 256–260.

One of the most striking characteristics of our times is the universal tendency to band together in societies for the promotion of all sorts of purposes.[1] This tendency is the natural outgrowth of an age of popular rights and representative institutions. It is also in accordance with the spirit of the Church, whose aim, as indicated by her name Catholic, is to unite all mankind in brotherhood. It is consonant also with the spirit of Christ, who came to break down all walls of division, and to gather all in the one family of the one heavenly Father.

But there are few good things which have not their counterfeits, and few tendencies which have not their dangers. It is obvious to any reflecting mind that men form bad and rash as well as good and wise designs; and that they may band together for carrying out evil or dangerous as well as laudable and useful purposes. And this does not necessarily imply deliberate malice, because, while it is unquestionably

---

[1] That the bishops were not exaggerating the phenomenon may be seen from the fact that between 1880–1900 at least 490 new societies were organized in the United States, and by 1900 there were over six million names on the rolls of these societies. Arthur M. Schlesinger has stated, "So thoroughly did the 'habit of forming associations' — James Bryce's phrase — interpenetrate American life that it becomes possible to understand practically all the important economic and social developments merely by examining the activities of voluntary organizations" ("Biography of a Nation of Joiners," *American Historical Review*, L [October, 1944], 16).

true that there are powers at work in the world which deliberately antagonize the cause of Christian truth and virtue, still the evil or the danger of purposes and associations need not always spring from so bad a root. Honest but weak and erring human nature is apt to be so taken up with one side of a question as to do injustice to the other; to be so enamored of favorite principles as to carry them to unjustifiable extremes; to be so intent upon securing some laudable end as to ignore the rules of prudence, and bring about ruin instead of restoration. But no intention, no matter how honest, can make lawful what is unlawful. For it is a fundamental rule of Christian morals that "evil must not be done that good may come of it," and "the end can never justify the means," if the means are evil. Hence it is the evident duty of every reasonable man, before allowing himself to be drawn into any society, to make sure that both its ends and its means are consistent with truth, justice, and conscience.

In making such a decision, every Catholic ought to be convinced that his surest guide is the Church of Christ. She has in her custody the sacred deposit of Christian truth and morals; she has the experience of all ages and all nations; she has at heart the true welfare of mankind; she has the perpetual guidance of the Holy Ghost in her authoritative decisions. In her teaching and her warnings therefore, we are sure to hear the voice of wisdom, prudence, justice and charity. From the hill-top of her Divine mission and her world-wide experience, she sees events and their consequences far more clearly than they who are down in the tangled plain of daily life. She has seen associations that were once praiseworthy, become pernicious by change of circumstances. She has seen others, which won the admiration of the world by their early achievements, corrupted by power or passion or evil guidance, and she has been forced to condemn them. She has beheld associations which had their origin in the spirit of the Ages of Faith, transformed by lapse of time, and loss of faith, and the manipulation of designing leaders, into the open or hidden enemies of religion and human weal. Thus our Holy Father Leo XIII has lately shown that the Masonic and kindred societies, — although the offspring of the ancient Guilds, which aimed at sanctifying trades and tradesmen with the blessings of religion; and although retaining, perhaps, in their "ritual," much that tells of the religiousness of their origin; and although in some countries still professing entire friendliness toward the Christian religion, — have nevertheless already gone so far, in many countries, as to array themselves in avowed hostility against Christianity, and against the Catholic Church as its embodiment; that they virtually aim at substituting a world-wide fraternity of their own, for the universal brotherhood of Jesus Christ, and at disseminating mere Naturalism for the supernatural revealed religion bestowed upon mankind by the Saviour of the world. He has shown, too, that, even in countries where they are as yet far from acknowledging such purposes, they nevertheless have in them the germs, which under favorable circumstances, would inevitably blossom forth in similar results.[2] The Church, consequently, forbids her children to have any connection with such societies, because they are either an open evil to be shunned or a hidden danger to be avoided. She would fail in her duty if she did not speak the word of warning, and her children would equally fail in theirs, if they did not heed it.

Whenever, therefore, the Church has spoken authoritatively with regard to any society, her decision ought to be final for every Catholic. He ought to know that the Church has not acted hastily or unwisely, or mistakenly; he should be convinced that any worldly advantages which he might derive from his membership of such society, would be a poor substitute for the membership, the sacraments, and the blessings of the Church of Christ; he should have the courage of his religious convictions, and stand firm to faith and conscience. But if he be inclined or asked to join a society on which the Church has passed no sentence, then let him, as a reasonable and Christian man, examine into it carefully, and not join the society until he is satisfied as to its lawful character.

There is one characteristic which is always a strong presumption against a society, and that is secrecy. Our Divine Lord Himself has laid down the rule: "Every one that doth evil, hateth the light and cometh not to the light, that his works may not be reproved. But he that doth truth cometh to the light that his works may be made manifest, because they are done in God."[3] When, therefore associations veil themselves in secrecy and darkness, the presumption is against them, and it rests with them to prove that there is nothing evil in them.

But if any society's obligation be such as to bind its members to secrecy, even when rightly questioned by competent authority, then such a society puts itself outside the limits of approval; and no one can be a member of it and at the same time be admitted to the

---

[2] Cf. Leo XIII's encyclical *Humanum genus*, April 20, 1884, in John J. Wynne, S.J. (ed.), *The Great Encyclical Letters of Pope Leo XIII* (New York, 1903), pp. 83–106.

[3] Jn. 3:20–21.

sacraments of the Catholic Church. The same is true of any organization that binds its members to a promise of blind obedience — to accept in advance and to obey whatsoever orders, lawful or unlawful, that may emanate from its chief authorities; because such a promise is contrary both to reason and conscience. And if a society works or plots, either openly or in secret, against the Church, or against lawful authorities, then to be a member of it is to be excluded from the membership of the Catholic Church.

These authoritative rules, therefore, ought to be the guide of all Catholics in their relations with societies. No Catholic can conscientiously join, or continue in, a body in which he knows that any of these condemned features exist. If he has joined it in good faith and the objectionable features become known to him afterwards, or if any of these evil elements creep into a society which was originally good, it becomes his duty to leave it at once. And even if he were to suffer loss or run the risk by leaving such a society or refusing to join it, he should do his duty and brave the consequences regardless of human consideration.

To these laws of the Church, the justice of which must be manifest to all impartial minds, we deem it necessary to add the following admonition of the Second Plenary Council: "Care must be taken lest workingman's societies, under the pretext of mutual assistance and protection, should commit any of the evils of condemned societies; and lest the members should be induced by the artifices of designing men to break the laws of justice, by withholding labor to which they are rightfully bound, or by otherwise unlawfully violating the rights of their employers."[4]

But while the Church is thus careful to guard her children against whatever is contrary to Christian duty, she is no less careful that no injustice should be done to any association, however unintentionally. While therefore the Church, before prohibiting any society, will take every precaution to ascertain its true nature, we positively forbid any pastor, or other ecclesiastic, to pass sentence on any association or to impose ecclesiastical penalties or disabilities on its members without the previous explicit authorization of the rightful authorities. . . .[5]

[4] *Concilii plenarii Baltimorensis II. . . . Acta et decreta* (Baltimore, 1868), p. 263.

[5] The plenary council of 1884 constituted the archbishops of the United States as a commission to investigate and pass judgment on all suspect societies. For a treatment of how the commission operated, the condemnation of three American societies by the Holy Office in August, 1894, and the final solution given to the problem cf. Fergus Macdonald, *The Catholic Church and the Secret Societies in the United States* (New York, 1946), p. 100 ff.

123. John Gilmary Shea Discusses His Problems and Methods in Writing the *History of the Catholic Church in the United States*, March, 1885–September 26, 1890

IT MAY truthfully be said that were it not for John Gilmary Shea (1824–1892) the history of the Catholic Church in the United States could never have been written. The bibliography of this devoted scholar, who never had any formal professional training, numbered nearly 250 titles, including translations and editions of important source materials, studies in American Indian linguistics, general works in American and American Catholic history, biographies, devotional treatises, and miscellaneous writings (cf. Edward Spillane, S.J., "Bibliography of John Gilmary Shea," *Historical Records and Studies*, VI, Part II [December, 1912], 249–274). His principal successor in the field of American Catholic history, Peter Guilday (1884–1947), was not exaggerating, therefore, when he stated, "The prodigious activity of Dr. Shea is unique in American historiography" (Guilday, *op. cit.*, p. 155). Moreover, Shea's work was of a high scientific character, and it earned the admiration of contemporary professionals like Jared Sparks, Justin Winsor, and Edmund B. O'Callaghan with whom he maintained friendly contacts. His *magnum opus*, however, was the four-volume *History of the Catholic Church in the United States* (New York, 1886–1892), the final volume of which was published a few months after Shea's death by his wife. In the writing of that major work Shea often experienced a heart-breaking lack of interest and support from American Catholics generally as the following letters reveal, a fact which may be taken as an indication of the absence of interest in intellectual matters among his coreligionists at the time. In fact, it was only in the last two years of his life that the historian was finally relieved of financial anxiety for the support of himself and his family. In December, 1944, the American Catholic Historical Association instituted at its silver jubilee meeting in Chicago the annual John Gilmary Shea Prize of $200 for the best work in the history of the Church in order to help perpetuate Shea's memory. Source: Peter Guilday, "John Gilmary Shea," *Historical Records and Studies*, XVII (July, 1926), 99–100, 103–107, 109, 117–120, 124–127.

An appeal to prospective subscribers, March, 1885.

Most of the leisure hours of my life and much of my means have been devoted to studies, as well as to the acquisition of every book, periodical, paper, and document, whose existence I could trace, bearing on the early and actual history of the Church in this country, the efforts of the pioneer Catholics and their clergy, the Indian missions, the organization of the Church under English, French, and Spanish rule, the religious life and discipline that grew up, the vicissitudes of the Church and its ultimate steady development to its present condition.

It has been the purpose of my life to write this history, hoping that the evening of my days would give me the means and leisure to accomplish the task. Little fitted by studious habits for active business life, I have maintained myself by literary labor comfortably, but no more; and year by year my leisure has been required by work needed for my support, so that a competence on which to retire is now out of the question.

This disappointment I accept without repining and without a murmur. Recently some of the Most Rev. Archbishops and Right Rev. Bishops, with several of the Clergy, have, unexpectedly to me, taken the matter into consideration,[1] regarding it as important for the Church in this country that the knowledge of the subject acquired by so many years of study should be published and made accessible; they have debated on the best means of securing me the necessary leisure, and of completing my collections, where printed or manuscript matter becomes accessible.

To Archbishop Gibbons, May 1, 1885.[2]

The encouragement and aid which you have so generously accorded to my projected History of the Church in response to the action of the Committee places me under new and increased obligations. The sense of my inability to meet as I should desire the confidence placed in me, and the estimate formed of my ability, absolutely discourages me. I feel that I must produce a work that will justify my Patrons in the course they have adopted. To Your Grace in an especial manner, I consider my obligation extreme, as your name comes with all the historic weight of our most ancient See. Never have I seen so clearly that I must pray and work — *ora et labora* — to attain the desired end.

To Archbishop Corrigan, May 1, 1885.[3]

I called to thank you in person for the interest Your Grace has taken in the project to enable me to devote myself to writing the

---

[1] Early in 1885 a committee was formed in New York to assist Shea financially in the writing of his history. The subject had been discussed informally by some of the bishops during the Third Plenary Council of Baltimore in November–December, 1884, and as a result the committee had the backing of about twenty bishops and around fifty priests and laymen who were interested in the project.

[2] From the time he became Archbishop of Baltimore in October, 1877, Gibbons gave strong moral and monetary support to Shea.

[3] Michael Augustine Corrigan (1839–1902) was Bishop of Newark, 1873–1880, Coadjutor Archbishop of New York, 1880–1885, and Archbishop of New York from 1885 to his death. Corrigan acted as chairman of the committee organized in 1885 to assist Shea.

History of the Church. But for Your Grace's direction and influence little I am certain would have been effected but with it all difficulties seemed to vanish.

The confidence felt in me and the result that you and the kind patrons, who led by Your Grace's influence, have co-operated, may justly expect at my hands, have completely discouraged me now that I am brought face to face with the task. The last week has been one of the most miserable of my life so easily am I depressed. I have set to work studying up the whole field to learn first what the great deficiences of material are and where to look for the information to supply them. Sabin's *Dictionary of Books relating to America*[4] with nearly 100,000 titles and the Catalogues of all great libraries will be thoroughly examined that nothing in print may escape me. Collections of documents in public and private depositories are less easily reached but many will be accessible. For those in the archives of dioceses which formerly had jurisdiction over parts of this country I need a letter to the present Archbishop or Bishop. Enclosed is a facsimile of a hand that you recognize, my warm and kind friend Archbishop Bayley.[5] That letter opened to me many avenues of research. If a similar letter of introduction in the name of His Eminence[6] signed by Your Grace, also by the Most Rev. Archbishop of Baltimore, can be drawn up in which it would appear that I am now at work under the direct sanction of such members of our Hierarchy, I would reproduce it and feel assured that every facility will be afforded me.

To Archbishop Corrigan, September 21, 1885.

How can I thank you for your kindness in again addressing the Secretary of the Propaganda.[7] Mr. Maziere Brady[8] had access to documents giving some light on our Maryland Missions and I hope to obtain from him more information than he printed. The connection of events seemed so probable that I could not refrain from asking to see

---

[4] Joseph Sabin, *et al.* (eds.), *Bibliotheca Americana. A Dictionary of Books relating to America, from its Discovery to the Present Time* (New York, 1868 ff.). This work reached twenty-nine volumes by 1936.

[5] James Roosevelt Bayley (1814–1877) was first Bishop of Newark, 1853–1872, and eighth Archbishop of Baltimore, from 1872 to his death.

[6] John McCloskey (1810–1885) was Bishop of Albany, 1847–1864, and second Archbishop of New York, 1864–1885. He was made a cardinal in 1875.

[7] Archbishop Domenico Jacobini was Secretary of the Congregation of Propaganda de Fide, 1882–1891.

[8] W. Maziere Brady (1825–1894) was an Irish-born Protestant minister who wrote many volumes on the history of the Church. He was converted to Catholicism in 1873 at Rome while working in the Vatican Archives.

whether the papers examined by Mr. Brady did not contain more. From England, though I fail to obtain any details as to the Franciscans, information comes very unexpected to me in regard to projects of Catholic colonization before Lord Baltimore and there is every reason to believe that the famous voyage of Sir Humphrey Gilbert[9] in Queen Elizabeth's reign is connected with a Catholic project, and that a plan formed at a later day was defeated by the famous Jesuit Father Persons,[10] although supported by the brave Lord Arundel [*sic*] of Wardour.[11] That the early Franciscan Mission in Maryland is not altogether imaginary is proved by two facts recently elicited, one, that in 1712, and some years before, Lord Baltimore allowed them 1000 lbs. of tobacco a year, and the other that a library in Maryland has two books bearing the name. It must not be supposed that Father Haddoc [*sic*][12] was such a smoker that he required an allowance of three pounds a day; in justice to the old missionary I will add that all values in Maryland were then estimated in tobacco. The Minister of the established Church received from every person Catholic as well as Protestants 40 lbs. of tobacco every year. There are complaints extant from these worthy gentlemen that, as the law did not fix the quality to be delivered, most that came to their hands was very bad. I do not suppose that a Catholic so taxed would pick out the best of his stock of tobacco to pay so unjust a tax.

To Archbishop Leray, December 1, 1885.[13]

In compliance with the wish of several Archbishops and Bishops and encouraged by the subscription made in advance I have been working in earnest at the *History of the Church* in this country most of this year. The first volume includes all down to 1783 [*sic*].[14] For the most

---

[9] Sir Humphrey Gilbert (c. 1539–1583) made a voyage to the New World in 1578–1579; he took possession of Newfoundland in 1583 in the name of Queen Elizabeth and lost his life on the return voyage.

[10] Robert Persons (1546–1610) was the leader of the first Jesuit mission for the reconversion of England in 1580.

[11] Thomas, first Lord Arundell of Wardour (1560–1639), was one of the leading English Catholic noblemen of the late Elizabethan and early Stuart periods.

[12] James Haddock, O.F.M., was one of the members of the Franciscan mission in Maryland which lasted from 1672 to c. 1725.

[13] Francis X. Leray (1825–1887) was Bishop of Natchitoches, 1877–1879, Coadjutor Archbishop of New Orleans, 1879–1883, and Archbishop of New Orleans from 1883 to his death.

[14] Volume I, entitled *The Catholic Church in Colonial Days, 1521–1763* (New York: John Gilmary Shea, 1886), actually came only to 1763, not 1783. It was dedicated to the patrons "by whose request and aid this work has been undertaken" (p. iii).

part in the English colonies I have collected all material that I can trace and most of the narrative is written. For the Spanish part I have most encouraging success for Florida, Texas, and New Mexico. The French part touches Maine, and of which I have much, some hitherto unknown. For the Mission in New York I have also abundant material. For Michigan, Wisconsin and Illinois my documents are also rich. But for Louisiana, I now appeal to Your Grace. My first published work in 1853 was on the *Discovery of the Mississippi*[15] by Father Marquette followed by the Recollect Fathers under La Salle. I have Iberville's[16] Voyage, in which he was accompanied by a Recollect and Jesuit. Some years ago I printed letters from Messrs. Montigny[17] and his associates, sent out from the Seminary of Quebec by St. Vallier,[18] with his Lordship's act founding the Mission.

I have Abp. Taschereau's[19] history of that Mission which finally centered at Tamarois in Illinois. This includes the very curious history of Rev. M. Le Maire's[20] coming to Louisiana.

I have recently discovered a protest of Bp. St. Vallier against the action of the Pope who erected some Vicariates-Apostolic [*sic*][21] in the Mississippi Valley, which on his protest were suppressed. Investigation is now in progress at Rome to find all about this. For the

[15] *The Discovery and Exploration of the Mississippi Valley* (New York: Redfield, 1852) was dedicated to Jared Sparks of Harvard University who then encouraged Shea to write on the Catholic missions of Canada and the West, a volume which he brought out under the title *History of the Catholic Missions among the Indian Tribes of the United States, 1529–1854* (New York: Dunigan, 1854).

[16] Pierre Le Moyne Iberville (1661–1706) was a Canadian-born explorer who laid the foundations for Louisiana.

[17] François Jolliet de Montigny was the leader of the seminary priests of Quebec in 1698 to the missions along the Mississippi River.

[18] Jean-Baptiste de Saint-Vallier (1653–1727) was the successor of the famous Laval as second Bishop of Quebec.

[19] Elzéar-Alexandre Taschereau (1820–1898) was made Archbishop of Quebec in 1871 and the first Canadian cardinal in 1887. He wrote a manuscript history of the seminary of Quebec.

[20] F. Le Maire was a French priest who left a comfortable post in Paris to serve as a missionary in Louisiana for some years in the early eighteenth century.

[21] The very confused jurisdictional problem in Louisiana that arose during the last years of Pope Clement XI (1700–1721) and the first years of Pope Innocent XIII (1721–1724) became further involved by the Gallican controversy between the Holy See and France. The jurisdictions in question were prefectures-apostolic and not vicariates-apostolic as Shea said.

Jesuit Mission there are letters in the *Lettres Edifiantes*,[22] the *Bannissement des Jesuites de la Louisiane* and a few letters recently found. My great want is documents to give anything like a connected sketch of the history of the Church among the settlers of Louisiana while the Capuchin Fathers[23] were in control. There is nothing in the Archives at Quebec either in the Archévêché or in the Seminary. Will Your Grace permit your Rev. Secretary to inform me what the archives of your See can supply? 1. Are there any reports, sketches or statements made by Capuchins between 1725 and 1783? 2. Are there any documents by Rt. Rev. Cyril de Barcelona, Bishop of Tricali,[24] who, as auxiliary Bishop, administered that portion of the diocese of Cuba and, after its division, of St. Christopher of Havana from 1776 to 1783? 3. At what date do the oldest Registers begin and are they perfect from the beginning? 4. Is the Bull erecting the Diocese of Louisiana and the Floridas (1793) preserved in the archives? 5. Which are the oldest parishes outside New Orleans and which of them have ancient Registers?

If your Grace will permit your Rev. Secretary to have an examination made I will meet all expense: and I can then know what material I can hope to obtain for my work. I wish to make it full and faithful for every part of the country; and feeling that my material is not complete for Louisiana, I beg Your Grace's favor and indulgence.

To Monsignor Farley, October 18, 1888.[25]

The Life and Times of Archbishop Carroll is, as you know, ready; and it has cost me great labor, absorbing all my leisure and impairing my health seriously. It covers an important period, and really the history of the Church during it has not hitherto been known. Not only are errors and misrepresentations corrected, but whole chapters are new contributions.

---

[22] The series of Jesuit missionary sources entitled *Lettres edifiantes et curieuses, écrites des missions etrangères* (Paris, 1702 ff.) contained some material on North America for the years 1702–1776, but they were devoted mainly to the Jesuit missions elsewhere. The other title mentioned here by Shea was François Philibert Watrin, S.J.'s account of the banishment of the Jesuits from Louisiana, which will be found in No. 24 of this collection.

[23] The French Capuchins opened their mission in Louisiana in 1722.

[24] The Spanish Capuchin, Cirilo Sieni, known as Cyril of Barcelona, was consecrated as Auxiliary Bishop of Santiago de Cuba in 1781 and served in Louisiana, which was then part of the Cuban see, until 1793.

[25] John M. Farley (1842–1918), then secretary to Archbishop Corrigan, was Auxiliary Bishop of New York, 1895–1902, Archbishop of New York, 1902 to his death. Farley was made a cardinal in 1911.

I have made the volume so large and expensive, that I am in considerable debt; and I see no way except to have another appeal for patrons of the work. There have been eight deaths, and there were when I issued the volume eight delinquents, some of whom wish to withdraw altogether.

By making up a list of 250 prominent Catholics in the United States, it seems to me that 25 or 30 new patrons ought to be secured. With that number I can complete the work without anxiety. . . .

To Archbishop Corrigan, May 21, 1889.

In full consciousness of the many calls upon your time and thoughts I am most reluctant to make a personal appeal; but I am in a sore strait. When the matter of the *History of the Church* was proposed, it was suggested that I should withdraw from Leslie's[26] establishment. This I was reluctant to do, as I regarded my position secure and permanent, but I leaned upon a straw. Leaving a meeting of the Committee of the Catholic Historical Society[27] on the 2nd of January, I fell in stepping from an ill-constructed elevator and so injured my knee that I have been laid up and am now barely able to get about on crutches and even with them dare not attempt to walk in the street. During my enforced absence from the office, advantage was taken of this; although I continued to keep up my work. The prominence given to me directly and indirectly by my *History* prompted hostility, and I have recently been deprived of my position, a mere temporary position at a pittance being offered me.

Nothing would be more congenial to me than Church work and if there be any position in the Chancery Office, Calvary Cemetery Office, or in connection with any of the institutions, where I could be sure of a moderate salary I should be only too grateful to Your Grace for enabling me to obtain it.

I am able to work and willing. My aspirations are not high; and I do not ask to be a mere pensioner. If I can obtain a position in New York where I can earn my living, I can devote my leisure to the completion of the *History,* but if I am thrown upon precarious pieces of work, my labor on it must of necessity be fitful and uncertain. I commend the whole matter to Your Grace's kind consideration, and I feel certain from the friendly interest you have always manifested in

[26] Frank Leslie's Publishing House, 53–57 Park Place, New York City.

[27] It was due to the initiative of Shea that the United States Catholic Historical Society of New York was founded in December, 1884, with the active assistance of Richard H. Clarke (1827–1911) and Charles G. Herbermann (1840–1916).

me, that you will not feel offended at my thus intruding my private troubles on your attention. It was with great reluctance that I now address you, and do so only after efforts made in various directions, which have tended to discourage me.

Whether you could exert influence in any other field than those I have named I do not know, but leaving the matter in Your Grace's hands, I remain with deep and sincere respect.

To Archbishop Corrigan, June 2, 1889.

I must thank you sincerely for your kind letter to Mgr. Donnelly[28] in regard to my affairs. When I called on him yesterday my position was talked over at some length. It is far from my wish to be a pensioner or have a place made for me. I felt that if there were an opening anywhere for work which I was competent to do, Your Grace would exert influence in my favor. . . . Another proposal has just been made to me. Mr. Ridder[29] asks me to assume the editorship of the *Catholic News* and to give some days of the week to do it. As the editorship of a Catholic paper or periodical was never before offered me, I should not like to undertake it without Your Grace's sanction and entire approval. If I assumed the position it would be with the hope that I might, when occasion required, learn Your Grace's wishes as to the tone to be adopted, or the mode in which subjects should be treated. I can certainly conduct it prudently and temperately, how ably or successfully I cannot presume to say.

An Announcement in the *Catholic News,* May 4, 1890.

Some years since I was invited to write the History of the Catholic Church in this country, and subscriptions were advanced by several of the hierarchy, clergy and laity sufficient to cover the cost of the volumes as they were undertaken. Of these generous friends nearly one-third have already passed from this world. Two volumes were written and published. Soon after the appearance of the second volume, 'The Life and Times of Archbishop Carroll,' an accident laid me up for months a cripple. Though I endeavored successfully in this state

---

[28] Arthur J. Donnelly (1820–1890) was treasurer of the committee formed in 1885 to assist Shea. Monsignor Donnelly founded St. Michael's Parish, New York, in September, 1857.

[29] Herman Ridder (1851–1915) had founded the weekly *Katolisches Volksblatt* of New York in 1878 which he discontinued for the *Catholic News* in 1886. In 1890 Ridder became manager of the *New-Yorker Staats-Zeitung,* the foremost German daily in the United States, which he managed until his death.

to fulfill my usual editorial duties, I was deprived of nearly my whole income by an unjust and cruel act that I never anticipated. While in this position the proprietor of the *Catholic News* offered me the editorial charge of his paper, and, aided by the intelligent and well-informed staff connected with that journal, I have till the present time labored to meet his expectations and those of the Catholic body.

Meanwhile my History was virtually suspended, beyond the collection of material and studies of particular phases of periods. Understanding this, some friends in the clergy of the State[30] where I reside made an effort to enable me to lay aside all other work and apply myself to the completion of the History. Since the first of January I have done nothing else, except the editorial work of the *Catholic News,* notwithstanding which, my third volume is so far advanced that it will appear early this summer unless some unforeseen event intervenes.

I notified the proprietor of the *Catholic News* of the position of affairs, and of my relinquishment of all other work. As he had made heavy outlay, based on my continuance as editor of the *News,* he had felt great reluctance to sever the connection which will involve loss, and require a change in the management of the paper.

For my own part I should without hesitation retire at once from the editorial chair, did I find that it interfered with my special work. Hitherto it has been no obstacle, but, on the contrary, by the wide circulation it enjoys, the *News* brings me in contact with Catholics in all parts of the country, enables me to see all the Catholic journals, and profit by all historical reminiscences, biographical sketches and the like. It has also enabled me to obtain important and valuable material. My presence in the office is limited to two days, and the change of scene for that short time is beneficial to my health.

My great desire is to complete the History of the Church. To it I will sacrifice all other matters, and even the editorship of the *News,* if it proves the slightest bar, shall be relinquished on due notice, whenever I feel and my kind friends see that it retards the work.

To Father Corrigan,[31] May 5, 1890.

I inserted in the last number of the *News* a statement which you

---

[30] The names of this committee in the Diocese of Newark were listed in the final volume of Shea's work which appeared some months after his death in 1892 (IV, vii–viii).

[31] Patrick Corrigan (1830–1893), pastor of St. Mary's Church, Hoboken, New Jersey, was well known for his feud with his ordinary, Winand M. Wigger (1841–1901), over the question of priests' rights. He was the author of a brochure entitled *What the Catholic Church Most Needs in the United States, or, The Voice of the Priests in the Election of the Bishops* (New York, 1884).

have seen, as Mr. Ridder promised to send you copies. It defines my position and leaves me free to withdraw whenever I find it necessary. Last week I did an immense deal of work at Baltimore, and today I hear of a large batch of documents coming from Rome. My volume, so far as my actual material goes, is half done, and I am arranging to begin the printing at once. I got out volumes I and II by night work, about 25 hours a week, after a hard day's work in the office in New York. Now by the help coming from you and the large-hearted friends who have responded to you, I have devoted 55 hours a week to the History, and I certainly can complete the three volumes in two years or very little more. The connection with the *News* is a diversion that helps rather than retards the work, and of course when my book is completed, leaves me a foothold for the future. My chief aim is now to close up the work on the history with as little delay as possible, so as not to tax the generosity of my friends a day longer than is necessary. If, however, my name on Ridder's paper at all affects your appeal, it must come off and my work there cease.

To Father Corrigan, September 26, 1890.

While enclosing receipt for $1,000, being the third payment made by you this year, I must express more deeply than ever how much I owe you personally and all Catholics owe to your disinterested exertions and to the generous friends whom you have interested in the Church History of this country.

The accident which befell me and the consequence it entailed, made it very difficult for me to continue the work, and I began to feel that no one for a century would attempt to go so systematically over the whole ground. Your action enabled me to complete the work as I projected it. Besides adding steadily to my stock of documents from Rome and collections in dioceses here, I have acquired many necessary books, newspapers, pamphlets, letters of Bishops, priests, religious, giving me a rich mine of material.[32] Since the commencement of the year I have labored steadily on my third volume, and have nearly six hundred pages in type, so that I can certainly issue next month. I shall then set out for the West in search of documents and letters, and on my return, begin writing the fourth volume, which I hope, God willing, to complete by the first of May.

The fifth and concluding volume I aim and trust to have entirely

---

[32] Three days before Shea's death he signed an agreement with J. Havens Richards, S.J. (1851–1923), thirtieth president of Georgetown University, for the transfer of all his historical materials to Georgetown.

written by the end of the year, so as to issue it early in 1892. My aim
is to be able to show the whole work brought to a conclusion before
the Columbus centenary. In the volume about to appear I shall express
my gratitude for the appreciation already manifested in my work, but
I hope to receive from you a complete list of those who so nobly
co-operate with you that I may dedicate my fifth volume and the work
it crowns to those who deserve to be remembered as long as the work
can preserve their memory.

124. John Boyle O'Reilly's Speech in Behalf of the Negro, December 7, 1885, and His Editorial on the Excommunication of Dr. McGlynn, July 16, 1887

AMERICAN Catholic journalism had no more popular and influential figure
in the late nineteenth century than John Boyle O'Reilly (1844–1890). De-
ported to Australia by the British government in 1867 for his Fenian activities in behalf of Irish freedom, O'Reilly escaped and reached the United
States in 1869. He settled in Boston where he was soon on the staff of the
Pilot, becoming editor in 1876 and within a few years bringing that Catholic
weekly to a position of national prominence. O'Reilly combined the talents
of a poet and prose writer with a ringing patriotism and a deep devotion to
the Church. He was so attractive and gifted a personality that he was chosen
to compose verse for such occasions as the memorial to Wendel Phillips and
the unveiling of the monuments to Crispus Attucks and Plymouth Rock,
honors which, it has been said, "ordinarily only the most proper native
Protestant would have received" (Arthur Mann, *Yankee Reformers in the
Urban Age* [Cambridge, 1954], pp. 28–29). As a consequence of O'Reilly's
campaign against racism and his personal popularity, by the time of his
death he had done a good deal to close the breach between the Irish Catholics and Yankee Puritans of Boston. The documents that follow illustrate
two aspects of O'Reilly's thought: first, his championing of the cause of the
Negro, a stand that came naturally to one who had spent a lifetime opposing
the injustice practiced by England against the land of his birth; second,
his loyalty to the Church in the case of Father Edward McGlynn (1837–
1900) whose excommunication was pronounced by the Holy See when
McGlynn refused to go to Rome to explain his adherence to the land
theories of Henry George, and this in spite of O'Reilly's sympathies with
the ideas of McGlynn and George. Sources: James Jeffrey Roche, *Life of
John Boyle O'Reilly* (New York: Cassell Publishing Co., 1891), pp. 738–
742; Boston *Pilot,* July 16, 1887.

THE NEGRO-AMERICAN

Mr. President and Gentlemen: I was quite unaware of the nature of this meeting when I came here. I learn from Mr. Downing's speech that it is more or less a political meeting; that you are going to express preferences this way or that. I came here because I was asked to speak at a colored men's meeting in Boston. I don't care what your political preferences or parties are. I don't care whether you vote the Republican or Democratic ticket, but I know that if I were a colored man I should use parties as I would a club — to break down prejudices against my people. I shouldn't talk about being true to any party, except so far as that party was true to me. Parties care nothing for you only to use you. You should use parties; the highest party you have in this country is your own manhood. That is the thing in danger from all parties; that is the thing that every colored American is bound in his duty to himself and his children to defend and protect.

I think it is as wicked and unreasonable to discriminate against a man because of the color of his skin as it would be because of the color of his hair. He is no more responsible for the one than for the other, and one is no more significant than the òther. A previous speaker's reference to Mr. Parnell[1] and his growing power as a reformer ought to suggest to you that Parnell is to-day a powerful man because he is pledged to no party. He would smash the Tories tomorrow as readily as he smashed the Liberals yesterday. That is the meaning of politics. The highest interest of politics is the selfish interest of the people. You are never going to change the things, that affect you colored men, by law. If my children were not allowed into Northern schools, if I myself were not allowed into Northern hotels, I would change my party and my politics every day until I changed and wiped out that outrage.

I was in Tennessee last spring, and when I got out of the cars at Nashville I saw over the door of an apartment, "Colored people's waiting room." I went into it and found a wretched, poorly-furnished room, crowded with men, women, and children. Mothers with little children sat on the unwashed floor, and young men and young women filled the bare, uncomfortable seats that were fastened to the walls. Then I went out and found over another door, "Waiting-room." In there were the white people, carefully attended and comfortable; separate rooms for white men and women, well ventilated and well kept. I spent two days in Nashville, and every hour I saw things that

---

[1] Charles Stewart Parnell (1846–1891) was the leader of the Irish nationalists in the British House of Commons.

made me feel that something was the matter either with God or humanity in the South; and I said going away, "If ever the colored question comes up again as long as I live, I shall be counted in with the black men."

But this disregard for the colored people does not only exist in the South; I know there are many hotels in Boston, where, if any one of you were to ask for a room, they would tell you that all the rooms were filled.

The thing that most deeply afflicts the colored American is not going to be cured by politics. You have received from politics already about all it can give you.

You may change the law by politics, but it is not the law that is going to insult and outrage and excommunicate every colored American for generations to come. You can't cure the conceit of the white people that they are better than you by politics, nor their ignorance, nor their prejudice, nor their bigotry, nor any of the insolences which they cherish against their colored fellow-citizens.

Politics is the snare and delusion of white men as well as black. Politics tickles the skin of the social order; but this disease, and other diseases of class, privilege, and inheritance, lie deep in the internal organs. Social equity is based on principles of justice; political change on the opinion of a time. The black man's skin will be a mark of social inferiority so long as white men are conceited, ignorant and prejudiced. You cannot legislate these qualities out of the whites — you must steal and reason them out by teaching, illustration, and example.

No man ever came into the world with a grander opportunity than the American negro. He is like new metal dug out of the mine. He stands at this late day on the threshold of history, with everything to learn and less to unlearn, than any civilized man in the world. In his heart still ring the free sounds of the desert. In his mind he carries the traditions of Africa. The songs with which he charms American ears are refrains from the tropical forests, from the great inland seas and rivers of the dark continent.

At worst, the colored American has only a century or so of degrading civilized tradition and habit to forget and unlearn. His nature has only been injured on the outside by these late circumstances of his existence. Inside he is a new man, fresh from nature — a color-lover, an enthusiast, a believer by the heart, a philosopher, a cheerful, natural, good-natured man. I believe the colored American to be the kindliest human being in existence. All the inhumanities of slavery have not made him cruel or sullen or revengeful. He has all the qualities that fit him to be a good citizen of any country; he does not worry his soul to-day with the fear of next week or next year. He has feelings and convictions, and he loves to show them. He sees no reason why he should hide them. He will be a great natural expression if he dares to express the beauty, the color, the harmony of God's world as he sees it with a negro's eyes. That is the meaning of race distinction — that it should help us to see God's beauty in the world in various ways.

What this splendid man needs most is confidence in himself and his race. He is a dependent man at present. He is not sure of himself. He underrates his own qualities. He must be a self-respecting man. Not all men can be distinguished, but assuredly some distinct expression of genius will come out of any considerable community of colored people who believe in themselves, who contemn and despise the man of their blood who apes white men and their ways, who is proud to be a negro, who will bear himself according to his own ideas of a colored man, who will encourage his women to dress themselves by their own taste, to select the rich colors they love, to follow out their own natural bent, and not to adopt other people's stupid and shop-made fashions. The negro woman has the best artistic eye for color of all the women in America.

The negro is the only graceful, musical, color-loving American. He is the only American who has written new songs and composed new music. He is the most spiritual of Americans, for he worships with soul and not with narrow mind. For him religion is to be believed, accepted like the very voice of God, and not invented, contrived, reasoned about, shaded, and made fashionably lucrative and marketable, as it is made by too many white Americans.

The negro is a new man, a free man, a spiritual man, a hearty man; and he can be a great man if he will avoid modeling himself on the whites. No race ever became illustrious on borrowed ideas or the imitated qualities of another race.

No race or nation is great or illustrious except by one test — the breeding of great men. Not great merchants or traders, not rich men, bankers, insurance-mongers, or directors of gas companies. But great thinkers — great seers of the world through their own eyes — great tellers of the truths and beauties and colors and equities as they alone see them. Great poets — ah, great poets above all — and their brothers, great painters and musicians, fashioners of God's beautiful shapes in clay and marble and harmony.

The negro will never take his full stand beside the white man till he has given the world proof of the truth and beauty of heroism and power that are in his soul. And only by the organs of the soul are these delivered — by self-respect and self-reflection, by philosophy, religion, poetry, art, love, and sacrifice. One great poet will be worth a hundred bankers and brokers, worth ten Presidents of the United States, to the negro race. One great musician will speak to the world for the black man as no thousand editors or politicians can.

The wealth of our Western soil, in its endless miles of fertility, is less to America than the unworked wealth of the rich negro nature. The negro poet of the future will be worth two Mexicos to America. God send wise guides to my black fellow-countrymen, who shall lead them to understand and accept what is true and great and perennial, and to reject what is deceptive and changeable in life, purpose, and hope.

It is a great pleasure to me to say these things that I have long believed to a colored meeting in Boston. It would be a greater pleasure to go down to Nashville and address a colored meeting there; and God grant that it may be soon possible for a Boston white man to go down to Nashville and address colored men. As I said in the beginning, so long as American citizens and their children are excluded from schools, theaters, hotels, or common conveyances, there ought not to be and there is not among those who love justice and liberty, any question of race, creed, or color; every heart that beats for humanity, beats with the oppressed.

DR. McGLYNN

It is hard to find words to express the pain felt by the Catholics of America over the excommunication of Dr. McGlynn. Grief for the insubordination of a priest once deeply loved and respected is strangely mixed with astonishment and perplexity at his stubborn refusal to abide by the primary elements of Church discipline.

In this excommunication there is no question whatever of political or social principles. It is wholly a matter of Church discipline. Dr. McGlynn directly refused to obey the order of the Sacred Congregation of the Propaganda, to go to Rome and be heard in his own behalf. For this insubordination the threatened excommunication falls upon him, his own hand bringing down the blow.

No matter what following Dr. McGlynn may win outside the Church, either of children of the Church or others, those who love him best and wish him most happiness will continue to pray that his pride may be put under his feet, that he may come back to the altar like a child to its mother, humble and sorrowful for his rebellion.

Right or wrong, submission to the authority of the Church is the manly as well as the priestly and Christian duty of Dr. McGlynn. Because he submits, no true principle which he may hold will die. Because he rebels, whatever truth or virtue may lie in his land doctrine is set back, discountenanced and weighted down. No cause ever suffered by the humiliation of its apostles.

It is nonsense for Dr. McGlynn to say that he has been excommunicated because he taught that God made the land for the people. It is not true. The Sacred Congregation of Propaganda has never considered Henry George's theories. Dr. McGlynn is simply like a soldier who refuses to keep step or rank or direction.

But he will come back — he will surely stay his feet in time. Believe it, the heart of the priest is true, and the passion will not hold it long. He will wash away the stains of the scandal with tears. Too many love him and pray for him to let him go too far. *Soggarth Aroon, Soggarth Aroon,* remember the little ones who do not know!

125. Bishop Keane's Admonitions to Cardinal Gibbons, December 29, 1886

JOHN J. KEANE (1839–1918) was one of the most colorful and forthright prelates in the group of remarkable bishops who governed the American Church in the late nineteenth and early twentieth centuries. Irish-born, he came to the United States at the age of seven, and twelve years after his ordination he was named fifth Bishop of Richmond in 1878. In August, 1888, he was formally appointed first rector of the Catholic University of America, a post for which he had no training but which brought out his talents for imaginative leadership, arresting public address, and enthusiastic promotion of a cause to which he had committed himself. Keane learned his job by serious reading and by visits to various institutions where he counseled with leading university executives. Thoroughly American in his sentiments, forthright in his view, and convinced of the necessity for a closer relationship between American Catholics and their fellow countrymen, at times his enthusiasm outran his discretion. The result was that he incurred enmity and suspicion as a liberal whose orthodoxy was not entirely sound. In September, 1896, he was summarily dismissed from the university, spent several years of exile in Rome, and was vindicated only in September, 1900, when he was named second Archbishop of Dubuque, a position he held until his resignation was accepted by the Holy See in April, 1911. Few bishops served the American Church more unselfishly and few experienced more reverses and humiliations than Keane. Yet he bore it all in a spirit of deep religious faith and at no time was known to have succumbed to embitterment. The following letter, written from Rome to Cardinal Gibbons at a time when the latter showed signs of wavering on several important questions before the Roman Curia, offers a good example of Keane's candor, courage, and steadfast devotion to what his biographer characterizes as "the best interests of the Catholic Church in the United States even though it could have meant the loss of a powerful friend" (Patrick H. Ahern, *The Life of John J. Keane, Educator and Archbishop, 1839–1918* [Milwaukee, 1955], p. 37). It was a measure of the cardinal's magnanimity that this letter did nothing to impair their friendship and, in fact, he may even be said to have shown thereafter more resolution in his policies. Source: Archives of the Archdiocese of Baltimore, 82–J–4, Keane to Gibbons, Rome, December 29, 1886.

Your Eminence:

We were delighted to receive yesterday your letter of the 17th. Its references to the three important points of the German question,[1] the coadjutorship of N. Orleans,[2] & the Knights of Labor,[3] were most valuable & welcome. I at once put them into three Latin documents, and handed them in to the Propaganda this morning. They will be sure to have great weight. I was very glad to be thus enabled to put your Eminence in a proper light in the Propaganda on the N. Orleans question. You were there identified with the advocacy of Dr. Chapelle's[4] nomination; and as he is sure to be the losing man, you were going down with him on the losing side. Your present advocacy of Bishop Janssens[5] puts you once more on the winning side, where you ought to be.

But I beg that you will permit me, dear and venerated friend, to go on and mention things which it is exceedingly painful for me to pen, and which only my high regard for yourself personally and for the exalted office which you hold, could induce me to write, for it is a hard task and often a risky one, to write painful truths to a friend, especially when he is a superior. Only *real* friendship can nerve one to the duty.

[1] At the time Keane wrote there was serious dissension within the Church of the United States between the Irish and German elements over the petition which Father Peter M. Abbelen of Milwaukee had presented to the Holy See in November, 1886, charging the hierarchy with neglect of the German Catholic immigrants.

[2] The question of a coadjutor with the right of succession to Francis X. Leray (1825–1887), Archbishop of New Orleans, was also in dispute.

[3] In August, 1884, the Knights of Labor in Canada had been condemned by Rome as a forbidden secret society. An effort to secure a unanimous judgment of the archbishops of the United States in favor of the knights in this country was not successful and, therefore, the question had to be referred to the Holy See for a final decision.

[4] Placide L. Chapelle (1842–1905) was named Coadjutor Archbishop of Santa Fe in 1891 and in December, 1897, was promoted to the See of New Orleans.

[5] Francis Janssens (1843–1897) had been Bishop of Natchez since 1881. In August, 1888, he was named Archbishop of New Orleans.

I find, to my intense regret, that an impression has taken shape in Rome to the effect that your Eminence is changeable in views, weak and vacillating in purpose, anxious to conciliate both parties on nearly every question; that it is hard to know, therefore upon which side you stand concerning any important question, or what weight to attach to your utterances. Hence I find a growing inclination to look elsewhere than to your Eminence for reliable information & judgments, — a tendency, not only here but among the Bishops of the United States, to look to New York rather than to Baltimore for the representative & leader of our Hierarchy.

Against this I protest with all earnestness; but they allege fact after fact in defence of their position. They say that, just as in the change of front in regard to New Orleans there is evidence that the former letter was written to please the Archbishop, and did not represent your real views as to the best & safest man, which was what they expected of you, so there was a somewhat similar change of front in regard to poor Dr. Foley,[6] whose friends, notwithstanding all explanations, feel quite sore over his having been finally abandonment [*sic*]. They offset your sentiments on the German question by the fact that the emissary of this attack secretly directed against our Hierarchy by a few German prelates, comes to Rome with a letter of introduction from your Eminence.[7] And they further allege the case of Bishop Dwenger,[8] who may be considered an arch-mover in this bad cause, who, in order to make much of himself & of his cause, had himself sent on here by your Eminence as the representative of our Hierarchy in regard to the Plenary Council, — and they overwhelm me by adding that whereas your Eminence at first asserted that you did not intend to send him, and denied that you had sent him, you later acknowledged that you had done so. We have lately

[6] John S. Foley (1833–1918). Foley had been on the *terne* for both the See of Savannah in 1885 and the vacancy in the Diocese of Wilmington in 1886, but in each case opposition to his candidacy arose and he was not appointed. In November, 1888, however, he was consecrated as Bishop of Detroit, a post which he filled until his death.

[7] Before he sailed for Rome on October 13, 1886, Abbelen had received a letter of recommendation from Gibbons to Giovanni Cardinal Simeoni, Prefect of the Congregation of Propaganda de Fide. The Cardinal of Baltimore had known Abbelen's good work in the Third Plenary Council of 1884, but he was not aware of the real nature of the petition which Abbelen was taking to the Holy See.

[8] Joseph Dwenger, C.PP.S. (1837–1893), was Bishop of Fort Wayne from 1872 to his death. Keane was referring here to Gibbons' appointment of Dwenger as one of the two American bishops who were charged with getting the legislation of the Third Plenary Council approved in Rome. Dwenger's conduct of that mission aroused a considerable amount of opposition among his fellow bishops.

been pouring out our[9] honest indignation at the charge that the signatures of the Prelates to the University petition could not be implicitly trusted as giving the real sentiment of the signers;[10] but I cannot help recognizing with what crushing force they can say to us: "Why look, even your Cardinal puts his name to statements & recommendations which he will afterwards take back or modify; if even he can send us important documents, not because he believes them best for the interests of the Church, but in order to please this one or that one, what confidence can we repose in any of these signatures?" They do not always say this in honest words; but they say it quite gallantly in meaning shrugs, and smiles, and insinuations. Even the Holy Father himself has thus intimated his apprehension that your Eminence was uncertain & vacillating in your views as to the University's location, etc.

I know well, dear & venerated friend, that whatever truth there may be in all this has its real source in your kindness of heart, your anxiety to be gracious and yielding to every one as far as you possibly can. But, as happened to the old man in the fable, by endeavoring to be over prudent and to please all, there is great danger that you eventually will please no one, — that both here and at home they will come to mistrust your consistency & strength of character, and to look elsewhere than to our beloved Cardinal for our exponent & our leader. It galls me to the heart to think that such injustice should be done to our Cardinal; to the leader whom Providence has given to us, — and it is this thought that has given me courage to write so plainly on so painful a subject. Let me hope that you will not be offended, that you will appreciate the affectionate devotedness which, next to my desire for the Church's best welfare, has been my only motive in thus writing; and let me hope that henceforth your Eminence will more than regain the lost ground, by showing such singleness, such consistency, such firmness, such nobleness, in every word and act, as to fully realize the grand ideal of your position in the fore-front of the foremost Hierarchy of the world.

---

[9] Keane's use of the plural throughout his letter referred to John Ireland (1838–1918), then Bishop of St. Paul, who was with him in Rome and who co-operated closely with Keane on all the problems of the American Church which were before the Roman Curia.

[10] At a meeting of the committee for the university held at Baltimore on October 27, 1886, they had drawn up documents for Pope Leo XIII and Cardinal Simeoni approving the plans so far made for the university. Since five other archbishops were in Baltimore at the time they were asked to sign the documents and did so. The opposition party, however, later made it known at the Holy See that some of those who signed were not really in favor of the project.

From the depths of my heart I wish you a blessed & happy new year, and am ever

Your devoted servant & friend in Christ,

John J. Keane, Bp. of Rd.[11]

126. John LaFarge Describes His Painting of "The Ascension," 1887

OF JOHN LA FARGE (1835–1910) it has been said, "With his learning, his imagination, and his skill he gave rank to American art more than any other of the craft. For that reason he is to-day hailed as master and written down in our annals as belonging with the Olympians" (John G. Van Dyke, *American Painting and Its Tradition* [New York, 1919], p. 146). LaFarge was a man who left the imprint of his genius not only on painting and stained glass but upon the lives of many of the leading American men of art and letters of his time. His extraordinary mind began to manifest itself at a very early age. For example, in a little over two months while he was in boarding school — and before he had reached his sixteenth birthday — he requested his father to send him works of Herodotus, Plautus, Catullus, Dryden, Goldsmith, Michelet, Molière, Corneille, and Victor Hugo for his reading (cf. "Schoolboy Letters between John LaFarge and His Father," *Historical Records and Studies*, XVIII [March, 1928], 74–120). LaFarge graduated on June 29, 1853, from Mount Saint Mary's College, Emmitsburg, with Silas M. Chatard (1838–1918), later fifth Bishop of Vincennes as a classmate, and Orestes Brownson delivering an address on "Liberal Studies." By the time he was thirty his reputation as an artist was widespread and his glass for the windows of Trinity Church, Boston, in 1876 brought him international fame. Among his principal works was the great mural painting of "The Ascension" for the Protestant Episcopal Church of the Ascension in New York. Of that picture his biographer remarked, "LaFarge never painted anything more purely beautiful than 'The Ascension' and it might not unreasonably be taken as summing up his qualities as a mural decorator. . . ." (Cortissoz, *op. cit.*, p. 171). In the following letter to Cortissoz, undated, LaFarge described some of the problems he encountered in painting "The Ascension." Source: Royal Cortissoz, *John LaFarge. A Memoir and A Study* (Boston: Houghton Mifflin Co., 1911), pp. 161–166.

In the picture of "The Ascension" in the Tenth Street church there were some very curious problems. The clergyman had liked a drawing which I had made many years before, let us say some thirty years ago,

---

[11] There was no answer to this letter among the Keane Papers, nor a copy of such found in the archives at Baltimore. In Gibbons' diary under date of January 14, 1887, there was the unrevealing entry: "Wrote to Bp. Keane in reply to his letter from Rome of Dec. 29" (Archives of the Archdiocese of Baltimore, Diary of Cardinal Gibbons, p. 213).

of that subject, with a similar grouping. This was to be a very narrow high window for a memorial chapel out West. It was never carried out; in fact it was nothing but one of those projects forced upon unfortunate artists by enthusiastic millionaires who forget almost immediately what their last plans had been. I do not even know if anything was done about it, but the proposed patron was interesting, owing to his having very many works of art, some of which were fine and the others not usually seen in this country even to-day — not that they were good.

The Dr. Donald,[1] the clergyman, happening to see this, wished to have this long and narrow window carried out where you now see the painting; there being a recess in the wall, it might be used. At that time I was very anxious to have Saint-Gaudens[2] get a chance to do work and to show his capacity. Remember that I am talking of very many years ago. I proposed that he might, perhaps, be tempted to make a great bas-relief of this to fill that space; but there were too many reasons against it, among others those of money. A painting can be done, it is supposed, quite cheaply compared to a piece of sculpture, even if that sculpture is only in plaster at a few cents a foot.

By and by, when Stanford White[3] took charge of the church, the questions came together and it was proposed that I should paint the picture upon the wide space which he left for it. But that space was many, many times wider than the sketch or study and even enlarging the figures in enormous proportions would not fill it. Even now the picture is almost square, so that I had a problem of widening my space of figures and of settling their proportion in a given space. Nothing that I could do, and keep the original intention, would allow the change to be done to cover enough space, so that I proposed a frame which should both cut a little space, indicate the Gothic character of the church, and help what I thought I was going to do to carry out the painting — that was to place these figures in a very big landscape. The landscape I wished to have extremely natural, because I depended on it to make my figures also look natural and to account for the floating of some twenty figures or more in the air. We do not see this ever, as you know, but I knew that by a combination of the clouds and figures I might help this look of what the mystic people call levitation.

---

[1] The Reverend Dr. E. W. Donald was rector of the Church of the Ascension.

[2] Augustus Saint-Gaudens (1848–1907), the sculptor, was greatly influenced by LaFarge.

[3] Stanford White (1853–1906) was a famous American architect of the period.

Of course you may well suppose that I studied what I could of all the people who are swung in ropes and other arrangements across theatres and circuses. The question of the composition of the figures had to meet certain geometric conditions in my mind; that is to say, to fit a given pattern which I thought fortunate in the space. I forget whether it was an arrangement of hexagons but I have a faint belief that it was, owing to the arithmetical figures of the proportions of the space. That could be settled, but my landscape, — I was much troubled.

At that moment I was asked to go to Japan by my friend Henry Adams,[4] and I went there in 1886. I had a vague belief that I might find there certain conditions of line in the mountains which might help me. Of course the Judean mountains were entirely out of question, all the more that they implied a given place. I kept all this in mind and on one given day I saw before me a space of mountain and cloud and flat land which seemed to me to be what was needed. I gave up my other work and made thereupon a rapid but very careful study, so complete that the big picture is only a part of the amount of work put into the study of that afternoon. There are turns of the tide which allow you at times to do an amount of work incredible in sober moments; as you know, there are very many such cases; I do not understand it myself. When I returned I was still of the same mind. My studies of separate figures were almost ready and all I had to do was to stretch the canvas and begin the work.

Perhaps you do not know that I got into great difficulties thereupon. The weight of such a canvas is something very great. The mere lead paint used to fasten it was far over five hundred pounds. The wall, that is to say, the plaster wall, was a new one, just made, and I felt dubious about its standing this weight, when, as you know, the canvas is fastened down and then pulled flat by a great many men. It was just as I surmised. The wall tumbled down as soon as the canvas was put up, or, rather, when the first part of it was fastened. They were careful about the next wall and I believe that it is now a safe one.

After that I had only pleasure out of my work. During that summer

---

[4] Henry Adams (1838–1918), the historian, was another man who was strongly influenced by LaFarge. In his own memoirs Adams said, "Of all the men who had deeply affected their friends since 1850 John LaFarge was certainly the foremost, and for Henry Adams, who had sat at his feet since 1872, the question of how much he owed to LaFarge could be answered only by admitting that he had no standards to measure it by" (*The Education of Henry Adams. An Autobiography* [Boston, 1918], p. 369).

my friend Okakura[5] spent a great deal of his time with me and I
could paint, and then, in the intervals, we could talk about spiritual
manifestations and all that beautiful wonderland which they have;
that is to say, the Buddhists, where the spiritual bodies take form
and disappear again and the edges of the real and the imaginary melt.
I had one objection brought up by a friend, a lady, who was
troubled by certain news she had heard. That was that I had made
these studies of clouds in a pagan country, while a true Episcopalian
would make them, I suppose, in England. Otherwise I think people
have liked this and everybody has been very kind about it. At a
distance the picture is not injured, I think, by the rapidity of its
execution, only a summer and an autumn, during which I carried out
several other large things.

127. Cardinal Gibbons' Defense of the Knights of Labor, February 20, 1887

THROUGHOUT the nineteenth century which witnessed the most rapid
growth of the Church in this country, the great majority of American
Catholics belonged to the working classes. In a period marked by the rise
of grave evils in the system of industrial capitalism it was not surprising
that the workers should have resorted to secret organizations to defend
their rights. In so doing there were at times real abuses, which became the
source of deep anxiety to the American bishops lest these secret societies
should alienate Catholics from their religious obligations. Fortunately, the
hierarchy had at the time a man who possessed the wisdom to weigh the
issues judiciously and the foresight to see that a severe condemnation by
the Church of the Knights of Labor, the greatest labor organization of the
day, would endanger the faith of thousands of Catholic workers. That man
was James Cardinal Gibbons, Archbishop of Baltimore (1834–1921). In
September, 1884, the Holy See had condemned the K. of L. in Canada at
the request of the Archbishop of Quebec. But Gibbons was intent that this
action should not be extended to his own country. Upon a visit to Rome
in 1887 he prepared — with the assistance of Bishops John Ireland and
John Keane — a forceful protest against such a possibility which he submitted to the Congregation de Propaganda Fide. The result was that the
condemnation which some of the American bishops had sought was not
issued, and Gibbons' memorial became the deciding factor in averting what
would have proved a major calamity. As a consequence the tradition of
friendliness between the Church and labor in the United States was established and has endured, and the alienation of the Catholic workers — which
constituted so heavy a loss to the Church in the countries of western Europe
— has never had a counterpart in the United States. Source: Henry J.

[5] Okakura was a Japanese friend of LaFarge's not otherwise identified.

Browne, *The Catholic Church and the Knights of Labor* (Washington: The Catholic University of America Press, 1949), pp. 365–378.

Your Eminence:

In submitting to the Holy See the conclusions which after several months of attentive observation and reflection,[1] seem to me to sum up the truth concerning the association of the Knights of Labor, I feel profoundly convinced of the vast importance of the consequences attaching to this question, which forms but a link in the great chain of the social problems of our day, and especially of our country.

In weighing [treating — jugeant] this question I have been very careful to follow as my constant guide the spirit of the Encyclicals, in which our Holy Father, Leo XIII, has so admirably set forth the dangers of our time and their remedies, as well as the principles by which we are to recognize associations condemned by the Holy See. Such was also the guide of the Third Plenary Council of Baltimore in its teaching concerning the principles to be followed and the dangers to be shunned by the faithful either in the choice or in the establishment of those associations toward which the spirit of our popular institutions so strongly impels them. And considering the dire [evil — funestes] consequences that might result from a mistake in the treatment of organizations which often count their members by the thousands and hundred of thousands, the council wisely ordained (n. 255) [n. 225] that when an association is spread over several dioceses, not even the bishop of one of these dioceses shall condemn it, but shall refer the case to a standing committee of all the archbishops of the United States; and even these are not authorized to condemn unless their sentence be unanimous; and in case they fail to agree unanimously, then only the supreme tribunal of the Holy See can impose a condemnation; all this in order to avoid error and confusion of discipline.

This committee of archbishops held a meeting, in fact, toward the end of last October, especially to consider the association of the Knights of Labor [at which the Knights of Labor was specially considered — spécialement pour consider]. We were not persuaded to

[1] Archives of the Archdiocese of Baltimore, 82-N-3. The "official" English version, first published in the *Moniteur de Rome* on March 28, 1887, was reproduced in a number of works, among them Allen Sinclair Will, *Life of Cardinal Gibbons, Archbishop of Baltimore* (New York, 1922), I, 337–352. The lesser differences in the readings which usually show the toning down of the original French for American readers, are indicated in brackets within the text. The other variations are cited in the notes.

hold this meeting because of any request on the part of our bishops, for none of them had asked for it; and it should also be said that, among all the bishops we know, only two or three desire the condemnation. But the importance of the question in itself, and in the estimation of the Holy See led us to examine it with greatest attention. After our discussion, the results of which have already been communicated to the Sacred Congregation of the Propaganda, only two out of the twelve archbishops voted for condemnation, and their reasons were powerless to convince the others of either the justice or the prudence of such a condemnation.

In the following considerations I wish to state in detail the reasons which determined the vote of the great majority of the committee — reasons whose truth and force seem to me all the more evident today; I shall try at the same time to do justice to the arguments advanced by the opposition.

1. In the first place, in the constitution, laws and official declarations of the Knights of Labor, there can clearly be found assertions and rules [though there may be found . . . things — peuvent bien se trouver des assertions ou des règles] which we would not approve; but we have not found in them those elements so clearly pointed out by the Holy See, which places them among condemned associations.

(a) In their form of initiation there is no oath.

(b) The obligation to secrecy by which they keep the knowledge of their business from strangers or enemies, in no wise prevents Catholics from manifesting everything to competent ecclesiastical authority, even outside of confession. This has been positively declared to us by their president [their chief officers — leur président].

(c) They make no promise of blind obedience. The object and laws of the association are distinctly declared, and the obligation of obedience does not go beyond these limits.

(d) They not only profess no hostility against religion or the Church, but their declarations are quite to the contrary. The Third Plenary Council commands that we should not condemn an association without giving a hearing to its officers or representatives: "auditis ducibus, corypheis vel sociis praecipuis" (n. 254).[2] Now, their president in sending me a copy of their constitution, says that he is a Catholic from the bottom of his heart [devoted Catholic — Catholique du fond de son coeur]; that he practices his religion faithfully and receives the sacraments regularly; that he belongs to no Masonic or other society condemned by the Church; that he knows of nothing

---

[2] The Latin phrase was omitted in the English version.

in the association of the Knights of Labor contrary to the laws of the Church; that, with filial submission he begs the Pastors of the Church to examine all the details of their organization [their constitution and laws — tous les détails de leur organisation], and, if they find anything worthy of condemnation, they should indicate it, and he promises its correction. Assuredly one does not perceive in all this any hostility to the authority of the Church, but on the contrary a spirit in every way praiseworthy. After their convention last year at Richmond, he and several of the officers and members, devout Catholics [principal members — officiers et members], made similar declarations concerning their feelings[3] and the action of that convention, the documents of which we are expecting to receive.

(e) Nor do we find in this organization any hostility to the authority and laws of our country. Not only does nothing of the kind appear in their constitution and laws, but the heads of our civil government treat with the greatest respect [with respect — avec le plus grand respect] the cause which they represent. The President of the United States told me personally, a month ago [a few weeks ago — il y a un mois] that he was then examining a law for the amelioration of certain social grievances and that he had just had a long conference on the subject with Mr. Powderly,[4] president of the Knights of Labor. The Congress of the United States, following the advice of President Cleveland is busying itself at the present time with the amelioration of the working classes, in whose complaints they acknowledge openly[5] there is a great deal of truth. And our political parties, far from regarding them as enemies of the country, vie with each other in championing the evident rights of the poor workmen [workmen — pauvres travailleurs], who seek not to resist[6] the laws, but only to obtain just legislation by constitutional and legitimate means.

These considerations, which show that in this association [these associations — cette association] those elements are not to be found which the Holy See condemns, lead us to study, in the second place, the evils which the associations contend against, and the nature of the conflict.

2. That there exist among us, as in the other countries of the

---

[3] "Leurs sentiments" was not translated.

[4] Terence V. Powderly (1849–1924), a Catholic at the time, was elected Grand Master Workman of the K. of L. in September, 1879, and held that office until November, 1893. After mentioning that Congress followed the advice of Cleveland, the English version inserted "in his annual message."

[5] "Ouvertement" was not translated.

[6] "Or overthrow" was inserted.

world, grave and threatening social evils, public injustices, which call for strong resistance and legal remedy, is a fact which no one dares to deny, and the truth of which has been already acknowledged by the Congress and the President of the United States. Without entering into the sad details of these wrongs, — which does not seem necessary here, — it may suffice to mention only that monopolies on the part of both individuals and of corporations, have already called forth not only the complaints of our working classes, but also the opposition of our public men and legislators; that the efforts of these monopolists, not always without success, to control legislation to their own profit, cause serious apprehension among the disinterested friends of liberty; that the heartless avarice which, through greed of gain, pitilessly grinds not only the men, but particularly the women and children in various employments, makes it clear to all who love humanity and justice that it is not only the right of the laboring classes to protect themselves, but the duty of the whole people to aid them in finding a remedy against the dangers with which both civilization and the social order are menaced by avarice, oppression and corruption.

It would be vain to deny either the existence of the evils, the right of legitimate resistance, or the necessity of a remedy. At most doubt might be raised about the legitimacy of the form of resistance and the remedy employed by the Knights of Labor. This then ought to be the next point of our examination.

3. It can hardly be doubted that for the attainment of any public end, association — the organization of all interested persons — is the most efficacious means, a means altogether natural and just. This is so evident, and besides so conformable to the genius of our country, of our essentially popular social conditions, that it is unnecessary to insist upon it. It is almost the only means to invite public attention, to give force to the most legitimate resistance, to add weight to the most just demands.

Now there already exists an organization which presents a thousand attractions and advantages, but which our Catholic workingmen, with filial obedience to the Holy See, refuse to join; this is the *Masonic* organization, which exists everywhere in our country, and which, as Mr. Powderly has expressly pointed out to us, unites employer and worker in a brotherhood very advantageous for the latter, but which numbers in its ranks hardly a single Catholic. Freely [nobly — de grand coeur] renouncing the advantages which the Church and their consciences forbid, workingmen form associations [join — se forment], having nothing in common with the deadly designs of the enemies of religion and seeking only mutual protection and help, and the legitimate assertion of their rights. But here they also find themselves threatened with condemnation, and so deprived of [hindered from — privés] their only means of defense. Is it surprising that they should be astonished at this and that they ask *Why?*[7]

4. Let us now consider the objections made against this sort of organization.

(a) It is objected that in these organizations Catholics are mixed with Protestants, to the peril of their faith. Naturally, yes, they are mixed with Protestants in the workers' associations,[8] precisely as they are at their work; for in a mixed people like ours, the separation of religious in social affairs is not possible. But to suppose that the faith of our Catholics suffers thereby is not to know the Catholic workers of America who are not like the workingmen of so many European countries — misguided and perverted children, looking on their Mother the Church as a hostile stepmother — but they are intelligent, well instructed and devoted children ready to give their blood, as they continually give their means (although small and hard-earned) [hard-earned — chétifs et péniblement gagnés] for her support and protection. And in fact it is not in the present case that Catholics are mixed with Protestants, but rather that Protestants are admitted to the advantages of an association, two-thirds of whose members and the principal officers [many of whose members and officers — des deux tiers des membres et les officiers principaux] are Catholics; and in a country like ours their exclusion would be simply impossible.

(b) But it is said, could there not be substituted for such an organization confraternities which would unite the workingmen under the direction of the priests and the direct influence of religion? I answer frankly that I do not believe that either possible or necessary in our country. I sincerely admire the efforts of this sort which are made in countries where the workers are led astray by the enemies of religion; but thanks be to God, that is not our condition. We find that in our country the presence and explicit influence of the clergy would not be advisable where our citizens, without distinction of religious belief, come together in regard to their industrial interests alone. Without going so far, we have abundant means for making our

---

[7] The last sentence of the paragraph was entirely omitted in the English version.

[8] The first part of the parallel was omitted in English: "avec les Protestants dans les associations des travailleurs, précisément comme ils sont dans le travaux mêmes."

working people faithful Catholics, and simple good sense advises us not to go to extremes.

(c) Again, it is objected that the liberty of such an organization exposes Catholics to the evil influences of the most dangerous associates, even of atheists, communists, and anarchists. That is true; but it is one of the trials of faith which our brave American Catholics are accustomed to meet almost daily, and which they know how to disregard with good sense and firmness. The press of our country tells us and the president of the Knights of Labor has related to us, how these violent and aggressive elements have endeavored to seize authority in their councils, or to inject their poison into the principles of the association; but they also verify with what determination these evil spirits [machinators — mauvais esprits] have been repulsed and defeated. The presence among our citizens of this destructive element, which has come for the most part from certain nations of Europe, is assuredly for us an occasion of lively regrets and careful precautions; it is an inevitable fact, however, but one which the union between the Church and her children in our country renders comparatively free from danger. In truth, the only grave danger would come from an alienation between the Church and her children, which nothing would more certainly occasion than imprudent condemnations.

(d) An especially weighty charge is drawn from the outbursts of violence, even to bloodshed, which have characterized [accompanied — charactérizé] several of the strikes inaugurated by labor organizations. Concerning this, three things are to be remarked: first, strikes are not an invention of the Knights of Labor, but a means almost everywhere and always resorted to by employees in our land and elsewhere to protest against what they consider unjust and to demand their rights; secondly in such a struggle of the poor and indignant multitudes against hard and obstinate monopoly, anger and violence [outbursts of anger — colère et le violence] are often as inevitable as they are regrettable; thirdly, the laws and chief authorities of the Knights of Labor, far from encouraging violence or the occasions of it, exercise a powerful influence to hinder it, and to keep strikes within the limits of good order and legitimate action. A careful examination of the acts of violence which have marked the struggle between capital and labor during the past year, leaves us convinced that it would be unjust to attribute them to the association of the Knights of Labor. This was but one of several associations of workers that took part in the strikes, and their chief officers, according to disinterested witnesses, used every possible effort to appease the anger of the crowds and to prevent the excesses which, in my judgment, could not justly be attributed to them. Doubtless among the Knights of Labor as among thousands of other workingmen, there are violent, or even wicked and criminal men, who have committed inexcusable deeds of violence, and have urged their associates to do the same; but to attribute this to the organization, it seems to me, would be as unreasonable as to attribute to the Church the follies and crimes of her children against which she protests.[9] I repeat that in such a struggle of the great masses of the people against the mail-clad power, which, as it is acknowledged, often refuses them the simple rights of humanity and justice, it is vain to expect that every error and every act of violence can be avoided; and to dream that this struggle can be prevented, or that we can deter the multitudes from organizing, which is their only practical means [hope — moyen pratique] of success, would be to ignore the nature and forces of human society in times like ours. The part of Christian prudence evidently is to try to hold the hearts of the multitude by the bonds of love, in order to control their actions by the principles of faith, justice and charity, to acknowledge frankly the truth and justice in their cause, in order to deter them from what would be false and criminal, and thus to turn into a legitimate, peaceable and beneficent contest what could easily become for the masses of our people a volcanic abyss, like that which society fears and the Church deplores in Europe.

Upon this point I insist strongly, because, from an intimate acquaintance with the social conditions of our country I am profoundly convinced that here we are touching upon a subject which not only concerns the rights of the working classes, who ought to be especially dear to the Church which our Divine Lord sent to evangelize the poor, but with which are bound up the fundamental interests of the Church and of human society for the future. This is a point which I desire, in a few additional words to develop more clearly.

5. Whoever meditates upon the ways in which divine Providence is guiding contemporary history cannot fail to remark how important is the part which the power of the people takes therein at present and must take in the future. We behold, with profound sadness, the efforts of the prince of darkness to make this power dangerous to the social weal by withdrawing the masses of the people from the influence of religion, and impelling them towards the ruinous paths of license and anarchy. Until now our country presents a picture of altogether different [most consolingly different — tout différent] char-

---

[9] "Proteste" was translated "strives and protests."

acter — that of a popular power regulated by love of good order, by respect for religion, by obedience to the authority of the laws, not a democracy of license and violence, but that true democracy which aims at the general prosperity through the means of sound principles and good social order.

In order to preserve so desirable a state of things it is absolutely necessary that religion should continue to hold the affections, and thus rule the conduct of the multitudes. As Cardinal Manning has so well written,[10] "In the future era the Church has no longer to deal with princes and parliaments, but with the masses, with the people. Whether we will or no this is our work; we need a new spirit, a new direction of our life and activity." To lose influence over the people would be to lose the future altogether; and it is by the heart, far more than by the understanding, that we must hold and guide this immense power, so mighty either for good or for evil. Among all the glorious titles of the Church which her history has merited for her, there is not one which at present gives her so great influence as that of *Friend of the People*. Assuredly, in our democratic country, it is this title which wins for the Catholic Church not only the enthusiastic devotedness of the millions of her children, but also the respect and admiration of all our citizens, whatever be their religious belief. It is the power of precisely this title which renders persecution almost an impossibility, and which draws toward our holy Church the great heart of the American people.

And since it is acknowledged by all that the great questions of the future are not those of war, of commerce or finance, but the social questions, the questions which concern the improvement of the condition of the great masses of the people, and especially of the working people, it is evidently of supreme importance that the Church should always be found on the side of humanity, of justice toward the multitudes who compose the body of the human family. As the same Cardinal Manning very wisely wrote, "We must admit and accept calmly and with good will that industries and profits must be considered in second place; the moral state and domestic condition of the whole working population must be considered first. I will not venture to formulate the acts of parliament, but here is precisely their fundamental principle for the future. The conditions of the lower classes as are found at present among our people, can not

---

[10] In the English version this quotation is introduced with the words, "A new task is before us."

and must not continue. On such a basis no social edifice can stand."[11] In our country, especially, this is the inevitable program of the future, and the position which the Church must hold toward the solution is sufficiently obvious. She must certainly not favor the extremes to which the poor multitudes are naturally inclined, but, I repeat, she must withhold them from these extremes by the bonds of affection, by the maternal desire which she will manifest for the concession of all that is just and reasonable in their demands, and by the maternal blessing which she will bestow upon every legitimate means for improving the condition of the people.

6. Now let us consider for a moment the consequences which would inevitably follow from a contrary course, from a lack of sympathy for the working class, from a suspicion of their aims, from a hasty condemnation of their methods.

(a) First, there is the evident danger of the Church's losing in popular estimation her right to be considered the friend of the people. The logic of men's hearts goes swiftly to its conclusions, and this conclusion would be a pernicious one for the people and for the Church. To lose the heart of the people would be a misfortune for which the friendship of the few rich and powerful would be no compensation.

(b) There is a great danger of rendering hostile to the Church the political power of our country, which openly takes sides with the millions who are demanding justice and the improvement of their condition. The accusation of being, *"un-American,"* that is to say, alien to our national spirit, is the most powerful weapon which the enemies of the Church know how to employ against her. It was this cry which aroused the Know-Nothing persecution thirty years ago, and the same would be quickly used again if the opportunity offered itself. To appreciate the gravity of this danger it is well to remark that not only are the rights of the working classes loudly proclaimed by each of our two great political parties, but it is very probably [not im-

---

[11] The *Moniteur* version of Manning's text was cited as from, "Miscellanies, Vol. 2, p. 81," and read as follows: "I know I am treading on a very difficult subject, but I feel confident of this, that we must face it, and that we must face it calmly, justly, and with a willingness to put labor and the profits of labor second — the moral state and domestic life of the whole working population first. I will not venture to draw up such an act of Parliament further than to lay down this principle. These things (the present condition of the poor in England) cannot go on; these things ought not to go on. The accumulation of wealth in the land, the piling up of wealth like mountains, in the possession of classes or individuals, cannot go on. No commonwealth can rest on such foundations."

probable — très probable] that, in our approaching national elections there will be a candidate for the office of President of the United States as the special representative of these complaints and demands of the masses. Now, to seek to crush by an ecclesiastical condemnation an organization which represents nearly [more than — presque] 500,000 votes, and which has already so respectable and so universally recognized a place in the political arena, would to speak frankly, be considered by the American people as not less ridiculous as it is rash. To alienate from ourselves the friendship of the people would be to run great risk of losing the respect which the Church has won in the estimation of the American nation, and of destroying the state of peace and prosperity which form so admirable a contrast with her condition in some so-called Catholic countries. Already in these months past, a murmur of popular anger and of threats against the Church has made itself heard, and it is necessary that we should move with much precaution.[12]

(c) A third danger, and the one which touches our hearts the most, is the risk of losing the love of the children of the Church, and of pushing them into an attitude of resistance against their Mother. The whole world presents no more beautiful spectable than that of their filial devotion and obedience. But it is necessary to recognize that, in our age and in our country, obedience cannot be blind. We would greatly deceive ourselves if we expected it. Our Catholic working men sincerely believe that they are only seeking justice, and seeking it by legitimate means. A condemnation would be considered both false and unjust, and would not be accepted [and therefore, not binding — et ne serait pas acceptée]. We might indeed preach to them submission and confidence in the Church, but these good dispositions could hardly go so far. They love the Church, and they wish to save their souls, but they must also earn their living, and labor is now so organized that without belonging to the organization there is little chance to earn one's living.

Behold, then, the consequences to be feared. Thousands of the most devoted children of the Church would believe themselves repulsed by their Mother and would live without practicing their religion. The revenues of the Church, which with us come entirely from the free offerings of the people, would suffer immensely, and it would be the same with Peter's pence. The ranks of the secret societies would be

---

[12] The English read, "Angry utterances have not been wanting of late, and it is well that we should act prudently."

filled with Catholics, who had been up to now faithful.[13] The Holy See, which has constantly received from the Catholics of America proofs of almost unparalleled devotedness, would be considered not as a paternal authority, but as a harsh and unjust power. Here are assuredly effects, the occasion of which wisdom and prudence must avoid.

In a word, we have seen quite recently the sad and threatening confusion caused by the condemnation inflicted by an Archbishop upon a single priest in vindication of discipline — a condemnation which the Archbishop believed to be just and necessary, but which fell upon a priest who was regarded as the friend of the people. Now, if the consequences have been so deplorable for the peace of the Church from the condemnation of only one priest, because he was considered to be the friend of the people, what will not be the consequences to be feared from a condemnation which would fall directly upon the people themselves in the exercise of what they consider their legitimate right?[14]

7. But besides the danger which would result from such a condemnation and the impossibility of having it respected and observed [putting it into effect — de la faire respecter et observer] one should note that the form of this organization is so little permanent, as the press indicates nearly every day, that in the estimation of practical men in our country, it cannot last very many years.[15] Whence it follows that it is not necessary, even if it were just and prudent, to level the solemn condemnations of the Church against something which will vanish of itself. The social agitation will, indeed, last as long as there are social evils to be remedied; but the forms of organization and procedure meant for the attainment of this end are necessarily provisional and transient. They are also very numerous, for I have already remarked that the Knights of Labor is only one among several forms of labor organizations. To strike, then, at one of these forms would be to commence a war without system and without

---

[13] The variant reading in English was, "Thousands of the Church's most devoted children, whose affection is her greatest comfort, and whose free offerings are her chief support, would consider themselves repulsed by their Mother, and would live without practising their religion. Catholics who have hitherto shunned the secret societies, would be sorely tempted to join their ranks."

[14] This whole paragraph referring to the case of Dr. Edward McGlynn was elided in the English version.

[15] The English read: "It is also very important that we should carefully consider another reason against condemnation, arising from the unstable and transient character of the organization in question. It is frequently remarked by the press and by attentive observers that this special form of association has in it so little permanence that, in its present shape, it is not likely to last many years."

end; it would be to exhaust the forces of the Church in chasing a crowd of changing and uncertain phantasms. The American people behold with perfect composure and confidence the progress of our social contest, and have not the least fear of not being able to protect themselves against any excesses or dangers that may occasionally arise. And, to speak with the most profound respect, but also with the frankness which duty requires of me, it seems to me that prudence suggests, and that even the dignity of the Church demands that we should not offer to America an ecclesiastical protection for which she does not ask, and of which she believes she has no need.

8. In all this discussion I have not at all spoken of Canada, nor of the condemnation concerning the Knights of Labor in Canada. For we would consider it an impertinence to involve ourselves in the ecclesiastical affairs of another country which has a hierarchy of its own, and with whose needs and social conditions we do not pretend to be acquainted.[16] We believe, however, that the circumstances of a people almost entirely Catholic, as in lower Canada, must be very different from those of a mixed population like ours; moreover, that the documents submitted to the Holy Office are not the present constitution of the organization in our country, and that we, therefore, ask nothing involving an inconsistency on the part of the Holy See, which passed sentence *juxta exposita*.[17] It is of the condition of things in the United States that we speak, and we trust that in these matters we are not presumptuous in believing that we are competent to judge. Now, as I have already indicated, out of the seventy-five archbishops and bishops of the United States, there are about five who would desire a condemnation of the Knights of Labor, such as we know them in our country; so that our hierarchy are almost unanimous in protesting against such a condemnation. Surely, such a fact ought to have great weight in deciding the question. If there are difficulties in the case, it seems to me that the prudence and experience of our bishops and the wise rules of the Third Plenary Council ought to suffice for their solution.

9. Finally, to sum it all up, it seems clear to me that the Holy See should not entertain the idea of condemning an association:

1. When the condemnation does not seem to be *justified* either by the letter or the spirit of its constitution, its law and the declaration of its leaders.

---

16 "Les besoins" was not translated.
17 In the *Moniteur*, it read *"localiter et juxta exposita."*

2. When the condemnation does not seem *necessary,* in view of the transient form of the organization and the social condition of the United States.

3. When it does not seem to be *prudent,* because of the reality of the grievances of the workers, and the admission of them made by the American people.

4. When it would be *dangerous* for the reputation of the Church in our democratic country, and possibly even arouse persecution.

5. When it would be *ineffectual* in compelling the obedience of our Catholic workers, who would regard it as false and unjust.[18]

6. When it would be *destructive* instead of beneficial in its effects, impelling the children of the Church to disobey their Mother, and even to join condemned societies, which they have thus far shunned.

7. When it would be almost *ruinous* for the financial maintenance of the Church in our country, and for the Peter's pence.[19]

8. When it would turn into suspicion and hostility the outstanding devotedness of our Catholic people toward the Holy See.

9. When it would be regarded as a cruel blow to the authority of the bishops of the United States, who, it is well known, protest against such a condemnation.

Now, I hope the considerations here presented have shown with sufficient clearness that such would be the condemnation[20] of the Knights of Labor in the United States.

Therefore, with complete confidence, I leave the case[21] to the wisdom and prudence of your Eminence and the Holy See.

Rome, February 20, 1887.

J. Cardinal Gibbons,
Archbishop of Baltimore.

128. Cardinal Gibbons Opposes the Condemnation of the Works of Henry George, February 25, 1887

A SECOND major social question which agitated American Catholic circles in the 1880's centered around the single tax proposals of Henry George (1839–1897), and the advocacy of George's theories by Father Edward

---

[18] The fifth reason in the official English version was: "When it would probably be inefficacious, owing to the general conviction that it would be unjust."

[19] This point was completely omitted in the *Moniteur* translation.

[20] The official English read "the effect of condemnation."

[21] The English inserted "the decision of the case."

McGlynn (1837–1900), pastor of St. Stephen's Church, New York City. McGlynn's superior, Archbishop Michael A. Corrigan, forbade him to participate in the movement, but McGlynn refused to obey and was removed from his pastorate in January, 1887, and later excommunicated by the Holy See. The New York pastor was a powerful orator and had an immense following which gave the controversy very wide publicity. A number of Catholic churchmen believed that George's ideas on the single tax undermined the right of private property, and they urged the Holy See, therefore, to put his books on the Index. Cardinal Gibbons felt that this would be a serious mistake, and he took occasion during his visit to Rome in the winter of 1887 to address a letter to Cardinal Simeoni, Prefect of Propaganda, in which he strongly deprecated any action of this kind. Gibbons' protest delayed matters, but it did not prevent the Holy Office from condemning George's teachings in February, 1889, although it was stated that by reason of the highly controversial nature of the case the condemnation need not be published. Following is the text of the letter of Gibbons to Simeoni. Source: Archives of the Archdiocese of Baltimore, unclassified, printed copy in French entitled "La question des écrits de Henri George."

Your Eminence:

I have already had the honor of presenting to your Eminence my views on the social questions which agitate America, especially with regard to their bearing on the association of the Knights of Labor. But recently another form of social debate has developed relating to the doctrines of Mr. Henry George, an American author identified with the working classes. And since my arrival in Rome I have heard the idea discussed that the writings of Henry George should be put on the Index.[1] After having fully thought over the subject I believe it my duty to submit to your Eminence the reasons which seem to me to demonstrate that a formal condemnation of the works of Henry George would be neither opportune nor useful.

1. Henry George is in no way the originator of the theory which he advocates concerning the right of ownership in land. In his principal book, "Progress and Poverty," he cites precisely the teachings of Herbert Spencer and John Stuart Mill, two of England's chief authors. And in the English periodical work, the "Contemporary Review," of November 1886, a distinguished Professor quotes them more fully to prove, as he says, that Mr. George is only a plagiarist of these celebrated authors.[2] Now it seems to me that the world will judge it a bit singular if the Holy See attacks the work of a humble American artisan instead of attacking his great masters. And if there

[1] Up to 1887 George's principal works were *Progress and Poverty* (1879); *Social Problems* (1883); *Protection or Free Trade* (1886).

[2] H. Sidgwick, "Economic Socialism," *Contemporary Review,* L (November, 1886), 629.

are some who, therefore, think that it is the duty of the Holy See to pronounce judgment on Spencer and Mill, perhaps it would be prudent first to take counsel with their Eminences Cardinals Manning and Newman on the opportuneness of such action.[3]

2. It is well to remark that the theory of Henry George differs from that which is ordinarily called Communism and Socialism. Because as Father Valentine Steccanella shows very well in his work on Communism, published by the Propaganda Press in 1882,[4] this implies "the abolition of private property and the collectivization of all goods in the hands of the State." Now anyone who has read the books of Henry George ought to recognize that he neither teaches this nor does he at all wish it. On the contrary, he maintains the absolute ownership of all the fruits of human energy and industry, even when they amount to great riches acquired either by labor or heredity. It is only with regard to land itself that he would wish to limit the ownership of individuals by an extension of the *supremum dominum* of the state; and on this point he has expressly stated that he would in no way dispossess the actual owners; but he would desire simply that our system of taxation be changed in such a way that only the land would provide taxes and not the fruits of human industry. One can see, therefore, that in the practical form in which the controversy presents itself to the American public it is simply a question of the government's power over individual ownership of land. And on that there is this to be noted:

a) Anyone who studies properly the question of the relations of the State to the right of ownership of land, as it is treated by Father Steccanella and by other Catholic writers, or as it is regulated by the laws of taxation and the care of the poor in some countries, and especially in England, cannot help but understand that it is a very complex question, very much subject to the diverse circumstances of time and place, and not yet ready to be resolved by a decisive judgment.

b) The question is already before the American public as a political issue, and in so practical an arena it will soon find its end;[5]

---

[3] "Perhaps the only ecclesiast who knew George personally was Cardinal Manning, who, in the previous year [1885], had discussed with him his proposals to alleviate the world as written in his book, *Progress and Poverty*" (Shane Leslie, *Henry Edward Manning. His Life and Labours* [London, 1921], p. 353).

[4] Valentino Steccanella, S.J., *Del communismo esame critico filosofico e politico* (Rome, 1882).

[5] Gibbons was referring to George's unsuccessful effort to be elected Mayor of New York City in the fall elections of 1886 when he was defeated by Abram S. Hewitt.

c) As Mr. George himself realizes, it is only the legislative power of the country which could bring about such a disposition of affairs; and it is quite certain that neither a Congress nor a legislature will ever be found that would vote for such a profound change in social relations, nor a President who would approve it,

d) In a country such as ours, which is by no means a country of doctrinaires and visionaries, speculative theory will not be dangerous, nor will it live long after its practical application will have been rejected; one may, therefore, in all certainty, let it die by itself.

3. Certain recent events in our country have occasioned a profound and widespread popular excitement having an intimate relation to this question.[6] Therefore, your Eminence understands better than I how necessary it is for us to have care not only to speak the truth, but also to choose well the time and the circumstances to say it, so that our action may produce salutary and not fatal results. It seems evident, therefore, that even if there is certainly a need for condemnation, now is not the time to speak out.

4. Finally, it would be prudent to apply here the principle of morality which counsels one not to pronounce a sentence the consequences of which will probably be adverse rather than favorable to the good end proposed. Now I am sure that such would be the result of a condemnation of the works of Mr. George. It would give them a popular importance that they would not ever otherwise have, and would excite an appetite of curiosity that would make them sell by the thousands of copies, and would thus extend immensely the influences that the condemnation sought to restrain and prevent.

Once again, in dealing with so practicable a people as the Americans, in whose genius bizarre and impractical ideas quickly find their grave, it seems to me that prudence suggests that absurdities and fallacies be allowed to perish by themselves, and not run the risk of giving them an importance, a life and an artificial force by the intervention of the tribunals of the Church.

J. Card. Gibbons
Archbishop of Baltimore.

Rome, February 25, 1887.

---

[6] Here the cardinal was alluding to the removal of Father Edward McGlynn from the pastorate of St. Stephen's Church, New York, by Archbishop Corrigan on January 14, 1887, and the storm that this action stirred up among McGlynn's many followers. For the role of McGlynn in the single tax movement of Henry George, cf. John Tracy Ellis, *The Life of James Cardinal Gibbons, Archbishop of Baltimore, 1834–1921* (Milwaukee, 1952), I, 547–594.

129. The Roman Sermon of the American Cardinal on Church and State in the United States, March 25, 1887

FEW subjects in American religious history have held more interest, or caused more controversy, than that of the relations of Church and State. From the time of Archbishop Carroll to our own day the Catholic hierarchy of the United States has repeatedly expressed its approval of the separation of Church and State as it has existed in this country since the beginning of the Republic (cf. John Tracy Ellis, "Church and State: An American Catholic Tradition," *Harper's Magazine*, CCVII [November, 1953], 63–67). The first time these views were publicly voiced in Rome was on the occasion when Cardinal Gibbons took possession of his titular Church of Santa Maria in Trastevere. The sermon was of more than ordinary significance in view of the severely strained relations at that time between the Church and the anticlerical governments of Germany, Italy, and France, countries where there had been a long tradition of union of Church and State. American Catholics were pleased with their new cardinal's pronouncement, and Father Isaac Hecker was doubtless expressing the reaction of the great majority when he remarked how well fitted Gibbons was by his "thorough-going American spirit to interpret us to the peoples and powers of the Old World" ("Cardinal Gibbons and American Institutions," *Catholic World*, XLV [June, 1887], 331). Source: *Catholic Mirror* (Baltimore), April 2, 1887.

It is to me exceedingly gratifying that the Holy Father has assigned as my titular church this beautiful and historic basilica, the first church ever erected in honor of the Virgin Mother of God; and I regard it as an auspicious circumstance that my own Cathedral Church of Baltimore, the oldest cathedral in the United States, is also dedicated to our Blessed Lady. The venerable temple in which we are assembled leads us back to the days of the catacombs. It was founded by Pope St. Callixtus in the year 224.[1] It was reconstructed by Pope Julius in the fourth century, and renovated by another Supreme Pontiff in the twelfth.

That ceaseless solicitude which the Roman Pontiffs have exhibited in erecting the material temples which adorn this city, they have also manifested on a larger scale in building up the spiritual walls of Sion in every age.

Every student of history must be deeply impressed with the overruling action of the Papacy in the evangelization and civilization of

---

[1] The Basilica of Santa Maria in Trastevere dates from Pope Julius I (337–352), not from Pope Callixtus I who reigned over a century before.

the Christian world. I place these words together, for a nation is civilized in proportion as it receives the light of the Gospel. It was the vigilant zeal of the Holy See that sent Augustine to England, and Patrick to Ireland, and Pelagius to Scotland, and that sent Francis Xavier to evangelize the Indies; and all those other heroes of Christ's Church who bore, amid the sufferings and trials, the bright light of truth into the regions of pagan darkness. And coming down to a later period, scarcely were the United States formed into an independent government when Pius VI, of happy memory, established there the Catholic hierarchy and appointed the illustrious John Carroll first Bishop of Baltimore. This event, so important to us, occurred less than a hundred years ago — a long period, indeed, in our history, but how brief in that of Rome eternal! Our Catholic community in those days numbered only a few thousand souls, scattered chiefly through the States of New York, Pennsylvania, and Maryland, and were served by the merest handful of priests. Thanks to the fructifying grace of God, the grain of mustard seed then planted has grown to be a large tree, spreading its branches over the length and the width of our fair land. Where only one bishop was found in the beginning of this century, there are now seventy-five serving as many dioceses and vicariates. For their great progress under God and the fostering care of the Holy See we are indebted in no small degree to the civil liberty we enjoy in our enlightened republic.

Our Holy Father, Leo XIII, in his luminous encyclical on the constitution of Christian States,[2] declares that the Church is not committed to any particular form of civil government. She adapts herself to all; she leavens all with the sacred leaven of the Gospel. She has lived under absolute empires; she thrives under constitutional monarchies; she grows and expands under the free republic. She has often, indeed, been hampered in her divine mission and has had to struggle for a footing wherever despotism has cast its dark shadow like the plant excluded from the sunlight of heaven, but in the genial air of liberty she blossoms like the rose!

For myself, as a citizen of the United States, without closing my eyes to our defects as a nation, I proclaim, with a deep sense of pride and gratitude, and in this great capitol of Christendom, that I belong to a country where the civil government holds over us the aegis of its protection without interfering in the legitimate exercise of our sublime mission as ministers of the Gospel of Jesus Christ.

---

[2] *Immortale Dei*, November 1, 1885, John J. Wynne, S.J. (Ed.), *The Great Encyclical Letters of Pope Leo XIII* (New York, 1903), p. 109.

Our country has liberty without license, authority without despotism. Hers is no spirit of exclusiveness. She has no frowning fortifications to repel the invader, for we are at peace with all the world. In the consciousness of her strength and of her good will to all nations she rests secure. Her harbors are open in the Atlantic and Pacific to welcome the honest immigrant who comes to advance his temporal interest and to find a peaceful home.

But, while we are acknowledged to have a free government, we do not, perhaps, receive due credit for possessing also a strong government. Yes, our nation is strong, and her strength lies, under Providence, in the majesty and supremacy of the law, in the loyalty of her citizens to that law, and in the affection of our people for their free institutions.

There are, indeed, grave social problems which are now engaging the earnest attention of the citizens of the United States. But I have no doubt that, with God's blessings, these problems will be solved by the calm judgment and sound sense of the American people without violence, or revolution, or injury to individual right.

As an evidence of his benevolence and good will to the great republic of the West, as evidence of his appreciation of the venerable hierarchy of the United States, and as an expression of his kind condescension for the ancient See of Baltimore, our Holy Father, Leo XIII, has been graciously pleased to exalt its present incumbent in my humble person to the dignity of the purple.

For this mark of exalted favor I offer the Holy Father my profound thanks in my own name and in the name of the clergy and people under my charge. I venture also to thank him in the name of my venerable colleagues the bishops, the clergy, as well as the Catholic laity of the United States. I presume to thank him also in the name of our separated brethren of America who, though not sharing our faith, have shown that they are not insensible to the honor conferred on our common country, and have again and again expressed their warm admiration of the enlightened statesmanship, the apostolic virtues, and benevolent charities of the illustrious Pontiff who now sits in the Chair of Peter.

130. The Laying of the Cornerstone of the Catholic University of America, May 24, 1888

AT THE Second Plenary Council of Baltimore in October, 1866, the idea of a university for American Catholics was seriously discussed for the first time by the hierarchy, although nothing came of it at that time. In the interval between the plenary councils of 1866 and 1884 the subject continued to be urged by a number of leaders such as Thomas A. Becker (1832–1899), first Bishop of Wilmington, Isaac T. Hecker (1819–1888), founder of the Paulists, and by none more insistently than Bishop Spalding of Peoria. It was Spalding's notable sermon of November 16, 1884, during the Third Plenary Council, and the fact that he was able to secure the first substantial grant of funds, that helped to make the project a reality. It was fitting, therefore, that when the cornerstone of Caldwell Hall, the original building, was laid in the presence of President Grover Cleveland and a large assembly of distinguished guests, Spalding should have been chosen to deliver the principal address. The university opened on November 13, 1889, with forty-six students; the enrollment in February, 1956, was 3350 students divided among the ten schools of the university. Source: John Lancaster Spalding, "University Education," *Education and the Higher Life* (Chicago: A. C. McClurg and Co., 1891), pp. 178–179, 193, 195–198.

The special significance of our American Catholic history is not found in the phases of our life which attract attention, and are a common theme for declamation; but it lies in the fact that our example proves that the Church can thrive where it is neither protected nor persecuted, but is simply left to itself to manage its own affairs and to do its work. Such an experiment had never been made when we became an independent people, and its success is of worldwide import, because this is the modern tendency and the position toward the Church which all the nations will sooner or later assume; just as they all will be forced finally to accept popular rule. The great underlying principle of democracy, — that men are brothers and have equal rights, and that God clothes the soul with freedom, — is a truth taught by Christ, is a truth proclaimed by the Church; and the faith of Christians in this principle, in spite of hesitations and misgivings, of oppositions and obstacles and inconceivable difficulties, has finally given to it its modern vigor and beneficent power. . . .

The aim the best now propose to themselves is to provide not wealth or pleasure, or better machinery or more leisure, but a higher and more effective kind of education; and hence whatever one's preoccupation, whether social, political, religious, or industrial, the question of education forces itself upon his attention. Pedagogy has grown to be a science, and chairs are founded in universities to expound the theory and art of teaching. The learning of former times has become the ignorance of our own; and the classical writings have ceased to be the treasure-house of knowledge, and in consequence their educational value has diminished. . . . The ancients, indeed, excel us in the sense for form and symmetry. There is also a freshness in their words, a joyousness in their life, a certain heroic temper in their thinking and acting, which give them power to engage the emotions; and hence to deny them exceptional educational value is to take a partial view. But even though we grant that the study of their literatures is in certain respects the best intellectual discipline, education, it must be admitted, means knowledge as well as training; and thorough training is something more than refined taste. It is strength as well, and ability to think in many directions and on many subjects. Nothing known to men should escape the attention of the wise; for the knowledge of the age determines what is demanded of the scholar. And since it is our privilege to live at a time when knowledge is increasing more rapidly even than population and wealth, we must, if we hope to stand in the front ranks of those who know, keep pace with the onward movement of mind. To turn away from this outburst of splendor and power; to look back to pagan civilization or Christian barbarism, — is to love darkness more than light. Aristotle is a great mind, but his learning is crude and his ideas of Nature are frequently grotesque. Saint Thomas is a powerful intellect; but his point of view in all that concerns natural knowledge has long since vanished from sight. What poverty of learning does not the early mediaeval scheme of education reveal; and when in the twelfth century the idea of a university rises in the best minds, how incomplete and vague it is! Amid the ruins of castles and cathedrals we grow humble, and think ourselves inferior to men who thus could build. But they were not as strong as we, and they led a more ignorant and blinder life; and so when we read of great names of the past, the mists of illusion fill the skies, and our eyes are dimmed by the glory of clouds tinged with the splendors of a sun that has set.

Certainly a true university will be the home both of ancient wisdom and of new learning; it will teach the best that is known, and encourage research; it will stimulate thought, refine taste, and awaken the love of excellence; it will be at once a scientific institute, a school of culture, and a training ground for the business of life; it will educate the minds that give direction to the age; it will be a nursery of ideas, a centre of influence. The good we do men is quickly lost, the truth we leave them remains forever; and therefore the aim of the best education is to enable students to see what is true, and to inspire them with the love of all truth. Professional knowledge brings most profit to the individual; but philosophy and literature, science and art, elevate and refine the spirit of a whole people, and hence the university will make culture its first aim, and its scope will widen as the thoughts and attainments of men are enlarged and multiplied. Here if anywhere shall be found teachers whose one passion is the love of truth, which is the love of God and of man; who look on all things with a serene eye; who bring to every question a calm, unbiassed mind; who, where the light of the intellect fails, walk by faith and accept the omen of hope; who understand that to be distrustful of science is to lack culture, to doubt the good of progress is to lack knowledge, and to question the necessity of religion is to want wisdom; who know that in a God-made and God-governed world it must lie in the nature of things that reason and virtue should tend to prevail, in spite of the fact that in every age the majority of men think foolishly and act unwisely. . . .

131. Pope Leo XIII's Plea for the Italian Immigrants in America, December 10, 1888

THE first great wave of immigration to the United States before the Civil War had stamped the Catholic Church as the Church of the immigrant. That character became even more indelibly impressed during the so-called New Immigration of the years after 1880. Among the new arrivals the Italians occupied a prominent place, and since they were practically all at least nominal Catholics, it put a severe strain on the Church to provide adequate ministration for them. In 1880 there were only 44,230 Italian-born persons in the country, but by 1900 the number had risen to 484,027, and in the first decade of the twentieth century 2,104,309 arrived from Italy. Not all of these remained, however, for of all the late immigrants the Italians showed a greater tendency to return home after a time, and by 1910 it was estimated that about 800,000 had gone back to Italy. The plight of the Italians was aggravated by the abuses practiced against them through tricky labor contracts. Their condition became well known abroad and it was with a view to helping these unfortunate people, both spiritually and materially, that Pope Leo XIII addressed a special plea to the American hierarchy in December, 1888, in which he asked for their assistance in alleviating the lot of the Italian immigrants in this country. Source: Latin text, *American Ecclesiastical Review*, I (February, 1889), 43–48; English translation adapted from the New York *Freeman's Journal*, January 5, 1889.

How toilsome and disastrous is the condition of those who for some years have been migrating out of Italy to the regions of America in search of a livelihood is so well known to you that nothing is to be gained by dwelling on it. Indeed, you see these evils at first hand and several of you have sorrowfully called our attention to them in repeated letters. It is to be deplored that so many unfortunate Italians, forced by poverty to change their residence, should rush into evils which are often worse than the ones they have desired to flee from. For very often to labors of various kinds that take away the life of the body, there is added the ruin of souls. At the outset the emigrants' crossing itself is full of dangers and injuries; for many of them fall into the hands of avaricious men whose slaves, as it were, they become, and then herded in ships and inhumanly treated, they are gradually depraved in their nature. And when they have reached the desired land, being ignorant of both the language and the locale, and engrossed in their daily toil, they become the victims of the trickery of the dishonest or the powerful by whom they are employed.[1] Those who by their own industry succeed sufficiently to assure for themselves a livelihood, associating constantly with people who regard everything from the point of view of business or profit, little by little lose the nobler feelings of human nature and learn to live like those who have set all their hopes and thoughts on this earth. To all this are added the ever present excitement of the passions, and the deceits practiced by the sects which flourish widely there to the injury of religion and which draw many into the path leading to destruction.

What is more lamentable among these evils is that because of the great multitude of these emigrants, the extent of the territory, and the local difficulties, it is by no means easy to provide these people with the saving care of ministers of God familiar with the Italian language, who would teach them the word of life, administer to them the sacraments, and provide for them timely help by which their souls might be lifted up in the hope of heavenly goods and their spiritual life be sustained and invigorated. In many places, therefore, there are very few who have a priest when they are dying, and there are many of the newly-born for whom there is none to administer the sacrament of regeneration. There are many who enter into marriage without regard

---

[1] Leo XIII was referring here to the notorious treatment of the Italian immigrants under the *padrone* system which made them virtual slaves to their greedy fellow countrymen and others who exploited them through labor contracts in the United States and other countries. For these abuses cf. Robert F. Foerster, *The Italian Emigration of Our Times* (Cambridge, 1919), p. 390 ff.

to the Church's laws, and thereby give rise to an offspring similar to their parents. Thus there is everywhere with this people a decay of Christian morality and a growth of wickedness.[2]

Reflecting on all these things, and grieving at the wretched lot of so many whom we perceive to be wandering like sheep without a shepherd through steep paths and dangerous places, and at the same time mindful of the eternal Shepherd's love and warning, we have thought it our duty to render every possible help to them, to prepare wholesome nourishment, and to consult in every practical way for their good and salvation. We have been all the more inclined to enter upon this undertaking because of our love for men sprung from the same soil as ourselves, and because a sure hope inspires us that we shall not lack your own interest in the matter and your helpful assistance. Wherefore, we have taken care to have this matter considered by the Sacred Congregation of the Propaganda, and we have commanded it diligently to seek out and to examine the remedies by which so many evils and inconveniences can be removed, or at least be alleviated, and to propose to us what especially can be done both for the salvation of souls and for softening, as far as may be, the emigrants' hardships. But since the most potent cause of the growing evils is the lack of a priestly ministry through which heavenly grace is imparted and increased, we have determined to send to your country a number of priests from Italy accustomed to the language of their countrymen, to teach them the doctrine of faith and the unknown or neglected precepts of Christian life, to provide among them a salutary administration of the sacraments, to form the growing offspring to religion and good conduct, to help them in every way by advice and assistance, and to foster them by priestly care. To effect this the more conveniently we established by our letter of the 16th of November of last year, under the Fisherman's ring, an apostolic college of priests in the episcopal see of Piacenza, under the charge of our Venerable Brother John Baptist, Bishop of Piacenza,[3] so that ecclesiastics who are moved by a love of

---

[2] That the spiritual plight of the Italian immigrants was real may be gleaned from the statement made by Archbishop Corrigan of New York to Cardinal Manning on February 10, 1888, when he said, "There are 80,000 Italians in this city, of whom only two per cent have been in the habit of hearing Mass" (quoted in Shane Leslie, *Henry Edward Manning. His Life and Labours* [London, 1921], p. 358). For the question of the Church and the Italian immigrants cf. Henry J. Browne, "The 'Italian Problem' in the Catholic Church of the United States, 1880–1900," *Historical Records and Studies*, XXXV (1946), 46–72.

[3] Giovanni B. Scalabrini (1839–1905), Bishop of Piacenza, founded the Congregation of Missionaries of St. Charles Borromeo of which two priests and a lay brother arrived in New York in July, 1888, to begin work among the

Christ may there cultivate those studies and be exercised in those employments and that sort of training by means of which they may earnestly and successfully perform the ministry of Christ for the scattered Italians and become fit dispensers of God's mysteries.

Among the students of this college, which we wish to be regarded as a sort of seminary of ministers of God for the salvation of Italians dwelling in America, we desire also that young men from your own country, children of Italian parents, be received and instructed; providing they are called to the vineyard of the Lord and have a wish to be initiated into Holy Orders, so that, having been ordained and returning to you, as many of them as there shall be need of will fulfill under your pastoral authority the work of the apostolic ministry. Nor do we doubt that on their return they will be received by you with fatherly love, and that also they will receive the necessary faculties for exercising the sacred ministry among their countrymen, subject to the admonition of the parish priest. For they will come to you to labor under the authority of those of you in whose dioceses they dwell. Especially at the outset of the work there will not, by any means, be so many of these helpers as the circumstances and times demand, nor will the labors of those who are sent be on a par with the number and needs of the faithful in such a way that the priests assigned to the care of souls can be appointed to separate and remote places. Wherefore, we deem it best that in dioceses where Italians are numerous there be common residences for these priests, so that they may go forth separately into the neighboring areas and perform their sacred functions on these expeditions. But in what manner or in what places these can best be established will be for your foresight to decide. All these things which we have thought to belong to our apostolic providence we have taken pains to signify to you in this letter. If any of you should discover, either by his own sense and judgment, or by consultation with his brethren, anything further that can be done by us for the welfare or comfort of those in whose behalf we are writing, let him know that he will do us a favor if he will carefully relate his proposal to the Sacred Congregation of the Propaganda.

From this work which we have undertaken for the care and defence of many souls that lack every comfort of the Catholic religion, we promise ourselves much fruit, especially if, as we hope, there be added

---

Italian immigrants. In the following year the Missionary Sisters of the Sacred Heart of St. Francesca Cabrini (1850–1917) opened the first of their numerous American houses for the spiritual care of their fellow countrymen when Archbishop Corrigan blessed the ophanage on 59th Street, New York, on May 3, 1889.

for its support and protection, the interest and assistance of the faithful whose means are equal to their piety. As for the rest, praying the most benign God, Who wishes that all men shall be saved and come to the knowledge of the truth, that He will propitiously inspire this undertaking and give prosperous increase to it, we lovingly in the Lord, impart the apostolic benediction of our inmost affection to you, Venerable Brethren, and to the entire clergy and faithful over whom you are set.

Given at Rome, in St. Peter's, the 10th of December, 1888, in the eleventh year of our pontificate.

Leo XIII., Pope

132. Charles J. Bonaparte on the American Experience of Separation of Church and State, July 11, 1889

CHARLES J. BONAPARTE (1851–1921) was one of the most distinguished Catholic laymen of his generation. Baltimore-born grandson of King Jerome of Westphalia, brother of Emperor Napoleon I, Harvard-trained, and from a family of wealth, Bonaparte enjoyed all the advantages which such a background afforded. He was especially noted for his zeal in behalf of good government and civil-service reform, having been one of the founders of the National Municipal League and later its president. Theodore Roosevelt appointed Bonaparte to a number of federal offices, naming him Secretary of the Navy in May, 1905, and Attorney General of the United States in December, 1906, where he continued to the end of the administration in March, 1909, and earned for himself widespread fame as a trust-buster. He was always a devout Catholic and had very pronounced views about the need for keeping the Church free from politics and the State out of religious affairs. The excerpts from one of his public addresses that follow were all the more pertinent in being spoken at a time when the A.P.A. were on the rise. The speech was delivered at the centennial celebration of the Catholic societies of the Archdiocese of Baltimore at Bay Ridge, Maryland. Source: Charles J. Bonaparte, *The Catholic Church and American Institutions* (Baltimore: William K. Boyle & Son, 1889), pp. 16–21.

You have all heard and read, many of you, no doubt, often, some, perhaps, *ad nauseam,* that there is an "incompatability" between American institutions and the Catholic Church. . . . Even now it may be, perhaps, sincerely said by a Catholic who is not an American, or an American who is not a Catholic, but I cannot think this opinion is shared by any American Catholic, sufficiently informed to have an intelligent opinion. Nor need I disprove it *a priori;* we have met to commemorate its refutation by the one unanswerable test of experience.

The mustard seed planted on these shores a hundred years ago fell on no ungrateful soil; of this no better proof can be given or reasonably asked than Time has furnished in the stately tree with its deep roots and spreading branches, which has grown from that seed. . . . If we apply to the sum of American institutions the vague and much abused term "liberty," a century's history proves that liberty is good for the Catholic Church, and this is a conclusion of such moment that I feel justified in a further trespass on your patience to briefly weigh its import.

I claim the fact to have been established by a decisive experiment, but opinions may of course, differ as to its explanation; to understand, however, why American liberty has proved thus congenial to the Church, we must first appreciate what, in its essentials, our liberty is, and how it differs from political systems abroad, which usurp or masquerade in the same name. A competent and candid observer asked to indicate the countries whose history during the present century could be read with most pleasure by devout Catholics would unhesitatingly group with the United States, the great English colonies. In old Catholic countries, the Church has often contended with hostility and spoliation from the State; elsewhere she has been steadfast under persecution from non-catholic rulers of arbitrary power; but among all English speaking peoples she has gained ground, and in Canada and Australia and the United States her prosperity has been manifest and her progress rapid. What suits her in our country, then, is something we share with our Northern neighbors and our kinsmen in the great island of the Southern sea, and we share with them a large measure of individual freedom under a popular government.

The genius of our common institutions, is to let each citizen work out his own happiness with little hindrance and little help from the State; the government protects his person and property and enforces his contracts, then leaves him as nearly to himself as the exigencies of national defence and public order permit. To the ephemeral republics which this century has seen rise and fall in Europe, this spirit has been utterly alien; they may have committed the State's authority to many hands, but have made that authority ever more and more arbitrary and far-reaching; in such a republic,

That worst of tyrants, a usurping crowd

intrudes upon every phase of a man's life, assumes to watch over his coming in and his going out, the management of his property, the education of his children, the care of his health, to dictate even the words he shall use and the clothes he shall wear. The legitimate outcome of the first system is complete religious liberty, to give any creed, not grossly repugnant to the accepted standard of public morals, a fair field, but no favor, for the State to ask only the things of Caesar, leaving to the conscience of each citizen to care for the more lasting interests which lie beyond its humbler sphere.

Under the second system, the State becomes itself a church, a church wanting, indeed, in almost all that makes a church a means of good, but with a potent influence for evil. To be consistent, a paternal government must provide a legal religion; it cannot, in the words of the Great Frederic, "let its subjects go to Hell by the road they like best," and under such a government, the Catholic Church stands face to face with a rival. The Bill of Rights of Maryland declares:

> That, as it is the duty of every man to worship God in such manner as he thinks most acceptable to Him, all persons are equally entitled to protection in their religious liberty. . . .

The aim of ecclesiastical legislation in many European countries is precisely to make all places of worship, public buildings, and all ministers of religion, of whatsoever creed or order, public functionaries, controlled by the State and maintained from the proceeds of taxation. Here the Church goes her way and does her work without caring, almost without thinking, whether the civil rulers for the time being are within or without her fold; there she may be hampered in every function of her ministry by the hostility of such rulers or more gravely embarrassed, more permanently discredited by their compromising friendship. For, even if I scandalize some worthy people by so thinking, I yet think the civil power less dangerous to the Church as a rival, even as an oppressor, than as a patron. The Church of Christ should be no hot-house plant:

> Moored in the rifted rock,
> Proof to the tempests' shock,
> The firmer they root her the harder they blow,

but when fenced about with laws, when sheltered behind privileges and prescriptions, her rugged fibre grows soft and her sturdy frame dainty. When the time of trial comes, — and come it will, for dynasties and their kingdoms, laws and the nations that made them, man and all man's works, must sometime change and pass away, — when all these screens and safe guards of a day fall around her, and she faces again the whirlwind of human error and human passion, many sapped boughs shall break and much dead wood claim the pruning knife. It is no trick of theologian's jargon that calls the Church "militant"; she is indeed a fighting body, and her conquests must be held as they were made by valor and discipline and well kept arms, not by a Chinese Wall of timid isolation. Moreover Caesar does not work for nothing: he must be paid for his protection; if he makes heresy treason, he asks that she make treason heresy, and this is little less than a ruinous price for a less than doubtful service.

Here the Church hires no mercenary defender, she guards her own by her own might; no prince or magistrate, no parliament or judge, wielding the clumsy weapon of unconvincing force, is called on to fill a mission for which her clergy have grown unworthy. Her soldiers cannot rust in barracks or cower behind intrenchments; they must meet their foes of to-day as all the countless spiritual heroes of her history met and conquered theirs, in the open field of argument and example with the armament of zeal and eloquence, learning and saintly life. The American priesthood is no refuge for cowardice and sloth either intellectual or physical. It has a work to do, a vast and hard and endless work, which no one else will do or try or pretend to do for it; and to-day, as we look back along these hundred years and then around us, we say with a just pride in the past, with a reasonable confidence in the future, and, above all, with perfect trust in the proven and abiding guidance of Almighty God, that work has been and is and will be well done!

133. Archbishop Ireland Explains His Stand on Public and Parochial Schools, December, 1890

THE controversial issue of public versus parochial schools, already seen in connection with the Blaine Amendment of 1875, continued to occupy American educators in the years thereafter. When John Ireland (1838–1918), first Archbishop of St. Paul, was invited to speak before the annual convention of the National Education Association in his see city on July 10, 1890, he seized the chance to put forth a compromise solution which would make it possible for the parochial schools to be absorbed into the public system with provision made for the teaching of religion. The speech was vigorously assailed both by critics outside the Church, who claimed it was a ruse by which the Catholics sought to gain control of the public schools, and by certain elements within the Church to whom Ireland's plan constituted a threat to the integrity of the religious schools. When the address was reported adversely to the Holy See and Cardinal Gibbons was asked for his opinion by Pope Leo XIII, the cardinal came strongly to Ireland's defense. In order to put Gibbons in possession of all the necessary facts, the archbishop wrote him the following lengthy letter in which he explained in detail what he had said and what he had meant in those passages especially under fire from his critics. Source: Daniel F. Reilly, O.P., *The School Controversy, 1891–1893* (Washington: The Catholic University of America Press, 1943), Appendix B, pp. 237–241.

Your Eminence,

I beg leave to pen down a few lines, with the intent of making somewhat clear the meaning of my address on "Schools."[1]

I am free to say that it is difficult for me to see anything in it calling for or deserving censure. I have read all the objections raised against it in German papers, and my judgment is that those objections arise from malice prepense in wresting certain phrases from the context, and giving to them an interpretation which antecedent and subsequent declarations do not permit. It is possible, too, that they are in some degree due to ignorance of the true ethical principles which underlie the school question, and to the dislike which so many Catholics entertain for American institutions, or American ideas. I cannot bring myself to believe that those in Rome, finding fault with me, could have had my whole discourse before their eyes: garbled extracts were sent to them, & from these their judgment is formed. My best defense is a perusal of the whole discourse.

The general purpose of the discourse was to state plainly to the country the grounds of Catholic opposition to the State Schools, & to lead up, if possible, to an alteration permitting the removal of this opposition. I was anxious, too, incidentally to allay the angry feeling which reigns between non-Catholic Americans & Catholics, in so far as this feeling rests on misunderstanding of our position. These misunderstandings derive fully as much from exaggerations and misstatements made by Catholics as from ill will or prejudice on the part of non-Catholics.

I had a grand opportunity opened to me; the country was my audience.

The impression is abroad that the Church is opposed to State Schools and to State interference in education, because she is opposed to the

---

[1] The text of the address, entitled "State Schools and Parish Schools," may be found in John Ireland, *The Church and Modern Society* (St. Paul, 1905), I, 215–232.

education of the children of the people. I desire to set her right before the country on these points.

I admitted in principle the State School — Thus the State, I said, has the right to establish & maintain Schools. Instruction being so necessary in America for good citizenship, and the means of instruction being beyond the reach of many children, thro' poverty or ill will of parents, I asserted the duty on the part of the State, to maintain Schools, in which all children, the poorest & the most abandoned, would be instructed. Of course, in this point, I am dealing with abstract right & duty: in the concrete, as my whole discourse plainly shows, I require that this right be so exercised that while the State obtain its purposes, the purposes of the Church be not frustrated.

I upheld compulsory education, & in this I have with me numerous Catholic writers, Rickaby,[2] Bouquillon,[3] etc. German papers raise a great clamor against me on this point as if I denied to parents that right to control the education of their children. Well, I am most plain & strong in declaring that this right belongs primarily to the parents, and that the State has no right to give itself instruction except when parents neglect their duty. Nor do I allow the State to demand attendance in its own Schools — except when parents neglect absolutely their children. Abundant room is left for home schools, parish schools, etc. Bishop Katzer[4] took publicly the position that the State must enact no school-law, erect no school-building, that the parent had the right, if he desired, to bring up his child in ignorance, total ignorance. Of course, he thinks me heretical.

"Free Schools! Blessed indeed is the nation whose vales and hill sides they adorn, and blessed the generations upon whose souls are poured their treasures!"

A fearful cry went out against those words, as if I extolled the present free-schools of America as being perfect. Well, it is clear that I am talking of free schools in the abstract — free instruction, to be had by all for the asking. Later on, I will show emphatically what free schools in the concrete must be — schools in which religion is taught.

"It were idle for me to praise the State-School of America in the

---

[2] Joseph Rickaby (1845–1932), English Jesuit, who wrote extensively on theological and philosophical subjects.

[3] Thomas Bouquillon (1840–1902), Belgian-born professor of moral theology in the Catholic University of America. Bouquillon's brochure entitled *Education: To Whom Does It Belong?* (Baltimore, 1891) played an important part in the controversy over the schools in American and European Catholic circles.

[4] Frederick F. X. Katzer (1844–1903) was Bishop of Green Bay, 1886–1891, and from the latter year to his death Archbishop of Milwaukee.

imparting of secular instruction. It is our pride and our glory." German papers have kept for weeks a garbled version of these words in large headlines, actually cutting the sentence in twain, so as to take out of it my meaning. "It were idle for me to praise the State School of America. It is our pride and our glory" — So they wrote. I restricted my praise to the "imparting of secular instruction," and in this matter who will contradict me?

I granted to the State School its full quota of merit, so that my censure of it might not seem to come from prejudice. And that censure came — clear and unmistakable. How men — priests — bishops could write that I endorsed the public-school, passes my understanding. I said: "Can I be suspected of enmity to the State School — because I tell of defects which I seek to remedy? . . . There is dissatisfaction with the State School as at present organized." — and I consecrate two-thirds of the discourse to give the grounds of this dissatisfaction. I add "the dissatisfaction will exist as long as no change is made. It is founded on conscience."

"The free Schools of America! Withered be the hand raised in sign of their destruction!" — Another sentence for which I was threatened with excommunication. My meaning was that I would not destroy, but improve, correct, enlarge. "I fain would widen the expanse of their wings until all the children of the people find shelter beneath their cover — " "Not one stone of the wondrous edifice which Americans have built up in their devotion to education will Catholics remove, or permit to be removed. They would fain add to its splendor and majesty by putting side by side religion and the School" — I was addressing Protestants, the born defenders of the schools — teachers. What was I to do to gain their ear, but to confess to all the good in the system, and, then, when their sympathy is won, to tell of the defects!

"I turn to the parish school. It exists. I repeat my regret that there is the necessity for its existence. In behalf of the State School I call upon my fellow Americans to aid in the removal of this necessity." On this point Father Abbelen[5] of Milwaukee has raised a dreadful clamor in Milwaukee papers; German and English priests of Wisconsin replied to him.

I cannot but think I am right and that Abbelen is wrong. Be it understood that I always allow the right of a parish to have a parish school, no matter how perfect the state school may be. But my con-

5 Peter M. Abbelen (1843–1917) had been the emissary to Rome for the German Catholics of the Middle West in November, 1886, in their controversy with the Irish over national parishes and schools.

tention is that the state school, rightly organized — sustained by State funds, and yet granting to Catholic children all that is needed for the protection of the State, no absolute necessity exists for the parish school. In Ireland [and] England there is no strictly-speaking parish school. In Belgium and France, no parish-school was thought of until infidel governments had made the State school infidel. The necessity for parish-schools is hypothetical — the necessity being not a direct result of the Church's mission, but a provision in certain cases for the protection of the faith. The Church is not established to teach writing and ciphering, but to teach morals and faith, and she teaches writing and ciphering only when otherwise morals and faith could not be taught. Abbelen makes out that the "Docete gentes" implies teaching all that children have to learn — quod est absurdum.

Now, what is required in the State-School to make it acceptable to us, I develop in two-thirds of my discourse. I am sure you will find this part ultra abstract. I demand positive Catholic dogmatic teaching — rejecting mere moral teaching, rejecting totally the so-called "common Christianity" theory. Now, my opponents pass over in absolute silence this part of the discourse, which is the more important part, which secular papers took to be properly the discourse.

One point here has been criticized. It is this: "I am a Catholic, of course, to the tiniest fibre of my heart, unflinching and uncompromising in my faith. But God forbid that I desire to see in America the ground which protestantism occupies exposed to the chilling and devastating blast of unbelief. Let me be your ally in stemming the swelling tide of irreligion." — Why, said one priest in a German paper, Abp. Ireland has lost the faith: he is willing to keep up Protestantism. Of course, my meaning is that of words, spoken by Manning and Newman — that factional Christianity is better than materialism. Besides I took the standpoint of your Eminence's book — of speaking to Americans in the name of our "Christian Heritage"[6] — and in this name asking them to make the Schools Christian — Catholic for us, and Protestant for themselves. We cannot have Catholic State Schools without giving them Protestant State Schools.

My appeal for State Schools fit for Catholic children has been censured under the plea that a Protestant state should touch nothing Catholic. But America is not a "Protestant State," and if Catholics pay school taxes they should receive benefit from them. The burden upon our Catholics to maintain parish schools up to the required standard

---

[6] Ireland was referring here to Gibbon's volume, *Our Christian Heritage* (Baltimore, 1889).

for all the children of the Church is almost unbearable. There is danger that never shall we have schools for all Catholic children, or that Catholics will grow tired of contributing. At present nearly half the Catholic children of America do not attend parish-schools. The true solution, in my judgment, is to make the State-School satisfactory to Catholic consciences, and to use it. Can this be done? Let us try. If it cannot be done, let us do our best with our parish-schools.

Besides have not bishops and priests gone too far in their denunciations of the State School? Have they not, in their desire to protect the parish school, often belied, in their exaggerations of the evil, the State School? Have they not gone beyond the "Apostolic Instruction" of 1875?[7] Have they not needlessly brought upon us the odium of the country? Indeed, since our own schools are neither numerous enough, nor efficient enough for our children, and many of these must attend the public school, have we not done immense harm to souls by our anathemas? Catholics in many cases must use those schools, and yet they are denounced for it; their consciences are falsified — they are estranged from the Church. I am not afraid to say that in places where bishops have been very severe against Public schools, their parish schools have done more harm than good to religion.

It is well, too, to remark that our public schools, in many places at least, are not *positively* bad. They are not *hot beds* of vice; neither do they teach unbelief or Protestantism. Teachers are often good Catholics; or at least they are gentlemen or ladies, decorous in conduct, and generous toward our faith. I know well the immense advantage to children of positive dogmatic teaching in school; yet, where the school is as nearly neutral as can be — the family and the Sunday School can do much — tho' never all we should give if circumstances permit.

Our public-schools are better than those of France and Italy, and in those countries we hear no continuous anathemas.

At any rate, continuous anathemas only irritate. Germans have actually said I was disloyal to the Church when I did not stand up before the Convention and tell of the immoralities and the scepticism of the public-schools.

Now, as to my remedies for bringing together State and Church. Those remedies of mine were put forth tentatively, and as mere beginnings. We cannot have all at once; let us get an entering wedge. The

---

[7] The instruction of the Congregation of Propaganda de Fide on the danger to the faith of Catholic children attending public schools was dated November 24, 1875. Cf. No. 118.

system of payment by results is the system of England — to which Catholics gladly subscribe. The "Poughkeepsie Plan"[8] is the Irish System in vogue for 40 years — used by sisters and brothers — with the sole exception of the Christian brothers. In this system teachers and pupils are all Catholics; the atmosphere is Catholic; all secular teaching is from Catholic minds and from Catholic hearts. The one point is, that positive dogmatic teaching is before or after legal school-hours. Catechism, it is said, should be free at all hours: what does it matter whether it be taught at nine A.M. or eleven A.M.! It is not, as a fact, taught at all hours. But the crucifix is to be removed: Abp. Ireland is the enemy of the crucifix. But the crucifix often is not in Catholic schools, and religion is not dependent on one symbol. Nor is the atmosphere neutral: It cannot be neutral while teachers and pupils are Catholic.

I have myself no further remarks to make. If fault were to be found in Rome with the address, let the precise point with which fault is found be quickly pointed out to me and I will give explanation, or if necessary quietly withdraw it. A public condemnation from Rome of the address would set America in fury, as it would be a direct attack on principles which America will not give up, that is the right of the State to provide for the instruction of all children. As I am so clear on the need of religion in the Schools, Rome's condemnation will be understood to bear on the fact that I allow any right to the State.

I repeat — I have read all the objections to the discourse, and they come either from partial reading of my words, or from hatred of the American state.

The "Poughkeepsie Plan" is in existence in very many of our Catholic country settlements, with the best possible results. Sisters teach, and without the aid of state funds, Sisters could not be supported in those settlements. Had I made the effort, I could have had it in St. Paul.[9] But this war made on me disturbs me.

---

[8] The Poughkeepsie Plan arose out of the efforts of Father Patrick Mc-Sweeney, pastor of St. Peter's Church, Poughkeepsie, New York, who in 1873 arranged with the local school board to rent his parochial school for $1.00 a year and to give the school board power and responsibility over repair of the building, hiring and testing the teachers, etc., with the provision that religion would be taught outside the regular school hours. The system was likewise in vogue in local communities in Georgia, New Jersey, Connecticut, and Pennsylvania.

[9] Actually such a plan was instituted in the Archdiocese of St. Paul in August–October, 1891, when the parochial schools of Faribault and Stillwater, Minnesota, were rented to the local school boards for $1.00 a year and thus became a part of the public school system. But opposition to these cases caused the plan to be terminated in the two Minnesota towns by October, 1893.

I will write you again tomorrow. Meanwhile, I repeat my expression of deep gratitude and sincere affection, and remain,

Very respectfully,
John Ireland

134. The St. Raphaelsverein Protests the Neglect of Immigrant Catholics in the United States, February, 1891

THE addition of an estimated 2,475,000 immigrants from twenty or more countries to the Catholic population of the United States in the years 1880–1900 brought inevitable strains within the American Church. One of the most acute controversies among these varied national groups developed between the Irish and German Catholics over the demand of the latter for their own parishes, priests, and schools, and a higher proportion of bishops of German birth or extraction in the hierarchy. This situation led to a protest being lodged with the Holy See in November, 1886, by Father Peter Abbelen of the Archdiocese of Milwaukee which maintained that unless the demands were met there would be grave losses to the faith. In the succeeding years the question took on more serious proportions when it entered into the discussions of the various national branches of the St. Raphaelsverein, an organization founded in 1871 for the care of German Catholic emigrants. From an international conference of the St. Raphaelsverein held in Lucerne, Switzerland, on December 9–10, 1890, there emerged a document signed by officials of the society from seven different countries. This document, dated February, 1891, was presented to Pope Leo XIII on April 16, 1891, and on the following May 28 the full text was published in the New York *Herald*. Most of the American hierarchy protested vigorously against the implication that they had neglected the spiritual welfare of the immigrants and that there had been anywhere near the fantastic figure of ten million souls lost to the Church in this country. Source: Colman J. Barry, O.S.B., *The Catholic Church and German Americans* (Milwaukee: The Bruce Publishing Co., 1953), Appendix IV, pp. 313–315.

Most Holy Father,

The presidents, secretaries general, and delegates of the societies under the protection of the Holy Archangel Raphael for the protection of emigrants, encouraged by the benevolence which Your Holiness has shown them, assembled on December 9 of last year at an international conference in Lucerne to deliberate upon means best suited to serve the spiritual and material well-being of their Catholic compatriots who have emigrated to America, the number of which is in excess of 400,000 yearly.[1]

The above mentioned take the liberty to place before Your Holiness, with deepest respect, the fact that the numerous emigrants constitute a great strength, and could co-operate eminently in the expansion of the Catholic Church in the several states of America. In this way they could contribute to the moral stature of their new homeland, as well as to the stimulation of religious consciousness in the old European fatherlands.

Only the true Church, of which Your Holiness is the highest shepherd, can obtain these happy results because it is the true source of all progress and civilization.

But in order that European Catholics, in their adopted country, preserve and transmit to their children their faith and its inherent benefits, the undersigned have the honor to submit to Your Holiness the conditions, which in the light of experience and in the nature of things, appear to be indispensable for that purpose in the countries of immigration. The losses which the Church has suffered in the United States of North America number more than ten million souls.[2]

1. It seems necessary to unite the emigrant groups of each nationality in separate parishes, congregations, or missions wherever their numbers and means make such a practice possible.

2. It seems necessary to entrust the administration of these parishes to priests of the same nationality to which the faithful belong. The sweetest and dearest memories of their homeland would be constantly recalled, and they would love all the more the holy Church which procures these benefits for them.

---

[1] If the memorialists had in mind Catholic immigrants solely to the United States this figure was a gross exaggeration. The best authority on the subject estimated that in the years 1881–1890 inclusive there was a total increase of 1,250,000 to the American Catholic population through immigration, a figure that included 119,000 from Canada, Mexico, and other non-European countries. From those European countries whose delegates signed the Lucerne Memorial there had been in the entire period 1881–1890 approximately only 700,000 Catholics immigrants (Gerald Shaughnessy, S.M., *Has the Immigrant Kept the Faith?* [New York, 1925], p. 165).

[2] The recklessness with which figures on Catholic leakage were used by the ill informed in these years may be gauged by the fact that at an international Catholic congress held in Liège, Belgium, in September, 1890, a French-Canadian priest of the Diocese of Albany, Alphonse Villeneuve, presented a paper which alleged that out of twenty-five million Catholic immigrants who had entered the United States twenty million had been lost to the Church.

3. In areas settled by emigrants of several nationalities who are not numerous enough to organize separate national parishes, it is desirable as far as possible, that a pastor be chosen to guide them who understands the diverse languages of these groups. This priest should be strictly obliged to give catechetical instruction to each of the groups in its own language.

4. It will be especially necessary to establish parochial schools wherever Christian public schools are not available, and these schools should be separate, as far as possible, for each nationality.

The curriculum of these schools should always include the mother tongue as well as the language and history of the adopted country.

5. It seems necessary to grant to priests devoting themselves to the emigrants all rights, privileges, and prerogatives enjoyed by the priests of the country. This arrangement, which is only just, would have the result that zealous, pious, and apostolic priests of all nationalities will be attracted to immigrant work.

6. It seems desirable to establish and encourage societies of various kinds, confraternities, charitable organizations, mutual aid and protective associations, etc. By these means Catholics would be systematically organized and saved from the dangerous sects of Freemasons and organizations affiliated with it.

7. It seems very desirable that the Catholics of each nationality, wherever it is deemed possible, have in the episcopacy of the country where they immigrate, several bishops who are of the same origin. It seems that in this way the organization of the Church would be perfect, for in the assemblies of the bishops, every immigrant race would be represented, and its interests and needs would be protected.

8. Finally the undersigned wish to point out that for the attainment of the objectives which they have enumerated, it would be very desirable, and this they vigorously urge, that the Holy See foster and protect in the emigration countries: a) special seminaries and apostolic schools for training missionaries for emigrants; b) St. Raphael societies for the protection of emigrants, and that it recommend to the Most Rev. Bishops that they establish such societies in the emigration countries where they do not yet exist, and that the Holy See place them under the protection of a Cardinal Protector.

The undersigned hope for the happiest and most immediate results from this organization and these measures. Emigration missionaries trained under the direction of a distinguished Italian Bishop have already gone to America.[3] Others, members of neighboring nations, are waiting, before entering, upon their important and holy calling, for the Supreme Shepherd of the Church, by a decree of his wisdom, to guarantee the free exercise of their mission. If the Holy See will lend its indispensable co-operation, wonderful results should follow. The poor emigrants will find on American soil their priests, their parishes, their schools, their societies, their language, and thus cannot fail to extend the boundaries of the Kingdom of Jesus Christ on earth.

In giving solemn testimony of their loyal devotion to the Apostolic See, the undersigned humbly beg Your Holiness to grant paternal approbation to the propositions which they have proposed for the salvation of souls and the glory of our holy mother, the Church, in the different American nations. With the most loyal devotion, Your most devoted, humble, and obedient sons: [There then follow the signatures of the boards of directors of the St. Raphael Society in Germany, Austria-Hungary, Belgium, and Italy, with the signatures of a single delegate each from Switzerland and France. A duplicate of the memorial was attached in the interests of the French-speaking Canadian Catholics in the United States and was signed by fifteen Canadian Catholics, including Prime Minister Henri Mercier of Quebec].

135. The Secret Oath of the American Protective Association, October 31, 1893

AFTER the breakup of the Know-Nothings with the Civil War there was no organized movement against the Catholic Church in the United States until March, 1887, when Henry F. Bowers (1837–1911) and six associates founded the American Protective Association at Clinton, Iowa. The founders were drawn from no single political or religious group, there being among the original seven two Republicans, two Democrats, one Populist, and one Prohibitionist, with two of no religion and one each a Methodist, Lutheran, Baptist, Presbyterian, and Congregationalist. The A.P.A. grew slowly at first, but by 1894 they made significant gains in the elections of that year and by 1896 it was estimated that they numbered approximately a million members with the chief strength centered in the Middle West. The issue of Bryanism and free silver split their ranks in 1896, and as Arthur Meier Schlesinger remarked, "Both major parties snubbed the A.P.A., and the movement withered as suddenly as it had grown" ("A Critical Period in

---

[3] Giovanni Battista Scalabrini (1839–1905), Bishop of Piacenza, founded the Congregation of Missionaries of St. Charles Borromeo, the first of whose members had arrived in the United States in July, 1888, for work among the Italian immigrants.

American Religion, 1875–1900," *Proceedings of the Massachusetts Histori-cal Society,* LXIV [1932], 546). The A.P.A. lingered on, however, until 1911 and during the 1890's they did a great deal of harm among many Americans who were taken in by their lying propaganda, the most fantastic item of which was published in the *Patriotic American* of Detroit on April 8, 1893, and purported to be an encyclical of Pope Leo XIII instructing the American Catholics to rise on the feast of St. Ignatius Loyola, July 31, 1893, and massacre all heretics in the country. The secret oath of the A.P.A., a copy of which follows, came to light late that year through the exposé of the St. Paul *Globe* and through the efforts of Henry M. Youmans (1832–1920), defeated congressman from the eighth district of Michigan, to unseat William S. Linton (1856–1927), his opponent, who, he contended, was a member of the A.P.A. Source: Michael Williams, *The Shadow of the Pope* (New York: McGraw-Hill Book Co., Inc., 1932), pp. 103–104.

I do most solemnly promise and swear that I will always, to the utmost of my ability, labor, plead and wage a continuous warfare against ignorance and fanaticism; that I will use my utmost power to strike the shackles and chains of blind obedience to the Roman Catholic church from the hampered and bound consciences of a priest-ridden and church-oppressed people; that I will never allow any one, a member of the Roman Catholic church, to become a member of this order, I knowing him to be such; that I will use my influence to promote the interest of all Protestants everywhere in the world that I may be; that I will not employ a Roman Catholic in any capacity if I can procure the services of a Protestant.[1]

I furthermore promise and swear that I will not aid in building or maintaining, by my resources, any Roman Catholic church or institution of their sect or creed whatsoever, but will do all in my power to retard and break down the power of the Pope, in this country or any other; that I will not enter into any controversy with a Roman Catholic upon the subject of this order, nor will I enter into any agree-ment with a Roman Catholic to strike or create a disturbance whereby the Catholic employes may undermine and substitute their Protestant co-workers; that in all grievances I will seek only Protestants and

---

[1] A sample of A.P.A. literature which made their intent clear was the 56-page pamphlet put out by a certain J. H. Jackson of Forth Worth, Texas, supreme vice-president of the organization, entitled *The American Protective Association. What It Is, Its Platform and Roman Intolerance* (n.p., n.d.). In the preface Jackson remarked that he had been a member for eighteen months and had read everything he could find on the Catholic Church and had become convinced that there was an urgent need to combat its power. When he learned "that the Roman pope gave his subjects no right to think for themselves," he declared "this is a false assumption of authority, which American manhood cannot, and will not, submit to" (p. 3).

counsel with them to the exclusion of all Roman Catholics, and will not make known to them anything of any nature matured at such conferences.

I furthermore promise and swear that I will not countenance the nomination, in any caucus or convention, of a Roman Catholic for any office in the gift of the American people, and that I will not vote for, or counsel others to vote for, any Roman Catholic, but will vote only for a Protestant, so far as may lie in my power. Should there be two Roman Catholics on opposite tickets, I will erase the name on the ticket I vote; that I will at all times endeavor to place the political positions of this government in the hands of Protestants, to the entire exclusion of the Roman Catholic church, of the members thereof, and the mandate of the Pope.

To all of which I do most solemnly promise and swear, so help me God. Amen.

136. George P. A. Healy Recounts His Beginnings as an Artist and His Painting of Pope Pius IX, 1894

WITH the exception of John LaFarge the most important painter among American Catholics was George P. A. Healy (1813–1894). Boston-born of an American mother and a father who had left Ireland in the uprising of 1798, Healy's fame rested chiefly on the portraits he painted of many of the great in both Church and State on both sides of the Atlantic. His subjects included such varied figures as Pius IX, Jenny Lind, Guizot, Carmen Sylva, King Louis Philippe, Franz Liszt, Lord Bulwer-Lytton, ten or more presidents of the United States, and the leading American statesmen of his time, including Henry Clay, John C. Calhoun, and Daniel Webster. Healy won prizes in Paris and Florence never before conferred on an American, and of his great picture, "Webster Replying to Hayne," which brought the gold medal of the Paris Exposition of 1855 and which hangs in Faneuil Hall, Boston, it was said, "No other American artist at any cost of time and energy could have produced the huge canvas which does not seem to have required any special effort from Healy, who as far as schooling and *technique* go was entirely Parisian" (Samuel Isham, *The History of American Painting*, rev. ed. by Royal Cortissoz [New York, 1927], p. 281). It is to Healy that we owe some of the best likenesses of the American hierarchy among them Cardinals McCloskey and Gibbons and Archbishops Francis Kenrick and Bayley. In his early manhood he had been quite indifferent about his religious duties, having married Louisa Phipps, an English girl, in London in 1839 in an Anglican ceremony. But through the influence of Catholic friends, and principally John B. Fitzpatrick, Bishop of Boston

(1812–1866) whose portrait he painted, the artist became an ardent Catholic, succeeded in persuading Mrs. Healy to become a convert in 1860, and for most of the remainder of his long life attended Mass daily. The following excerpts from his memoirs tell of how he began his artistic career and of his experiences while painting Pius IX. Source: George P. A. Healy, *Reminiscences of a Portrait Painter* (Chicago: A. C. McClurg and Co., 1894), pp. 17, 20–25, 135–137.

My grandmother, Mrs. Hicks, painted quite prettily in water-colors, and one of my delights as a child was to turn over a series of sketches she had made during a journey among the West Indian Islands. It is doubtless from her that I inherited my first liking for painting. . . . The first time I held a brush was when I was about sixteen years of age. One day I was to meet a friend of mine at his house, and we were then to go off together on some excursion. But as it began to rain violently, I found my friend and his two sisters amusing themselves with a paint-box. They made drawings which they afterwards colored. One of the little girls, holding up her work where bright reds, greens, and blues vied with each other, exclaimed: "You could not do as much, could you, George?" "I guess I could," said I in true Yankee fashion; and, nettled, I began to color one of the childish drawings on which the little girl obligingly wrote directions as to the tints I should use. When I had finished, my friends declared that I must have painted before. But I had not. I had shown at school much aptitude for map drawing, but that was the first time I had ever used a brush.

After that, however, I would do nothing else. I determined to be a painter. . . . My first small success came to me in rather an odd way. Miss Stuart,[1] who took some interest in me, lent me a print of Guido Reni's[2] "Ecce Homo." I copied this on a canvas, and then colored it as best I could, without any help except such as the study of my own face afforded for the flesh tints. Such as it was, I carried the picture to a good-natured bookseller, who consented to put it in his shop-window. I own that I often found an excuse for passing along that street, so as to give a rapid glance at my work. In later years I have never seen an artist hover about his picture at a public exhibition without thinking of my "Ecce Homo" in the friendly bookseller's window.

A Catholic priest from the country happened to pass that way,

---

[1] Miss Jane Stuart was the daughter of the famous painter, Gilbert Stuart (1755–1828).

[2] Guido Reni (1575–1642), an Italian painter.

and stopped to look at the picture. Catholic priests are not rich now; in those days they were terribly poor. After hesitating, he went in and asked whether that picture was for sale. My friend the bookseller must have had a twinkle in his eyes, as he answered that doubtless the artist would consent to part with his work — for a consideration. "I am not rich," said the priest; "all I could scrape together would be ten dollars." "I will speak to the artist, and give you an answer tommor- row." And on the morrow the priest carried away the "Ecce Homo," and the "artist" pocketed the ten dollars. I do not know which was the happier of the two; but I rather fancy it was the boy painter!

Some thirty years later, as I stood talking with some friends at the Capitol in Washington, I saw an old man wearing a Roman collar. On hearing my name pronounced by one of my friends he came up to me and said: "Are you Mr. Healy, the painter?" I bowed, and he con- tinued with a smile: "I believe that I am the happy possessor of one of your earliest works, if not the earliest. Do you remember an 'Ecce Homo' which you had placed in the window of a Boston bookseller? A country priest offered ten dollars for it. I am that priest, and your picture still hangs in my little church. Who knows? it perhaps brought down blessings on your head. I have always felt that I had something to do with your success in life!" I shook my first patron heartily by the hand, and told him what joy his ten dollars had given me. But somehow, in the confusion of the moment, I neglected to ask him for his name and address. I have always regretted this. I should greatly have liked to pay him a visit, and see how my copy of Guido Reni looked in the Yankee country church.

The first serious encouragement which I received came to me from Sully,[3] who, when I was about eighteen, was called to Boston to paint a portrait of Colonel Perkins[4] for the Athenaeum. Miss Jane Stuart, daughter of the great painter, spoke to him of "little Healy's" attempts, and he sent word to me that if I would make a sketch from Nature and a copy of one of Stuart's heads he would be glad to give me some advice. When I showed him what I had done, he looked at the canvases and exclaimed heartily: "My young friend, I advise you to make painting your profession!" . . .

During my stay in Rome I painted from memory a portrait of Pope

---

[3] Thomas Sully (1783–1872) was the ranking American painter after the deaths of Charles Willson Peale in 1827 and Gilbert Stuart in 1828. In 1838 Sully painted the young Queen Victoria from life.

[4] Thomas H. Perkins (1764–1854) was a leading Boston merchant and phi- lanthropist who was called "Colonel" by reason of his many years as an officer in the Massachusetts militia.

Pius IX.[5] His Holiness, having seen this unfinished work, liked it, and consented to give me a few sittings. This was a great favor, which I highly appreciated. So far I had only seen the Pope, with other strangers, at the Vatican receptions, or from afar when he officiated at St. Peter's, before the events of 1870.

I was introduced one morning into Pius IX's library; a pleasant room, simply enough furnished, full of books, the table covered with papers. The Pope was dressed all in white cloth, with scarlet shoes; the hair was white, the face rather pale, with very bright eyes, not incapable of sparkle, for his Holiness knew how to take a joke. He was a pretty good sitter, but somewhat restless, and curious also as to what his painter was about. On one occasion he arose from his seat to look over my shoulder. When I am earnestly at work, I wish my sitters to help me, and do their duty by remaining in the attitude I have chosen. I exclaimed, perhaps a little abruptly: "I beg your Holiness to sit down." The Pope laughed and said: "I am accustomed to give orders, not to receive them. But you see, Mr. Healy, that I also know how to obey," and submissively went back to his chair.

Pius IX has been dead now many a year. I like to think of the few short sittings he gave me in his cheerful library; I like to remember his quiet, pleasant talk, his rather Italian-sounding French, his judgments of men and things. One day, speaking of a monk who had left the Church and married, he observed, not without glee: "He has taken his punishment in his own hands."[6] I like especially to feel as though the hours spent in his presence had cast a glow on my later years, as the glorious setting sun behind St. Peter's throws a glamour over Rome, its domes and gardens. I often think, also, of Pius IX's gentle reproach to one of my countrymen who, in his American pride, refused to bend before him: "My son, an old man's blessing never did harm to any one."

----

[5] Healy painted Pius IX in the winter of 1870–1871 for which the artist was made a Knight of St. Gregory.

[6] According to Marie De Mare, *G. P. A. Healy, American Artist* (New York, 1954), p. 252, this was the French Carmelite, Père Hyacinthe [Charles Loyson] (1827–1912), who left the Church after the Vatican Council, attached himself to Döllinger, married, and founded an Old Catholic congregation in Paris.

137. Archbishop Ireland's Views on Socialism, October 14, 1894

BY THE 1890's the advance of socialism had become the cause of serious concern to many men in both Europe and the United States. This concern was heightened by the bloody Homestead Strike of 1892 and the turbulent year 1894 which saw the huge strikes of the Pullman Company and the western railroads and the march of Coxey's Army of unemployed on Washington. No American bishop was more alive to the necessity of finding correct solutions to social problems than John Ireland, first Archbishop of St. Paul (1838–1918). In the summer of 1892 Ireland had attracted national attention in France by a series of addresses, and it was not surprising, therefore, that Jules Huret, dean of the Paris correspondents, should seek an interview with him which was published in *Le Figaro* on August 29, 1894. The following reprint of the interview embodied a number of ideas which Ireland later expanded and published from his lectures in the two-volume work, *The Church and Modern Society* (St. Paul, 1905). The archbishop was a friend of the laboring man, as his strong support to Cardinal Gibbons in 1887 in the case of the Knights of Labor made evident. But he was not an uncritical admirer as he made clear in the interview he gave to the press in July of this same year when violence broke out among the strikers in Chicago. Source: New York *Times*, October 14, 1894.

The interviewer laureate of the Paris press, Jules Huret[1] reports in *Le Figaro*[2] the following conversation with Archbishop Ireland:

Q. — What do you think of the Socialist predictions? Do you believe that transformations in social organizations are imminent?

A. — The transformations predicted by the Socialists seem to me to be neither imminent nor probable. What is probable, what I desire to realize as soon as possible is improvement in the condition of the mass of working men, their elevation from an intellectual and moral point of view, as much as from a material point of view. This improvement and this elevation shall have as consequences the advent of democracy and the disappearance of what is called, in Europe, the reign of the bourgeoisie. This will be accomplished without much resistance. As was said to me by a Belgian statesman, Minister

---

[1] Jules Huret (1864–1915) was a famous French journalist who won early notice by his series of articles on controverted questions for *l'Echo de Paris,* and later for a series on European social questions for *Le Figaro.*

[2] *Le Figaro* began in 1825 and went through a number of changes, becoming in 1866 a daily paper which was monarchical in sympathies after the Franco-Prussian War and which continued to be an organ of conservative opinion.

Northamb:[3] "In our days, more than ever, nobody remains immovable. Some turn to reaction, others to democracy."

Observe that true democracy does not exclude, but, on the contrary, presupposes social influences. There shall always be in society men of genius, men of talent, and men of elevated character, and these men will always exert influence. A society where social influences are weak, where natural legitimate influences are replaced by others, is a society in an abnormal state. It was a great mistake of writers in France to write of directing classes. The expression is unfortunate; there are no directing classes, but there are, and there always will be, directing men.

I do not believe that there will be an extreme condensation of capital in the future. I think, on the contrary, that money shall be more generally distributed, that the workingmen shall be better paid, and, consequently, shall have more instruction. Notice what Leo XIII[4] says of diffusion of property, while talking of capital. Doubtless there shall always be great fortunes, but great fortunes are an evil only when they have been acquired by fraud and injustice, and, moreover, they are not incompatible with small fortunes; on the contrary, often small fortunes are formed in the shadow of great ones. No other country possesses as many millionaires as the United States, and no other country possesses as small a number of poor people, whereas, no country possesses a smaller number of millionaires than Russia, and no other country contains more poor people. There shall always be great capitalists, great capitalists shall always have influence, and this influence will be increased naturally by association, but association in its turn will protect small capitalists and workingmen. Between the interests of the two classes, independently of moral and religious influences, there is and will remain the civil power, the mission of which is to enact wise laws which insure liberty, rights, the activity of all, especially of the weakest. In transitory times these laws are not easily made. But this is a fault inherent in human nature.

Q. — You are called here "the Socialist Bishop." Do you accept the adjective? Would your ideas be accepted by the Scholastic schools?

A. — The word "Socialist" has an evil ring, and before applying it to my ideas it should be defined. If by Socialists you understand those who are preoccupied by social necessities and miseries, who desire to improve the state of society, and who ask, in view of this improve-

---

[3] An effort to identify Northamb was not successful.

[4] Leo XIII's encyclical *Rerum novarum* on the condition of the working classes had been issued on May 15, 1891.

ment, not only action of individuals and influence of voluntary associations, but also a reasonable intervention of the civil power, yes, I am a Socialist. But if by "Socialist" you understand those who share the theories of Marx, of Benoit Malon,[5] of Greef, and others — theories which consist in denying the rightfulness of private property in land and in instruments of labor — no, I am not a Socialist.

I do not doubt that my ideas would be rejected by the Socialistic sects. Everywhere the Socialist sects are opposed to the Christian social movement. In laboring for the disappearance of the just grievances of the working class, the Christian movement takes from sectarian socialism the reason for its existence.

This is not because the promoters of the Christian social movement preach only charity and resignation. Far from this, they preach, above all, right and justice; natural right of the workingman; complete justice, social as well as individual. It is said that justice is a foundation of societies; it is also the foundation of economic order. Therefore, in the first place, justice; after justice, charity; charity may not be substituted for justice; one completes the other; in places where justice has ceased to command, charity intervenes.

Doubtless our conception of life differs essentially from that of the materialists; our reason and our faith teach us that present life is a preparation for a better life. But we are not led by this to neglect material welfare. Material welfare is not our end; it is our means. Its profession to a reasonable degree is of the highest importance for the moral and religious life of men.

Q. — Do you admit as legitimate the actual aspirations of the masses toward absolute social equality? Do you think that the natural inequalities might be reconciled with social equality?

A. — Aspirations of the masses toward social equality — I mean reasonable equality — are perfectly legitimate. Social equality is, after all, only the expression of equality from the point of view of human dignity and of Christian dignity. We must take care, however, that social equality should not be opposed to social hierarchy; parentage, service, and authority engender rights and social duties which are not the same for all; genius, talent, virtue, and riches entail consideration and give a certain moral pre-eminence which shall always be admitted. This observation is sufficient to show that social equality may be

---

[5] Benôit Malon (1841–1893) was a French socialist who participated in the Paris Commune of 1870–1871 and later fled to Geneva where he founded *La Revanche;* Guillaume-Joseph de Greef (1842–1924) was a professor of sociology in the University of Brussels.

reconciled with natural inequality. Natural inequality is that of intelligence, of strength, and of health. This inequality is more or less corrected by society, which protects the weak. Social hierarchy is natural and indestructible. Something not as natural, and which may be abolished, is the great distance between the two ends of this hierarchy. It is not necessary that some should be so elevated and that others should be so degraded.

Q. — Since you admit that societies may pass through transformations, think you that the trilogy — family, religion, and property — should necessarily escape these transformations?

A. — The action of Providence, which brings everything to its end, does not prevent the natural course of things and does not suppress the liberty of man. Modifications in the form of societies are therefore possible, but family, religion, and property are essential elements of all human society. Family is the principle of human society; religion is its crown; property — considered in itself, independently of variable forms — is a condition of life, of liberty, and of progress.

The form of the family is determined by the nature of man, his physical forces, his intellectual faculties, his sentiments, and his instincts, and this form was sanctioned by Christ. It will not change, but what may be desired, what may be hoped, is more perfect realization of this form, and this realization may not be obtained except by progress in manners, customs, and laws.

The form of religion is also determined in a general manner by nature as regards its object and its principal acts. It was also determined in a special and positive manner by Christ. There shall not therefore be a new form of religion, but one may hope for a more complete intelligence and a more general and more perfect realization of the Christian idea, and consequently a more powerful influence of the Gospel on the life of individuals and of nations. Outside of Christianity there may be new religious forms, as was Mohammedanism, but these forms shall not be progressive. As for Neo-Christianity,[6] it will never be anything but amateurish religion.

Property is essential, but there is nothing absolute in its forms. These depend on the social, industrial, political, and moral situation of peoples. The history of property has occupied in France and elsewhere many learned men. Their studies cannot but throw light on questions of social philosophy.

---

[6] Ireland may have been referring here to the followers of Claude-Henri de Rouvroy, Comte de Saint-Simon (1760–1825), who fostered in his last years a sort of mystical fraternalism.

Q. — Among the possible modifications of property, which ones would you regard favorably? What do you think of the communist theory?

A. — The form of property was not always the same at all epochs, and even to-day it is not absolutely the same in all countries. What modifications are possible, useful, and necessary depends on the conditions under which each people finds itself. Modifications may not be made by legislation. This can only give sanction. They are accomplished slowly, by progress in manners and under the sway of circumstances. An example of such modifications is the introduction and disappearance of feudal property.

The system of property which appears to me to be the most desirable should reunite the following qualities: Stimulate human activity and individual labor by assurance of just retribution; maintain the stability of the family, and favor an equitable distribution of the good things of this world.

The Communist theory takes no account of the nature of things or of the nature of man. It does not seem possible to me that it may be realized, and if it were realized the result would be fatal to civilization. Herbert Spencer[7] recently demonstrated this in the introduction which he wrote for "The Man Versus the State." Community of goods may exist among a certain number of men devoted to celibacy and to the cult of God. It might have existed in the age of gold and in a state of innocence; but it does not answer to the real state of present humanity.

Yet the present movement contains very complex elements, which may not be judged in their entirety from the point of view of morality and of civilization. There are few theories, however false they may be in their entirety, which do not contain elements of truth and of justice. The errors which they contain are often an occasion determining a more complete intelligence of the truth. Thus, it may not be denied that the Communist agitation has provoked a more adequate understanding of certain social principles and a more profound sentiment of social justice.

Q. — What is the state of the social question in America? Where, think you, do the Socialist theories have a better chance to succeed, in Europe or in the United States?

A. — The social question exists in America. Read on this subject

---

[7] *Man versus the State,* to which Herbert Spencer (1820–1903) wrote an introduction, was first published in 1884 and was reprinted in 1940 by the Caxton Printers, Caldwell, Idaho.

Prof. Ely's[8] book, "The Labor Movement in America." In my opinion, the difference between our situation and that of Europe is as follows:

The social movement is expressed in the United States by numerous and powerful workingmen's associations. These associations have for their principal object to maintain good wages; they are preoccupied by the morality of their members and by professional education. You know that there are some associations which labor to maintain harmony between bosses and workmen, and to prevent strikes. I think that among the American people there are few Anarchists, few Communists, and that the number of collectivists cannot be large. They come from other countries. European immigration supplies their principal contingent. The details which Mr. Ely gives on these subjects are very interesting. As for Henry George's[9] agrarian movement, it is far from powerful.

Socialist theories have far less chance in America than in Europe. In the first place, the sentiment of personal dignity and responsibility and the spirit of enterprise are much developed in the American people. It likes and appreciates individual liberty and respects the law. These dispositions do not lead to social revolution. Furthermore, there is room in the United States for all kinds of energy. Labor there insures honorable life; then, the greater number of Americans have conquered their situation by personal valor, at the price of efforts, perils, and heroic sacrifices. They are not disposed to share with others what they have gained by so much work. Then there are philosophical, moral, and political causes which elsewhere favor the development of Socialism, and have no force in the United States. I allude to administrative centralization, intervention of the Government in the affairs of citizens, to the military regime, and to authoritative traditions.

138. The Americanism Controversy Foreshadowed in the Writings of a French Visitor, 1895

IN THE late nineteenth century the Catholic Church suffered severe pressure from the governments of France, Italy, and Spain. The progress which had meanwhile been made in the United States where there was a separa-

---

[8] Richard T. Ely (1854–1943), at this time professor of political economy in the University of Wisconsin, was a prolific writer on social and economic questions. The latest edition of his volume, *The Labor Movement in America*, appeared in 1905.

[9] Henry George (1839–1897) was chiefly notable for his theory of the single tax on land.

tion of Church and State excited the admiration of leading European Catholic liberals who sought to have the Church in their own countries model itself on the American pattern. In their enthusiasm at times they used careless and extravagant language concerning the American Catholics which aroused the distrust of conservative ecclesiastics and which led eventually to charges of a lack of orthodoxy in the controversy over the so-called heresy of Americanism. The controversy was especially heated in France where the writings of men like Max Leclerc (1864——) served to heighten suspicions concerning the doctrines taught in the burgeoning branch of the universal Church in the United States. Leclerc, one of the editors of the *Journal des débats,* after a visit to this country in July–October, 1890, wrote a series of articles in that paper and in the *Revue bleue* which he published in book form in 1895. It is easily seen how his descriptions of American Catholicism could lead to misunderstanding and contribute to the quarrel which broke in France on this subject two years after the publication of his book. Source: Max Leclerc, *Choses d'Amérique. Les crises économique et religieuse aux États-Unis* (Paris: Armand Colin et Cie, 1895), pp. 220, 222–225, 236–240.

The Church enjoys an absolute freedom, in virtue of common right and within the limits of the nation's laws; she is self-sufficient; she expects nothing from the State which demands nothing of her. She even congratulates herself on being left to her unaided might; she owes to this form of government a vigor, an eternal youthfulness which she certainly does not have elsewhere; she gathers the fruits of independence; she waxes strong under the necessity of making her way in the bright world of competition . . .

The Church has known how to make its place in the State. Accustomed in the old world to rely on the State, or at any rate to reckon with it, in America she has been able to disregard it. But how has she conducted herself in regard to the people themselves? Experienced in dealing with old western societies, how has she handled the contact with this developing society?

With an amazing flexibility and that unflagging faculty for adaptation which Macaulay recognized in her, she has become acclimated to her new environment: she has modelled her spirit on the very spirit of the nation; she has made herself tolerant, democratic, American.

Doctor Carroll, who was the first Archbishop of Baltimore and the founder of the hierarchy, showed his clergy and his successors an example of independence and broadness of outlook. It is he who declared: "It was never our doctrine that salvation could be obtained only by those who are in actual communion with the Church." It is he who expressed the desire that the liturgy be allowed to employ

English for the greatest good of the poor people and the illiterate Negroes. Cardinal Gibbons, the present head of the American Church, has faithfully continued to teach the same doctrines. 'He never speaks of the Protestant sects as irreconcilable enemies; he calls them rather "our separated brethren," "our dissident brothers." He condemns in a dogmatic book, *The Faith of Our Fathers,*[1] the Inquisition and the persecutions; he reproves in indignant terms the massacre of St. Bartholomew. He brings together some very happy arguments to demonstrate that the Catholic Church has been and remains the friend of civil liberties and of tolerance. He is pleased that the Church should be free in a free State and that these two powers should be equally respectful of the rights of each other. He shows that the American Catholics have played a noble role in the national history, that they have given the example of tolerance, offering asylum in their colony of Maryland to the Protestants who were persecuted among their own.

In this land of liberty the Catholic Church has realized that she should preach and practice tolerance; likewise, she has made a point of proving that she is not an aristocratic organization, that she is, on the contrary, sincerely devoted to democracy. She is openly arrayed on the side of the poor and the weak; she has espoused the cause of the lowly. And if one keeps in mind that her clientele is almost entirely composed of the proletariat, of workers, of the little people, one will recognize that she has been right and discerning in her own interest in defending the interests of her faithful. The attitude taken four years ago by Cardinal Gibbons in the affair of the Knights of Labor is a striking proof of it.

The Church is tolerant, she is democratic, she is, in fine, American. She has known nothing but rapid development in the soil of the Union from the day when the hierarchy was founded, when she passed from the hands of missionaries dependent on Rome to the hands of an autonomous clergy to the present when she has become one of the institutions of the country, one of the organs of the national life. . . .

She wishes to be called American; she has entered into the spirit of the nation; but she sensed, indeed, that she has very much to do, more so every day, to transform and to assimilate the heterogeneous elements who come to her without ceasing from Europe. She foresees and she fears the reproaches which they are able to make that she is an immigrant, a stranger; she is very anxious to avoid this. She is

[1] Baltimore: John Murphy & Co., 1876.

sincerely searching for every means of Americanizing herself from top to bottom. . . .

While Europe toils along the well-worn rut of race hatreds, of bloody quarrels between nation and nation, of rivalries between ministers and sovereigns, — an occurrence of capital significance in the history of the world took place on the other side of the ocean and went almost unnoticed: the Catholic Church, the most powerful and most ancient of religious organizations, met up with the youngest and most enterprising of recent societies. The Roman Church, for the first time, found herself at grips with a people of a modern civilization without the interposition of governments, local authorities, intrigues of courts or the schemes of diplomacy. I would like to examine what has been, what may be the influence of this important event upon the guiding spirit and upon the destinies of the Church.

The Church has conquered in America a vast territory inhabited by an English-speaking people. Among the Catholics of Europe, those who speak English form a tiny minority: the American nation, the most populous even now of the nations of western civilization, the fastest to reproduce, finally the most active agent for the diffusion of the English language, brings to the Church a contingent of faithful which disturbs the balance in Catholicity, and doubles the hold of the Church of Rome upon the world: one can foresee the day in which the Catholics speaking English will be more numerous than the Catholics speaking any other language.

But at this point several questions arrest us: what is the future of religious opinion on the American continent? A difficult mystery to penetrate. One can foresee that as time marches on, the more vigorously will the Catholic Church have to struggle against growing indifference, against the advance of materialism or the spirit of skepticism. The American civilization is profoundly materialistic. When the new settlers, when the sons of the docile recruits of the Catholic Church have been imbued with the American spirit, will there remain a place in their hearts for the precepts of Rome and for the faith?

Be that as it may, the Catholic Church cannot fail to be deeply stirred by this inroad of the Anglo-Saxon race, with its concept of life, its democratic instincts, its relish for action and independence, and a whole long civilization behind it remaining up to then alien to the Church of Rome. The Latin influence will cease to exercise uncontested domination in the Church; the Anglo-Saxon influence will establish for itself a usurping stronghold there, and the history of the world will be swerved by it. Old Europe, shackled by its past, introspective, reduced to helplessness, will cease to attract the constant attention of the Church which will turn toward the new lands with their innumerable inhabitants, for she will recognize that the future is with them. Rome will no longer be in Rome, but in Baltimore or in Carthage.

Already the strong and solemn voice of the Anglo-Saxons has made itself heard and hearkened to in the councils of the Church; it is that voice which thrust upon Rome, by threatening an appeal to the people, the solicitude about social problems, and an inexorably democratic policy. It is by the voice of Cardinal Manning, of Cardinal Gibbons, an English prelate and an American prelate, that modern democracy, the power of tomorrow, has indicated to the Church that she must turn her attention from the powerful of the present in order to bring it to bear on itself. One still remembers the voyage to Rome in June, 1886,[2] of Cardinal Gibbons who came to plead the cause of democracy in the name of the interests of the American Church and to demand the withdrawal of the interdict issued by the Holy See against the powerful secret association of the Knights of Labor. M. E.-M. de Vogüé[3] told a year later, in some prophetic pages, of "this eruption of the new World in the midst of the Roman prelacy, little concerned up to now with social problems." I will not return to this. M. de Vogüé said then, and subsequent history has proven him correct: "The term 'revolution' is not excessive. One felt the wind of tomorrow which was blowing, one perceived its force."

The American Church, after having been a simple external appendage of the Church of Rome, a remote extension and loosely attached, has become one of the inmost motive forces; and all the more so since Rome, following the example of the great European powers, has taken upon herself to formulate in some sense a colonial policy. . . . the ten million American Catholics have, on several memorable occasions, weighed heavier in the scales of the Holy See than the hundreds of millions of faithful in old Europe. . . .

---

[2] Gibbons' visit to Rome took place in February–March, 1887, not in June, 1886.

[3] Eugène Marie Melchoir Vicomte de Vogüé (1848–1910), frequent contributor in these years to the *Revue des deux mondes* and the *Journal des débats*. Leclerc was referring here to De Vogüé's *Souvenirs et visions* (Paris, 1887), a travelogue.

139. Pope Leo XIII's Encyclical *Longinqua oceani* to the Church of the United States, January 6, 1895

THE last twenty years of the nineteenth century was one of the stormiest periods in the history of American Catholicism. Attacked from without by the American Protective Association (A.P.A.) as un-American and a threat to the Republic, and subject within to feuds among the bishops by reason of their conflicting interpretations on the role of the Church in public affairs, there was little peace until after the opening of the new century. The Holy See was, of course, aware of these tensions, and in an effort to restore unity and harmony Leo XIII addressed an encyclical to the hierarchy in which he analyzed the strengths and weaknesses of American society, and was at special pains to emphasize the function of the recently established Apostolic Delegation in the life of the American Church. Source: John J. Wynne, S.J. (Ed.), *The Great Encyclical Letters of Pope Leo XIII* (New York: Benziger Bros., 1903), pp. 320–335.

We traverse in spirit and thought the wide expanse of ocean; and although We have at other times addressed you in writing — chiefly when We directed Encyclical Letters to the bishops of the Catholic world — yet have We now resolved to speak to you separately, trusting that We shall be, God willing, of some assistance to the Catholic cause amongst you. To this We apply Ourselves with the utmost zeal and care; because We highly esteem and love exceedingly the young and vigorous American nation, in which We plainly discern latent forces for the advancement alike of civilization and of Christianity.

Not long ago, when your whole nation, as was fitting, celebrated, with grateful recollection and every manifestation of joy, the completion of the fourth century since the discovery of America, We, too, commemorated together with you that most auspicious event, sharing in your rejoicings with equal good-will. Nor were We on that occasion content with offering prayers at a distance for your welfare and greatness. It was Our wish to be in some manner present with you in your festivities. Hence We cheerfully sent one who should represent Our person.[1] Not without good reason did We take part in your celebration. For when America was, as yet, but a new-born babe, uttering in its cradle its first feeble cries, the Church took it to her

---

[1] Francesco Satolli (1839–1910), Archbishop of Lepanto, came to the United States in October, 1892, as Leo XIII's representative at the World's Columbian Exposition in Chicago.

bosom and motherly embrace. Columbus, as We have elsewhere expressly shown, sought, as the primary fruit of his voyages and labors, to open a pathway for the Christian faith into the new lands and new seas. Keeping this thought constantly in view, his first solicitude, wherever he disembarked, was to plant upon the shore the sacred emblem of the cross. Wherefore, like as the Ark of Noe, surmounting the overflowing waters, bore the seed of Israel together with the remnants of the human race, even thus did the barks launched by Columbus upon the ocean carry into regions beyond the seas as well the germs of mighty States as the principles of the Catholic religion.

This is not the place to give a detailed account of what thereupon ensued. Very rapidly did the light of the Gospel shine upon the savage tribes discovered by the Ligurian. For it is sufficiently well known how many of the children of Francis, as well as of Dominic and of Loyola, were accustomed during the two following centuries to voyage thither for this purpose; how they cared for the colonies brought over from Europe; but primarily and chiefly how they converted the natives from superstition to Christianity, sealing their labors in many instances with the testimony of their blood. The names newly given to so many of your towns and rivers and mountains and lakes teach and clearly witness how deeply your beginnings were marked with the footprints of the Catholic Church.

Nor, perchance, did the fact which We now recall take place without some design of divine Providence. Precisely at the epoch when the American colonies, having with Catholic aid, achieved liberty and independence, coalesced into a constitutional Republic the ecclesiastical hierarchy was happily established amongst you; and at the very time when the popular suffrage placed the great Washington at the helm of the Republic, the first bishop was set by apostolic authority over the American Church.[2] The well-known friendship and familiar intercourse which subsisted between these two men seems to be an evidence that the United States ought to be conjoined in concord and amity with the Catholic Church. And not without cause; for without morality the State cannot endure — a truth which that illustrious citizen of yours, whom We have just mentioned, with a keenness of insight worthy of his genius and statesmanship perceived and proclaimed. But the best and strongest support of morality is religion. She, by her very nature, guards and defends all the principles on

---

[2] George Washington was inaugurated as first President of the United States on April 30, 1789; John Carroll was appointed as first Bishop of Baltimore on November 6, 1789.

which duties are founded, and, setting before us the motives most powerful to influence us, commands us to live virtuously and forbids us to transgress. Now what is the Church other than a legitimate society, founded by the will and ordinance of Jesus Christ for the preservation of morality and the defence of religion? For this reason have We repeatedly endeavored, from the summit of the pontifical dignity, to inculcate that the Church, whilst directly and immediately aiming at the salvation of souls and the beatitude which is to be attained in heaven, is yet, even in the order of temporal things, the fountain of blessings so numerous and great that they could not have been greater or more numerous had the original purpose of her institution been the pursuit of happiness during the life which is spent on earth.

That your Republic is progressing and developing by giant strides is patent to all; and this holds good in religious matters also. For even as your cities, in the course of one century, have made a marvellous increase in wealth and power, so do we behold the Church, from scant and slender beginnings, grown with rapidity to be great and exceedingly flourishing. Now if, on the one hand, the increased riches and resources of your cities are justly attributed to the talents and active industry of the American people, on the other hand, the prosperous condition of Catholicity must be ascribed, first indeed, to the virtue, the ability, and the prudence of the bishops and clergy; but in no slight measure also, to the faith and generosity of the Catholic laity. Thus, while the different classes exerted their best energies, you were enabled to erect unnumbered religious and useful institutions, sacred edifices, schools for the instruction of youth, colleges for the higher branches, homes for the poor, hospitals for the sick, and convents and monasteries. As for what more closely touches spiritual interests, which are based upon the exercise of Christian virtues, many facts have been brought to Our notice, whereby We are animated with hope and filled with joy, namely, that the numbers of the secular and regular clergy are steadily augmenting, that pious sodalities and confraternities are held in esteem, that the Catholic parochial schools, the Sunday-schools for imparting Christian doctrine, and summer schools are in a flourishing condition; moreover, associations for mutual aid, for the relief of the indigent, for the promotion of temperate living, add to all this the many evidences of popular piety.

The main factor, no doubt, in bringing things into this happy state were the ordinances and decrees of your synods, especially of those which in more recent times were convened and confirmed by the authority of the Apostolic See. But, moreover (a fact which it gives pleasure to acknowledge), thanks are due to the equity of the laws which obtain in America and to the customs of the well-ordered Republic. For the Church amongst you, unopposed by the Constitution and government of your nation, fettered by no hostile legislation, protected against violence by the common laws and the impartiality of the tribunals, is free to live and act without hindrance. Yet, though all this is true, it would be very erroneous to draw the conclusion that in America is to be sought the type of the most desirable status of the Church, or that it would be universally lawful or expedient for State and Church to be, as in America, dissevered and divorced.[3] The fact that Catholicity with you is in good condition, nay, is even enjoying a prosperous growth, is by all means to be attributed to the fecundity with which God has endowed His Church, in virtue of which unless men or circumstances interfere, she spontaneously expands and propagates herself; but she would bring forth more abundant fruits if, in addition to liberty, she enjoyed the favor of the laws and the patronage of the public authority.

For Our part We have left nothing undone, as far as circumstances permitted, to preserve and more solidly establish amongst you the Catholic religion. With this intent, We have, as you are well aware, turned Our attention to two special objects: first, the advancement of learning; second, a perfecting of methods in the management of Church affairs. There already, indeed, existed several distinguished universities. We, however, thought it advisable that there should be one founded by authority of the Apostolic See and endowed by Us with all suitable powers, in which Catholic professors might instruct those devoted to the pursuit of learning. The design was to begin with philosophy and theology, adding, as means and circumstances would allow, the remaining branches, those particularly which the present age has introduced or perfected. An education cannot be deemed complete which takes no notice of modern sciences. It is obvious that in the existing keen competition of talents, and the widespread and, in itself, noble and praiseworthy passion for knowledge, Catholics ought to be not followers but leaders. It is necessary, therefore, that they should cultivate every refinement of learning, and

---

[3] This remark caused some uneasiness on the part of certain American bishops as to its possible effect on non-Catholics. Cf. John Tracy Ellis, *The Life of James Cardinal Gibbons, Archbishop of Baltimore, 1834–1921* (Milwaukee, 1952), II, 28–30.

zealously train their minds to the discovery of truth and the investigation, so far as it is possible, of the entire domain of nature. This in every age has been the desire of the Church; upon the enlargement of the boundaries of the sciences has she been wont to bestow all possible labor and energy. By a letter, therefore, dated the seventh day of March, in the year of Our Lord, 1889, directed to you, Venerable Brethren, We established at Washington, your capital city, esteemed by a majority of you a very proper seat for the higher studies, a university for the instruction of young men desirous of pursuing advanced courses. In announcing this matter to Our Venerable Brethren, the Cardinals of the Holy Roman Church, in Consistory, We expressed the wish that it should be regarded as the fixed law of the university to unite erudition and learning with soundness of faith and to imbue its students not less with religion than with scientific culture. To the Bishops of the United States We entrusted the task of establishing a suitable course of studies and of supervising the discipline of the students; and We conferred the office and authority of Chancellor, as it is called, upon the Archbishop of Baltimore. And, by divine favor, a quite happy beginning was made. For, without any delay, whilst you were celebrating the hundredth anniversary of the establishment of your ecclesiastical hierarchy, under the brightest auspices, in the presence of Our delegate, the divinity classes were opened.[4] From that time onward We know that theological science has been imparted by the diligence of eminent men the renown of whose talents and learning receives a fitting crown in their recognized loyalty and devotion to the Apostolic See. Nor is it long since We were apprised that, thanks to the liberality of a pious priest, a new building had been constructed, in which young men, as well cleric as lay, are to receive instruction in the natural sciences and in literature.[5] From Our knowledge of the American character, We are fully confident that the example set by this noble man will incite others of your citizens to imitate him; they will not fail to realize that liberality exercised towards such an object will be repaid by the very greatest advantages to the public.

No one can be ignorant how powerfully similar institutions of learning, whether originally founded by the Roman Church herself from time to time, or approved and promoted by her legislation, have

---

[4] The Catholic University of America was opened on November 13, 1889.

[5] McMahon Hall, the second building of the university, was formally dedicated on October 1, 1895. It had been made possible through the generosity of James McMahon (1817–1901), former pastor of St. Andrew's Church, New York.

contributed to the spread of knowledge and civilization in every part of Europe. Even in Our own day, though other instances might be given, it is enough to mention the University of Louvain, to which the entire Belgian nation ascribes its almost daily increase in prosperity and glory. Equally abundant will be the benefits proceeding from the Washington University, if the professors and students (as We doubt not they will) be mindful of Our injunctions, and, shunning party spirit and strife, conciliate the good opinion of the people and the clergy.

We wish now, Venerable Brethren, to commend to your affection and to the generosity of your people the college which Our predecessor, Pius IX, founded in this city for the ecclesiastical training of young men from North America,[6] and which We took care to place upon a firm basis by a letter dated the twenty-fifth day of October, in the year of Our Lord 1884. We can make this appeal the more confidently, because the results obtained from this institution have by no means belied the expectations commonly entertained regarding it. You yourselves can testify that during its brief existence it has sent forth a very large number of exemplary priests, some of whom have been promoted for their virtue and learning to the highest degrees of ecclesiastical dignity. We are, therefore, thoroughly persuaded that you will continue to be solicitous to send hither select young men who are in training to become the hope of the Church. For they will carry back to their homes and utilize for the general good the wealth of intellectual attainments and moral excellence which they shall have acquired in the city of Rome.

The love which We cherish towards the Catholics of your nation moved Us, likewise, to turn Our attention at the very beginning of Our Pontificate to the convocation of a third Plenary Council of Baltimore.[7] Subsequently, when the archbishops, at Our invitation, had come to Rome, We diligently inquired from them what they deemed most conducive to the common good. We finally, and after mature deliberation, ratified by apostolic authority the decrees of the prelates assembled at Baltimore. In truth the event has proven, and still proves, that the decrees of Baltimore were salutary and timely in the extreme. Experience has demonstrated their power for the maintenance of discipline; for stimulating the intelligence and zeal of the clergy for defending and developing the Catholic education of

---

[6] The North American College, Rome, was opened on December 8, 1859.

[7] The Third Plenary Council of Baltimore was held November 9–December 7, 1884.

youth. Wherefore, Venerable Brethren, if We make acknowledgment of your activity in these matters, if We laud your firmness tempered with prudence, We but pay tribute due to your merit; for We are fully sensible that so great a harvest of blessings could by no means have so swiftly ripened to maturity, had you not exerted yourselves, each to the utmost of his ability, sedulously and faithfully to carry into effect the statutes you had wisely framed at Baltimore.

But when the Council of Baltimore had concluded its labors, the duty still remained of putting, so to speak, a proper and becoming crown upon the work. This, We perceived, could scarcely be done in a more fitting manner than through the due establishment by the Apostolic See of an American Legation. Accordingly, as you are well aware, We have done this.[8] By this action, as We have elsewhere intimated, We have wished, first of all, to certify that, in Our judgment and affection, America occupies the same place and rights as other States, be they ever so mighty and imperial. In addition to this We had in mind to draw more closely the bonds of duty and friendship which connect you and so many thousands of Catholics with the Apostolic See. In fact, the mass of the Catholics understood how salutary Our action was destined to be; they saw, moreover, that it accorded with the usage and policy of the Apostolic See. For it has been, from earliest antiquity, the custom of the Roman Pontiffs in the exercise of the divinely bestowed gift of the primacy in the administration of the Church of Christ to send forth legates to Christian nations and peoples. And they did this, not by an adventitious but an inherent right. For "the Roman Pontiff, upon whom Christ has conferred ordinary and immediate jurisdiction, as well over all and singular churches, as over all and singular pastors and faithful [Con. Vat. Sess., iv. c. 3], since he cannot personally visit the different regions and thus exercise the pastoral office over the flock entrusted to him, finds it necessary, from time to time, in the discharge of the ministry imposed on him, to despatch legates into different parts of the world, according as the need arises; who, supplying his place, may correct errors, make the rough ways plain, and administer to the people confided to their care increased means of salvation" [Cap. Un. Extrav. Comm. De Consuet., 1. 1].

But how unjust and baseless would be the suspicion, should it anywhere exist, that the powers conferred on the legate are an obstacle to the authority of the bishops! Sacred to Us (more than to any other) are the rights of those *"whom the Holy Ghost has placed as*

---

[8] The Apostolic Delegation at Washington was established on January 21, 1893.

bishops to rule the Church of God." That these rights should remain intact in every nation in every part of the globe, We both desire and ought to desire, the more so since the dignity of the individual bishop is by nature so interwoven with the dignity of the Roman Pontiff that any measure which benefits the one necessarily protects the other. "My honor is the honor of the Universal Church. My honor is the unimpaired vigor of My brethren. Then am I truly honored when to each one due honor is not denied" [S. Gregorius Epis. ad Eulog. Alax. lib. viii. ep. 30]. Therefore, since it is the office and function of an apostolic legate, with whatsoever powers he may be vested, to execute the mandates and interpret the will of the Pontiff who sends him, thus, so far from his being of any detriment to the ordinary power of the bishops, he will rather bring an accession of stability and strength. His authority will possess no slight weight for preserving in the multitude a submissive spirit; in the clergy discipline and due reverence for the bishops, and in the bishops mutual charity and an intimate union of souls. And since this union, so salutary and desirable, consists mainly in harmony of thought and action, he will, no doubt, bring it to pass that each one of you shall persevere in the diligent administration of his diocesan affairs; that one shall not impede another in matters of government; that one shall not pry into the counsels and conduct of another; finally, that with disagreements eradicated and mutual esteem maintained, you may all work together with combined energies to promote the glory of the American Church and the general welfare. It is difficult to estimate the good results which will flow from this concord of the bishops. Our own people will receive edification; and the force of example will have its effect on those without — who will be persuaded by this argument alone that the divine apostolate has passed by inheritance to the ranks of the Catholic episcopate.

Another consideration claims our earnest attention. All intelligent men are agreed, and We Ourselves have with pleasure intimated it above, that America seems destined for greater things. Now it is Our wish that the Catholic Church should not only share in, but help to bring about, this prospective greatness. We deem it right and proper that she should, by availing herself of the opportunities daily presented to her, keep equal step with the Republic in the march of improvement, at the same time striving to the utmost, by her virtue and her institutions, to aid in the rapid growth of the States. Now, she will attain both these objects the more easily and abundantly, in proportion to the degree in which the future shall find her constitution perfected. But what is the meaning of the legation of which we are speaking, or what is its ultimate aim except to bring it about that the constitution of the Church shall be strengthened, her discipline better fortified? Wherefore, We ardently desire that this truth should sink day by day more deeply into the minds of Catholics — namely, that they can in no better way safeguard their own individual interests and the common good than by yielding a hearty submission and obedience to the Church. Your faithful people, however, are scarcely in need of exhortation on this point; for they are accustomed to adhere to the institutions of Catholicity with willing souls and a constancy worthy of all praise.

To one matter of the first importance and fraught with the greatest blessings it is a pleasure at this place to refer, on account of the holy firmness in principle and practice respecting it which, as a rule, rightly prevails amongst you; We mean the Christian dogma of the unity and indissolubility of marriage; which supplies the firmest bond of safety not merely to the family but to society at large. Not a few of your citizens, even of those who dissent from us in other doctrines, terrified by the licentiousness of divorce, admire and approve in this regard the Catholic teaching and the Catholic customs. They are led to this judgment not less by love of country than by the wisdom of the doctrine. For difficult it is to imagine a more deadly pest to the community than the wish to declare dissoluble a bond which the law of God has made perpetual and inseverable. Divorce "is the fruitful cause of mutable marriage contracts; it diminishes mutual affection; it supplies a pernicious stimulus to unfaithfulness; it is injurious to the care and education of children; it gives occasion to the breaking up of domestic society; it scatters the seeds of discord among families; it lessens and degrades the dignity of women, who incur the danger of being abandoned when they shall have subserved the lust of their husbands. And since nothing tends so effectually as the corruption of morals to ruin families and undermine the strength of kingdoms, it may easily be perceived that divorce is especially hostile to the prosperity of families and States" [Encyc. *Arcanum*].

As regards civil affairs, experience has shown how important it is that the citizens should be upright and virtuous. In a free State, unless justice be generally cultivated, unless the people be repeatedly and diligently urged to observe the precepts and laws of the Gospel, liberty itself may be pernicious. Let those of the clergy, therefore, who are occupied with the instruction of the multitude, treat plainly this topic of the duties of citizens, so that all may understand and feel the necessity, in political life, of conscientiousness, self-restraint, and integrity; for that cannot be lawful in public which is unlawful in private affairs. On this whole subject there are to be found, as you know, in the encyclical letters written by Us from time to time in the course of Our pontificate, many things which Catholics should attend to and observe. In these writings and expositions We have treated of human liberty, of the chief Christian duties, of civil government, and of the Christian constitution of States, drawing Our principles as well from the teaching of the Gospels as from reason.[9] They, then, who wish to be good citizens and discharge their duties faithfully may readily learn from Our Letters the ideal of an upright life. In like manner, let the priests be persistent in keeping before the minds of the people the enactments of the Third Council of Baltimore, particularly those which inculcate the virtue of temperance, the frequent use of the sacraments, and the observance of the just laws and institutions of the Republic.

Now, with regard to entering societies, extreme care should be taken not to be ensnared by error. And We wish to be understood as referring in a special manner to the working classes, who assuredly have the right to unite in associations for the promotion of their interests; a right acknowledged by the Church and unopposed by nature. But it is very important to take heed with whom they are to associate, lest whilst seeking aid for the improvement of their condition, they may be imperilling far weightier interests. The most effectual precaution against this peril is to determine with themselves at no time or in any matter to be parties to the violation of justice. Any society, therefore, which is ruled by and servilely obeys persons who are not steadfast for the right and friendly to religion is capable of being extremely prejudicial to the interests as well of individuals as of the community; beneficial it cannot be. Let this conclusion, therefore, remain firm — to shun not only those associations which have been openly condemned by the judgment of the Church, but those also which, in the opinion of intelligent men, and especially of the bishops, are regarded as suspicious and dangerous.[10]

Nay, rather, unless forced by necessity to do otherwise, Catholics ought to prefer to associate with Catholics, a course which will be very conducive to the safeguarding of their faith. As presidents of

---

[9] Cf. Wynne, *op. cit.*, for the encyclicals *Immortale Dei*, November 1, 1885 (pp. 107–134); *Libertas praestantissimum*, June 20, 1888 (pp. 135–163); and *Sapientiae christianae*, January 10, 1890 (pp. 180–207).

[10] Cf. Wynne, *op. cit.*, pp. 83–106, for Leo XIII's encyclical *Humanum genus*, April 20, 1884, on Freemasonry.

societies thus formed among themselves, it will be well to appoint either priests or upright laymen of weight and character, guided by whose counsels they should endeavor peacefully to adopt and carry into effect such measures as may seem most advantageous to their interests, keeping in view the rules laid down by Us in Our Encyclical, *Rerum Novarum*.[11] Let them, however, never allow this to escape their memory: that whilst it is proper and desirable to assert and secure the rights of the many, yet this is not to be done by a violation of duty; and that these are very important duties; not to touch what belongs to another; to allow every one to be free in the management of his own affairs; not to hinder any one to dispose of his services when he please and where he please. The scenes of violence and riot which you witnessed last year in your own country[12] sufficiently admonish you that America too is threatened with the audacity and ferocity of the enemies of public order. The state of the times, therefore, bids Catholics to labor for the tranquillity of the commonwealth, and for this purpose to obey the laws, abhor violence, and seek no more than equity or justice permits.

Towards these objects much may be contributed by those who have devoted themselves to writing, and in particular by those who are engaged on the daily press. We are aware that already there labor in this field many men of skill and experience, whose diligence demands words of praise rather than of encouragement. Nevertheless, since the thirst for reading and knowledge is so vehement and widespread amongst you, and since, according to circumstances, it can be productive either of good or evil, every effort should be made to increase the number of intelligent and well-disposed writers who take religion for their guide and virtue for their constant companion. And this seems all the more necessary in America, on account of the familiar intercourse and intimacy between Catholics and those who are estranged from the Catholic name, a condition of things which certainly exacts from our people great circumspection and more than ordinary firmness. It is necessary to instruct, admonish, strengthen and urge them on to the pursuit of virtue and to the faithful observance, amid so many occasions of stumbling, of their duties towards the Church. It is, of course, the proper function of the clergy to devote their care and energies to this great work; but the age and

---

[11] *Rerum novarum* was published on May 15, 1891. For the text, cf. Wynne, *op. cit.*, pp. 208–248.

[12] Between March and August, 1894, there had occurred the march of Coxey's Army on Washington, the Pullman strike, and a general strike on the western railroads.

the country require that journalists should be equally zealous in this same cause and labor in it to the full extent of their powers. Let them, however, seriously reflect that their writings, if not positively prejudicial to religion, will surely be of slight service to it unless in concord of minds they all seek the same end. They who desire to be of real service to the Church, and with their pens heartily to defend the Catholic cause, should carry on the conflict with perfect unanimity, and, as it were, with serried ranks, for they rather inflict than repel war if they waste their strength by discord. In like manner their work, instead of being profitable and fruitful, becomes injurious and disastrous whenever they presume to call before their tribunal the decisions and acts of bishops, and, casting off due reverence, cavil and find fault; not perceiving how great a disturbance of order, how many evils are thereby produced. Let them, then, be mindful of their duty, and not overstep the proper limits of moderation. The bishops, placed in the lofty position of authority, are to be obeyed, and suitable honor befitting the magnitude and sanctity of their office should be paid them. Now, this reverence, "which it is lawful to no one to neglect," should of necessity be eminently conspicuous and exemplary in Catholic journalists. For journals, naturally circulating far and wide, come daily into the hands of everybody, and exert no small influence upon the opinions and morals of the multitude [Ep. Cognita Nobis ad Archiepp. et Epp. Provinciarum, Taurinen. Mediolanen, et Vercellen., XXV., Jan. an. MDCCCLXXXII].

We have Ourselves, on frequent occasions, laid down many rules respecting the duties of a good writer; many of which were unanimously inculcated as well by the Third Council of Baltimore as by the archbishops in their meeting at Chicago in the year 1893. Let Catholic writers, therefore, bear impressed on their minds Our teachings on this point as well as yours; and let them resolve that their entire method of writing shall be thereby guided, if they indeed desire, as they ought to desire, to discharge their duty well.

Our thoughts now turn to those who dissent from us in matters of Christian faith; and who shall deny that, with not a few of them, dissent is a matter rather of inheritance than of will? How solicitous We are of their salvation, with what ardor of soul We wish that they should be at length restored to the embrace of the Church, the common mother of all, Our Apostolic Epistle, *"Praeclara,"* has in very recent times declared.[13] Nor are we destitute of all hope; for He is

---

[13] For Leo XIII's views on the reunion of Christendom, cf. the encyclical *Praeclara gratulationis publicae*, June 20, 1894, in Wynne, *op. cit.*, pp. 303–319.

present and hath a care whom all things obey and who laid down His life that He might "gather in one the children of God who were dispersed" (John xi. 52).

Surely we ought not to desert them nor leave them to their fancies; but with mildness and charity draw them to us, using every means of persuasion to induce them to examine closely every part of the Catholic doctrine, and to free themselves from preconceived notions. In this matter, if the first place belongs to the bishops and clergy, the second belongs to the laity, who have it in their power to aid the apostolic efforts of the clergy by the probity of their morals and the integrity of their lives. Great is the force of example; particularly with those who are earnestly seeking the truth, and who, from a certain inborn virtuous disposition, are striving to live an honorable and upright life, to which class very many of your fellow-citizens belong. If the spectacle of Christian virtues exerted the powerful influence over the heathens blinded, as they were, by inveterate superstition, which the records of history attest, shall we think it powerless to eradicate error in the case of those who have been initiated into the Christian religion?

Finally, We cannot pass over in silence those whose long-continued unhappy lot implores and demands succor from men of apostolic zeal; We refer to the Indians and the negroes who are to be found within the confines of America, the greatest portion of whom have not yet dispelled the darkness of superstition. How wide a field for cultivation! How great a multitude of human beings to be made partakers of the blessing derived through Jesus Christ!

Meanwhile, as a presage of heavenly graces and a testimony of Our benevolence, We most lovingly in the Lord impart to you, Venerable Brethren, and to your clergy and people, Our Apostolic Benediction.

140. Bishop Keane's Views on the Role of Legislation in a Democratic Government, September 11, 1895

DURING the years 1887–1896 while John J. Keane (1839–1918) served as first rector of the Catholic University of America, he gave many public addresses throughout the country. From the earliest days of his priesthood he had been an ardent temperance advocate, an interest which he maintained until his death. When an interdenominational temperance group in Buffalo,

New York, invited him to speak to them in September, 1895, he responded. The following excerpts from that speech embodied Keane's views concerning the nature and object of civil legislation in a democratic government. Source: John J. Keane, *The Catholic Church and the American Sunday* (Buffalo: Catholic Truth Society, 1895).

What is the proper end and object and matter of civil legislation? The Christian maxim that rulers represent God's authority only for the popular welfare has come to be understood almost the wide world over. The inalienable rights of man as man have been so forcibly proclaimed and emphasized, especially by our own country, that all the peoples of the earth have come to appreciate that the classes, just like the sovereign, have reason to exist only in so far as they contribute to the general welfare, and that this, once more, must be the aim of legislation. — The civilized world now never loses sight of the great truth that the general welfare must be the main consideration, the chief test of legislation, and that corporations, industrial and financial organizations of any sort whatsoever, can receive legislative recognition only in so far as they are compatible with the common weal, can claim legislative privileges only in so far as this conduces to the welfare of the people at large.

The end and object of legislation is "the greatest good of the greatest number."

What is the greatest good of the greatest number? — that which will turn them into the best men; what will spread abroad the reign of the true and the right and fill the lives of the people with peace. We are human beings, and it is human welfare that we seek, the welfare of the whole being of man, physical, intellectual, moral. The true aim of legislation is the promotion of civilization along all the lines of human activity that constitute it and perfect it. It is not merely to repress the violence and wrong-doing that would hinder civilization, but to encourage and help on the right-doing that conduces to civilization. Civilization means not merely the machinery for producing wealth, for transporting and distributing wealth, for multiplying the conveniences of life, for increasing its comfort and physical well-being. It means all that, but it means much more; because man is much more than that and needs much more than that. It means the advance of human welfare along the lines of man's complex being, physical, intellectual, moral. The function of law and government is to promote civilization; it is to promote man's physical welfare by fostering industries, securing justice to both employers and employed, multiplying means of popular comfort; it is to promote man's intellectual welfare, by fostering the multiplication of schools and the improvement of educational methods; it is to promote man's aesthetic welfare, by seeing to the beauty of cities as well as to their healthfulness and orderliness; it is to promote man's moral welfare by repressing incentives to public immorality and encouraging all institutions that aim at making both public and private life better, purer and nobler. This is the aim of civilization, and this is the aim of legislation.

Legislation like civilization must be Ethical. The basis of human life, of human progress, of human civilization, is ethical, is moral. That ethics, morals, are not nature's instinct but nature's rule and guide, a rule and guide imposed on nature for nature's good, its source and sanction are not to be sought in nature's self, but above nature, in the Supreme Good to which nature tends as its perfection and its destiny. [Here Keane quoted Washington's dictum, "Of all the dispositions and habits that lead to political prosperity, religion and morality are indispensable supports."]

Whatever fosters religion and morality in the lives of our people, strengthens the foundations of our national prosperity, and it is our duty as Americans to encourage and uphold it and vice versa. . . .

141. Cardinal Satolli's Visit to New Orleans, February 15–21, 1896

ON JANUARY 21, 1893, Pope Leo XIII established the Apostolic Delegation in Washington after lengthy and sometimes heated negotiations between the Holy See and the American hierarchy. The man selected as first delegate was Francesco Satolli (1839–1910), Archbishop of Lepanto and a favorite of the pontiff's since their days together in Perugia. To the A.P.A. the event became, as might be expected, something of a *cause célèbre,* and its principal founder later stated that it had "very materially" stimulated the growth of the organization, for as he said, "We looked upon Satolli as a representative of the Propaganda at Rome to direct and influence legislation . . ." and the opinion was circulated "that he was interfering with the public institutions of this country" (Henry F. Bowers to Humphrey J. Desmond, Clinton, Iowa, March 1, 1899, Desmond, *The A.P.A. Movement. A Sketch* [Washington, 1912], p. 15). At the outset of his residence in the United States, Satolli leaned toward the more liberal-minded bishops like Gibbons and Ireland, but as time went on his sympathies shifted to their conservative colleagues led by Archbishop Corrigan and the prelates of German birth or extraction. In the consistory of November, 1895, he was created a cardinal, but he remained prodelegate until the arrival of his successor, Sebastiano Martinelli, O.S.A. (1848–1918), in October, 1896.

During his last months in the country the prodelegate made an extensive trip through the South and West with Alexis Orban (1850–1915), a French-born Sulpician, who acted as his secretary, and who since November, 1889, had been acting librarian and assistant spiritual director at the Catholic University of America. Both Satolli and Orban were strongly opposed to Bishop Keane, rector of the university, whom they regarded as an ultra-liberal. When, therefore, they encountered Keane at the inauguration of the Catholic Winter School in New Orleans the meeting was not a cordial one. A few months later Orban was recalled by the Superior-General of St. Sulpice at the request of the university administration, and that only a few weeks before Keane himself was dismissed as rector. Orban kept an account in French of his trip with Satolli in which he recorded not only the bias against Keane and his own uncomplimentary views about the Irish clergy in the United States, but also some valuable impressions of local customs in the areas visited.* The following excerpt describes the prodelegate's stay in New Orleans where the carnival, the Catholic immigrant groups, the Winter School, and other items come in for comment. The document was discovered in 1951 by Colman J. Barry, O.S.B., in the library of the Collegio di Sant' Anselmo in Rome. Father Barry kindly supplied the editor with a copy of the English translation. Satolli had spent the years 1872–1874 at Monte Cassino with the intention of becoming a Benedictine, and it was that, plus his desire that the students should profit from his library of Thomistic works, that prompted him to leave his books and papers to Sant' Anselmo. Source: Archives of St. John's Abbey, Collegeville, Minnesota (microfilm). For the entire document cf. Colman J. Barry, O.S.B. (Ed.), "Tour of His Eminence Cardinal Francesco Satolli, Pro-Apostolic Delegate, through the United States (of the North) from 12 February to 13 March 1896," *Historical Records and Studies,* XLIII (1955), 27–94.

The "Southern Railway" Company had given free passage from Washington to Atlanta to Cardinal Satolli and his secretary. The same favor was granted from Atlanta to New Orleans. Suffice it to say, on a trip of 5,000 kilometers His Eminence did not pay travel expenses, and almost nothing for the other incidentals of his journey; the committees set up to receive him took charge of everything. Toward six o'clock we awoke in the state of Mississippi after having crossed Alabama, with its capital Montgomery, and its episcopal see of Mobile. Mississippi comprises the territory assigned to the diocese of Natchez. At one of the railroad stations on the gulf, in a pretty little place called Bay St. Louis (a name which indeed recalls the origin of the colony), some religious were present in spite of the

---

* Although Orban's signature appears nowhere on the original document, there would seem to be little doubt that he was the author. Cf. Patrick H. Ahern, *The Life of John J. Keane, Educator and Archbishop, 1839–1918* (Milwaukee, 1955), p. 171.

early hour. They were the Brothers of the Sacred Heart from Puy-en-Velais (France) brought here by one of the French bishops who had established Catholicism in this area.[1] They had come to the station at five o'clock in the morning with a small number of their novices and students, in order to present their respects to the Cardinal Pro-Delegate.

At eight-thirty in the morning [February 15, 1896] we came into New Orleans. The Archbishop, Monsignor Janssens,[2] with his chancellor and Father Semple, S.J., Rector of the Jesuit College,[3] were at the station to receive His Eminence. We were scarcely in the carriage before two reporters came up to offer their services. In a few minutes we were at the Archbishop's palace. One would have thought himself in Europe. It was the convent of the Ursulines erected shortly after their arrival from France in 1732.[4] Built around a court and garden, in the center of the old town, which is now called the French Quarter, it truly had a grand air with its imposing carriage gate and circular wall. After passing the porter's office, we crossed the court in front of the main building decorated with palms, cactus, banana and magnolia trees, to a grand stairway with iron balustrade which led to the rooms. A 17th century clock, brought from Paris by the Ursulines, still keeps time as exactly under the republic as it did under the kings. On the left a corridor led to the chapel where we went immediately to offer holy Mass. A person would have believed himself to be in one of the good, old chapels of France. It was of Louis XIV Renaissance style, with its scrolled volutes, its corners ornamented at the top, and its rounded friezes. There was a miraculous statue of the Virgin under the title of Our Lady of Perpetual Help which Leo XIII had recently crowned, and to which was attributed a great number of favors, both public and private. Every good creole of New Orleans has the greatest veneration for this statue.

After breakfast His Eminence wanted his first talk to be for the

---

[1] The Brothers of the Sacred Heart had originally been brought to the United States in January, 1847, by Michael Portier (1795–1859), first Bishop of Mobile. They opened their St. Stanislaus College at St. Louis, Mississippi, in 1855.
[2] Francis Janssens (1843–1897), the Dutch-born Archbishop of New Orleans, had been promoted to that see from the Diocese of Natchez in August, 1888. The chancellor at the time was the Very Reverend Joseph A. Thebault.
[3] Henry C. Semple, S.J. (1853–1925), pastor of the Church of the Immaculate Conception and president of the college of the same name, was the editor of *The Ursulines in New Orleans and Our Lady of Prompt Succor. A Record of Two Centuries, 1727–1925* (New York, 1925).
[4] The Ursulines arrived in New Orleans in August, 1727, not 1732.

Italian Sisters (the Salesians) [*sic*] who conduct a school here for Italian immigrants.[5] The Italians have two churches here reserved by the priests for their nationality.[6] One of these priests is unfortunately old and infirm. But the other has his own church and rectory, so that the Ordinary does not feel free to replace the former with a younger and more active pastor. The good Sisters were hoping for this visit from the Cardinal, but they did not expect him so soon, and his unannounced arrival at such an early hour upset the whole community. The portress on duty ran to the cloister and made the greatest possible noise while at the same time making desperate signs to the Sisters who were no more prepared than she to receive a visit. However, soon re-assured by the evident simplicity and cordiality of the Cardinal, they regained their calm a little, and they began to converse about their community and its work. This was a foretaste of the more complete visit which His Eminence promised to make with them on his first free day.

We had luncheon at the Archbishop's palace. We had as guests Bishop Gabriels of Ogdensburg (New York), Bishop Van de Vyver of Richmond (Virginia), and Bishop Meerschaert, Vicar-Apostolic of the Indian Territory, all of whom were Belgians by birth as was Archbishop Janssens.[7] Cardinal Gibbons, who had arrived the evening before, was staying with his brother who was a prominent citizen of the city.[8] He had left a note at the Archbishop's palace inviting His Eminence and his secretary to dine with him. We arrived there at the appointed hour to find the Cardinal Archbishop of Baltimore surrounded by a charming family of nephews and nieces who strove among themselves to entertain him. Beside me at dinner was an old Jesuit who had been chaplain of the prison for forty-eight years,

---

[5] The Missionary Sisters of the Sacred Heart, founded by St. Frances Xavier Cabrini (1850–1917), got their start in New Orleans when three sisters arrived from New York in July, 1892, and took up residence in rented rooms in a tenement house on St. Philip Street. The foundress herself had visited New Orleans in the spring of 1892 and had responded to the request of Archbishop Janssens that she establish a house in his see city for the spiritual and material care of the Italian immigrants.

[6] St. Anthony of Padua Church at Rampart and Conti Streets was for the Italians, but the Chapel of St. Francis of Assisi at Chartres and Decatur Streets which had been opened in 1891 was discontinued after 1893.

[7] Henry Gabriels (1838–1921) was consecrated as second Bishop of Ogdensburg in May, 1892; Augustine Van de Vyver (1844–1911) was named sixth Bishop of Richmond in 1889; Theophile Meerschaert (1847–1924) was appointed first Vicar Apostolic of Indian Territory in June, 1891. Archbishop Janssens had been born in the Netherlands, not in Belgium.

[8] John T. Gibbons (1837–1924), brother of the cardinal, was a wealthy grain merchant in New Orleans.

who had assisted at the hanging of forty prisoners condemned to death, and who had endured eighteen epidemics of yellow fever. During one of these epidemics he was almost the only priest, and all his time from morning to evening was taken up in administering the sacraments to the sick. He found time to say his breviary only upon his return in the evening which often was very late at night. He recited it entirely, fatigued as he was. What a beautiful life! What a venerable priest! His superiors have commissioned him to write his memoirs. They will be without doubt a very edifying page in the history of this mission.

Sunday, February 16 at eleven o'clock, was set for pontifical Mass. It was a superb day: an Italian sky with a spring sun. At ten-thirty a detachment of troops took up their position in the Archbishop's court. The Archbishop asked His Eminence to come to the balcony where the soldiers gave him a military salute. Then the clergy formed in procession before the Cardinal's chamber and the procession began: the soldiers, the band playing a march, then the different orders of the clergy, finally the prelates each escorted by two assistants, the deacons of honor and the deacons of the Mass, the assistant priest, and at the end His Eminence Cardinal Satolli in pontificals. They crossed the city streets (it is the custom here), through a respectful crowd. In front of the cathedral there was a large crowd. Police sergeants had great difficulty in making a passage way for the procession. The Cathedral of St. Louis, a grand edifice built during the interval of Spanish domination, was packed in spite of its two tiers of galleries and the fact that admissions were by ticket only. In the first benches near the sanctuary the Governor of Louisiana,[9] the Mayor of the city,[10] the Judges of the Superior Court, the Consuls-General of France and Spain with their personnel had taken their places. One of the secretaries of the French Embassy had even come from Washington, and he had presented his card to Cardinal Satolli soon after his arrival. The ceremonies were impressive, since they were presided over by the Cardinal Delegate of the Sovereign Pontiff, in the presence of another prince of the Roman Court, Cardinal Gibbons, Archbishop of Baltimore, the Archbishop of Cincinnati,[11] and three other Bishops of the New Orleans province who had come for the occasion. Since here we were so far distant from any Catholic

---

[9] Murphy J. Foster (1849–1921) was Governor of Louisiana, 1892–1900.

[10] John Fitzpatrick (1844–1919) was Mayor of New Orleans at the time.

[11] William Henry Elder (1819–1904) became Archbishop of Cincinnati in July, 1883, after having served for three years as coadjutor to John B. Purcell.

nation, it is not astonishing to say that such a spectacle had never been seen in this city. Cardinal Gibbons gave a short homily on the gospel of the day. At the end of the Mass, Cardinal Satolli took off his pontificals and returned to the throne. Then the Archbishop, in a discourse which came from the heart, expressed the appreciation of his people and himself for the honor given to them, the respect which they had for the person of the august and well-beloved Pontiff, Leo XIII, whom he represented. Then the recessional was formed to lead the clergy and eminent prelates back to the Archbishop's palace, where a dinner awaited them. It was almost two o'clock in the afternoon.

After a few minutes of necessary rest a deputation of Italian immigrants waited upon His Eminence. These sons of Italy were about sixty in number, some born in New Orleans, but most of them came from the old world. Their spokesman made a truly touching address, filled with sentiments of love for their native land which they had left, and also of respect and attachment for the Papacy. Cardinal Satolli responded eloquently, thanking them, felicitating them on their patriotic and Catholic sentiments. Then he added that without doubt they should be most appreciative of their adopted homeland which gave them, as to its own children, bread and liberty. They should not forget, however, that they were Italian in origin, that they should be proud of being sons of Italy, that land of the fine arts, of the Papacy, center of true civilization. He developed these ideas with a force which uplifted his audience. All left full of encouragement and admiration for their eminent compatriot.

That evening at seven-thirty, a reception was held in honor of the two cardinals at the home of Mr. Thomas Semmes,[12] an excellent Catholic and one of the prominent citizens of the city. These receptions entail, for the person who is the object of them, standing throughout the ceremony and receiving the "hand shakes" of all the visitors. At Mr. Semmes' home we met the most distinguished society of New Orleans and consequently of the whole of America. All indeed agree that nothing is comparable in any city to the old plantation families. Many had been ruined by the Civil War of 1862 [*sic*]–1865, but they still preserve a distinction of language and customs. The French spoken in New Orleans is as pure as the language of the best Parisian society, and now the

---

[12] Thomas J. Semmes (1824–1899), a prominent Catholic lawyer of New Orleans, was professor of law in Tulane University and president of the American Bar Association in 1886.

people of New Orleans have the advantage of knowing English as well as their mother tongue.

After Mass on Monday morning at the archbishopric, the brother of His Eminence, Cardinal Gibbons, came to conduct us on a carriage tour, and to visit the cemeteries as well as other charitable institutions on route. Of all cities New Orleans has the most cemeteries. Along one long road completely bordered with them, I counted seven, one of which was especially extensive. The reason for multiplying these cemeteries is that the people never inter anyone where another body has been laid. The soil here is dark alluvial; it is like a big raft floating on the water. The river flows at the base of this mass. Each family, with the little means they have, build a funeral chapel on top of the ground. Inside the chapel on both sides shelves are recessed in the form of bureau drawers, and in these the coffins are placed. Then the heavy door of iron or stone is closed just as a big strong box is closed after a treasure is enclosed. Mausoleums are found everywhere with respective family names on the front. The Jews who here as elsewhere have control of the banking system and trade, and who already possess the most beautiful homes, have also the richest cemetery. On returning from this mournful but interesting tour and after visiting the "Maison du Bon Pasteur" (an Angers foundation),[13] we crossed the "Bayou" Saint Jean (here they call a "bayou" a natural canal formed by one of the many branches of the Mississippi across the delta) and then went along Esplanade Street, the popular planters' quarter before the war. A number of their residences can still be seen, but a good number have passed into other hands.

The day before Mardi Gras we participated in all the customs brought here by the French since the carnival is still held in great honor in New Orleans. People come from all sections of the Union to see it, and during these days of the feast the hotels are filled. One of the nephews of Cardinal Gibbons took us to await after dinner the arrival of "Rex," or the king of the carnival. At the close of the preceding carnival a king is named by the majority vote of the club members of the city. His nomination is kept secret. Several days before Shrove Monday he goes with his court to one of the islands of the Gulf, and on Monday afternoon he leaves it on a magnificent steamer beautifully

---

[13] The first Sisters of the Good Shepherd arrived in New Orleans in February, 1859, from their convent in St. Louis. The original House of the Good Shepherd was located on Magazine Street, but was later moved to the location at Bienville and Broad Streets.

decorated. The port authorities are on the look-out and as soon as he is sighted, many yachts and barges, with carnival flags flying from their masts, conduct him into the port. At a cannon signal the crowd closes in on the quay, the garrison soldiers precede with fanfare announcing the march, and when "Rex" disembarks, he and his court are solemnly conducted in carriages to the city hall. The king, as well as his officials, are clad in bright oriental costumes, his head is crowned, he carries a sceptre, and he majestically bows to right and left. At the city hall, the mayor and his council receive him on a platform and present the keys of the city to him. The king is then led to the council chamber where a throne has been prepared. There he distributes his favors as gifts of the joyous event, naming his friends duke of this or count of that, etc.

We assisted at this spectacle coming down from the Middle Ages, where all the people, rich and poor, old and young, white and black, forgetting life's anxieties for two or three days, give themselves entirely to the innocent joys of simple celebrations.

On Tuesday morning (February 18) His Eminence offered holy Mass at the convent of the Salesian Sisters (Italians). The little chapel was filled. Besides the children, their parents were there as well as friends of the institution. After the Gospel, His Eminence turned to the congregation and delivered a short exhortation, taking as his theme the life of Saint Agatha whose feast it was. After holy Mass we had breakfast which, thanks to the generosity of benefactors, was more like a full dinner. Then we were conducted to a parlor (very small; it is believed to be the original room) where the children presented an "academia" in honor of His Eminence. First they played a lovely little selection from Mascagni, then one of them came forward and read an address in Italian. A "ragazzetta" presented a bouquet of picked flowers "sul terreno del amore." "Mi tocca il cuore," the little one said; however she recited her piece without pause. A Sister then read a very interesting exposition of the work which the Salesians had come to undertake for poor Italian immigrants two years previously. She told of their difficulties, fears, and consolations as well as their hopes. Everything about this family reunion in this poor school was so touching that tears came involuntarily to the eyes. His Eminence was truly inspired by the occasion, and gave a talk to the children, parents and Sisters that was full of paternal charity. All the little black eyes, brightened with the sun of Italy, so lively, so intelligent, were fixed on the Pope's representative, on the cardinal born as they on Italian soil. His Eminence encouraged them to love their fatherland of adoption which had been so willing to receive them, and to offer them the same advantages as its own citizens.

Italian immigrants in the United States are generally very poor and suffer intellectual and moral disadvantages which ordinarily accompany poverty. From this fact arises that despising of the Italian name among the mass of the American people. But with the passing of a few years, these immigrant children who combine physical vitality with vivacity and an intellectual sharpness which other nations certainly do not possess to the same degree, will become men who will make their mark and be counted among the best elements of the American population. A person does not need to be a prophet to predict this.

After this family celebration, so moving for the invited guests and so encouraging to the good Sisters, His Eminence returned to the archbishop's palace.

During the remainder of the day the Cardinal remained there, occupied with his correspondence, but a part of the time was given to viewing the carnival parade. We set out on foot at two o'clock, and guided by the Archbishop, we arrived at the home of a French family on the canal. This street is almost three times as wide as the "Via nazionale."[14] As we passed the street was literally filled with people, and the three tramways could scarcely care for the crowd in spite of the desperate shouts of their shrill guides. We could hardly cross this street with its crowd and three lines of carriages, coming and going, in order to reach the balcony where we were expected. The Archbishop, big and vivacious, opened a passage for us, and with him in the lead and me in the rear, Cardinal Satolli managed to bring himself safe and sound to the other side. From the height of our balcony the sight was fairy-like. This immense street was completely covered with people; as far as the eye could see there were only heads in the midst of which the three long parallel lines of tramways slowly came and went with difficulty. Across the street the windows and balconies were also filled. People drove their carriages on both sides of the street in order to open the necessary free space for the parade to pass. Suddenly the advance guard appeared, and then the first float. The crowd below pushed about and surged like an eddy toward the central point of attraction. The float was so beautiful, so rich, so artistic, that the crowd applauded from every side. The first parade, the main one of the day, symbolized the different seasons and scenes from daily life. Each of the floats was symbolic and carried people dressed according to the dominant idea. From time to time a flourish

---

[14] The Via Nazionale is one of the principal thoroughfares of Rome.

of trumpets with joyous airs diverted attention and tingled the ears. In all this immense crowd of spectators there was not one cry, one disorder or one inconvenience. Everyone was happy with simple and innocent mirth, and the troubled times could not affect this celebration of the whole city and of all the people. The good God Himself had a part in it, for He made the day beautiful, neither too hot nor cold, with a blue, pure sky like beautiful turquoise. That evening at eight o'clock we came to the same street to watch the passing of a second parade. It had the same good taste, the same beauty of arrangement, of color and of costume, and the same order among the people. The whole shone forth with a beauty perhaps even greater than the electric lights which cast most irregular and weird reflections on the gathering, and which caused beads and ornaments to sparkle. It was said that these floats were purchased in Paris a year in advance and that they cost almost 200,000 francs. New Orleans thinks much of its carnival, and the civil and ecclesiastical authorities, far from discouraging the custom, concurred that it was a happy diversion, as innocent amusement, if controlled in the limits of good taste. Consequently, all encourage it. They tell me that only men over thirty and members of the best families are allowed to impersonate characters on the floats. They are masqued and disguised as sphynxes, as birds, or as allegorical persons, and no one recognizes them. But they are able to see and they greet their parents and friends whom they see in the balconies as they pass. They even throw objects, gifts and flowers, to them. These parades are truly beautiful and entertained the Cardinal. They also reminded him regretfully of the old carnivals of Rome which the usurping government thought best to suppress.

On Ash Wednesday His Eminence offered Mass at the Convent of the Daughters of St. Teresa on Rampart Street.[15] This convent is a branch of the one at Baltimore from which the Sisters came in 1877. Several years ago they had difficulties with the diocesan administration over the building of their chapel. The Jesuit priest who directed them, built it large and made it, in the opinion of the pastor, a public chapel. All was settled, thanks to the intervention of Cardinal Satolli, who in this case as in all others had been an angel of peace. Although the chapel was only semi-public, yet for this occasion a large number of people had assembled. The chaplain, a Jesuit Father, had already blessed and distributed the ashes. After His Eminence had celebrated Mass he also wished, for the edification of the participants, to receive

[15] The Carmelite convent of New Orleans had been founded in November, 1877, by four nuns from the convent in St. Louis.

ashes. The faithful then came forward to kiss his ring. His Eminence was afterward led to a parlor where breakfast was served. Then we visited the convent. The Sisters formed two lines, and with candles in hand, led His Eminence to the entrance of the convent and went before him singing the "Domini est terra" in a very low tone. When we arrived at the chapter room the chants, or rather the groanings, ceased. The prioress sang several versicles and an oration, and then all sat down with veils drawn. The cardinal spoke a few appropriate words in English about their holy state so perfectly detached from the world, blessed them and retired. Then he had a conversation with the prioress at the grill. She asked as a favor from him that he would destroy all the papers concerning their past difficulties, assuring him that all loved their Archbishop, and that the ill-will that was thought to exist had emanated from one or two Sisters, especially the prioress, who had been replaced.

In the afternoon we accompanied the Archbishop to visit what they call a jetty. Jetties play a big role here, a role indispensable to the cultivation of the fields, and even to the existence of the city. They have broad terraces, one of twenty meters in height and sixty at the base, built along the various branches of the river and its principal course in order to retain the water in its bed and to prevent inundations. Without this precaution the entire city and countryside would certainly be under water; for the height of the river is noticeably higher than the fields which it erodes, and even of the houses of the town built on its banks. This maximum water height comes from the enormous deposits which form each day at its mouth, especially from its numerous tributaries. These accumulated alluvial deposits built up incessantly to a point where equilibrium is reached between swiftness of the current and the deposit of accumulated debris, and consequently the point where these materials are deposited. Hence the bed of the river and its branches are always rising. Without these protective ramparts New Orleans would be enveloped instantly, and when from the height of the jetty a person sees on one side the city below, and on the other the enormous mass of water, he cannot but shudder. The disaster would not be so frightful, but yet especially deplorable if the fields should be flooded. That is what often happens each time an unforeseen hole breaks through one of the jetties built along the irrigation canals. Such an accident is usually caused by a crevice which unluckily works through the humid soil. Thus it moves little by little across the jetty and pierces it one part at a time. The enclosed water by its own movement rushes through a small opening, enlarges it little by little and soon there is a disaster. Thus there are usually guards walking around the jetties looking for weak points and to prevent accidents.

On our return we visited several churches, all truly beautiful, the one of the Lazarist Fathers first,[16] then that of the Redemptorist Fathers.[17] The one of the Lazarist Fathers covered the whole street. When they first came to this section they found only a small French church. But since the population moved in from the coast the church was found to be much too small. Furthermore, the newcomers were chiefly of English and German ancestry. The good Fathers then built two other churches on their property, and two large schools adjacent; the whole with their residence constitute a number of truly imposing buildings which front two sides of the street on a rather extended area. The Jesuit Fathers also have several churches, one in the new section near the new buildings of "Tulane University."[18] They acquired a plot of land there which already had great value and which would become more and more valuable. St. Francis Xavier, the church adjoining their college, is truly large and beautiful.

The next day, Thursday, Mass was celebrated at the Madames of the Sacred Heart. These Madames have two convents in New Orleans. One, in the city, has the appearance of a beautiful country house. The other is located on Maine Street [*sic*] in the old French quarter.[19] In this quarter all the buildings are very old. This is especially inappropriate. It is now as it was 300 years ago, at the beginning of the colony: the streets are narrow, badly paved, dirty water collects on each side from the open sky, everything is dirty, old rags, old shoes, dead animals, etc., collect here. It is worthy of Constantinople. The Archbishop assured us it was a very healthy section. The reason he gave is pleasant enough to record: "the microbes thrive on filth; since the streets are more dirty in the quarter, the microbes attach themselves to the dirt and leave the world in peace." (!) After holy Mass at the Madames

---

[16] The Vincentians' principal parish was St. Joseph's at Tulane Avenue and Derbigny Street; they also had St. Stephen's Church at Napoleon Avenue and Camp Street.

[17] The Church of Our Lady of the Assumption had been dedicated in April, 1844. The Redemptorists also had St. Alphonsus Church and the French parish of Notre Dame de Bon Secours.

[18] This was the Church of the Holy Name of Jesus on St. Charles Avenue. The Jesuits also were in charge of the Church of the Immaculate Conception at Baronne and Canal Streets.

[19] The first Religious of the Sacred Heart had arrived in Louisiana in May, 1818, under the leadership of Blessed Philippine Duchesne (1769–1852). In 1896 they had two academies — both called Sacred Heart — at Dumaine Street and on St. Charles Avenue, as well as the cathedral school for girls.

of the Sacred Heart, Maine Street, the Archbishop joined His Eminence, and the young girls of the convent gave a program during which they recited, in poetry and in music, the praises of the Holy Father and his representative. One of them recited some French poetry composed for the occasion; it was excellent in form and pronunciation; it could not have been done better nor spoken better in an old French city. We ate dinner at the Archbishop's house. There were several new guests: Bishop O'Sullivan of Mobile, Bishop Dunne of Dallas, Bishop Heslin of Natchez, Rev. Brucker [*sic*], pastor of Willimantic (diocese of Hartford) who as a Belgian had been invited by the Archbishop, finally Bishop Keane, Rector of the Catholic University who had come to give three addresses on "Modern Philosophical Thought." (!)[20] I was seated beside the venerable pastor of Willimantic and I benefited by it by asking what people in New England thought of the Catholic University (New England comprises the ecclesiastical provinces of Boston and New York).[21] He answered: "They say absolutely nothing about it. They are absolutely indifferent on this matter when they are not hostile. You see they do not like Bishop Keane," he continued. "They know he is ultra-liberal and that he has no practical judgment. They know also that Doctor Bouquillon has great influence with him, and people challenge Dr. Bouquillon especially regarding his intemperate campaign on the topic of education.[22] Besides, the time had not yet come to establish a Catholic University. Our bishops do not have ecclesiastical personnel to send to it; vocations are becoming very rare, and they have great need for all their priests. As for the lay students, our Catholics are either rich or poor. If they are rich they would more readily go to the great Protestant Universities like Harvard, Yale, Princeton, etc., where they are now easily received, where they are encouraged to come, and where they find an opportunity of associating with the children of the more important families of the Republic. If they are poor, they can go to Washington and live there on scholar-

---

[20] Jeremiah O'Sullivan (1842–1896) was consecrated as the fourth Bishop of Mobile in September, 1885; Edward J. Dunne (1848–1910) was named second Bishop of Dallas in September, 1893; Thomas Heslin (1845–1911) was consecrated fifth Bishop of Natchez in June, 1889; Florien de Bruycker was pastor of St. Joseph's Church in Willimantic, Connecticut; John J. Keane (1839–1918) was Bishop of Richmond, 1878–1887, before his appointment as first rector of the Catholic University of America.

[21] New England comprised only the Province of Boston, not that of New York.

[22] Thomas Bouquillon (1840–1902) was the Belgian-born professor of moral theology in the Catholic University of America whose writings on the right of the State in education had been the subject of severe controversy during the years 1891–1893.

ships. There are hardly any parishes entirely free of debt or where the necessary Catholic institutions have been built. Before asking Catholics to donate to the University it is necessary to think of establishing our parishes on firm foundations and to insure the existence of our parochial schools. The general conviction is that they have built a University fifty years too soon and that they have placed at its head a man least capable of this office. Consequently a great number of the clergy think that before they are old, it will be a fiasco." I myself was thoroughly convinced that he was correct in his opposition, and I was aware that a complete understanding of the true condition of things would only confirm the public in these dark views on the future of the Catholic University. I understood the venerable priest to say that an institution, founded by the Pope himself and which already possessed considerable property, could not be a fiasco; that it could be in trouble for some time, but that it would not die; that as for personnel, if they would become an obstacle, Providence would indeed be able to remove them. I terminated the conversation by asking him to look favorably upon the work according to the viewpoint of the Holy Father so that it might become a blessing for the American Church (which up to now had scarcely appeared as it ought to be).

The official opening of the Winter School took place at five o'clock in the great hall of Tulane University. The ceremony consisted of an address of welcome to the two Cardinals by the Governor of Louisiana and by the mayor of the city. The Archbishop also made a few remarks and then a public reception in honor of Cardinal Satolli took place.

This "Winter School" of which we speak, and which was the occasion of the visit of the Cardinal Pro-Delegate to New Orleans, is the counterpart of the "Summer School" which is held in July at Plattsburg, diocese of Ogdensburg, for the East, and at Madison, diocese of Green Bay, for the West.[23] This work consists of giving a series of public addresses on diverse topics of philosophy, religion, history, Science, literature. For a long time the Protestants had an institution of this kind and lay Catholics prevailed upon the clergy to procure for them the same advantages (!). There is no doubt as to the intrinsic good of this school, and it would appear difficult in the circumstances to refuse to grant this request. But there are those who are convinced

---

[23] The Catholic Summer School of America was first opened in New London, Connecticut, in July, 1892, and then moved to Plattsburg, New York, in July, 1893. The Catholic Summer School in the Middle West met in various places after holding its first session in Madison, Wisconsin, in 1895.

that the intellectual advantages are rather insignificant and that, among the "non-Catholics" at least it is an application of the general plan of advancing *"Modern Science,"* in order to diminish the religious idea and to weaken as a result the influence of the priest. In that at least which most concerns Catholics, the Bishops have taken over the movement and have exerted themselves in turning it to good.

That evening at six o'clock there was a reception at the Jesuit Fathers given by former students, the "alumni" as they say in America. A young lawyer first gave a fine speech for the Cardinal Pro-Delegate; the Father Rector delivered a well thought-out address. Cardinal Satolli gave a eulogy in Latin on the Society of Jesus, the "dextera Ecclesiae Christi," and then warmly commended classical studies. Cardinal Gibbons, who was also present, recalled *his* study, now stereotyped, of Alexander and Aristotle drawn from the "Lives" of Plutarch. The speeches were then ended. After the reception we went to supper in the community refectory. Then the real opening of the "Winter School" began with an address by Cardinal Satolli followed by another by Bishop Keane. Cardinal Satolli spoke for more than an hour in Latin on the "Magisterium" of God, man and the Church. It was a magnificent discourse, a "sursum corda," giving the tone to the whole endeavor. He had spoken with such fire and conviction that the audience, although made up of a great number of people who did not know Latin, evidenced every sign of attention and interest up to the end. A large number of priests was also there. They were literally rapt in admiration and often expressed it with the warmest applause. One lady told me later: "I understand nothing, but the delivery was so animated, so expressive, that I would willingly have listened to His Eminence for a still longer time." After His Eminence, Bishop Keane appeared, and tried to give for those who did not understand, a resume of the magnificent address which they had just heard. But he forgot precisely the principal point, that is, concerning the magisterium of the Church, without which we would be led back to the condition of the Protestants. Then he began his topic: an exposition of the philosophy of the ancients touching on God, the human soul, and future life. He took one after another the great philosophers of Greece and Rome and made them say things which often they had not said at all. His Eminence was not able to prevent a show of impatience and resentment; also, he chose to leave the platform quietly under pretext of the advanced hour (10:15 p.m.). Bishop Keane spoke until 11:30 p.m. His success, they say was negligible. The priests, who had heard him for the first time, clearly evidenced their disappointment. But as he had facility in speaking, the good people did not notice the basic inaccuracies, taking it all in and finding no fault.

In the list of visits which His Eminence wished to make to the different institutions of New Orleans there are two which I omitted to relate in their proper place: the visit to the Sisters of the Holy Family and to the Ursulines. The Sisters of the Holy Family were Negro Religious,[24] founded forty years previously by a French priest, whose aim is to care for the orphans and poor of their race. The motherhouse, very large, was built near the Archbishop's house. These Sisters grew fast enough and the Archbishop testified to their spirit of humility, simplicity and devotion. Among the Sisters all shades of color are to be found, from the black of shoe polish to the color of soot. The Superior who appeared very intelligent was also as black as if she had recently arrived from the Congo. Their little Moors sang several chants and performed several well-executed dances for us. Christian charity is ingenious: it has an ointment for all wounds and a solace·for all miseries. But what a thing it is to be a Negro, especially in the United States! It is precisely in this professedly classical land of equality that society makes the Negro feel most that he is not white. The Church alone does not make this distinction and embraces all her children with the same tenderness.

One of the most interesting visits was that at the Ursulines. Coming from France in 1732 [*sic*], the Ursulines were identified with the foundation and the progress of the French colony in Louisiana. They are for this city what they have been in Quebec,[25] and the religious of the Congregation of Notre Dame for Montreal in Canada.[26] We found them in the suburbs of the city on a street which previously had been their farm. Their first convent, the one which had received their founders and where all the admirable Christians had been formed who would later be the mothers of the colony, is now, as we have already said, the residence of the Archbishop and still belongs to the Ursulines. These good religious live faithful to their traditions of regularity, piety, and noble simplicity. Their young girls gave a reception worthy of the

---

[24] The Sisters of the Holy Family had been founded in New Orleans in November, 1842, under the auspices of Antoine Blanc (1792–1860), fourth bishop and first Archbishop of New Orleans. In 1896 they had in the city, besides their mother house, orphan asylums for both boys and girls, a home for the aged, and four parochial schools.

[25] The Ursulines had been established in July, 1639, at Quebec by Venerable Marie de l'Incarnation Guyard (1599–1672).

[26] Blessed Marguerite Bourgeoys (1620–1700) arrived in Montreal from France in 1653 and soon thereafter founded the Congregation de Notre Dame.

venerable institution. Two living tableaus were especially remarkable: Eleazer and Rebecca at the well of Jacob, and Esther interceding for the safety of her people. The perfection, grace of poise, richness of costume and blending of colors made an incomparable production.

Since we had to leave on Friday evening, His Eminence paid a visit to Cardinal Gibbons on that morning, as well as to Archbishop Elder of Cincinnati, who had called on the Pro-Delegate the previous evening. After these courtesy calls Cardinal Satolli was taken to a large school conducted by the Sisters of St. Vincent de Paul ("St. Simeon's Academy").[27] Extraordinary preparations had been made for the reception of His Eminence. The small boys, in military uniforms and with drawn swords, formed a line at the entrance to the school. Two or three speeches were again delivered here, along with music and gifts of flowers. In this way the visit of His Eminence to New Orleans was ended. . . .

After dinner we had to pack our bags and prepared for the trip to Galveston. The Archbishop and his Chancellor wanted to accompany His Eminence to the ferry which crossed to the other side of the Mississippi where the South Station is located. It was a dark night, but we saw, by the light of electric lamps, the swift waters of the river churning rapidly and carrying along much wood and turf debris, actually small islands which will be deposited a little further on and thus continue the building up of the famous delta. What power! What majesty! Nevertheless, the steamboat passed through these powerful and swift waters without the slightest rocking. Soon we arrived on the other side of the river and boarded the train for Galveston.

We were now leaving this city whose people were still so French after almost a century of separation from their mother country, so Catholic in their traditions and their religious institutions. Now as they are a part of the Union, the English element penetrates little by little, and a new clergy accordingly replaces the old. The transition has already begun, and as a rule Belgians and Swiss are being used. The present Archbishop, who is worthy of his office, marks the end of the old regime and the beginning of the new.[28] The French clergy is

---

[27] St. Simeon's Select School had been opened by the Daughters of St. Vincent de Paul in 1860.

[28] This prediction proved untrue. On the death of Janssens in June, 1897, the French-born Placide L. Chapelle (1842–1905) became Archbishop of New Orleans; there then succeeded the German-born James H. Blenk, S.M. (1856–1917). It was only in January, 1918, that John W. Shaw (1863–1934), born in Mobile, Alabama, became the first native American to occupy the See of New Orleans. The present Archbishop Joseph F. Rummel (1876 –), who was installed in May, 1935, was born in Germany.

going to disappear gradually, and the Irish will move as quickly as possible into the parishes which yield a sufficient income. Let us hope that the Church and souls not only will not lose but even gain by the change. . . .

142. The Charter of the First Catholic Women's College in the United States, April 2, 1896

THE development of American Catholic higher education since Georgetown, the first Catholic college in the United States, opened in September, 1791, with a single student, has been an impressive one. At the present time there are 254 Catholic colleges and universities with a total enrollment of 241,709 students. In this movement Catholic colleges for women have played an increasingly important role. The first of these institutions was the College of Notre Dame of Maryland in Baltimore which held its first commencement on June 14, 1899, when six young women received the bachelor's degree. The college was staffed by the School Sisters of Notre Dame who had originally come to this country in July, 1847, for the purpose of teaching the children of German immigrants. Thus about a generation after Vassar College received its charter in 1861, college education for American Catholic women got underway. There are now 139 colleges for women under Catholic auspices in the United States, of which 118 are four-year institutions and twenty-one are junior colleges. Their combined enrollment is 77,446 with an additional 57,266 women students in Catholic institutions which admit both men and women. Source: *Laws of the State of Maryland*. . . . (Baltimore: King Bros., 1896), pp. 204–205.

Section 1. *Be it enacted by the General Assembly of Maryland.* That the body politic and corporate created by the Act of the General Assembly of Maryland of 1864, Chapter 357, for the instruction and education of females and the promotion of learning, and the faculty of the professors and teachers in said corporation, be, and they are hereby, authorized and empowered to grant to the graduates of the said institution of learning thereby created, who, in the judgment of the said faculty, may merit the distinction, the degree of Bachelor of Arts, and also the degree of Master of Arts; and to those students of the collegiate scientific department, who may merit the distinction, the degree of Bachelor of Science; and to those students of the department of English literature, who may merit the distinction, the degree of Bachelor of Literature; and to the students of the music department, who may merit the distinction, the degree of Bachelor of Music; and to those who may complete a full graduate or post-graduate course in said institution, having previously received from said institution the degrees of A.B., A.M., or B.S., or any others, who, in the judgment of said faculty, may merit the distinction, the degree of Doctor of Philosophy; and to the students in said institution such certificate of proficiency and attainments in any special study as the faculty of said institution may see fit and proper to confer, and further to confer the honorary degree of Ph.D., A.B., A.M., B.S., B.Lit. [*sic*], or such other degrees as are or may be conferred by any college or institution of learning of this State, upon any woman, who, in the judgment of the said faculty, may merit such distinctions, whether such woman be a student or graduate of the said institution or not.

Sec. 2. *And be it further enacted,* That the General Assembly shall have the right at any time to repeal or amend this Act.

Sec. 3. *And be it further enacted,* That this Act shall take effect from the date of its passage.

Approved April 2ᵈ, 1896.

Lloyd Lowndes, *Governor.*

William Cabell Bruce, *President of the Senate*

Sidney E. Mudd, *Speaker of the House of Delegates*

143. Mr. Dooley's Comments on Keeping the Philippines, a Church Fair, and the Democratic National Convention of 1924

NO AMERICAN humorist since Mark Twain captivated the reading public so completely as Finley Peter Dunne (1867–1936). Dunne's career as a journalist on several Chicago newspapers brought him local prominence in the late 1880's but it was his creation of the lovable and entertaining character of Mr. Dooley in 1893, and that character's sage and witty comments on the Spanish American War, that earned Dunne national fame. Speaking of the closing years of the century, Henry Steele Commager said, "Perhaps the most penetrating literary commentary on the changing nature of politics came . . . from Finley Peter Dunne, whose transcriptions of the wit and wisdom of 'Mr. Dooley' pricked every political bubble and exposed every political fraud of these transition years" (*The American Mind* [New Haven, 1950], p. 63). Dunne was born and raised a Catholic, having been baptized in old St. Patrick's Church, Chicago, by his first cousin, Patrick W. Riordan (1841–1914), who in 1884 became second Archbishop of San Francisco. Although he did not practice his faith with the fidelity that his thoroughly Irish background would suggest, he never tolerated any disrespect of his religion, was deeply moved by audiences of Leo XIII in 1901 and 1902, and was reconciled to the Church at death and buried with a requiem Mass from St. Patrick's Cathedral, New York. The examples from Mr. Dooley which follow illustrate Dunne's satirical merrymaking with political themes and his understanding of Irish parish life at the end of the century. In the political realm he reflected the national uncertainty about what should be done with the Philippines after their conquest from Spain in 1898, while the last piece shows how Dunne, a lifelong Democrat, capitalized on the Teapot Dome scandals of the Coolidge administration which broke in March, 1924, and the spirit in which he took the Democratic national convention that nominated John W. Davis (1873–1955) in July, 1924. Sources: Elmer Ellis (Ed.), *Mr. Dooley at His Best* (New York: Charles Scribner's Sons, 1938), pp. 59–62, 93–96; Finley Peter Dunne, *Mr. Dooley in the Hearts of His Countrymen* (Boston: Small, Maynard & Co., 1899), pp. 135–138.

THE PHILIPPINE PEACE

"I know what I'd do if I was Mack,"[1] said Mr. Hennessy. "I'd hist a flag over th' Ph'lippeens, an' I'd take in th' whole lot iv thim."

"An' yet," said Mr. Dooley, "'tis not more thin two months since ye larned whether they were islands or canned goods. Ye'er back yard is so small that ye'er cow can't turn r-round without buttin' th' woodshed off th' premises, an' ye wudden't go out to th' stock yards without takin' out a policy on yer life. Suppose ye was standin' at the corner iv State Sthreet an' Ar-rchy Road, wud ye know what car to take to get to th' Ph'lippeens? If yer son Packy was to ask ye where th' Ph'lippeens is, cud ye give him anny good idea whether they was in Rooshia or jus' west iv th' thracks?"

"Mebbe I cudden't," said Mr. Hennessy, haughtily, "but I'm f'r takin' thim in, annyhow."

"So might I be," said Mr. Dooley, "if I cud on'y get me mind on it. Wan iv the worst things about this here war is th' way it's makin' puzzles f'r our poor, tired heads. Whin I wint into it, I thought all I'd have to do was to set up here behind th' bar with a good tin-cint see-gar in me teeth, an' toss dinnymite bombs into th' hated city iv Havana. But look at me now. Th' war is still goin' on; an' ivry night, when I'm countin' up th' cash, I'm askin' mesilf will I annex Cubia or lave it to the Cubians? Will I take Porther Ricky or put it by? An' what shud I do with th' Ph'lippeens? Oh, what shud I do with thim? I can't annex thim because I don't know where they ar-re. I can't let go iv thim because some wan else'll take thim if I do. They are eight thousan' iv thim islands, with a population iv wan hundherd millyon naked savages; an' me bedroom's crowded now with me an' the bed. How

[1] William McKinley (1843–1901), President of the United States, March, 1898–September 14, 1901.

can I take thim in, an' how on earth am I'm goin' to cover th' naked-
ness iv thim savages with me wan shoot iv clothes? An' yet 'twud break
me heart to think iv givin' people I niver see or heerd tell iv back to
other people I don't know. An' if I don't take thim, Schwartzmeister
down th' sthreet, that has half me thrade already, will grab thim sure.

"It ain't that I'm afraid iv not doin' th' r-right thing in th' end,
Hinnissy. Some mornin' I'll wake up an' know jus' what to do, an'
that I'll do. But 'tis th' annoyance in th' mane time. I've been r-readin'
about th' counthry. 'Tis over beyant ye'er left shoulder whin ye're
facin' east. Jus' throw ye'er thumb back, an' yet have it as ac'rate as
anny man in town. 'Tis farther thin Boohlgahrya an' not so far as
Blewchoochoo. It's near Chiny, an' it's not so near; an', if a man was
to bore a well through fr'm Goshen, Indianny, he might sthrike it, an'
thin again he might not. It's a poverty-sthricken counthry, full iv goold
and precious stones, where th' people can pick dinner off th' threes
an' ar-re starvin' because they have no stepladders. Th' inhabitants is
mostly naygurs an' Chinnymen, peaceful, industhrus, an' lawabidin',
but savage an' bloodthirsty in their methods. They were no clothes
except what they have on, an' each woman has five husbands an' each
man has five wives. Th' r-rest goes into th' discard, th' same as here.
Th' islands has been owned by Spain since befure th' fire; an' she's
threated thim so well they're now up in ar-rms again her, except a
majority iv thim which is thurly loyal. Th' natives seldom fight, but
whin they get mad at wan another they r-run-a-muck. Whin a man
r-runs-a-muck, sometimes they hang him an' sometimes they discharge
him an' hire a new motorman. Th' women ar-re beautiful, with lan-
guishin' black eyes, an' they smoke see-gars, but ar-re hurried an' incomplete in their dhress. I see a pitcher iv wan th' other day with
nawthin' on her but a basket of cocoanuts an' a hoop-skirt. They're
no prudes. We import juke, hemp, cigar wrappers, sugar, an' fairy
tales fr'm th' Ph'lippeens, an' export six-inch shells an' th' like. Iv
late th' Ph'lippeens has awaked to th' fact that they're behind th' times,
an' has received much American amminition in their midst. They say
th' Spanyards is all tore up about it.

"I larned all this fr'm th' papers, an' I know 'tis sthraight. An' yet,
Hinnissy, I dinnaw what to do about th' Ph'lippeens. An' I'm all alone
in th' wurruld. Ivrybody else has made up his mind. Ye ask anny conducthor on Ar-rchy Road, an' he'll tell ye. Ye can find out fr'm th'
paper; an' if ye really want to know, all ye have to do is to ask a
prom'nent citizen who can mow all th' law he owns with a safety razor.
But I don't know."

"Hang on to thim," said Mr. Hennessy, stoutly. "What we've got we must hold."

"Well," said Mr. Dooley, "If I was Mack, I'd lave it to George.[2] I'd say: 'George,' I'd say, 'if ye're f'r hangin' on, hang on it is. If ye say, lave go, I dhrop thim.' 'Twas George won thim with th' shells, an' th' question's up to him."

THE CHURCH FAIR

"Wanst I knew a man," said Mr. Dooley, laying down his newspaper, "be th' name iv Burke, that come fr'm somewhere around Derry, though he was Presbyteryan. He was iv th' right sort. Well, he was feelin' how-come-ye-so, an' he dhrifted over to where we was holdin' a fair. They was a band outside, an' he thought it was a grand openin'. So he come in with a cigar in th' side iv his mouth an' his hat hangin' onto his ear. It was th' last night iv th' fair, an' ivrything was wide open; f'r th' priest had gone home, an' we wanted f'r to break th' record. This Burke was f'r lavin' whin he see where he was; but we run him again th' shootin' gallery, where ye got twenty-five cints, a quarther iv a dollar, f'r ivry time ye rang th' bell. Th' ol' gun we had was crooked as a ram's horn, but it must 've fitted the Burke's squint; f'r he made that there bell ring as if he was a conducthor iv a grip-car roundin' a curve. He had th' shootin' gallery on its last legs whin we run him again th' wheel iv fortune. He broke it. Thin we thried him on th' grab-bag. They was four goold watches an' anny quantity iv brickbats an' chunks iv coal in th' bag. He had four dives, an' got a watch each time. He took a chanst on ivrything; an' he won a foldin'-bed, a doll that cud talk like an old gate, a pianny, a lamp-shade, a Life iv St. Aloysius, a pair iv shoes, a baseball bat, an ice-cream freezer, an' th' pomes iv Mike Scanlan.

"Th' comity was disthracted. Here was a man that'd break th' fair, an' do it with th' best iv humor; f'r he come fr'm another parish. So we held a private session. 'What'll we do?' says Dorgan, th' chairman. They was a man be th' name iv Flaherty, a good man thin an' a betther now; f'r he's dead, may he rest in peace! An' Flaherty says: 'We've got to take th' bull by th' horns,' he says. 'If ye lave him to me,' he says, 'I'll fix him,' he says.

"So he injooced this man Burke to come down back iv th' shootin' gallery, an' says he to Burke, 'Ye're lucky to-night.' 'Not so very,' says Burke. ''Twud be a shame to lave ye get away with all ye won,' says Flaherty. ''Twill be a great inconvanience,' says Burke. 'I'll have

---

[2] Admiral George Dewey (1837–1917) occupied Manila in August, 1898.

to hire two or three dhrays,' he says; 'an' 'tis late.' 'Well,' says Flaherty, 'I'm appinted be th' parish to cut th' ca-ards with ye,' he says, 'whether ye're to give back what ye won or take what's left.' ''Tis fair,' says Burke; 'an', whoiver wins, 'tis f'r a good cause.' An' he puts th' watches an' th' money on th' table.

" 'High man,' says Flaherty. 'High man,' says Burke. Flaherty cut th' king iv spades. Burke, th' robber, cut th' ace iv hearts. He was reachin' out f'r th' money, whin Flaherty put his hands over it. 'Wud ye yet take it?' says he. 'I wud,' says Burke. 'Wud ye rob th' church?' says Flaherty. 'I wud,' says Burke. 'Thin,' says Flaherty, scoopin' it in, 'ye're a heretic; an' they'se nawthin' comin' to ye.'

"Burke looked at him, an' he looked at th' comity; an' he says, 'Gintlemen, if iver ye come over in th' Sixth Ward, dhrop in an' see me,' he says. 'I'll thry an' make it plisint f'r ye," he says. An' he wint away.

"Th' story got out, an' th' good man heerd iv it. He was mighty mad about it; an' th' nex' sermon he preached was on th' evils iv gamblin', but he asked Flaherty f'r to take up th' colliction."

1924

"Am I goin' to th' Dimmycrat convintion?" said Mr. Dooley. "Ye can bet I am, I'm goin' if I have to hitch onto a freight. In th' first place I want to have a look at th' great wicked me-thropolus. I haven't see that vain, corrupt, but fascinatin' Babylon since I thramped acrost it on me way to fame an' fortune in th' goolden West. I don't think New York is as bad as it's painted be Bill White[1] an' Hinnery Allen,[2] but I sincerely hope it is. 'Twud be a turr'ble disappointment to me to spind me good money an' find mesilf landed in a varchous, hard-workin' community like th' wan I've been. livin' in these manny years. If New York expicts to live up to its repytation among us austere, but curyous Westhern Dimmycrats it'd betther begin to put on its paint an' bob its hair at wanst. If Vice ain't dazzlin' and' rampant whin I get there I'll take th' next train back. An' thin there's th' convintion. Iv all th' circuses, 15-round bouts or endurance contests that Tex Richard[3] iver managed this will be th' noblest. It's goin' to be a gr-reat episode in th' life iv a quite Chicago merchant, who had no

---

[1] William Allen White (1868–1944) was editor of the *Gazette*, Emporia, Kansas.

[2] Henry J. Allen (1868–1950) was a newspaper publisher and Governor of Kansas, 1919–1923.

[3] George L. (Tex) Rickard (1871–1929) was a sports promoter.

divarsions but bein' stuck up ivry week or two be a gunman. An' they do say, with all our boastin', there's ten gunmen in New York to wan in Chicago.

"That goes to show us Dimmycrats ought niver to despair iv a good time. Not that Dimmycrats, Hinnissy, as a rule, are iv a repinin' nature. To be a Dimmycrat a man must be as hopeful as an investor in a policy ticket. A few months ago I looked f'r a monotonous convintion an' a teejous campaign. Th' cards were shuffled an' marked. We wud hold a four-card heart flush; we wud bet it like th' cheerful souls we are; on iliction day we'd draw th' customary two spot iv clubs. Uncle Cal⁴ wud set in th' White House in front iv th' fire with his slippers on broadcastin' bedtime stores an' old New England sayin's f'r the voters. Billy Mack⁵ wud tear around th' counthry denouncin' railroad comp'nies fr'm th' back platform iv a private care an' that's all there be to it. Th' votes wud be counted be a quarther to eight an' at half-past I'd be undher th' comforter before th' band began to insult me ears with 'Marchin' Thro Georgia.'

"But, thank th' Lord f'r th' gin'rous open-handed ile men, that's all changed f'r th' betther an' th' sunshine has begun to break through th' clouds f'r our grand ol' party. I niver see a campaign open, as Hogan says, under more fav'rable or more disagreeable auspices. Scandal that wanst was resarved f'r th' mornin' iv iliction day is in full bloom at this minyit, an' th' bad language that we used to save up f'r October is now freely exchanged whereiver thoughtful men gather together. Th' intelligent ilictors are already layin' in their store iv hard coal, brick bats an' cabbageheads to greet th' candydates whin they appear on th' hustings. Before Siptimber dawns I look to be gettin' a little sense into Larkin's head be hammerin' it with a thransparency while he feebly retorts be thryin' to get fire to me with a karosene torch. Th' intilligent American voter ain't goin' to set around th' radio listenin' to solemn wurrds iv wisdom this year. Polyticks was niver meant f'r th' home annyhow. All us voters iver gets fr'm it is a chance to go out nights an' frolic, an' th' fellow that thries to appeal to our reason will have about as much of an aujeence as a lecturer on th' League iv Nations at a chicken fight. Be th' look iv things there'll be no home life f'r Uncle Cal this comin' Fall. Before th' punkin's on th' vine he'll have to put on his linen duster an' circylate

---

⁴ Calvin Coolidge (1872–1933) became president on August 3, 1923, on the death of Warren Harding.
⁵ William G. McAdoo (1863–1941), Secretary of the Treasury in the Wilson administration, was a leading contender for the Democratic nomination in 1924.

amongst th' inhabitants tellin' thim what he thinks iv his opponent, which ain't much.

"What will our platform be like? How do I know? I don't care. No wan iver reads a platform but th' boy that wrote it. Th' Dimmycrat platform this year will be wan sintince: 'We pint with pride to th' rottenness iv th' Raypublicans.' We're goin' to appeal on their record. 'Tis a wise policy. I heerd it first fr'm th' lips iv our sainted leader, Willum O'Brien. A fellow be th' name iv Flannigan was runnin' again him f'r alderman. 'Willum,' says I to th' gr-reat man, f'r we were very intimate, mind ye, in thim days an' I've often held his hat whin he was rollin' on th' flure in a discussion iv some important public question, 'Willum,' says I, 'ar-re ye goin' to stand on ye'er record?' 'I shud think not,' says he. 'I might fall through. I'm goin' to stand on Flannigan's. What's more,' he says, 'I'm goin' to jump on it,' he says. . . ."

"I'd like to go down to th' convintion," said Mr. Hennessy. "How long d'ye think it will last?"

"That depinds on how much self-resthaint New York shows," said Dr. Dooley. "I figure that about th' end iv th' first week th' gr-reat, gin'rous, warmhearted methropolus will say: 'Th' boys have been away fr'm home long enough. They've had a good time. Their show is funny, but th' action dhrags. Let's break 'em tonight.' An' th' nex' day we'll pull th' name iv our standard bearer out iv a hat an' go home on th' break beams."

144. Pope Leo XIII's Encyclical *Testem benevolentiae* on Americanism, January 22, 1899

ONLY once in the history of the Catholic Church in the United States was its orthodoxy of doctrine called in question. The episode grew out of a series of differences within the hierarchy due to the liberal and conservative approach of the bishops to problems such as the secret societies, the teachings of Henry George, and Catholic participation in the World's Parliament of Religions at Chicago in 1893. The flourishing state of American Catholicism had meanwhile attracted the attention of European observers, especially in France where the Church was harassed by the policies of anticlerical governments. As a consequence some French Catholic leaders advocated a closer imitation of the Church in the United States, a policy which aroused violent dissent among the more conservative leaders of the French Church. A crisis ensued when a careless French translation of *The Life of Father Hecker* (New York, 1891) by Walter Elliott, C.S.P., appeared in 1897. The controversy became so heated on both sides of the

Atlantic over American teaching and methods that Leo XIII finally took the matter into his own hands and after careful investigation issued a letter to Cardinal Gibbons on the subject. The pope was careful to say that the erring doctrines had been imputed to the American Catholics by a foreign source, that the issue had nothing to do with the legitimate patriotism of the Americans, and that he was not accusing the Catholics of the United States of holding these views; he was merely warning that if such doctrines were being taught, they were erroneous. Following the publication of the pope's letter the bishops of the Provinces of Milwaukee and New York thanked Leo XIII for saving the American Church from the threat of heresy. The more common reaction in the United States, however, was that embodied in the reply of Cardinal Gibbons to the pontiff on March 17, 1899, when he said: "This doctrine, which I deliberately call extravagant and absurd, this Americanism as it has been called, has nothing in common with the views, aspirations, doctrine and conduct of Americans" (John Tracy Ellis, *The Life of James Cardinal Gibbons, Archbishop of Baltimore, 1834–1921* [Milwaukee, 1952], II, 71). Source: John J. Wynne, S.J. (Ed.), *The Great Encyclical Letters of Pope Leo XIII* (New York: Benziger Bros., 1903), pp. 441–453.

We send you this letter as a testimony of that devoted affection in your regard, which during the long course of Our Pontificate, We have never ceased to profess for you, for your colleagues in the Episcopate, and for the whole American people, willingly availing Ourselves of every occasion to do so, whether it was the happy increase of your church, or the works which you have done so wisely and well in furthering and protecting the interests of Catholicity. The opportunity also often presented itself of regarding with admiration that exceptional disposition of your nation, so eager for what is great, and so ready to pursue whatever might be conducive to social progress and the splendor of the State. But although the object of this letter is not to repeat the praise so often accorded, but rather to point out certain things which are to be avoided and corrected, yet because it is written with that same apostolic charity which We have always shown you, and in which We have often addressed you, We trust that you will regard it likewise as a proof of Our love; and all the more so as it is conceived and intended to put an end to certain contentions which have arisen lately among you, and which disturb the minds, if not of all, at least of many, to the no slight detriment of peace.

You are aware, beloved Son, that the book entitled, "The Life of Isaac Thomas Hecker," chiefly through the action of those who have undertaken to publish and interpret it in a foreign language, has excited no small controversy on account of certain opinions which are introduced concerning the manner of leading a Christian life. We, therefore, on account of Our apostolic office, in order to provide for the integrity of the faith, and to guard the security of the faithful, desire to write to you more at length upon the whole matter.

The principles on which the new opinions We have mentioned are based may be reduced to this: that, in order the more easily to bring over to Catholic doctrine those who dissent from it, the Church ought to adapt herself somewhat to our advanced civilization, and, relaxing her ancient rigor, show some indulgence to modern popular theories and methods. Many think that this is to be understood not only with regard to the rule of life, but also to the doctrines in which the *deposit of faith* is contained. For they contend that it is opportune, in order to work in a more attractive way upon the wills of those who are not in accord with us, to pass over certain heads of doctrines, as if of lesser moment, or to so soften them that they may not have the same meaning which the Church has invariably held. Now, Beloved Son, few words are needed to show how reprehensible is the plan that is thus conceived, if we but consider the character and origin of the doctrine which the Church hands down to us. On that point the Vatican Council says: "The doctrine of faith which God has revealed is not proposed like a theory of philosophy which is to be elaborated by the human understanding, but as a divine deposit delivered to the Spouse of Christ to be faithfully guarded and infallibly declared. . . . That sense of the sacred dogmas is to be faithfully kept which Holy Mother Church has once declared, and is not to be departed from under the specious pretext of a more profound understanding" (*Const. de Fid. cath.,* c. iv).

Nor is the suppression to be considered altogether free from blame, which designedly omits certain principles of Catholic doctrine and buries them, as it were, in oblivion. For there is the one and the same Author and Master of all the truths that Christian teaching comprises: *The only-begotten Son who is in the bosom of the Father* (*John,* i, 18). That they are adapted to all ages and nations is plainly deduced from the words which Christ addressed to His apostles: *Going therefore teach ye all nations: teaching them to observe all things whatsoever I have commanded you: and behold I am with you all days even to the consummation of the world* (*Matthew,* xxviii, 19). Wherefore the same Vatican Council says: "By the divine and Catholic faith those things are to be believed which are contained in the word of God either written or handed down, and are proposed by the Church whether in solemn decision or by the ordinary universal magisterium, to be believed as having been divinely revealed" (*Const. de Fid. cath.*, c. iii). Far be it, then, for any one to diminish or for any reason whatever to pass over anything of this divinely delivered doctrine; whosoever would do so, would rather wish to alienate Catholics from the Church than to bring over to the Church those who dissent from it. Let them return; indeed, nothing is nearer to Our heart; let all those who are wandering far from the sheepfold of Christ return; but let it not be by any other road than that which Christ has pointed out.

The rule of life which is laid down for Catholics is not of such a nature as not to admit modifications, according to the diversity of time and place. The Church, indeed, possesses what her Author has bestowed on her, a kind and merciful disposition; for which reason from the very beginning she willingly showed herself to be what Paul proclaimed in his own regard: *I became all things to all men, that I might save all* (*Corinthians*, ix, 22). The history of all past ages is witness that the Apostolic See, to which not only the office of teaching but also the supreme government of the whole Church was committed, has constantly adhered *to the same doctrine, in the same sense and in the same mind* (Conc. Vatic., *ibid.*, c. iv): but it has always been accustomed to so modify the rule of life that, while keeping the divine right inviolate, it has never disregarded the manners and customs of the various nations which it embraces. If required for the salvation of souls, who will doubt that it is ready to do so at the present time? But this is not to be determined by the will of private individuals, who are mostly deceived by the appearance of right, but ought to be left to the judgment of the Church. In this all must acquiesce who wish to avoid the censure of Our predecessor Pius VI, who proclaimed the 18th proposition of the Synod of Pistoia "to be injurious to the Church and to the Spirit of God which governs her, inasmuch as it subjects to scrutiny the discipline established and approved by the Church, as if the Church could establish a useless discipline or one which would be too onerous for Christian liberty to bear."

But in the matter of which we are now speaking, Beloved Son, the project involves a greater danger and is more hostile to Catholic doctrine and discipline, inasmuch as the followers of these novelties judge that a certain liberty ought to be introduced into the Church, so that, limiting the exercise and vigilance of its powers, each one of the faithful may act more freely in pursuance of his own natural bent and capacity. They affirm, namely, that this is called for in order to imitate that liberty which, though quite recently introduced, is now the law and the foundation of almost every civil community. On that point We have spoken very much at length in the Letter written to all the bishops about the constitution of States;[1] where We have also shown the difference between the Church, which is of divine right, and all other associations which subsist by the free will of men. It is of importance, therefore, to note particularly an opinion which is adduced as a sort of argument to urge the granting of such liberty to Catholics. For they say, in speaking of the infallible teaching of the Roman Pontiff, that after the solemn decision formulated in the Vatican Council, there is no more need of solicitude in that regard, and, because of its being now out of dispute, a wider field of thought and action is thrown open to individuals. A preposterous method of arguing, surely. For if anything is suggested by the infallible teaching of the Church, it is certainly that no one should wish to withdraw from it; nay, that all should strive to be thoroughly imbued with and be guided by its spirit, so as to be the more easily preserved from any private error whatsoever. To this we may add that those who argue in that wise quite set aside the wisdom and providence of God; who when He desired it especially in order the more efficaciously to guard the minds of Catholics from the dangers of the present times. The license which is commonly confounded with liberty; the passion for saying and reviling everything; the habit of thinking and of expressing everything in print, have cast such deep shadows on men's minds, that there is now greater utility and necessity for this office of teaching than ever before, lest men should be drawn away from conscience and duty. It is far, indeed, from Our intention to repudiate all that the genius of the time begets; nay, rather, whatever the search for truth attains, or the effort after good achieves, will always be welcomed by Us, for it increases the patrimony of doctrine and enlarges the limits of public prosperity. But all this, to possess real utility, should thrive without setting aside the authority and wisdom of the Church.

We come now in due course to what are adduced as consequences from the opinions which We have touched upon; in which if the intention seem not wrong, as We believe, the things themselves assuredly will not appear by any means free from suspicion. For, in the first place, all external guidance is rejected as superfluous, nay even as somewhat of a disadvantage, for those who desire to devote

---

[1] For the encyclical *Immortale Dei* of November 1, 1885, cf. Wynne, *op. cit.,* pp. 107–134.

themselves to the acquisition of Christian perfection; for the Holy Ghost, they say, pours greater and richer gifts into the hearts of the faithful now than in times past; and by a certain hidden instinct teaches and moves them with no one as an intermediary. It is indeed not a little rash to wish to determine the degree in which God communicates with men; for that depends solely on His will; and He Himself is the absolutely free giver of His own gifts. *The Spirit breatheth where He will* (*John* iii, 8). *But to every one of us is given grace according to the measure of the giving of Christ* (*Ephesians,* iv, 7). For who, when going over the history of the apostles, the faith of the rising Church, the struggles and slaughter of the valiant martyrs, and finally most of the ages past so abundantly rich in holy men, will presume to compare the past with the present times and to assert that they received a lesser outpouring of the Holy Ghost? But, aside from that, no one doubts that the Holy Ghost, by His secret incoming into the souls of the just, influences and arouses them by admonition and impulse. If it were otherwise, any external help and guidance would be useless. "If any one positively affirms that he can consent to the saving preaching of the Gospel without the illumination of the Holy Ghost, who imparts sweetness to all to consent to and accept the truth, he is misled by a heretical spirit" (*Conc. Arausic.,* II, can. vii). But as we know by experience these promptings and impulses of the Holy Ghost for the most part are not discerned without the help, and, as it were, without the preparation of an external guidance. In this matter Augustine says: "It is he who in good trees co-operates in their fruiting, who both waters and cultivates them by any servant whatever from without, and who by himself gives increase within" (*De grat. Christi,* c. xix). That is to say, the whole matter is according to the common law by which God in His infinite providence has decreed that men for the most part should be saved by men; hence He has appointed that those whom He calls to a loftier degree of holiness should be led thereto by men, "in order that," as Chrysostom says, "we should be taught by God through men" (*Hom. i. in Inscr. altar.*). We have an illustrious example of this put before us in the very beginning of the Church, for although Saul, who was *breathing threatenings and slaughter* (*Acts* c. ix), heard the voice of Christ Himself, and asked from Him, *Lord what wilt Thou have me to do?* he was nevertheless sent to Ananias at Damascus: *Arise and go into the city, and there it shall be told thee what thou must do.* It must also be kept in mind that those who follow what is more perfect are by the very fact entering upon a way of life which for most men is untried and more exposed to error, and therefore they, more than others, stand in need of a teacher and a guide. This manner of acting has invariably obtained in the Church. All, without exception, who in the course of ages have been remarkable for science and holiness have taught this doctrine. Those who reject it, assuredly do so rashly and at their peril.

For one who examines the matter thoroughly, it is hard to see, if we do away with all external guidance as these innovators propose, what purpose the more abundant influence of the Holy Ghost, which they make so much of, is to serve. In point of fact, it is especially in the cultivation of virtue that the assistance of the Holy Spirit is indispensable; but those who affect these novelties extol beyond measure the natural virtues as more in accordance with the ways and requirements of the present day, and consider it an advantage to be richly endowed with them, because they make a man more ready and more strenuous in action. It is hard to understand how those who are imbued with Christian principles can place the natural ahead of the supernatural virtues, and attribute to them greater power and fecundity. Is nature, then, with grace added to it, weaker than when left to its own strength? and have the eminently holy men whom the Church reveres and pays homage to, shown themselves weak and incompetent in the natural order, because they have excelled in Christian virtue? Even if we admire the sometimes splendid acts of the natural virtues, how rare is the man who really possesses the habit of these natural virtues? Who is there who is not disturbed by passions, sometimes of a violent nature, for the persevering conquest of which, just as for the observance of the whole natural law, man must needs have some divine help? If we scrutinize more closely the particular acts We have above referred to, we shall discover that oftentimes they have more the appearance than the reality of virtue. But let us grant that these are real. If we do not wish *to run in vain,* if we do not wish to lose sight of the eternal blessedness to which God in His goodness has destined us, of what use are the natural virtues unless the gift and strength of divine grace be added? Aptly does St. Augustine say: "Great power, and a rapid pace, but out of the course" (*In Ps.,* xxxi, 4). For as the nature of man, because of our common misfortune, fell into vice and dishonor, yet by the assistance of grace is lifted up and borne onward with new honor and strength; so also the virtues which are exercised not by the unaided powers of nature, but by the help of the same grace, are made productive of a supernatural beatitude and become solid and enduring.

With this opinion about natural virtue, another is intimately connected, according to which all Christian virtues are divided as it were
into two classes, *passive* as they say, and *active;* and they add the
former were better suited for the past times, but the latter are more
in keeping with the present. It is plain what is to be thought of such
division of the virtues. There is not and cannot be a virtue which is
really passive. "Virtue," says St. Thomas, "denotes a certain perfection of a power; but the object of a power is an act; and an act of
virtue is nothing else than the good use of our free will" (I. II. a. I),
the divine grace of course helping, if the act of virtue is supernatural.
The one who would have Christian virtues to be adapted, some to one
age and others to another, has forgotten the words of the Apostle:
*Whom he foreknew he also predestinated to be made conformable to
the image of His Son* (*Romans,* viii, 29). The Master and exemplar
of all sanctity is Christ, to whose rule all must conform who wish to
attain to the thrones of the blessed. Now, then, Christ does not at all
change with the progress of the ages, but is *yesterday and to-day, and
the same forever* (*Hebrews,* xiii, 8). To the men of all ages, the
phrase is to be applied: *Learn of Me because I am meek, and humble
of heart* (*Matthew,* xi, 29) and at all times Christ shows Himself to
us as becoming *obedient unto death* (*Philippians,* ii, 8) and in every
age also the word of the Apostle holds: *And they that are Christ's
have crucified their flesh with the vices and concupiscences* (*Galatians,*
v, 24). Would that more would cultivate those virtues in our days,
as did the holy men of bygone times! Those who by humbleness of
spirit, by obedience and abstinence, were *powerful in word and work,*
were of the greatest help not only to religion but to the State and
society.

From this species of contempt of the evangelical virtues, which
are wrongly called *passive,* it naturally follows that the mind is
imbued little by little with a feeling of disdain for the religious life.
And that this is common to the advocates of these new opinions
we gather from certain expressions of theirs about the vows which
religious orders pronounce. For, say they, such vows are altogether
out of keeping with the spirit of our age, inasmuch as they narrow
the limits of human liberty; are better adapted to weak minds than
to strong ones; avail little for Christian perfection and the good of
human society, and rather obstruct and interfere with it. But how
false these assertions are, is evident from the usage and doctrine
of the Church, which has always given the highest approval to
religious life. And surely not undeservedly. For those who, not con-

tent with the common duties of the precepts, enter of their own accord upon the evangelical counsels, in obedience to a divine vocation, present themselves to Christ as His prompt and valiant soldiers. Are we to consider this a mark of weak minds? In the more perfect manner of life is it unprofitable or hurtful? Those who bind themselves by the vows of religion are so far from throwing away their liberty that they enjoy a nobler and fuller one — that, namely, *by which Christ has set us free* (*Galatians,* iv, 31).

What they add to this — namely, that religious life helps the Church not at all or very little — apart from being injurious to religious orders, will be admitted by no one who has read the history of the Church. Did not your own United States receive from the members of religious orders the beginning of its faith and civilization? For one of them recently, and it redounds to your credit, you have decreed that a statue should be publicly erected. And at this very time, with what alacrity and success are these religious orders doing their work wherever we find them! How many of them hasten to impart to new lands the life of the Gospel and to extend the boundaries of civilization with the greatest earnestness of soul and amid the greatest dangers! From them no less than from the rest of the clergy the Christian people obtain preachers of the Word of God, directors of conscience, instructors of youth, and the entire Church examples of holy lives. Nor is there any distinction of praise between those who lead an active life and those who, attracted by seclusion, give themselves up to prayer and mortification of the body. How gloriously they have merited from human society, and do still merit, they should be aware who are not ignorant of how *the continual prayer of a just man* (*James,* v, 16) especially when joined to affliction of the body, avails to propitiate and conciliate the majesty of God.

If there are any, therefore, who prefer to unite together in one society without the obligation of vows, let them do as they desire. That is not a new institution in the Church, nor is it to be disapproved. But let them beware of setting such association above religious orders; nay rather, since mankind is more prone now than heretofore to the enjoyment of pleasure, much greater esteem is to be accorded to those *who have left all things and have followed Christ.*

Lastly, not to delay too long, it is also maintained that the way and the method which Catholics have followed thus far for recalling those who differ from us is to be abandoned and another resorted to. In that matter, it suffices to advert that it is not prudent, Beloved Son, to neglect what antiquity, with its long experience, guided as it is by apostolic teaching, has stamped with its approval. From the word of God we have it that it is the office of all to labor in helping the salvation of our neighbor in the order and degree in which each one is. The faithful indeed will most usefully fulfil their duty by integrity of life, by the works of Christian charity, by instant and assiduous prayer to God. But the clergy should do so by a wise preaching of the Gospel, by the decorum and splendor of the sacred ceremonies, but especially by expressing in themselves the form of doctrine which the apostles delivered to Titus and Timothy. So that if among the different methods of preaching the word of God, that sometimes seems preferable by which those who dissent from us are spoken to, not in the church but in any private and proper place, not in disputation but in amicable conference, such method is indeed not to be reprehended; provided, however, that those who are devoted to that work by the authority of the bishop be men who have first given proof of science and virtue. For We think that there are very many among you who differ from Catholics rather through ignorance than because of any disposition of the will, who, perchance, if the truth is put before them in a familiar and friendly manner, may more easily be led to the one sheepfold of Christ.

Hence, from all that We have hitherto said, it is clear, Beloved Son, that We cannot approve the opinions which some comprise under the head of Americanism. If, indeed, by that name be designated the characteristic qualities which reflect honor on the people of America, just as other nations have what is special to them; or if it implies the condition of your commonwealths, or the laws and customs which prevail in them, there is surely no reason why We should deem that it ought to be discarded. But if it is to be used not only to signify, but even to commend the above doctrines, there can be no doubt but that our Venerable Brethren the bishops of America would be the first to repudiate and condemn it, as being especially unjust to them and to the entire nation as well. For it raises the suspicion that there are some among you who conceive of and desire a church in America different from that which is in the rest of the world. One in the unity of doctrine as in the unity of government, such is the Catholic Church, and, since God has established its centre and foundation in the Chair of Peter, one which is rightly called Roman, for where Peter is there is the Church. Wherefore he who wishes to be called by the name of Catholic ought to employ in truth the words of Jerome to Pope Damasus, "I following none as the first except

Christ am associated in communion with your Beatitude, that is, with the Chair of Peter; upon that Rock I know is built the Church; whoever gathereth not with thee scattereth" (*S. Ambr. in Ps.,* xi, 57).

What We write, Beloved Son, to you in particular, by reason of Our office, we shall take care to have communicated to the rest of the bishops of the United States, expressing again that love in which we include your whole nation, which as in times past has done much for religion and bids fair with God's good grace to do still more in the future.

To you and all the faithful of America We give most lovingly as an augury of divine assistance Our Apostolical Benediction.

145. Pope Leo XIII's Congratulations to the Church of the United States, April 15, 1902

ON FEBRUARY 20, 1902, Pope Leo XIII entered upon the silver jubilee year of his pontificate. Cardinal Gibbons, speaking in the name of the American hierarchy, had sent him a letter of congratulations on March 2, to which the old pontiff replied on April 15 with the highest praise for the American Church. It was an extremely difficult time for the Holy See with the government of René Waldeck-Rousseau (1846–1904) of France at outright war with the Church and the governments of Italy and other countries unfriendly. Leo XIII had these events in mind when he told the American bishops that the condition of the Church in the United States cheered his heart by the success in spreading the faith, the provision of educational facilities, the advance of the Negro and Indian missions, the liberty granted the Church by American law, and the generosity of American Catholics in relieving the poverty of the Holy See. In contrast to all these favorable factors in the United States the pope found, as he said, that "the changes and tendencies of nearly all the nations which were Catholic for many centuries give cause for sorrow. . . ." Source: John J. Wynne, S.J. (Ed.), *The Great Encyclical Letters of Pope Leo XIII* (New York: Benziger Bros., 1903), pp. 513–516.

Certainly We have reason to rejoice, and the Catholic world, on account of its reverence for the Apostolic See, has reason to rejoice at the extraordinary fact that We are to be reckoned as the third in the long line of Roman Pontiffs to whom it has been happily given to enter upon the twenty-fifth year of the Supreme Priesthood. But in this circle of congratulations, while the voices of all are welcome to Us, that of the Bishops and faithful of the United States of North

America brings Us special joy, both on account of the conditions which give your country prominence over many others, and of the special love We entertain for you.

You have been pleased, beloved Son and Venerable Brothers, in your joint letter to Us to mention in detail what, prompted by love for you, We have done for your churches during the course of Our Pontificate. We, on the other hand, are glad to call to mind the many different ways in which you have ministered to Our consolation throughout this period. If We found pleasure in the state of things which prevailed among you when We first entered upon the charge of the Supreme Apostolate, now that We have advanced beyond twenty-four years in the same charge, We are constrained to confess that Our first pleasure has never been diminished, but, on the contrary, has increased from day to day by reason of the increase of Catholicity among you. The cause of this increase, although first of all to be attributed to the providence of God, must also be ascribed to your energy and activity. You have, in your prudent policy, promoted every kind of Catholic organization with such wisdom as to provide for all necessities and all contingencies, in harmony with the remarkable character of the people of your country.

Your chief praise is that you have promoted and sedulously continue to foster the union of your churches with this chief of churches and with the Vicar of Christ on earth. Herein, as you rightly confess, is the apex and centre of government, of teaching and of the priesthood; the source of that unity which Christ destined for His Church, and which is one of the most striking notes distinguishing it from all human sects. As We have never failed to exercise with advantage this most salutary office of teaching and government in every nation, so We have never permitted that you or your people should suffer the lack of it. For We have gladly availed Ourselves of every opportunity to testify the constancy of Our solicitude for you and for the interests of religion among you. And Our daily experience obliges Us to confess that We have found your people, through your influence, endowed with perfect docility of mind and alacrity of disposition. Therefore, while the changes and tendencies of nearly all the nations which were Catholic for many centuries give cause for sorrow, the state of your churches, in their flourishing youthfulness, cheers Our heart and fills it with delight. True, you are shown no special favor by the law of the land, but on the other hand your lawgivers are certainly entitled to praise for the fact that they do nothing to restrain you in your just liberty. You must, therefore, and with you the Catholic host behind, make strenuous use of the favorable time for action which is now at your disposal by spreading abroad as far as possible the light of truth against the errors and absurd imaginings of the sects that are springing up.

We are not unaware, Venerable Brothers, of all that has been done by every one of you for the establishment and the success of schools and academies for the proper education of children. By your zeal in this respect you have clearly acted in conformity with the exhortations of the Apostolic See and the prescriptions of the Council of Baltimore. Your magnificent work on behalf of the ecclesiastical seminaries has assuredly been calculated to increase the prospects of good to be done by the clergy and to add to their dignity. Nor is this all. You have wisely taken measures to enlighten dissidents and to draw them to the truth by appointing learned and worthy members of the clergy to go about from district to district to address them in public in familiar style in churches and other buildings, and to solve the difficulties that may be advanced. An excellent plan, and one which We know has already borne abundant fruit. Nor has your charity been unmindful of the sad lot of the negro and the Indian — you have sent them teachers, helped them liberally, and you are most zealously providing for their eternal salvation. We are glad to add a stimulus, if such be necessary, to enable you to continue these undertakings with full confidence that your work is worthy of commendation.

Finally, not to omit the expression of Our gratitude, We would have you know what satisfaction you have caused Us by the liberality with which your people are endeavoring to contribute by their offerings to relieve the penury of the Holy See. Many indeed and great are the necessities for which the Vicar of Christ as supreme Pastor and Father of the Church is bound to provide in order to avert evil and to promote the faith. Hence your generosity becomes an exercise and a testimony of your faith.

For all these reasons We wish to declare to you again and again Our affection for you. Let the Apostolic blessing, which We bestow most lovingly in the Lord upon you all and upon the flocks entrusted to each one of you, be taken as a token of this affection and an augury of divine gifts.

146. Abbé Klein's Impressions of Bishop McQuaid, 1903

BERNARD J. McQUAID (1823–1909), first Bishop of Rochester, was one of the outstanding Catholic prelates of the late nineteenth and early twentieth centuries. After a highly successful career in the Diocese of Newark as first president of Seton Hall College and vicar-general, he was promoted to the new See of Rochester in March, 1868, where for over forty years he displayed remarkable talents as an organizer, a promoter of education, and a controversialist. His conservative views put him in opposition to the so-called liberals in the hierarchy, and the strong influence of his direct, fearless, and intelligent approach on a number of his fellow bishops, especially Michael A. Corrigan (1839–1902), Archbishop of New York, was marked. McQuaid was justly proud of his diocesan institutions and when the Abbé Félix Klein (1862–1953), a professor of literature in the Catholic Institute of Paris, visited Rochester in the late summer of 1903, the bishop was at pains that he should see them. Klein had been deeply involved in the controversy over Americanism a few years before (cf. Volume IV of his *Souvenirs* entitled *Une hérésie fantôme. l'Américanisme* [Paris, 1949]). But Klein's sympathies with the more liberal-minded American bishops did not blind him to the admirable qualities of one who, as he said, was regarded in Europe "as the most conservative prelate in the United States." No American bishop of his day better represented the conservative wing of the hierarchy than McQuaid, but his conservatism was not the kind that prevented him from making solid contributions to his own diocese and to the Church of the nation. Source: Félix Klein, *In the Land of the Strenuous Life* (Chicago: A. C. McClurg & Co., 1905), pp. 96–104, 112–113.

Almost immediately the Bishop appears, and offers me his hand in the whole-souled fashion which I admire so much in Bishop Spalding.[1] Nothing that I have yet seen is so thoroughly American as this old man of eighty years, straight, thick-set, vigorous, with a frank and resolute bearing. Far from allowing me a word of excuse, he declares in a tone that admits of no denial that he is pleased to see me, and is at my disposal. "You come to look for ideas, of course, and for information?" "Just so, Monseigneur; the encouraging example of what is taking place in the United States. . . ." "Your countrymen, indeed, might profit much by what is good here, instead of . . . They do not see things in the right light, your countrymen. How much time can you spare me?" "I meant to take the ten o'clock train for Buffalo. Is there one at noon?" The only answer is a frown.

---

[1] John Lancaster Spalding (1840–1916), first Bishop of Peoria.

"Is there one at two o'clock?" "In that time we could do nothing at all; how many days can you stay?" "Well, then, frankly, I will stop till to-morrow morning." "I am sorry the stay is so short. Well, then, there is no time to lose. Here is your room; make yourself at home. I will order the carriage."

Ten minutes afterward I was rolling along in an open landau with the man who is regarded in Europe as the most conservative prelate in the United States. The conversation, which the Bishop maintained in French, was soon on a footing of confidence, and did not lag for an instant the entire day.

"I am going to show you first my Normal School for sisters.[2] They must receive a good education themselves before undertaking to teach others. A woman with some initiative, Marie du Sacré Coeur, tried to start that work among you; you did not understand her. When I founded this diocese, in 1868, — you know that I am its first bishop, — there were eight poor Sisters of St. Joseph here. I adopted them as a diocesan congregation.[3] To-day these are four hundred. I get whatever service I desire from them, without having to apply to distant superiors or to encounter regulations made for other conditions. They pass a State examination at Albany; this is not exacted by the Government, but I insist on it. You are going to see how they work."

We visit the laboratories, the library, the study halls, where, High Mass being over, several young sisters are reading or writing. What I see and what I hear give me the impression that the work is solid, the methods up-to-date, the courses of study sound and proportioned to the aptitude of each pupil. Some sisters are appointed to teach elementary and advanced science; others history, Latin, Greek, and various modern languages. Both sisters and novices are almost all from this diocese; a few are from other parts of America; two or three from Germany. "If you know," said the Bishop, turning to me, "of any young French women who have a true vocation as teachers, and cannot follow it at home, send them to Rochester." This invitation was seriously meant, and was seconded by the Mother Superior. In every room that we pass through, and in the kitchen, too, the Bishop is welcomed with evident joy. In his own blunt way he scatters jokes, counsel, and when requested, a brief blessing: "God bless you, God bless you." One feels that at a sign from him these

---

[2] Nazareth Normal School was formally dedicated on December 27, 1898.
[3] The Sisters of St. Joseph of Rochester were separated from their Buffalo mother house in 1868.

good sisters would be ready to fling themselves into the fire, and that he knows it.

The Normal School is now at the entrance of the city which continues to grow. The price of ground has risen a great deal since Bishop MacQuaid [*sic*] purchased sixty acres here for the sisters; he has recently sold twenty acres of it for a sum sufficient to cover not only the cost of the whole property, but of all the buildings also. He tells me all this, as the carriage conveys us to the gorges and falls of the Genesee River. We descend at a very picturesque bridge. The Bishop invites me to admire the landscape, which is very pretty. "And all that," says he, "is as instructive as it is beautiful. These grounds are very rich in fossil specimens; and, you observe, the river has cut through and exposed the different stratifications. It is a real geological museum which Providence has furnished to the seminarians of Rochester. We have gathered a fine collection from it, with abundant material for exchanges." He welcomed my offer of putting him, for this purpose, in communication with M. de Lapparent who superintends our collection in the Catholic Institute of Paris.

"Now," said the Bishop, "you are going to see my Seminary."[4] And one can guess from the tone of this simple phrase how much the good old Bishop's idea of *his* Seminary represents of work accomplished, of hopes still growing, and of conscience satisfied. Indeed, one quite understands, after having seen it, that it is something to be proud of. I am afraid of falling into the American abuse of superlatives; but, truly, nowhere have I seen a better plan, or a better adaptation of everything that may serve, materially, intellectually, and morally, to prepare young clerics for their great mission. From the very entrance, where you pass under the Gothic arches of the graceful tower which divides the building into two portions, you are struck with the harmony and amplitude of the general lines, as well as with the exact adaptation of all the interior details to the purpose in view. Everything must have been long meditated and settled by the founder before the construction was taken in hand. The Seminary has been built ten years; Bishop MacQuaid spent thirty years in planning it. In the execution, it is true, simplicity was everywhere consulted; but at the same time elegance and comfort as well. Electricity, steam-heating, scientific ventilation, numerous bathrooms, commodious furniture, a good door and window plan; a bakery equipped with machines for kneading; a refectory that is a real dining-room, with its separate tables, and its silver service; a reading room, which

---

[4] St. Bernard's Seminary was dedicated on August 20, 1893.

is a *salon,* with newspapers and periodicals; students' rooms furnished with sober elegance; corridors which are galleries filled with photographs and engravings fit to develop the artistic sense; everything, in short, speaks of culture, and bears witness to a noble solicitude to bring up as gentlemen these young men sprung from the people, yet destined to serve them as guides in the higher life. Even in a recent letter[5] to his priests, recommending to them both the Preparatory and the chief Seminary, Bishop MacQuaid vigorously insists upon the necessity of providing for the health and comfort of the students. "A mistaken notion prevails that only hardships and sufferings build up strong characters. This notion may have some force, but in a full estimation of the value of this system some account must be taken of the wrecks that line the road, wrecks of ruined stomachs, disordered nerves, weakened lungs, and premature corpses, that have paid the penalty of disregard of the laws of health."

The Bishop of Rochester can well judge of the life which his seminarians lead; for he shares it. On arriving, without being received by anybody, we go straight to his rooms. These are no solemn suites of apartments, occupied but twice a year; they consist of a bedroom which has been used yesterday and is ready for use today or tomorrow, and a study where there is a desk covered with books that are being read and letters waiting to be answered. When we go to the refectory, the Bishop's entrance, though unannounced, is not an event. It is merely a matter of two additional covers; in fact, not even that, because there are vacant places, several of the professors being absent assisting in the neighboring parishes for the Sunday.

The only exceptional feature of the meal is the number of wines served, — four or five, unless I mistake, which is something in America, and above all in a seminary, that calls for explanation. It must be observed that, like the late Cardinal Lavigerie,[6] whose characteristics Bishop MacQuaid more than once recalled to me, the latter is a great viticulturist. He grows, I do not know how many kinds of excellent wine-grapes; and he is as proud of the diploma his wines won at Bordeaux as he is of his Seminary. He questioned me, not without a little quib, as to what wines we were then drinking; and I, who despite his injunctions, had been drowning my wine with water, took a mouthful of meat, wondering what I should reply. At a venture, — or, to be frank, after casting a hasty glance at the

---

[5] A pastoral letter of August 20, 1903.
[6] Charles Cardinal Lavigerie (1825–1892), Archbishop of Algiers.

oblong form of the bottles, — with the air of a connoisseur I pronounced it to be Moselle, or, more probably still, Rhenish. I hit it exactly; for the vintages of the Bishop of Rochester claim, perhaps not without reason, to rival the Deidesheimer and Liebfrauenmilch ones. I believe it was at this point that the Bishop's tone toward me passed from kindness to sympathy. My sentiments toward him had already changed from fear into curiosity, then to respect, and next to admiration.

I should have no reservation whatever to make regarding him, if he had not, from one o'clock to three during a terrible heat and after a sleepless night, led me, notwithstanding my timid hints, through all the marvels of his Seminary, from the well-filled wine-cellars to the top stories wisely arranged as gymnasiums and recreation halls for rainy days. Hence I have retained only a rather vague impression about many highly interesting things, — the library, museums, laboratories, and the chapel itself; all I can say is that many a university would be glad to see itself so well equipped. At last, however, as the hour fixed for a conference which the Bishop was to give to the students was approaching, I flatly declared that I could not take advantage of it unless I should get a nap. The indefatigable patriarch looked at me with astonishment, but directed me to a sofa, upon which I dropped like a log. Waking up in time, thoroughly refreshed, I listened with the greatest interest to his talk of an hour and a quarter.

He spoke to a select audience, in which every face shone with intelligence, uprightness, candor, and health, both moral and physical. Doubtful and incapable candidates are got rid of without hesitation; vocations are surely numerous enough to permit of a rigorous selection, and the Bishop tolerates no mediocrity in the priesthood. Of the one hundred and thirty-four seminarians, eighty-nine come from here, there, and everywhere, on account of the high reputation which the course enjoys. To Rochester belong forty-five, a number sufficient for a diocese of one hundred and ten thousand souls. Between this fine body of young men and this wonderful old man who addressed them the current of sympathy is not for a moment broken, nor ceases to manifest itself. From the beginning to the end of his discourse, he remains master of all these souls, carrying them along with him from laughter to deep emotion, from lofty ideas to familiar ones, from reasoning to enthusiasm. Nothing could be more animated and picturesque. But who can give a summary of such an address? "The opening retreat," he said in substance, "finished yesterday, and hearts were opened to the love of God; now minds are to be opened to science. The students of St. Bernard's are fortunate in having such facilities for work; the collections, the laboratories, the latest books; the professors above all, the fifteen professors, who for their sakes have been sent to qualify themselves in the old universities of Europe. Ah! in my time it was not so. Learning Latin in America at the beginning of the nineteenth century was not an easy task. To do so, one had to go by boat and coach from New York to Montreal; and what adventures there were along the way![7] When you reached the seminary there were just two professors, who taught everything and knew nothing. There was scarcely time to study then; the year that I was born, there were in the State of New York just eight priests; now there are nine [six] dioceses." And thus he continued to contrast the obscure past with the brilliant present, and to point out the resulting obligations; following throughout only what Pascal calls the order of the heart, but following it so well that when he had finished talking the students, much affected, kept looking at him proudly, as though to say to me, "This man is *our* Bishop, and you see how things go with us!" In the presence of a Catholicism so prosperous, I could scarcely believe that all this had developed within the lifetime of one man; and when the octogenarian Bishop was speaking of the humble beginnings of the American Church, I pictured to myself the first apostles of the Gauls assisting at the opening of our thirteenth century. . . .

On leaving Rochester at ten o'clock A.M., just twenty-four hours after my arrival, I do not observe that my stay with the prelate whom some people in France represent as the most conservative and reactionary in America, has exactly led me to become much less progressive than formerly. . . .

147. A Picture of Hungarian Immigrant Parish Life in the United States, 1905

AMONG the more numerous groups of Catholics who came to this country during the New Immigration of the late nineteenth century were the Hungarians. By 1910 there were 338,151 Hungarians listed as residents of the United States. Most of these immigrants settled in the large industrial areas where many of them became factory workers. Insofar as possible, provision was made for them by the Church in separate parishes with their

---

[7] McQuaid made his preparatory studies for the priesthood at Chambly College in Canada. For full details on his career cf. Frederick J. Zwierlein, *The Life and Letters of Bishop McQuaid*, 3 vols. (Rochester, 1925–1927).

own priests. One who took a keen interest in their welfare was a Hungarian prelate, Péter Vay (1864–1948), who made several trips to the United States, acting as chaplain on an immigrant ship in 1895 that sailed from Fiume with over 2000 Hungarian immigrants on board. Ten years later he returned, this time as a guest at the inauguration of President Theodore Roosevelt in March, 1905. During this extended visit Vay spent a long period in New York where he worked among his compatriots in the parishes of St. Stephen and St. Elizabeth and preached and lectured in towns like Passaic, Paterson, and Hoboken, where there were large numbers of Hungarians. The following extracts from his memoirs describe his impressions of a new Hungarian parish in Chicago and of the mother parish of the Magyars in the United States at Cleveland. Source: Monsignor Count Vay de Vaya and Luskod, *The Inner Life of the United States* (New York: E. P. Dutton and Co., 1908), pp. 181–185, 336–340.

The reason of my visit to Chicago this time was, as already said, to inaugurate the little Catholic church,[1] erected by the immigrants recently arrived from the shores of the Danube and the Tisza. I had left the United States some time previously, and when the amiable invitation of my compatriots reached me, I was in the extreme north of Canada, on the shores of the Atlantic; I had just been visiting a colony of Hungarian artisans working in the iron foundries of Sidney (Nova Scotia). Although it was a long way back to Chicago, I willingly undertook the tedious journey — occupying three days and three nights — in order to comply with the complimentary request. On arriving at Chicago I found that the place of my destination was rather difficult to get at, and a good way off, being situated in the southernmost suburb of the town. First I had to travel by rail up to a certain point, then by the overhead railroad, and finally by street car. We went right through the city, past sumptuous palaces and warehouses, through labyrinths of modest streets, until at last I found myself democratically seated in an ordinary street car, which carried me away into what seemed the heart of the country. To right and left stretched endless fields of maize, and with the exception of a few tall chimneys on the horizon, the scene before me appeared in its primeval verdure, one immense expanse of untilled loneliness. No streets, no houses! — "But all that will come by and by," I was told, and on my next visit I should see this rural landscape transformed into blocks of houses and streets, just like all the rest of the town.

---

[1] Our Lady of Hungary Church, Chicago, was founded in 1904 by the Reverend Francis Grosz. The combined frame church and rectory opened on the occasion of Vay's visit was located at 9218 Drexel Street.

At a little distance among the marshy pasture land I detected the small wooden structure. From its roof waved the American and Hungarian flags, stars and stripes and the tricolour (red, white and green) harmoniously blending together. "That is the church, and the school is underneath," some one proudly volunteered. A humble edifice truly, but speaking of much sacrifice and labour. These simple folk have built it with their hard-earned savings, for the glory of God and the religious education of their children.

More than half the population of Chicago are foreigners.[2]. . . There are over 200,000 Italians, and the Hungarians proper, not included in other categories, must be estimated at nearly 15,000 new arrivals within the last few years. These latter are chiefly employed as butchers in the slaughter-houses, and as blacksmiths and carpenters in the Pullman establishment. It was at the expense of these people that the little church was built which now met my view. It stands like a beacon amid the surrounding marshes; it is the nucleus of a new suburb, which will spring up around it, and will certainly be no less important a part of the metropolis than the others which have arisen at 16 miles from the centre of the town. It is a first step towards progress, another foundation stone of civilisation and culture.

The workmen and their families awaited me at the entrance of the building. For the greater part they were still dressed in their simple costume "from over the sea," and their whole demeanour showed that they had not long since arrived in these parts. Set adrift in that great city, without knowing the language, without friends or any one to advise them, these poor folks are at the mercy of chance. And, in addition to all the other difficulties and problems which the municipal authorities have to face, we can well understand that this question of dealing with the foreign population of inferior civilisation is one of the greatest and hardest to solve. They have not only to be fed, they have also to be protected and educated. The church and the school are their only safeguards. As long as the people will go to church and are willing to have their children brought up on religious principles there is nothing to fear. As long as they recognize their duty towards God they will also recognise and fulfil their duty towards their neighbour.

The inauguration of that humble little church and its simple worshippers has left an indelible impression upon me. It was one of those never-to-be-forgotten scenes which, in spite of their apparent

---

[2] The 1900 census gave Chicago a population of 1,698,575, of whom 587,112 were listed as foreign-born.

unimportance, form a page in the annals of history. This small beginning, representing the accumulated savings of those hardy workmen, is
the centre of new efforts and new struggles. Let us hope these may
lead here to as successful an issue as they have done in other parts
of the town. Let us hope that its inhabitants may one day be as
prosperous and wealthy as their fellow-citizens in older Chicago. Above
all, let us hope that the little church may grow into a cathedral, and
its elementary school into a great scientific establishment. And although
in the past the place has so often been shaken by strikes and tumults,
let us hope that henceforth faith and culture may ensure peace and
prosperity to this marvellous city. . . .

Our church, a modest wooden building of two stories, used also
as a school and as a habitation of the priest, rises like a landmark
in the midst of a desert of factories, for here are the ironworks of
the Illinois Steel Trust, and the famous workshops of the Pullman
Car Company. In both of these great enterprises the number of hands
employed greatly exceeds 10,000, drawn for the most part from
Austro-Hungary. That is why this parish was formed. The population,
called into existence by these works, required the consolations of
religion, and their numerous progeny needed education and care, in an
atmosphere impregnated with smoke and alcohol.

When at last I arrived, after a long journey, I found the church
crammed with workmen and their families, all persons who earned
their daily bread by the sweat of their brow. This sympathetic crowd,
and the warmth of their reception, almost made me forget that the
congregation had gathered in an erection made of planks, more like
a barn than a place of worship.

What was my surprise at the end of my sermon when the priest
appealed to the generosity of the worshippers, and, a sheet of paper
in his hand, held a meeting of the congregation, asking them to
furnish the empty building. The altar-cloth, ornaments — everything
was subscribed with a truly Christian generosity, and if ever Providence should again take me back, I am certain that I should find
that humble parish a most flourishing centre.

At Chicago I witnessed the initiation of an American cure of souls,
with its preliminary work; at Cleveland, on the contrary, I was able
to admire the full development of one of these immigrant parishes.[3]

---

[3] St. Elizabeth's Church, Cleveland, was the first exclusively Magyar parish in
the United States. The church had been begun in 1893 by the Reverend Charles
Boehm, the pioneer Hungarian priest in the United States. Boehm sought out
Hungarian Catholics in various parts of the country and succeeded in getting

This was the first and incontestably the most important of the Hungarian communities. The number of Magyars alone exceeds 30,000. They have numerous churches, several newspapers published in their language, and many societies and clubs. I knew all this beforehand, and yet on my arrival was surprised at the importance and size of the church of the first Hungarian parish in the United States.

I had promised to pass the feast of Whitsuntide there, and, thanks to my stay of several days, I was able to understand the phenomenal growth and immense influence attained in so short a period. The Church of Cleveland, like that of Chicago, had been founded only a few years before, in a suburb far from the town. The priest arrived there alone, without either help or acquaintance, finding nothing, knowing nobody. It would have been difficult to believe that such had been the state of affairs if I had not already known something of the work and the marvels accomplished by the faithful in these new States. My reception, in which all the different associations took part, their banners unfurled, was a most touching exhibition of hospitality and affection. The church and all the galleries were crowded with worshippers, thousands of voices sang the hymns, and the ground was strewn with flowers which perfumed the air, laden with incense which mounted in silvery clouds toward the blue heavens — the priests prostrate before the altars of God, made a beautiful picture, and was quite the most edifying scene in the whole of my mission, rich though it was in heart-warming recollections. Good Father B—— may well be proud of his work, and of the results of his apostolate.

Such results, attained in the short duration of a single life, are only possible in new countries. They afford the greatest encouragement to the humblest parsons in their work. The bishops on their side give full liberty of action, so that it may vary with the necessities of the different localities, and in order that the activity of each place in their diocese may be developed to the very utmost. Thus both agent and work increase in force, and existing parishes make new ones. Gradually independent dioceses are formed, for as soon as a parish priest has more members in his congregation than it is possible

---

parishes started for them, as well as editing a Magyar prayer book and founding a Magyar newspaper. By 1907 St. Elizabeth's was attended by two priests and had a parish school with 531 pupils taught by eight Ursuline Sisters. Cleveland was one of the most important centers for Hungarian settlement, having in the *Szabadsag* one of the earliest Hungarian daily newspapers in the country. The Diocese of Cleveland had by 1940 ten Hungarian parishes of the Latin Rite and four of the Byzantine Rite. Cf. Michael J. Hynes, *History of the Diocese of Cleveland. Origin and Growth, 1847–1952* (Cleveland, 1953), pp. 256, 260, 326.

for him to know and care for, a further division is made. In Europe there are parishes of forty or fifty thousand souls. In America, on the contrary, the number rarely exceeds twelve or fourteen thousand. The dwellers in each parish form, so to speak, a large family, in which the members know one another, at least by sight, and each is known to the priest. Thus they constitute, as I have said, large families, each member contributing according to his power to the welfare of the community. This is how the success to-day recognised by the world is made possible, and why the Catholic Church in the United States has risen to her place of general respect and honour.

148. The Origins of the Catholic Church Extension Society, October 18, 1905

THE predominantly urban character of American Catholicism is strikingly illustrated by the fact that out of 3070 counties in the United States there are 819 counties — embracing an area of 757,000 square miles or about one fourth of the country — where there is no resident priest. Moreover, there are 73,000 small towns and hamlets with no priest to serve the religious needs of the Catholic people. Early in the present century Francis Clement Kelley (1870–1948), then pastor of Immaculate Conception Church, Lapeer, Michigan, became convinced of the necessity to do something to remedy this situation. The result of his efforts was the founding of the Catholic Church Extension Society which during the past fifty years has collected and dispersed to the American rural missions over $48,000,000 in providing churches, support to priests, and the facilities of religious worship in country districts. Campaigns for enlisting support have been conducted principally through the society's official organ, *Extension Magazine*, begun in 1906 and having at the present time a circulation of over 500,000 copies monthly. In the following document the society's founder, who was consecrated in October, 1924, as second Bishop of Oklahoma City, recounted the circumstances that brought the organization into existence. Source: Francis Clement Kelley, *The Bishop Jots It Down. An Autobiographical Strain on Memories* (New York: Harper & Bros., 1939), pp. 114–123.

The dream? It had been growing on me from the day when I read a letter of appeal for the Society for the Propagation of the Faith sent out by Abbé Magnien. . . . I was then too poor to help but hopeful enough to promise that some day I should. I felt as I read the Abbé's circular that the whole Church in America ought to help. It was not gratitude for what the great Society had done for the

Church of America that moved me, but the thought that we had a duty to vindicate our Catholicity in missionary action within and even beyond our borders. There was for me an effective lecture on that particular mark of the Church in the appeal of the Grand Old Man of Baltimore.[1]

Then came traveling and lecturing. I saw America, not the America of the great cities but the real America which feeds and sustains the other — the America of the small towns, villages, and countryside. In the West and South I ran into small groups of Catholics threatened with being swallowed up by indifference, pastorless people as well as churchless people. And the conviction came to me that our leaders had missed something great because they had been overwhelmed by numbers pouring out of ships into the cities. We had, I thought, been forced to neglect the minority that had gone to the little places. But these were the hope of the cities of the future, the fathers and mothers of the next and succeeding generations of city dwellers. Could we afford to lose them? I was sure we could not.

There is something substantial behind every dream no matter how fantasy may distort it. Dreams are the plays of the subconscious memory. The substantial behind mine was the Catholicity of the Church. So deep-rooted became my desire to help the rural places that I felt no discouragement would prevent me from planting a seed in soil I hoped would be fertile enough to give it strength and growth.

There came to Trinity Rectory one evening when I was there a stern, dignified, and aloof-appearing man whose name has already been mentioned. He was John Hennessy, Bishop of Wichita.[2] His bearing did not invite confidences — even conversation for that matter. But young men with dreams are not afraid. I talked of mine in his presence. He showed interest. To the Dean's astonishment he even invited me to pay him a visit if my lecturing brought me near Wichita. I thanked him for the invitation without determining to accept it. I was afraid to accept it. But when I did actually find myself near Wichita I recalled it and paid him a visit. He questioned me closely about the thing that was interesting me. I was launched into the subject of home missions before I knew it, because I was soon aware of the fact that I had a sympathetic listener. To my surprise the Bishop took

---

[1] Alphonse L. Magnien, S.S. (1837–1902), was superior of the Sulpicians in the United States from 1878 to his death. In November, 1896, he was appointed National Director of the Society for the Propagation of the Faith.

[2] John J. Hennessy (1847–1920) was consecrated for the new See of Wichita on November 30, 1888.

up the discussion when and where I left off and suggested that I should make an effort to found a Society dedicated to the work.

"What we need first of all," he said, "is financial help to put up chapels for small groups scattered here and there all over the West. Someone like you must make a study of the situation and begin the work."

When I suggested that I was too unimportant a person to do more than make the study, he answered, "For some good purpose of Divine Providence you have been forced out to see conditions from one end of the country to the other. Learn all you can about home mission societies elsewhere and write on the subject. That is the way to begin."

I did make the study but remained doubtful that I was indicated as the founder of such a work. Then something else happened, and again in Kansas. I visited Ellsworth to lecture for the high school of the town and there met the pastor, Father Arthur Luckey. What happened to me in Ellsworth was read by thousands when the appeal I felt forced to write was published in the *Ecclesiastical Review*[3] of Philadelphia and reprinted many times in pamphlet form. For years after the Church Extension was founded that appeal was known as the "Little Shanty Story.". . . [There follows the first part of the article which described the miserable shanty in which the pastor of Ellsworth lived and the equally deplorable condition of the little church.]

That Little Shanty Story founded the Catholic Church Extension Society both in the United States and Canada because it played a sympathy if not a symphony on the heartstrings of many people. In the spring of 1905 nothing was wanting for the founding of the society but a distinguished sponsor, definitely the archbishop of one of the large metropolitan sees of the United States. I wanted to go out searching for one but had no money to pay my way around. To my rescue came a group of the Knights of Columbus in Michigan and Ohio. They gave me a one hour job and paid well for it. I was invited to preach on my hobby at their summer outing at Cedar Point, Ohio, with the collection as recompense. That collection netted me about two hundred dollars. I could travel as far as that sum would carry me.

Naturally New York was my first objective. I wanted Archbishop Farley[4] to be the honorary head of the society. His refusal was kindly expressed but clearly definite. I tried Archbishop Ryan[5] of Philadelphia.

[3] "Church Extension," *American Ecclesiastical Review*, XXXII (June, 1905), 573–585.

[4] John Farley (1842–1918) became Archbishop of New York in 1902 and was made a cardinal in 1911.

[5] Patrick J. Ryan (1831–1911) was named Archbishop of Philadelphia in 1884.

His refusal, too, was kind and to it he added the saving bit of humor that was expected of the Episcopal wit of the day. But it too was definite. Archbishop Bourgade[6] of Santa Fe was willing to help but did not think himself important enough to lead. Archbishop Williams[7] of Boston was growing old. I knew that he would not consider adding burdens to the great one he already was carrying. I felt the same about Cardinal Gibbons.[8] While I was hesitating about approaching Archbishop Ireland[9] of St. Paul I learned that the "Little Shanty Story" had met with the approbation of Archbishop Quigley[10] of Chicago. Why not Chicago? It was the very gateway to the whole home mission field. At the suggestion of Archbishop Bourgade I put all my hopes on Chicago.

It was at the University of Notre Dame that I met Archbishop Quigley for the first time. He was seated on a rear veranda of the presbytery chatting with President Morrissey[11] and Dr. Zahm,[12] the scientist, when I was presented by the future president, Dr. Cavanaugh.[13] The sun was setting, but for yet a little while I had a chance to study the face of the Archbishop. It was a good face to look at because it seemed to be set in quiet repose. One had the feeling that its owner was a tranquil man who might let his heart's influence count. He had keen measuring eyes, both dark and deep; one did not know how deep they might be. . . . He was a good listener, like a judge hearing a case and anxious to follow and check the points of law involved in it, or an Oxford examiner intent on finding out from the way the student handles himself, rather than from a display of technical learning, if he really merits the honors he seeks. I got the impression that my arguments would count with the Archbishop much less than my per-

---

[6] Peter Bourgade (1845–1908) was promoted from the See of Tucson to become Archbishop of Santa Fe in 1899.

[7] John J. Williams (1822–1907) governed the See of Boston from 1866 to his death.

[8] For the rather aloof attitude assumed by Gibbons toward Kelley and the Catholic Church Extension Society in its first years, cf. John Tracy Ellis, *The Life of James Cardinal Gibbons, Archbishop of Baltimore, 1834–1921* (Milwaukee, 1952), II, 404–407.

[9] John Ireland (1838–1918) was made Archbishop of St. Paul in 1888.

[10] James E. Quigley (1854–1915) was Bishop of Buffalo, 1896–1903, and Archbishop of Chicago from 1903 until his death.

[11] Andrew Morrissey, C.S.C. (1860–1921), was eighth president of the University of Notre Dame during the years 1893–1905.

[12] John A. Zahm, C.S.C. (1851–1921), wrote extensively on the relations of religion and science.

[13] John W. Cavanaugh, C.S.C. (1870–1935), was ninth president of the University of Notre Dame during the years 1905–1919.

sonality. That worried me, for my confidence was all in the arguments. Truth was that the Archbishop knew them as well as I did, since for years he had had the same thought on the subject which in me was only developing. But what I had seen in my travels around the West and South interested him, and it was plain that he loved a story with a lesson to end it. The strong impression I got from watching and hearing him was that he was a man of wide vision. . . . I must admit that he frightened me. But I knew that here was a personality and a protector well worth winning. He proved easy to win, not because I had winning ways but because he himself had been over the ground. When the light faded and a bell called him to the chapel for the opening of the retreat he was there to attend, his mind was made up and he said so. I had found my protector and knew that if I lost him later it would not be because he failed to stick but because I failed to make good. . . .

The Catholic Church Extension Society was founded in Archbishop Quigley's house in Chicago on the 18th of October, 1905. I was given mountains to climb. I knew well what was on the other side of them but I never expected to see it. Yet I think that, through a narrow pass high upon the most desolate part of one of them, perhaps I caught a glimpse of it. Cryptic? No! I am only thinking of the advanced guard of a new generation of priests, imitating the poor man of Assisi in a modern world; or, if you will, imitating the Apostle to the Gentiles in his own good way — priests of the highways and hedges. . . .

"I can't understand you priests," said a business friend as he shook hands in farewell when I was leaving Lapeer for Chicago. "Here you are abandoning your new church and your fine new home almost the day after you got into them, to start all over again in a Chicago flat with nothing but a dream and not much of a dream at that."

A dream? The man did not know the compelling force and persistent glory of a dream. While I am now, as a bishop, committed to a dislike for dreamers, only yesterday a mother, my own sister, pouring out of her artist soul a prayer of resignation over her afflicted son, brought tears acknowledging the truth and power of a dream from my eyes. . . .

Had I been leaving for a promotion few would have thought or expressed any wonderment. But the business that has to wait for eternity to pay its dividend is another matter. Those who follow the red-gold lure of the Cross are mysterious, even to some who ought to understand.

I had a friend in Detroit, Edward H. Doyle,[14] who would have his

---

[14] Edward H. Doyle (1849–1919) was Commissioner of Banking for Michigan, 1911–1915.

joke. He was one of those who thought I was risking too much by the burning of my ships.

"Did you ever hear the definition for a promoter made by my unusual friend, Marcus Pollasky?" he asked when I called at his office in the Majestic Building to say good-by.

"Never. What is it?"

"He was on the witness stand in a court case. The examining lawyer asked his name and his business. Marcus gave his name and said that his business was that of a promoter."

"What is your definition of a promoter, Mr. Pollasky?"

"A promoter? Why, a promoter is a man who has nothing to sell and who sells it to a man who doesn't want to buy it."

I saw the point and tried to explain what my kind of promoter was and what he had to sell. My friend listened politely for awhile. Really I was only trying to give him information, not to "sell him" anything. "That will do. That will do," he interrupted. "Before you go you ought to meet my friend Marcus. He was right. But I'll buy it."

Buy it expensively he did. In him I landed my first big fish. It weighed ten thousand dollars.

The society stayed only one year in Lapeer. Then it was moved to Chicago and I had to go with it. The Bishop of Detroit[15] granted me the usual *Exeat* transferring me to the archdiocese of Chicago. I must admit that he seemed to take his loss in a spirit of resignation.

149. Chief Justice White's Decisions in Regard to Divorce, April 12, 1906, and to the Selective Draft Law, January 7, 1918

EDWARD DOUGLAS WHITE (1845–1921) was a member of the Supreme Court of the United States for twenty-seven years, having been appointed in 1894 and promoted to the rank of chief justice in 1910. During his service on the bench White wrote opinions in over 700 cases, but it is difficult to characterize his decisions since at times he sided with the so-called liberals and again showed a conservative interpretation of the law. He was the second southern Catholic Democrat to be chief justice, Roger Brooke Taney having held the office from 1836–1864. White was educated at Mount Saint Mary's College, Emmitsburg, and Georgetown College. Two of his more notable opinions are given below. In *Haddock* v. *Haddock* of April 12, 1906, he spoke for a court divided 5–4 in a divorce suit that remained the ruling and controlling decision for a quarter century until expressly overruled in *Williams* v. *North Carolina* in December, 1942,

[15] John S. Foley (1833–1918) became Bishop of Detroit in 1888

which recognized the validity of Nevada divorces as applying to persons living in other states. The Haddocks had originally been domiciled in New York, but the husband had left that state, taken up residence in Connecticut, and had there obtained a divorce by service upon his wife. The wife later sued for divorce in New York and was informed of the earlier action of her husband which would have prevented her from securing her rights to his estate, alimony, etc. The case came before the Supreme Court under the constitutional provision that one state is obliged to give full faith and credit to the public acts of every other state. In the second decision of White, handed down on January 7, 1918, for a unanimous court the constitutionality of the Selective Draft Law of May, 1917, enacted to augment the armed forces of the United States during World War I was upheld. An item of personal interest in the latter case was that White had himself left Georgetown college unofficially at the age of fifteen to enlist as a soldier in a Confederate regiment then forming in his native Louisiana. Source: *Haddock* v. *Haddock*, 201 U. S. 562 (pp. 575–576); *Arver* v. *United States; Grahl* v. *United States; Otto Wangerin* v. *United States; Walter Wangerin* v. *United States; Kramer* v. *United States; Graubard* v. *United States*, 245 U. S. 366 (pp. 377–378, 390).

HADDOCK vs. HADDOCK

No one denies that the States, at the time of the adoption of the Constitution, possessed full power over the subject of marriage and divorce. No one, moreover, can deny that, prior to the adoption of the Constitution, the extent to which the States would recognize a divorce obtained in a foreign jurisdiction depended upon their conceptions of duty and comity. Besides, it must be conceded that the Constitution delegated no authority to the Government of the United States on the subject of marriage and divorce. Yet, if the proposition be maintained, it would follow that the destruction of the power of the States over the dissolution of marriage, as to their own citizens, would be brought about by the operation of the full faith and credit clause of the Constitution. That is to say, it would come to pass that, although the Constitution of the United States does not interfere with the authority of the States over marriage, nevertheless the full faith and credit clause of that instrument destroyed the authority of the States over the marriage relation. And as the Government of the United States has no delegated authority on the subject, that Government would be powerless to prevent the evil thus brought about by the full faith and credit clause. Thus neither the States nor the National Government would be able to exert that authority over the marriage tie possessed by every other civilized government. Yet more remarkable would be such result when it is borne in mind that, when the Constitution was adopted, nowhere, either in the mother country or on the continent of Europe, either in adjudged cases or in the treatises of authoritative writers, had the theory ever been upheld or been taught or even suggested that one government, solely because of the domicile within its borders of one of the parties to a marriage, had authority, without the actual or constructive presence of the other, to exert its authority by a dissolution of the marriage tie, which exertion of power it would be the duty of other States to respect as to those subject to their jurisdiction. . . . As the husband, after wrongfully abandoning the wife in New York, never established a matrimonial domicile in Connecticut, it cannot be said that he took with him the marital relation from which he fled to Connecticut. Conceding, however, that he took with him to Connecticut so much of the marital relation as concerned his individual status, it cannot in reason be said that he did not leave in New York so much of the relation as pertained to the status of the wife. From any point of view, then . . . if the marriage relation be treated as the *res,* it follows that it was divisible, and therefore there was a *res* in the State of New York and one in the State of Connecticut. Thus considered, it is clear that the power of one State did not extend to affecting the thing situated in another State.

SELECTIVE DRAFT LAW CASES

As the mind cannot conceive an army without the men to compose it, on the face of the Constitution the objection that it does not give power to provide for such men would seem to be too frivolous for further notice. It is said, however, that since under the Constitution as originally framed state citizenship was primary and United States citizenship but derivative and dependent thereon, therefore the power conferred upon Congress to raise armies was only coterminous with United States citizenship and could not be exerted so as to cause that citizenship to lose its dependent character and dominate state citizenship. But the proposition simply denies to Congress the power to raise armies which the Constitution gives. That power by the very terms of the Constitution, being delegated, is supreme. Article VI. In truth the contention simply assails the wisdom of the framers of the Constitution in conferring authority on Congress and in not retaining it as it was under the Confederation in the several States. Further it is said, the right to provide is not denied by calling for volunteer enlistments, but it does not and cannot include the power to exact enforced military duty by the citizen. This however but challenges the existence of all power, for a governmental power which has no sanction to it and which therefore can only be exercised provided the citizen consents to its exertion is in no substantial sense a power. It is argued, however, that although this is abstractly true, it is not concretely so because as compelled military service is repugnant to a free government and in conflict with all the great guarantees of the Constitution as to individual liberty, it must be assumed that the authority to raise armies was intended to be limited to the right to call an army into existence counting alone upon the willingness of the citizen to do his duty in time of public need, that is, in time of war. But the premise of this proposition is so devoid of foundation that it leaves not even a shadow of ground upon which to base the conclusion. Let us see if this is not at once demonstrable. It may not be doubted that the very conception of a just government and its duty to the citizen includes the reciprocal obligation of the citizen to render military service in case of need and the right to compel it. Vattel, Law of Nations, Book III, c. 1 & 2. To do more than state the proposition is absolutely unnecessary in view of the practical illustration afforded by the almost universal legislation to that effect now in force. . . .

Finally, as we are unable to conceive upon what theory the exaction by government from the citizen of the performance of his supreme and noble duty of contributing to the defense of the rights and honor of the nation, as the result of a war declared by the great representative body of the people, can be said to be the imposition of involuntary servitude in violation of the prohibitions of the Thirteenth Amendment, we are constrained to the conclusion that the contention to that effect is refuted by its mere statement.

150. Louise Imogen Guiney on a Preference for Living in England, April, 1907

AMONG the relatively few American Catholics of literary fame was Louise Imogen Guiney (1861–1920). Two years before she graduated from Elmhurst, the Convent of the Sacred Heart in Providence, her Irish-born father, Patrick Robert Guiney, who had had a gallant career in the Civil War, died rather dramatically in a Boston street in March, 1877. Speaking of this episode in connection with the Boston resentment of the Irish, Van Wyck Brooks, who classes Miss Guiney among "The Epigoni," remarked that in her and John Boyle O'Reilly the Bostonians found compensations. He said: "Miss Guiney's spirit rode forward in her father's stirrups. None of this was lost upon the city of the Puritans. The Bostonians knew a soldier, as they knew a poet. . . . Heaven only knew what future gifts the conquerors had in store for a later New England; and the Yankees were not ungrateful to them" (*New England: Indian Summer, 1865–1915* [New York, 1940], pp. 412–413). Although by the late century Miss Guiney had gained fame and acceptance in literary circles, on two trips to England she had lost her heart to that country and in 1901 she went to live permanently in Oxford. In this she shared the sentiment of other American literary figures and artists like Henry James, James Whistler, Edith Wharton, and George P. A. Healy who lived much of their lives abroad. Among her best essays was *A Little English Gallery* (1894) and her best poems were gathered together in *Happy Ending* (1909). But American readers will, perhaps, find more interesting an unsigned essay of 1907, the identity of which was made known by Miss Guiney's biographer, E. M. Tenison, in a chapter entitled, "An American View of England," *Louise Imogen Guiney* (London, 1923), pp. 215–225. Source: "On A Preference for Living in England," *Atlantic Monthly*, XCXIX (April, 1907), 569–572.

When men pitch their life-tents far away, they have manifold causes and reasons: some sound, some questionable, some wholly weak and unworthy. It is one thing feloniously to cast off one's derivation, nurture, and responsibilities; and quite another thing to brave homesickness in order to outwit and escape too difficult outward conditions. It is the pride of absence to remember Argos forever, to rest upon its garnered glories, and brooding upon its future with thoughtful affection, to

> lean and hearken after it
> And grow erect as that comes home.

The purpose of this paper is to hold a brief not so much for those who go, as for those who cannot stay. European passports, for instance, must be cheerfully furnished to our artist fraternity. With us, the historical sense, the scholastic mind, the instinct for color and form, must bring, in time, their own obsession. Whoever has a rage for origin, a lust for things at first-hand, is foredoomed to chafe at a civilization which dates from this morning, and spends its energies on tasks far other than the effort to see life steadily and see it whole. There is something rational, surely, in an attraction which has already drained the United States of so much genius, literary and artistic; which has resulted in forming so many wise, devoted, and detached critics to whip us up to our ideals, and remind us of our sins.

But the fellow-citizen, of all others, who must have the right of way over the sea, is the wounded man, the tired man, the sufferer from *Hustlerium Tremens sive Americanitis*. Let that true lover of the Republic fear not, but sink his foot in alien turf for the most defensible reason in life; like Denham's hero, unblamed,

If here he frets, he finds at Rome,
At Paris, or Madrid, his home.

He has "gone to be a fairy," not for ambition, not for excitement, nor for vogue; but for the velvety feel of the Past under foot, like moss of the forest floor to a barefooted child; or for the hardly less gentle feel of the Present, whence noise and worry seem miraculously to have vanished away. Well for him, when at last, from his own foolish impetus, as well as from the epic newness, and startling developments, and too eager gynaccocracy of the States, he has fled into transmarine twilight, and the ever noble State of Suspended Animation!

An American living on the Continent suggests, somehow, a career of genius or of crime. An American in England, on the other hand, is a perfect working hypothesis. Scotland, Wales, Ireland (and Ireland especially), are bristling with ideas, as with so many spiritual burs and mosquitoes. But England, with her queer and meek climate, presents no such intimidations to the weary who would rest there. She is a heaven for retired and non-rheumatic racers, who are set only upon a smoke and a sleep. The quality of the Past and of the Peace proffered is incomparably the best, for these debased reasons: that the past is the very one, next his own, about which the average educated American knows most; and peace is certainly promoted, in the adult breast at least, when no necessity exists for the full dress of a foreign language. That ghostly encounter with "chaunt" or "gulph," in columns yet wet from the printing-press, that strange sea-change of what was a "spool of cotton" into a "reel of thread," — these and their like are pleasing titillations, and to the truly lazy mind are beatific substitutes for the diplomacies of Latin idiom, and the strangling vocabulary of the Fatherland.

Oh, the grave charm of rural England! Every hedgerow seems to imply a racial age-long deliberate choice of simplicity and sincerity over all which would dim them or drive them away. None can know this people at home well enough to poke fun at them, without reverencing them all the while: their moral etiquette is so sure, their standards so disinterested. Outside tainted London, loud success is accorded little preëminence. All other things being equal, the rich stranger, not the poor one, is put on his social probation. There is extraordinary trustfulness in business relations; fabrics are genuine; street noises come under legislation; a fare in any conveyance (except where Americans are in control) means a seat; the children are wholesomely childish, and the old fearlessly aged; the decorum and honor of life, excluding sensationalism, rule the national imagination. Here are some rather large towns (to say nothing of the country districts) which are no more agitating than a dove's note or a junket. You cannot walk through them for three minutes in any direction without seeing something famous and ancient and uniquely beautiful; nor beyond them, without meeting a landscape which is almost mystically dreamy. There is never, so far as one can make out, any fickle fashion in clothes, any fad in amusements. There is no highway army of poles and wires; no appreciable slush or drifts or icicles; no continuous agony of heat; no mosquitoes; no nerves! Work is lonely and unhurried, and recreation reasonable and calm. One can the better endure the scarcity of wild wood, moor, and river, when daily conventional pleasuring, even at its worst, is so near to Nature. The god of Tea is propitiated on a greensward, in the company of gentle dames who all say "Quite so!" and mannerly little girls with their mannerly dogs; "a summer shower," as Hazlitt says, "is dropping manna on your head, and an old crazy hand-organ is playing 'Robin Adair'" on the other side of the blessed ivied garden wall. This is to loaf and to reign.

You know now that you will never long to get anywhere in particular, or strain after anything except salvation. You set up for a smug, rich, intellectual Pharisee, with immaterial horizons which never were, nor can be, in the West. Time and eternity are pretty nearly one in the moist amethyst-colored air. You realize fully that the ozone is gone out of it, and that the sad heart of the earth beneath has bled for long. But you also realize that you are acquiring from contact with these an almost sportive sense of the unseen and the supernatural, and a sense which unravels essence from accident, true from plausible, lasting from uncertain, innocent from profane. Very grateful some outlanders are for this strange, painless stretching of their spirits. They have done with the Puritans. They have been kidnapped and catholicized. Small wonder if they feel that they have come home, body and soul, in coming near to the Simple Life and the Quiet Mind: not, mind you, to mere talk of these healthful and beatific things. Not that our happier natures in the United States have not at all times attained to them. But their exemption from the hurly-burly is a bought one: you do not have to buy it in England. It commends itself to the indigent, for it is a flowing fountain in the streets.

Our imaginary friend Fugacius, hungry for rest, may attain even that, and a better thing — anonymity. He may possibly be tired of keeping awake, of toeing the mark, of showing interest, and wearing an intelligent expression. He may have been martyred, more or less, by the Public Eye; but in England, if anywhere, he may indulge to the full a life-long passion for silence and seclusion. He will not be asked by an interviewer at 4 A.M., and at the point of the moral bayonet, for his impressions concerning problems fiscal or forensic. If he is understood to have exhibited in the Salon, or to have published a sonnet, not a living British creature will think any the better of him for it. Mention was made, a moment ago, of a garden wall: ubiquitous and beloved symbol; Conscious that it is stone, ten feet high, and ninety-one feet in circumference, the American memory runs across, in the wake of ships, to the exquisite suburban streets where the graceful houses, with their wooden gables and verandas, their lilacs and syringas, and wide graveled paths, lie open to one another and to the road. An American feels sure, of a sudden, that the English inclosure gives a freedom that he never knew, and that even a king, in such a fastness, could defy the demon of publicity. Too much praise cannot be given to the universal inviolable respect for privacy in the land of the garden wall. The human ear, even in a drawing-room, is as holy as any mediaeval ambry. There have been two celebrated instances, in our own generation, where real names of English writers, objects of curiosity to the whole reading world, were kept from it through many years, and up to the deaths of the authors, although the secret of identification had been quite casually shared, for long, by scores of discreet friends. Such instances commend the conditions (how unlike ours!) which make them possible. Indeed, they arouse enthusiasm in any natural enemy of newspaper headlines.

A wit once remarked that the English love Americans but not America, and that the Americans love England, but not the English. The truth of this discerning remark is obvious, whatever the explanation of it may be. But every day one hears some anecdote or other which makes one feel that shell and snail, at least with them, are inseparable: that an Englishman is just what he is, because England is just what she is. Here is one slight illustration of the point. During the August of 1906 a party of three Americans went north from Euston Station in London. The railway porter put them aboard the train, after his wont, observing, as it would appear, the name marking their luggage. The gentleman of the party asked the porter whether he should have to change carriages before reaching his destination; the porter answered in the negative, the door was slammed to, and the day-long journey began. Hours later, at a station, as the train slowed up, an inspector came along the corridor, repeating in a loud voice a name which the travelers recognized as their own. He held a telegram in his hand. This had been sent to him direct, asking him to find aboard a certain train Mr. ——, bound for ——, and to tell him that he had been misinformed and that he must make a change at —— Junction. Now that London porter must have known that the Americans were mere sightseeing strangers, that he would never see them or hear of them again, and that the odds were that they would inquire anew about changing on the journey, and find their way to —— as scheduled, or, for that matter, not lose their wits or lives if they did not: in fact, there was every inducement to make him wash his hands of them. Yet it was he who sent the wire, taking all that thoughtful trouble to set his blunder right. Could such a thing have happened under ordinary circumstances in our country? We have heroisms on every side; but we are too busy for contritions. Exercise of scrupulous conscience in official matters is precisely England and the English; the little fortuitous error, the abundant reparation, are not exceptional and individual, but as typical as they can possibly be. Here is a people which fumbles, which drops many stitches, which has its multiform inefficiencies. But it may boast truly that a passion for duty is in its very marrow; it will not in the end consciously go forward with unrepented wrong in its bosom. Is it any wonder if some children of a more heedless and elliptical nation, harassed by rude corporations and their units, think it pleasant to dwell among the million blood-relatives of that unknown adored railway porter? For so soothing a privilege, they will even endure the immemorial cabbage, the sacred Brussels sprouts of Great Britain and Ireland, for three hundred and sixty-five days of the gastronomical year.

In England, notably in middle England, flourishes the most unbelievable and ubiquitous density of mind. It is there indeed; and it is disciplinary; it is funny, it is maddening. Does it dash your joy, in some village of heavenly picturesqueness, to find (as you are always finding!) that the parson is a stock, and the laundress a stone? Well, never ultimately; for the stocks and stones are excellent to live with and have staying qualities. The secret of happiness for us, under their roof, as elsewhere, is the spirit of conformity and compromise. The English ethnological key seems to be D minor, and the household metronome to be set at *Adagio Marcato;* until you have tried the tune of Yankee Doodle in that unexpected key, and to that revolutionizing measure, you can have no idea of its moving effectiveness, and its powers of accommodation. The expatriate, if any one, should get a right perspective, and an unconfused sense of values. He knows that for the joy of life; for zest thorough and permeating; for organization and invention; for autumn forest pageantry in its perfection; for idyllic things to eat, and the magical cooking of the same; for the prevalence of personal and domestic taste; for true touchstones of human worth and worthlessness; for exquisite chivalry in the relations between men and women, — he knows that for these he must cross the bounding main: he must go home. But dear as these things are, deeply as these things (especially the last) are respected and lamented by all who knew them, one can do without them for a while. The Past, and Peace, are dearer yet. The faction which stays on and on, in a land not quite foreign, is agreed quite passionately about that.

151. Mother Katharine Drexel Drafts the Constitutions of Her Congregation, May 25, 1907

WHEN the history of twentieth-century Catholicism in the United States is finally written there will be no more honored name than that of Mother Katharine Drexel (1858–1955). Granddaughter of Francis M. Drexel (1792–1863), the Austrian-born immigrant who came to Philadelphia in 1817 and in 1838 opened a brokerage office that led in time to the world famous banking house of Drexel & Company, Katharine and her two sisters became the heiresses of an immense fortune upon the death of their father in 1885. Having been the recipient of the finest type of religious training from her pious father and step-mother, Katharine Drexel was deeply impressed by the appeal of the bishops of the Third Plenary Council in 1884 for help to the Indian and Negro missions. In a private audience of Leo XIII in January, 1887, she spoke of this interest, whereupon the pontiff was prompted to ask, "Why not become a missionary yourself, my child?" That settled Miss Drexel's vocation for life. Guided by James O'Connor (1832–1890), first Bishop of Omaha, who as the pastor of Homesburg, Pennsylvania, had known the Drexel family very well, she made her novitiate with the Sisters of Mercy in Pittsburgh and in February, 1891, she took the veil and with thirteen other women launched the Sisters of the Blessed Sacrament for Indians and Colored People. Even before her entry into the religious life Miss Drexel had given a million dollars to the missions for these two races, and all during the next sixty-four years she continued to pour her vast wealth into the cause by building dozens of churches, chapels, schools, and other missionary buildings. At Mother Katharine's death the community numbered 511 professed religious stationed in fifty-one houses located in twenty-one states and the District of Columbia. The sisters staff sixty-two schools, including forty-nine elementary, twelve high schools, and the only Catholic Negro university in the country, Xavier University of New Orleans, founded in 1925, and having a faculty of 115 with over 1100 men and women students. Not only did Mother Katharine use all of her tremendous income for the advancement of the Catholic faith among the American Indians and Negroes, but she and her congregation have likewise given generously to missions for these races in Alaska, Canada, Africa, and the British possessions. Mother Katharine herself drew up the first draft of the constitutions of her community after it had been in existence for sixteen years, and the following document — the original written in her own hand — embodied a rough outline of her aims and objectives. The decree of final approbation for the sisters' rule was granted by the Holy See in May, 1913. Source: Archives of St. Elizabeth's Convent, Cornwells Heights, Pennsylvania, Constitutions of the Sisters of the Blessed Sacrament for Indians and Colored People (photostat).

Concerning the Nature of the Congregation & the Manner of Living in the same.

Chapter I

Nature & Object of the Congregation.

1. The primary object which the Sisters of this religious Congregation purpose to themselves is their own personal sanctification.

2. The secondary & special object of the members of the Congregation is to apply themselves zealously to the service of Our Lord in the Blessed Sacrament by endeavoring to lead the Indian & Colored Races to the knowledge & love of God, & so make of them living temples of Our Lord's Divinity.

Chapter II

The Means of Carrying out the Object.

3. The principal means by which the Sisters of the Blessed Sacrament for Indians & Colored People are to procure their own perfection & the education, sanctification & salvation of the Indian & Colored Races are the following: —

(1 The faithful observance of the three simple vows of Poverty, Chastity & Obedience according to the approved Constitutions of the Congregation, & the faithful observance of these same Constitutions.

(2 A complete consecration of themselves, body & soul, to the service of their Eucharistic Lord, by a special devotion to the Blessed Sacrament, so that through Him they may sanctify in an especial manner their two-fold apostolate of prayer & work as set forth in these Constitutions.

(3 Frequent prayer, especially at the Holy Sacrifice of the Mass & at Holy Communion, to draw down upon themselves & upon the souls of the Indian & Colored the graces that will save them.

(4 As a further means of accomplishing this work, the members of this Congregation are according to circumstances, [to] undertake

    1) To instruct the Indian & Colored Races in religious & other

useful knowledge according to their needs & capacities;
2) To care for their orphans & spiritually or corporally destitute children;
3) To attend to their sick by visiting them in their homes, or by the conducting of hospitals;
4) To visit their homes in order to look after their spiritual & temporal welfare;
5) To visit & instruct Indian & Colored inmates of prisons;
6) To shelter distressed & deserving women of these Races;
7) To aid in as far as they are able needy priests, religious communities & other reliable persons engaged in missionary work among the Indian & Colored Races.

152. The Launching of the Catholic Foreign Mission Society of America (Maryknoll), March 25, 1911

ON JUNE 29, 1908, the constitution *Sapienti consilio* of Pope Pius X removed the Church of the United States from the jurisdiction of the Congregation de Propaganda Fide and thus officially declared that its missionary status was at an end. Long before this date, however, the American Church had attained a position of strength in both numbers and resources and, in fact, by 1910 there were an estimated 16,363,000 Catholics in the country. Throughout the nineteenth century American Catholics had done relatively little for the foreign missions, although in 1904 their monetary contributions passed the $100,000 mark and rose steadily in the years thereafter. As yet, however, no full-fledged effort had been made to enlist American personnel for the foreign-mission field. In September, 1910, two American priests, James Anthony Walsh and Thomas Frederick Price, who had long thought and planned for this cause met at the International Eucharistic Congress in Montreal, and from that meeting there stemmed the founding of the first distinctly American Catholic foreign-mission society. Walsh and Price secured the sponsorship of Cardinal Gibbons and the Apostolic Delegate, and at the annual meeting of the archbishops of the United States on April 27, 1911, at the Catholic University of America approval was given for the opening of a seminary for this purpose. Maryknoll, as it is popularly known, began modestly in 1911 and today the society numbers over 600 priests, more than 100 brothers, and nearly 750 students studying for either the priesthood or brotherhood in eight training centers. Other American religious orders and congregations meanwhile increased their participation in the work and by December, 1953, there was a total of 4755 American priests, brothers, and sisters serving abroad in mission stations all over the world. Source: Archives of Maryknoll Seminary, copy.

To the Most Reverend Archbishops of the United States:

VENERABLE BRETHREN:

At the request of His Excellency, the Apostolic Delegate,[1] I submit to your consideration a plan to establish an American Foreign Mission Seminary.

That such a Seminary is needed, and urgently, seems daily more evident. The prestige .of our country has become wide-spread; and Protestants, especially in the Far East, are profiting by it, to the positive hindrance of Catholic missioners. I understand that even the educated classes in China, misled by the almost complete absence of American Catholic priests, believe that the Church of Rome has no standing in America.[2]

Conscious that we are still short of priests in many dioceses, I would cite the words of Cardinal Manning referring to the foundation of Mill Hill:

It is quite true that we have need of men and means at home; and it is BECAUSE we have need of more men and more means, by a great deal, than we as yet possess, that I am convinced we ought to send both men and means abroad. . . . If we desire to find the surest way to multiply immensely our own material means for works at home, it is by not limiting the expansion of Charity and by not paralyzing the zeal of self-denial.[3]

The priests of the United States number more than 17,000 but I am informed that there are hardly sixteen on the foreign missions. This fact recalls a warning which the late Cardinal Vaughan gave in a kindly and brotherly letter addressed to me twenty-two years ago, urging us American Catholics not to delay participation in foreign missions, LEST OUR OWN FAITH SHOULD SUFFER.[4]

---

[1] Diomede Falconio, O.F.M. (1842–1917), was the third Apostolic Delegate to the United States, having served from 1902 to late in the year 1911.

[2] Between 1881–1888 five Franciscans had gone to China from the United States but only one of them was a native-born American; there were also two American-born Sisters of Charity in China in the late years of the nineteenth century.

[3] Gibbons took the Manning quotation from a letter he had received from Herbert Vaughan (1832–1903), Bishop of Salford and after 1892 Archbishop of Westminster. Vaughan's letter dated Mill Hill, October 28, 1889, used the occasion of the centennial of the American hierarchy to urge upon the Catholics of the United States participation in the foreign missions of the Church. "A Challenge to the American Church on Its One Hundredth Birthday," *Catholic Historical Review*, XXX (October, 1944), 297.

[4] The reference here was to the letter noted above, the full text of which is printed *op. cit.*, pp. 290–298.

We must confess that as a Catholic body we have only begun, while our Protestant fellow-countrymen have passed the century mark in foreign mission work and are represented today in the heathen world by some thousands of missioners, who are backed by yearly contributions running up into the millions.

A seminary, such as that contemplated, if established with the goodwill of the entire American Hierarchy, can hardly fail to draw, emphatically, the attention of American Catholics.

"It is time," to use the words of the Apostolic Delegate, "that the American Church should begin to move in this direction."

With pleasure, therefore, acting on His Excellency's request, I submit the following outline of the plan, secured after conference with those immediately interested:

It is proposed to establish an American Foreign Mission Seminary for the training of secular priests.

This Seminary, like those of Paris, London (Mill Hill), Milan,[5] et al., would necessarily be independent of any diocese, and directly under Propaganda, which would control its status, rules, etc., and apportion its fields of labor.

It would be national in its character, organized and sustained by priests of the United States, guided, of course, by the best traditions of similar institutions abroad. It would appeal to young men reared in this country.

It is proposed to begin the work on a small scale, near some established house of Catholic philosophy and theology. It would seek its PERMANENT home, well removed from the heart of city life, gradually securing its own professors, and developing an exclusively apostolic atmosphere. No definite location is suggested, although a preference has been expressed by the organizers for a center reasonably convenient to the more populous Catholic zones and, if possible,

---

[5] The French Society for Foreign Missions was founded in 1658 and the famous seminary of the society was opened in Paris in 1663. In July, 1850, the hierarchy of Lombardy, at the suggestion of Pius IX, founded the Pontifical Institute of SS. Peter and Paul and SS. Ambrose and Charles for the Foreign Missions. The headquarters of the institute were established in Milan in June, 1851. St. Joseph's College opened in March, 1866, in Mill Hill, a suburb of London, with Herbert Vaughan as the founder and first president. The first missionary field assigned to the Mill Hill Fathers by the Holy See was the apostolate to the American Negroes. Four of the members of the community began their original American foundation at St. Francis Xavier Church, Baltimore, late in 1871.

not too far removed from those states in which a knowledge of foreign missions has already been cultivated.[6]

It is expected that Preparatory Colleges will be needed, to serve later as feeders to the Seminary.

Two priests are immediately concerned in this undertaking, to which they are willing to devote their lives, — Rev. James Anthony Walsh of Boston and Rev. Thomas F. Price of North Carolina.

Fr. Walsh is a priest of the Boston Archdiocese.[7] He was ordained in 1892, and the late revered Archbishop Williams appointed him, more than eight years ago, Diocesan Director for the Propagation of the Faith. Under His Grace, Archbishop O'Connell, Fr. Walsh has been confirmed in this position, which he still holds. He also directs the Catholic Foreign Mission Bureau, editing THE FIELD AFAR and issuing other publications bearing on the subject of foreign missions.

Fr. Price has spent twenty-five years in difficult mission work. He is the Superior of the Apostolate of Secular Priests of North Carolina and editor of the magazine, TRUTH.[8]

His Excellency, the Apostolic Delegate, has advised that these two priests, having secured the encouragement of the Hierarchy, shall, with the permission of their Bishops, visit without delay the most important foreign mission Seminaries and apply in person to Rome for the authorization necessary to start.

Returned with proper credentials, they would aim to carry out, with the approval of the individual Bishops, the following plan:

a) To secure spiritual aid, asking prayers and Communions from seminaries, religious houses of men and women, institutions, etc., etc.

---

[6] In December, 1911, the Maryknoll community settled temporarily at Hawthorne, New York, and in September, 1912, they moved to a location near Ossining on the Hudson where the seminary opened that month with six students and five priests as teachers. There were also three aspirants for the Maryknoll Brothers, and nearby eight women formed the nucleus from which the Maryknoll Sisters would later take their rise.

[7] James Anthony Walsh (1867–1936) was cofounder of Maryknoll and first superior-general of the society until his death. He was consecrated titular Bishop of Syene on June 29, 1933.

[8] Thomas Frederick Price (1860–1919), cofounder of Maryknoll, headed the first group of Maryknoll missionaries to China in September, 1918. He died at Hong Kong on September 12, 1919.

b) To spread a knowledge of the missions, by means of conference and illustrated talks and by an output of mission literature.

c) To seek material support, chiefly by increasing the subscription list of THE FIELD AFAR, which has already a wide circle of interested and generous readers among the clergy and laity.

It is my purpose to ask the Most Reverend Archbishops at our next meeting:

1. If they will commend the proposed idea.
2. In the event of their favorable consideration, if they will fix, or at least suggest, one or more desirable locations from which a choice might be made, both for a provisional and for a permanent Seminary.

I would, therefore, ask the Most Reverend Archbishops to discuss with their suffragans this proposed schema, that the views and suggestions of all the Bishops of the country may be obtained and a common understanding arrived at, and our common desire and the united commendation of the Hierarchy be made known to Rome and to the Catholic body of the United States.

Faithfully yours in Christ,
J. Card. Gibbons

Feast of the Annunciation [March 25], 1911.

153. Thomas Fortune Ryan Explains His Most Striking Financial Transaction, August, 1913

ON THE day after the death of Thomas Fortune Ryan (1851–1928) the New York *Times* of November 24 stated, "The career of Thomas Fortune Ryan is as good an example as any in American history of the possibilities that this country offers to a poor, uneducated boy." It was altogether true, for he had been orphaned at an early age with no means of support and had worked as an errand boy in a grocery store in Baltimore and later as a messenger in a brokerage firm in Wall Street. But the contest over the New York street railways gave Ryan his chance and after 1883 he rose rapidly through the financing of the street railways, the American Tobacco Company, and the gold, diamond, and copper mines of the Belgian Congo. When he died his fortune was variously estimated to total from 100 to 500 million dollars. His most unusual financial deal — described in the document that follows — was his purchase in June, 1905, of the controlling block of shares in the Equitable Life Assurance Company. In doing this he stated that he had acted solely in the public interest in order to put the finances of the company in a sound condition, set up a trust to manage it, and then personally had withdrawn from the business. Ryan was generous in his dona-

tions to various Catholic causes, normally given through his first wife, and among the institutions that benefited most were the Cathedral of the Sacred Heart in Richmond, Virginia, his home state, and the Church of St. Jean Baptiste in New York from which he was buried. He was prominent in the Democratic Party and excited the ire of men like William Jennings Bryan who suspected him of wielding a sinister sort of influence by reason of his money. Because he was associated in the financial world with names like Morgan, Whitney, Harriman, etc., the New York *Times* editorial of November 24, 1928, spoke of Ryan as "the sole survivor" of a group of New York financiers "who posed for the first composite picture of 'Big Business.' "
Source: Thomas F. Ryan, "Why I Brought the Equitable," *North American Review*, CXCVIII (August, 1913), 161–169.

In spite of the many explanations that have been made both by me and on my behalf about the purchase of the shares of the Equitable Life Assurance Society in June, 1905, the question that has since been asked me oftener than any other has related to that particular act. As the term of the trust then created has expired, and, as I no longer bear any relation to the property, it seems to me that I may, perhaps, be justified in giving a somewhat more detailed account of my ownership of it and my reasons for buying it.

No more serious quarrel has disturbed business for a generation than that which rose out of conditions that became known as existing in the Equitable early in 1905. Revelations of one kind or another then began to appear, so that it was for weeks the question upon which newspapers were expected to make a display each day. To outward seeming, this quarrel came out of a clear sky, but as in similar cases, events showed that it had been in preparation for years, and that predictions had long been freely made that some kind of storm was brewing.

It will not be necessary, for the purpose I have in mind, to enter into the details as to the clashing individualities, the many and strong jealousies which combined to foment the trouble. It did not come, however, as the result of machinations by the great financial houses of the Street. In reality, it had only a slight relation to what is familiarly known as Wall Street. In each of the three large life insurance companies which had become a marvel of the time, both as business organizations and as providing the machinery for savings, there were some officials who became jealous either of each other or of those in like positions in rival companies; in other words, it was a fierce incriminating quarrel between insiders and those of the smaller and less responsible order. It was almost wholly factional — and the facts fixing this were fully brought forth by the examination of the counsel for the Armstrong Committee, Mr. Charles E. Hughes, later Governor of New York, and now an associate justice of the United States Supreme Court.[1]

It would be as difficult to exaggerate the intensity of this quarrel as it would be to measure its effect upon business. For a time, while a thousand groundless reports were set in motion, the impression was given to the public that the management of great fiduciary institutions, not only of life insurance companies, but of all the corporations or companies or individuals which carried on great business operations, was rotten to the core.

I had taken no part in the management of any insurance company, and had no official relations with them. I was interested in insurance, as I had been from my entrance into business life, but it was as a policyholder, a student and admirer of the development of agencies which had had such a rapid growth and which, at the same time, had so commended themselves to the country as to command public confidence and make their way in almost every country in the world as models of what such institutions should be. . . .

I could but note, with serious and growing concern, the unseemly contest, the bitterness of which was daily emphasized, and also the indifference to public interest which was manifested by many of the men who, as directors or officials, ought to have been the first to come to the rescue. The public good seemed to be almost entirely forgotten in the desire of most of those on the inside and many others on the outside to take advantage of any mistake that might be made by their opponents, and that their only idea was to make these quarrels serve their own purposes.

In spite of these facts I did not, in the beginning of the contest, feel myself called upon either to throw myself into the breach or to make any attempt to use what resources I might command for composing the trouble. For some time it did not seem possible to me that responsible men would permit really serious conditions to develop, and as I held an entirely independent position, it did not appeal to me as lying within the power of an individual so situated to intervene; but, as the contest became more and more bitter, and as the contestants showed, increasingly, a determination to consider themselves only, thus failing to realize their obligations to the community, the conviction forced itself upon me, that, if others did not come to the

[1] Charles Evans Hughes (1862–1948) was appointed an associate justice in 1910 and served as Chief Justice of the United States from 1930 until his retirement in 1941.

rescue, the task, great as it was, might not be beyond my powers. In thinking of this I did not fail to realize what it meant in sacrifice of resources, in risk to fortune and reputation, in misunderstanding and abuse, nor in any of the other penalties that would naturally follow such an act.

But the more I thought of the matter, the clearer it seemed to me that perhaps I might never have a better opportunity to perform a public service than by averting panic and restoring confidence. Although I had no technical knowledge of insurance, it appeared to me plain that if the institutions built up by genius and experience, founded upon the confidence of many millions of saving, prudent individuals, handling together fabulous sums each year, were to be torn to pieces by passion and faction, then our whole scheme of business, whether it related to transportation, banking, manufacturing or mining, would receive a shock from which it would recover only after many years of loss and suffering.

In many respects, so far as I was concerned, the crisis came at an important period of my life. I had been engaged for many years in organizing and carrying on, so far as my powers and resources permitted, large business schemes and enterprises. They had taken all my energies and had left me practically no time for doing those things which it seemed to me more and more incumbent upon every man to do, at some time, if he has been the recipient of anything like an average share of prosperity. I felt that a man's success in this country was to be judged mainly by what he did, and the more I thought of it the more I was convinced that this was something worth doing.

Moreover, I had reached a time of life and a position in the business world which led me to contemplate retirement from its grinding activities. I had long had in mind many things that I wanted to do, and not one of them had borne any relation to a desire to make more money or to add to the fortune I had already accumulated. It occurred to me that I might make this practically the culminating point of my active career. I knew perfectly that, whatever might be the sentiment of others toward me or toward the act I contemplated, what I intended would be a real service, and that whatever of misunderstanding might result, the end would show that I had acted unselfishly.

When this idea presented itself to my mind in concrete form I had made arrangements to visit Kentucky, for the double purpose of resting and purchasing stock for my Virginia farm. Thus remote from the scenes of activity and struggle, away from news and financial gossip, free from all interruption and yet cognizant of all the underlying conditions in the problem that presented itself, I could look over the whole situation much more critically than if I were on the ground. The matter was too delicate to be discussed with anybody, and, besides, as it finally presented itself to me, it did not concern any one else. It seemed to be my task. In the beginning I had thought that perhaps I would need financial co-operation, but when I looked about I found that two difficulties presented themselves in this respect. It became clear that if I limited my associates to those who, like myself, were only desirous of doing a public service, both the number and amount of the contributions they could make were too small to be of vital assistance; if, on the other hand, I accepted the offers of one or two men who wanted to participate, I was in danger of being overwhelmed not only with advice, which I would not take, but with an assistance which would have hampered me in every movement.

I returned to New York without reaching any definite conclusion but still deeply impressed with the necessity for action. But the whole question had taken possession of me, and so I went to my Virginia farm where, still without advisers, I could again concentrate my attention upon the matter that had been of absorbing interest to me. It was there and then that I finally saw my way clear to take up the task, still leaving unimportant details out of account.

From the beginning I had no other idea than that of purchasing the stock control of the Equitable at such a price as I must pay, and of placing it at once in the hands of Trustees, of whom ex-President Grover Cleveland[2] was to be one — and, naturally, the Chairman — and also of doing this only upon such terms as should immediately divest me of all control over the stock, and of detail management of the Society itself. I had determined to do these things with the one condition that, so far as the laws permitted, the management of the Society should be turned over to a majority of directors to be chosen by the policyholders, from their own numbers.

I had long been an admirer of Mr. Cleveland and, by reason of personal and political affiliations, had come into close relations with him. Knowing that I had no ambitions, he had often asked my advice and assistance, mainly in matters relating to currency and coinage. Thus, in perfect accord with his aims, whether partisan or patriotic, cognizant of his unrivaled position in the country, I had also noted,

[2] Grover Cleveland (1837–1908) occupied the White House for two terms, 1885–1889 and 1893–1897.

with sorrow, that he was hampered by lack of means to maintain the dignity of a man who had twice filled with such distinction the Presidency of the United States. I visited him in Princeton soon after his removal there and noticed with great concern this fact, which was confirmed by himself and further emphasized by friends who knew him even better than I did. It seemed to me that he ought to be removed from the necessity of doing literary work of the kind in which he was engaged in order to obtain the money necessary for keeping himself and family in the position that he felt incumbent upon him. I soon found that schemes, ranging from the management of a winter hotel to the presidency of a trust company, had been suggested for him, but none of them, unworthy as they were, came to anything. I then resolved and announced, especially to one friend, that I would, at some time, make an opportunity to bring about the desired result. But the only condition that I fixed in this was that the solution of the difficulty must be one which would bring no profit to me in any form and should at the same time enable the former President to do some public service really worthy of his position and character.

Further, I felt that the creation of an Equitable Trust, with Mr. Cleveland at its head, would meet the idea I had in mind, both so far as it related to him, and at the same time enable me, even without his knowledge, to do a great service to the country. It would solidify the new appreciation of him which had begun to come back about this time, and, best of all, it would save our financial institutions by restoring confidence. No business proposal of any kind was ever made to him by me or any one acting for me from the beginning until his relations to the trusteeship were ended by death. When the preliminaries were complete, an intimate friend of my own and of the former President was intrusted with the presentation of the matter. The rest of the story is well known. . . .

The announcement of the appointment of the trustees acted like magic upon the unwholesome business conditions prevailing at the time. From their first meeting — the only one I ever attended in order to execute the deed of trust — accompanied by the issue of a formal address, followed by the first list of directors chosen by them, confidence asserted itself. Sensational reports disappeared and even the threat of danger — much less danger itself — was no longer powerful. Mr. Cleveland's action thus taken, added to the prestige of a great name, had entirely cleared the air in a moment. . . .

After this preliminary work had been done, the rest was comparatively easy. Confidence was at once restored in the way that I have noted, and from that moment practically all danger of panic disappeared not only so far as the insurance companies were concerned, but from every branch of financial activity. . . .

154. Maurice Francis Egan Urges the Purchase of the Danish West Indies, March 8, 1915

A CONSIDERABLE number of Catholics have held high posts in the American diplomatic service, among them Maurice Francis Egan (1852–1924), who was Minister to Denmark from 1907 to 1918. Egan had been professor of English literature in the Catholic University of America since 1896 when he resigned to take the Copenhagen legation, having previously done newspaper work in New York (1878–1888) and taught at the University of Notre Dame (1888–1896). His diplomatic career is best remembered for the part he played in the purchase of the Danish West Indies. Twice before, in 1867 and 1902, treaties had been negotiated for their purchase but they were never ratified. World War I quickened American interest lest the islands should fall to Germany and become a base of operations for submarines. On August 4, 1916, a treaty was signed for their purchase at a figure of $25,000,000. Egan's tenure of the Copenhagen post during the war years brought him into more than ordinary prominence, and Henry van Dyke (1852–1933), professor of English literature at Princeton University and Minister to the Netherlands, stated after a visit to the Danish capital in 1916 that Egan was "not only the Dean of the Diplomatic Corps, he was its Prince Charming, the one to whom all turned for help in difficulty and for conciliation in dispute" (Introduction to Maurice Francis Egan, *Recollections of a Happy Life* [New York, 1924], p. x). Source: *Papers Relating to the Foreign Relations of the United States* (Washington: Government Printing Office, 1926), pp. 588–590.

MINISTER EGAN TO THE SECRETARY OF STATE
(William Jennings Bryan, 1860–1925)

No. 833

American Legation,
Copenhagen, March 8, 1915.

Sir: It may seem out of place for me, especially when the most terrible events are making a crisis in the world, to return to a subject on which in the past I have written many despatches,[1] the purchase

---

[1] As early as July 19, 1909, in a dispatch from Copenhagen to Alvey A. Adee, Assistant Secretary of State, Egan had stated: "I am quite sure that a time will come when it will be expedient, if our Government continues to hold it advisable, to open the question of the Danish Antilles. I am doing my best to pave the way for this" (*ibid.*, p. 557).

of the Danish Antilles. For seven years I have hoped that the Department might instruct me to make such suggestions to the Danish Government as would lead to an offer of these islands to the United States at a reasonable price. For good reason, I am sure, I received little encouragement; it was necessary to soften the suspicion of our arrogance and imperialistic tendencies which had arisen here and seemed fixed, and to make the Danish people feel that the Government of the United States has a sincere interest in their progress and sympathy with their national aspirations.

Once during the administration of President Taft there seemed to be some hope that the matter of the purchase of these islands might be considered as probable in the near future; the President went so far as to ask me whether they could be put under the same jurisdiction as Porto Rico and what price might be asked for them. This was sometime after a number of distinguished Danes had sent to me a memorial (September 23, 1910) proposing that our Government should accept Greenland in exchange for Mindanao, the Danish Government having the right to surrender Mindanao to Germany in exchange for Northern Schleswig. The hope that Danish Schleswig may one day again become part of Denmark is still cherished by a great number of the Danes, whose very delicate position, between two great Powers, does not depress their national ardor. The knowledge that this memorial had been presented to me produced a discussion in certain groups here as to whether the Danish Government would be willing to part with St. Thomas and the other Danish Antilles.

All this of course was purely academic, but interesting. It was made plain that if the pride of this small country in parting with such useless possessions as the Danish West Indies could be soothed, the islands might easily be made to come to us. The price of course would have had to be greater than it would have been previous to the opening of the Panama Canal or before the present improvements in the harbor of St. Thomas had begun. There would have been then no objection on the part of either England or Germany.

The main opponent of the sale, when the last attempt was made in 1902, was the East Asiatic Company, backed up by certain business men here; for instance Mr. Holger Petersen. Home politics too, played a part in the defeat of the project in the Upper House, — the Conservative Party fearing that the Deuntzer Ministry might strengthen itself by spending the money received for these islands. The interest of the business men in the holding of the islands has fallen off; the national subscription for the improving of the islands, which was opened in 1912 entirely failed. My argument with the principal opposers of the sale of the islands to us was to the effect that if they were to remain a burden to Denmark and a blot on the face of progress, as they were, it would be much better for the national reputation of Denmark that they should be sold to the United States. This attitude was looked upon as reasonable. Representing the ideas of our Government, I said publicly, that the United States would gladly sympathize with any attempt to make the population of the islands more contented and prosperous. The improvements in St. Thomas are still going on, but interest in them, on the part of the Danish people, has almost entirely ceased.

It is not necessary for me to comment on the importance of the great harbor of St. Thomas as a base of operations for any nation that possesses it. There is a rumor, widely spread, founded on the negotiations of 1902, that the United States had secured an option on the islands in question. This is without foundation, as far as I know.

It is not improbable that one day Denmark, in spite of the apparent drawing together of the three Scandinavian countries, may be absorbed by Germany, not by the breaking of her neutrality, which, however, is feared, but by what is called "peaceful penetration." If Germany should gain great advantages in the present war, neither England, nor Russia, nor France would be in a position to protest; and protests from other nations would of course be useless. The Danish West India Islands would then be the property of Germany, as Heligoland, under very different circumstances, became her property. A copy of the memorial sent by me to the Department on September 23, 1910, is appended.

I have been impressed by the fact that the Department, notwithstanding its present arduous and grievous occupations, has kept its eyes fastened on probable contingencies which may result from the present war and I take the liberty of calling attention to one of these possible contingencies.[2]

I have [etc.]

Maurice Francis Egan

---

[2] Three months after the receipt of this dispatch Robert Lansing (1864–1928), Secretary of State, cabled Egan on June 16 as follows: "Department is of the opinion that plan suggested in your despatch No. 833, March 8, is desirable and may be feasible and you may very discreetly approach the proper officials with a view to ascertaining whether a proposal such as contemplated would be received not unfavorably" (*ibid.*, p. 591). Egan's personal and more colorful account of the negotiations that followed may be read in his volume of memoirs, *Ten Years Near the German Frontier* (New York, 1919), pp. 263–288.

155. John A. Ryan and the Bishops' Program of Social Reconstruction, February 12, 1919

THE most influential Catholic in the field of American social reform was John A. Ryan (1869–1945). From 1915 to his retirement in 1939 he taught political economy and moral theology in the Catholic University of America. By means of books such as *A Living Wage* (New York, 1906) and *Distributive Justice* (New York, 1916), Ryan established a national reputation. But more famous, perhaps, was a pamphlet of his composition entitled *Social Reconstruction: A General Review of the Problems and Survey of Remedies* (Washington, 1919), the origins of which Ryan told in his memoirs, *Social Doctrine in Action* (New York, 1941), pp. 143–151. Near the close of World War I numerous programs of social reform appeared from various groups. Ryan tried his hand at such a program and after it had been read by the bishops who composed the Administrative Committee of the National Catholic War Council they were impressed to the point of making it their own and issuing it over their signatures. The proposals set forth were thought so radical at the time that Stephen C. Mason, president of the National Association of Manufacturers, protested to Cardinal Gibbons that it was "partisan, pro-labor union, socialistic propaganda" (Archives of the Archdiocese of Baltimore, Mason to Gibbons, New York, February 25, 1919). A decade later the pamphlet was described by a committee of the New York State Senate investigating seditious activities, in a report filed on April 24, 1929, as the work of "a certain group in the Catholic Church with leanings toward Socialism" (Ryan, *op. cit.*, p. 147). These reactions were evidence of the advanced thinking of Ryan and the bishops who adopted his draft as their official pronouncement. Of the eleven proposals contained in the pamphlet, all have now been either wholly or partially translated into fact. Only one, the participation of labor in management and a wider distribution of ownership, has made little progress. Source: *Bishops' Program of Social Reconstruction* [reprint] (Washington: National Catholic Welfare Conference, 1950).

FOREWORD

The ending of the Great War has brought peace. But the only safeguard of peace is social justice and a contented people. The deep unrest so emphatically and so widely voiced throughout the world is the most serious menace to the future peace of every nation and of the entire world. Great problems face us. They cannot be put aside; they must be met and solved with justice to all.

In the hope of stating the lines that will best guide us in our right solution the following pronouncement is issued by the Administrative Committee of the National Catholic War Council. Its practical applications are of course subject to discussion, but all its essential declarations are based upon the principles of charity and justice that have always been held and taught by the Catholic Church, while its practical proposals are merely an adaptation of those principles and that traditional teaching to the social and industrial conditions and needs of our own time.

✠ PETER J. MULDOON, *Chairman,*
     Bishop of Rockford.

✠ JOSEPH SCHREMBS,
     Bishop of Toledo.

✠ PATRICK J. HAYES,
     Bishop of Tagaste.

✠ WILLIAM T. RUSSELL,
     Bishop of Charleston.

Washington, D. C.
February 12, 1919.

"Reconstruction" has of late been so tiresomely reiterated, not to say violently abused, that it has become to many of us a word of aversion. Politicians, social students, labor leaders, business men, charity workers, clergymen and various other social groups have contributed their quota of spoken words and printed pages to the discussion of the subject; yet the majority of us still find ourselves rather bewildered and helpless. We are unable to say what parts of our social system imperatively need reconstruction; how much of that which is imperatively necessary is likely to be seriously undertaken; or what specific methods and measures are best suited to realize that amount of reconstruction which is at once imperatively necessary and immediately feasible.

Nevertheless it is worth while to review briefly some of the more important statements and proposals that have been made by various social groups and classes. Probably the most notable declaration from a Catholic source is that contained in a pastoral letter, written by Cardinal Bourne several months ago. "It is admitted on all hands," he says, "that a new order of things, new social conditions, new relations between the different sections in which society is divided, will arise as a consequence of the destruction of the formerly existing conditions. . . . The very foundations of political and social life, of our economic system, of morals and religion are being sharply scrutinized, and this not only by a few writers and speakers, but by a very large number of people in every class of life, especially among the workers."[1]

The Cardinal's special reference to the action of labor was undoubtedly suggested by the now famous "Social Reconstruction Program" of the British Labor Party.[2] This document was drawn up about one year ago, and is generally understood to be the work of the noted economist and Fabian Socialist, Mr. Sidney Webb.[3] Unquestionably, it is the most comprehensive and coherent program that has yet appeared on the industrial phase of reconstruction. In brief it sets up "four pillars" of the new social order:

(1) The enforcement by law of a national minimum of leisure, health, education and subsistence;

(2) The democratic control of industry, which means the nationalization of all monopolistic industries and possibly of other industries, sometime in the future, if that course be found advisable;

(3) A revolution in national finance; that is, a system of taxation which will compel capital to pay for the war, leaving undisturbed the national minimum of welfare for the masses;

(4) Use of the surplus wealth of the nation for the common good; that is, to provide capital, governmental industries, and funds for social, educational and artistic progress.

This program may properly be described as one of immediate radical reforms, leading ultimately to complete Socialism. Evidently this outcome cannot be approved by Catholics.

PROGRAM OF AMERICAN LABOR

Through its Committee on Reconstruction, the American Federation of Labor has issued a lengthy program of reform proposals and demands which may be grouped under the three heads of trade union action, labor legislation and general industrial and social legislation. The principal demands under the first head are: the legally guaranteed rights of the workers to organize and to carry on the normal activities of trade unions; a living wage; no reduction in present scales of

---

[1] Francis Cardinal Bourne (1861–1935) was fourth Archbishop of Westminster. The pastoral referred to was issued on Quinquagesima Sunday [February 10], 1918. Cf. the chapter "The 1918 Pastoral," in Ernest Oldmeadow, *Francis Cardinal Bourne* (London, 1944), II, 139–145.

[2] For the various programs mentioned in the Ryan document, cf. Estella T. Weeks, *Reconstruction Programs* (New York, 1919).

[3] Sidney Webb (1859–1947) had been one of the principal founders of the Fabian Society in 1883.

wages; the right of labor to fix its hours of work; the eight-hour day; equal pay for equal work by the two sexes; exclusive reliance by labor on trade-union effort to maintain fair wages; establishment of co-operative stores; and no organization of a political party by the workers. Labor laws demanded are: prohibition of wage working by children under sixteen years of age; abolition of private employment agencies; prohibition of all immigration for two years; and vocational education which will fit the young for life in an industrial society. By implication both the eight-hour day and the living wage are declared to be subjects for trade-union action, not for legislation. Among the measures of general social legislation recommended are: a special tax on "usable land" not cultivated by the owner, and taxes on land values which would make the holding of idle land unprofitable;[4] government housing; government ownership and operation of docks, wharves and water powers; taxes on excess profits, incomes and inheritances; and limitation of the power of the courts to declare laws unconstitutional.

While this program is more practical and more moderate and reasonable than that of the British Labor Congress, its proposal for taxing land into use could easily involve confiscation. On the other hand, it does not give sufficient consideration to the case of the weaker sections of the working class, those for whom trade union action is not practically adequate; nor does it demand or imply that the workers should ever aspire to become owners as well as users of the instruments of production.

BRITISH QUAKER EMPLOYERS

Probably the most definite and comprehensive statement from the opposite industrial class was put forth several months ago by a group of twenty Quaker employers in Great Britain. In outline their program is as follows: A family living wage for all male employees, and a secondary wage in excess of this for workers having special skill, training, physical strength, responsibility for human life; the right of labor to organize, to bargain collectively with the employer and to participate in the industrial part of business management; serious and practical measures to reduce the volume and hardship of unemployment; provisions of such working conditions as will safeguard health, physical integrity and morals; the reduction so far as practicable of profits and interest until both the basic and the second-

---

[4] The single tax movement of Henry George (1839–1897) was still a live issue at this time.

ary wage has been paid, and transfer to the community of the greater part of surplus profits.

The spirit and conception of responsibility that permeate every item of the program are reflected in this statement: "We would ask all employers to consider very carefully whether their style of living and personal expenditure are restricted to what is needed in order to insure the efficient performance of their functions in society. More than this is waste and is, moreover, a great cause of class divisions."

AMERICAN EMPLOYERS

The only formal statements on the subject of social reconstruction that have yet come to our attention from an important group of American employers, are a declaration of principles and certain proposals by the National Chamber of Commerce. The declaration of principles was made at a convention of the organization, in Atlantic city, December 6, 1918. Beyond a general commendation of peaceful and friendly relations between employers and employees, it included nothing of importance on the labor phase of reconstruction. It condemned government operation and ownership of railroads, telegraphs and telephones, and demanded more moderate taxes and a modification of the Sherman Anti-Trust Law. More recently the executive officials of the Chamber have submitted to a referendum vote of its membership a statement, "with a view to furnishing a basis on which American industry can build a national labor program." The main specific proposals in this statement are: recognition of the right of workers to organize; adequate representation of both parties in the determination of employment conditions; a decent home and proper social conditions; no reduction in wages until all other costs of production have been brought down to the lowest possible level; and a system of national employment offices. Inasmuch as this organization represents more employers than any other association in the country, the vote of its members on these proposals will be of the greatest significance.

AN INTERDENOMINATIONAL STATEMENT

In Great Britain an organization known as the Interdenominational Conference of Social Service Unions, comprising ten religious bodies, including Catholics, spent more than a year formulating a statement of Social Reconstruction. (See the summary and analysis contained in the Catholic Social Year Book for 1918.)[5] This statement deals with

---

[5] *A Christian Social Crusade: Catholic Social Year Book for 1918* (London, 1918), p. 1.

principles, evils, and remedies. Presuming that Christianity provides indispensable guiding principles and powerful motives of social reform, it lays down the basic proposition that every human being is of inestimable worth, and that legislation should recognize persons as more sacred than property, therefore the State should enforce a minimum living wage, enable the worker to obtain some control of industrial conditions; supplement private initiative in providing decent housing; prevent the occurrence of unemployment; safeguard the right of the laborer and his family to a reasonable amount of rest and recreation; remove those industrial and social conditions which hinder marriage and encourage an unnatural restriction of families, and afford ample opportunities for education of all children industrially, culturally, religiously and morally. On the other hand rights imply duties, and the individual is obliged to respect the rights of others, to cultivate self-control, to recognize that labor is the law of life, and that wealth is a trust. Finally, the statement points out that all social reform must take as its end and guide the maintenance of pure and wholesome family life.

Such in barest outline are the main propositions and principles of this remarkable program. The text contains adequate exposition of the development and application of all these points, and concrete specifications of the methods and measures by which the aims and principles may be brought into effect. In the latter respect the statement is not liable to the fatal objection that is frequently and fairly urged against the reform pronouncements of religious bodies: that they are abstract, platitudinous and usually harmless. The statement of the Interdenominational Conference points out specific remedies for the evils that it describes; specific measures, legislative and other, by which the principles may be realized in actual life. Especially practical and valuable for Catholics are the explanations and modifications supplied by the Year Book of the Catholic social Guild.

NO PROFOUND CHANGES IN THE UNITED STATES

It is not to be expected that as many or as great social changes will take place in the United States as in Europe. Neither our habits of thinking nor our ordinary ways of life have undergone a profound disturbance. The hackneyed phrase: "Things will never again be the same after the war," has a much more concrete and deeply felt meaning among the European peoples. Their minds are fully adjusted to the conviction and expectation that these words will come true.

In the second place, the devastation, the loss of capital and of men, the changes in individual relations and the increase in the activities of government have been much greater in Europe than in the United States. Moreover, our superior natural advantages and resources, the better industrial and social condition of our working classes still constitute an obstacle to anything like revolutionary changes. It is significant that no social group in America, not even among the wage-earners, has produced such a fundamental and radical program of reconstruction as the Labor Party of Great Britain.

A PRACTICAL AND MODERATE PROGRAM

No attempt will be made in these pages to formulate a comprehensive scheme of reconstruction. Such an undertaking would be a waste of time as regards immediate needs and purposes, for no important group or section of the American people is ready to consider a program of this magnitude. Attention will therefore be confined to those reforms that seem to be desirable and also obtainable within a reasonable time, and to a few general principles which should become a guide to more distant developments. A statement thus circumscribed will not merely present the objects that we wish to see attained, but will also serve as an imperative call to action. It will keep before our minds the necessity for translating our faith into works. In the statements of immediate proposals we shall start, wherever possible, from those governmental agencies and legislative measures which have been to some extent in operation during the war. These come before us with the prestige of experience and should therefore receive first consideration in any program that aims to be at once practical and persuasive.

The first problem in the process of reconstruction is the industrial replacement of the discharged soldiers and sailors. The majority of these will undoubtedly return to their previous occupations. However, a very large number of them will either find their previous places closed to them, or will be eager to consider the possibility of more attractive employments. The most important single measure for meeting this situation that has yet been suggested is the placement of such men on farms. Several months ago Secretary Lane recommended to Congress that returning soldiers and sailors should be given the opportunity to work at good wages upon some part of the millions upon millions of acres of arid, swamp, and cut-over timber lands, in order to prepare them for cultivation. President Wilson in his annual address to Congress endorsed the proposal.[6] As fast as this preliminary task has been performed, the men should be assisted by government loans to establish themselves as farmers, either as owners or as tenants having long-time leases. It is essential that both the work of preparation and the subsequent settlement of the land should be effected by groups or colonies, not by men living independently of one another and in depressing isolation. A plan of this sort is already in operation in England. The importance of the project as an item of any social reform program is obvious. It would afford employment to thousands upon thousands, would greatly increase the number of farm owners and independent farmers, and would tend to lower the cost of living by increasing the amount of agricultural products. If it is to assume any considerable proportions it must be carried out by the governments of the United States and of the several States. Should it be undertaken by these authorities and operated on a systematic and generous scale, it would easily become one of the most beneficial reform measures that has ever been attempted.

UNITED STATES EMPLOYMENT SERVICE

The reinstatement of the soldiers and sailors in urban industries will no doubt be facilitated by the United States Employment Service. This agency has attained a fair degree of development and efficiency during the war. Unfortunately there is some danger that it will go out of existence or be greatly weakened at the end of the period of demobilization. It is the obvious duty of Congress to continue and strengthen this important institution. The problem of unemployment is with us always. Its solution requires the co-operation of many agencies, and the use of many methods; but the primary and indispensable instrument is a national system of labor exchanges, acting in harmony with State, municipal, and private employment bureaus.

WOMEN WAR WORKERS

One of the most important problems of readjustment is that created by the presence in industry of immense numbers of women who have taken the places of men during the war. Mere justice, to say nothing of chivalry, dictates that these women should not be compelled to suffer any greater loss or inconvenience than is absolutely necessary;

---

[6] The address of Wilson was delivered on December 2, 1918. For the president's endorsement of the proposal of Secretary of the Interior Franklin K. Lane (1864–1921) concerning lands for the returning servicemen cf. *Congressional Record, 65th Congress, 3rd Session* (Washington, 1919), LVII, 7.

for their services to the nation have been second only to the services of the men whose places they were called upon to fill. One general principle is clear: No female worker should remain in any occupation that is harmful to health or morals. Women should disappear as quickly as possible from such tasks as conducting and guarding street cars, cleaning locomotives, and a great number of other activities for which conditions of life and their physique render them unfit. Another general principle is that the proportion of women in industry ought to be kept within the smallest practical limits. If we have an efficient national employment service, if a goodly number of the returned soldiers and sailors are placed on the land, and if wages and the demand for goods are kept up to the level which is easily attainable, all female workers who are displaced from tasks that they have been performing only since the beginning of the war will be able to find suitable employments in other parts of the industrial field, or in those domestic occupations which sorely need their presence. Those women who are engaged at the same tasks as men should receive equal pay for equal amounts and qualities of work.

NATIONAL WAR LABOR BOARD

One of the most beneficial governmental organizations of the war is the National War Labor Board.[7] Upon the basis of a few fundamental principles, unanimously adopted by the representatives of labor, capital, and the public, it has prevented innumerable strikes, and raised wages to decent levels in many different industries throughout the country. Its main guiding principles have been a family living wage for all male adult laborers; recognition of the right of labor to organize, and to deal with employers through its chosen representatives; and no coercion of non-union laborers by members of the union. The War Labor Board ought to be continued in existence by Congress, and endowed with all the power for effective action that it can possess under the Federal Constitution. The principles, methods, machinery and results of this institution constitute a definite and far-reaching gain for social justice. No part of this advantage should be lost or given up in time of peace.

PRESENT WAGE RATES SHOULD BE SUSTAINED

The general level of wages attained during the war should not be

---

[7] The National War Labor Board was appointed by President Wilson in April, 1918, and had as co-chairmen former President Taft (1857–1930) and Frank P. Walsh (1864–1939). It was intended to act as a court of last resort for labor disputes.

lowered. In a few industries, especially some directly and peculiarly connected with the carrying on of war, wages have reached a plane upon which they cannot possibly continue for this grade of occupations. But the number of workers in this situation is an extremely small proportion of the entire wage-earning population. The overwhelming majority should not be compelled or suffered to undergo any reduction in their rates of remuneration, for two reasons: First, because the average rate of pay has not increased faster than the cost of living; second, because a considerable majority of the wage-earners of the United States, both men and women, were not receiving living wages when prices began to rise in 1915. In that year, according to Lauck and Sydenstricker,[8] whose work is the most comprehensive on the subject, four-fifths of the heads of families obtained less than 800 dollars, while two-thirds of the female wage-earners were paid less than 400 dollars. Even if the price of goods should fall to the level on which they were in 1915 — something that cannot be hoped for within five years — the average present rates of wages would not exceed the equivalent of a decent livelihood in the case of the vast majority. The exceptional instances to the contrary are practically all among the skilled workers. Therefore, wages on the whole should not be reduced even when the cost of living recedes from its present high level.

Even if the great majority of workers were now in receipt of more than living wages, there are no good reasons why rates of pay should be lowered. After all, a living wage is not necessarily the full measure of justice. All the Catholic authorities on the subject explicitly declare that this is only the minimum of justice. In a country as rich as ours, there are very few cases in which it is possible to prove that the worker would be getting more than that to which he has a right if he were paid something in excess of this ethical minimum. Why then, should we assume that this is the normal share of almost the whole laboring population? Since our industrial resources and instrumentalities are sufficient to provide more than a living wage for a very large proportion of the workers, why should we acquiesce in a theory which denies them this measure of the comforts of life? Such a policy is not only of very questionable morality, but is unsound economically. The large demand for goods which is created and maintained by high rates of wages and high purchasing power by the masses is the surest guarantee of a continuous and general operation

[8] W. Jett Lauck and Edgar Sydenstricker, *Conditions of Labor in American Industries* (New York, 1917), p. 66.

of industrial establishments. It is the most effective instrument of prosperity for labor and capital alike. The principal beneficiaries of a general reduction of wages would be the less efficient among the capitalists, and the more comfortable sections of the consumers. The wage-earners would lose more in remuneration than they would gain from whatever fall in prices occurred as a direct result of the fall in wages. On grounds both of justice and sound economics, we should give our hearty support to all legitimate efforts made by labor to resist general wage reductions.

HOUSING FOR WORKING CLASSES

Housing projects for war workers which have been completed, or almost completed by the Government of the United States, have cost some forty million dollars, and are found in eleven cities. While the Federal Government cannot continue this work in time of peace, the example and precedent that it has set, and the experience and knowledge that it has developed, should not be forthwith neglected and lost. The great cities in which congestion and other forms of bad housing are disgracefully apparent ought to take up and continue the work, at least to such an extent as will remove the worst features of a social condition that is a menace at once to industrial efficiency, civic health, good morals and religion.

REDUCTION OF THE COST OF LIVING

During the war the cost of living has risen at least seventy-five per cent. above the level of 1913. Some check has been placed upon the upward trend by government fixing of prices in the case of bread and coal, and a few other commodities. Even if we believe it desirable, we cannot ask that the Government continue this action after the articles of peace have been signed; for neither public opinion nor Congress is ready for such a revolutionary policy. If the extortionate practices of monopoly were prevented by adequate laws and adequate law enforcement, prices would automatically be kept at as low a level as that to which they might be brought by direct government determination. Just what laws, in addition to those already on the statute books, are necessary to abolish monopolistic extortion is a question of detail that need not be considered here. In passing, it may be noted that government competition with monopolies that cannot be effectively restrained by the ordinary anti-trust laws deserves more serious consideration than it has yet received.

More important and more effective than any government regulation of prices would be the establishment of co-operative stores. The enormous toll taken from industry by the various classes of middle-men is now fully realized. The astonishing difference between the price received by the producer and that paid by the consumer has become a scandal of our industrial system. The obvious and direct means of reducing this discrepancy and abolishing unnecessary middle-men is the operation of retail and wholesale mercantile concerns under the ownership and management of the consumers. This is no Utopian scheme. It has been successfully carried out in England and Scotland through the Rochdale system.[9] Very few serious efforts of this kind have been made in this country because our people have not felt the need of these co-operative enterprises as keenly as the European working classes, and because we have been too impatient and too individualistic to make the necessary sacrifices and to be content with moderate benefits and gradual progress. Nevertheless, our superior energy, initiative and commercial capacity will enable us, once we set about the task earnestly, even to surpass what has been done in England and Scotland.

In addition to reducing the cost of living, the co-operative stores would train our working people and consumers generally in habits of saving, in careful expenditure, in business methods, and in the capacity for co-operation. When the working classes have learned to make the sacrifices and to exercise the patience required by the ownership and operation of co-operative stores, they will be equipped to undertake a great variety of tasks and projects which benefit the community immediately, and all its constituent members ultimately. They will then realize the folly of excessive selfishness and senseless individualism. Until they have acquired this knowledge, training and capacity, desirable extensions of governmental action in industry will not be attended by a normal amount of success. No machinery of government can operate automatically, and no official and bureaucratic administration of such machinery can ever be a substitute for intelligent interest and co-operation by the individuals of the community.

THE LEGAL MINIMUM WAGE

Turning now from those agencies and laws that have been put in operation during the war to the general subject of labor legislation and problems, we are glad to note that there is no longer any serious

---

[9] This system of co-operatives originated in 1844 at Rochdale, England, when a group of chartists and Owenite workmen opened a store of the so-called Rochdale Pioneers.

objection urged by impartial persons against the legal minimum wage. The several States should enact laws providing for the establishment of wage rates that will be at least sufficient for the decent maintenance of a family, in the case of all male adults, and adequate to the decent individual support of female workers. In the beginning the minimum wages for male workers should suffice only for the present needs of the family, but they should be gradually raised until they are adequate to future needs as well. That is, they should be ultimately high enough to make possible that amount of saving which is necessary to protect the worker and his family against sickness, accidents, invalidity and old age.

SOCIAL INSURANCE

Until this level of legal minimum wages is reached the worker stands in need of the device of insurance. The State should make comprehensive provision for insurance against illness, invalidity, unemployment, and old age. So far as possible the insurance fund should be raised by a levy on industry, as is now done in the case of accident compensation. The industry in which a man is employed should provide him with all that is necessary to meet all the needs of his entire life. Therefore, any contribution to the insurance fund from the general revenues of the State should be only slight and temporary. For the same reason no contribution should be exacted from any worker who is not getting a higher wage than is required to meet the present needs of himself and family. Those who are below that level can make such a contribution only at the expense of their present welfare. Finally, the administration of the insurance laws should be such as to interfere as little as possible with the individual freedom of the worker and his family. Any insurance scheme, or any administrative method, that tends to separate the workers into a distinct and dependent class, that offends against their domestic privacy and independence, or that threatens individual self-reliance and self-respect, should not be tolerated. The ideal to be kept in mind is a condition in which all the workers would themselves have the income and the responsibility of providing for all the needs and contingencies of life, both present and future. Hence all forms of State insurance should be regarded as merely a lesser evil, and should be so organized and administered as to hasten the coming of the normal condition.

The life insurance offered to soldiers and sailors during the war should be continued, so far as the enlisted men are concerned. It is very doubtful whether the time has yet arrived when public opinion would sanction the extension of general life insurance by the Government to all classes of the community.

The establishment and maintenance of municipal health inspection in all schools, public and private, is now pretty generally recognized as of great importance and benefit. Municipal clinics where the poorer classes could obtain the advantage of medical treatment by specialists at a reasonable cost would likewise seem to have become a necessity. A vast amount of unnecessary sickness and suffering exists among the poor and the lower middle classes because they cannot afford the advantages of any other treatment except that provided by the general practitioner. Every effort should be made to supply wage-earners and their families with specialized medical care through development of group medicine. Free medical care should be given only to those who cannot afford to pay.

LABOR PARTICIPATION IN INDUSTRIAL MANAGEMENT

The right of labor to organize and to deal with employers through representatives has been asserted above in connection with the discussion of the War Labor Board. It is to be hoped that this right will never again be called in question by any considerable number of employers. In addition to this, labor ought gradually to receive greater representation in what the English group of Quaker employers have called the "industrial" part of business management — "the control of processes and machinery; nature of product; engagement and dismissal of employees; hours of work, rates of pay, bonuses, etc.; welfare work; shop discipline; relations with trade unions." The establishment of shop committees, working wherever possible with the trade union, is the method suggested by this group of employers for giving the employees the proper share of industrial management. There can be no doubt that a frank adoption of these means and ends by employers would not only promote the welfare of the workers, but vastly improve the relations between them and their employers, and increase the efficiency and productiveness of each establishment.

There is no need here to emphasize the importance of safety and sanitation in work places, as this is pretty generally recognized by legislation. What is required is an extension and strengthening of many of the existing statutes, and a better administration and enforcement of such laws everywhere.

VOCATIONAL TRAINING

The need of industrial, or as it has come to be more generally called, vocational training, is now universally acknowledged. In the interest of the nation, as well as in that of the workers themselves, this training should be made substantially universal. While we cannot now discuss the subject in any detail, we do wish to set down two general observations. First, the vocational training should be offered in such forms and conditions as not to deprive the children of the working classes of at least the elements of a cultural education. A healthy democracy cannot tolerate a purely industrial or trade education for any class of its citizens. We do not want to have the children of the wage-earners put into a special class in which they are marked as outside the sphere of opportunities for culture. The second observation is that the system of vocational training should not operate so as to weaken in any degree our parochial schools or any other class of private schools. Indeed, the opportunities of the system should be extended to all qualified private schools on exactly the same basis as to public schools. We want neither class divisions in education nor a State monopoly of education.

CHILD LABOR

The question of education naturally suggests the subject of child labor. Public opinion in the majority of the States of our country has set its face inflexibly against the continuous employment of children in industry before the age of sixteen years. Within a reasonably short time all of our States, except some stagnant ones, will have laws providing for this reasonable standard. The education of public opinion must continue, but inasmuch as the process is slow, the abolition of child labor in certain sections seems unlikely to be brought about by the legislatures of those States, and since the Keating-Owen Act[10] has been declared unconstitutional, there seems to be no device by which this reproach to our country can be removed except that of taxing child labor out of existence. This method is embodied in an amendment to the Federal Revenue Bill which would impose a tax of ten per cent on all goods made by children.

---

[10] The Keating-Owen Act of 1916 had barred products of child labor from interstate commerce. In *Hammer* v. *Dagenhart* of June 3, 1918, the Supreme Court ruled it unconstitutional as a regulation of local labor conditions rather than commerce.

SUFFICIENT FOR THE PRESENT

Probably the foregoing proposals comprise everything that is likely to have practical value in a program of immediate social reconstruction for America. Substantially all of these methods, laws and recommendations have been recognized in principle by the United States during the war, or have been indorsed by important social and industrial groups and organizations. Therefore, they are objects that we can set before the people with good hope of obtaining a sympathetic and practical response. Were they all realized a great step would have been taken in the direction of social justice. When they are all put into operation the way will be easy and obvious to still greater and more beneficial result.

ULTIMATE AND FUNDAMENTAL REFORMS

Despite the practical and immediate character of the present statement, we cannot entirely neglect the question of ultimate aims and a systematic program; for other groups are busy issuing such systematic pronouncements, and we all need something of the kind as a philosophical foundation and as a satisfaction to our natural desire for comprehensive statements.

It seems clear that the present industrial system is destined to last for a long time in its main outlines. That is to say, private ownership of capital is not likely to be supplanted by a collectivist organization of industry at a date sufficiently near to justify any present action based on the hypothesis of its arrival. This forecast we recognize as not only extremely probable, but as highly desirable; for, other objections apart, Socialism would mean bureaucracy, political tyranny, the helplessness of the individual as a factor in the ordering of his own life, and in general social inefficiency and decadence.

MAIN DEFECTS OF THE PRESENT SYSTEM

Nevertheless, the present system stands in grievous need of considerable modifications and improvement. Its main defects are three: Enormous inefficiency and waste in the production and distribution of commodities; insufficient incomes for the great majority of wage-earners, and unnecessarily large incomes for a small minority of privileged capitalists. Inefficiency in the production and distribution of goods would be in great measure abolished by the reforms that have been outlined in the foregoing pages. Production would be greatly increased by universal living wages, by adequate industrial education, and by harmonious relations between labor and capital on the basis of adequate participation by the former in all the industrial aspects of business management. The wastes of commodity distribution could be practically all eliminated by co-operative mercantile establishments, and co-operative selling and marketing associations.

CO-OPERATION AND CO-PARTNERSHIP

Nevertheless, the full possibilities of increased production will not be realized so long as the majority of the workers remain mere wage-earners. The majority must somehow become owners, or at least in part, of the instruments of production. They can be enabled to reach this stage gradually through co-operative productive societies and co-partnership arrangements. In the former, the workers own and manage the industries themselves; in the latter they own a substantial part of the corporate stock and exercise a reasonable share in the management. However slow the attainments of these ends, they will have to be reached before we can have a thoroughly efficient system of production, or an industrial and social order that will be secure from the danger of revolution. It is to be noted that this particular modification of the existing order, though far-reaching and involving to a great extent the abolition of the wage system, would not mean the abolition of private ownership. The instruments of production would still be owned by individuals, not by the State.

INCREASED INCOMES FOR LABOR

The second great evil, that of insufficient income for the majority can be removed only by providing the workers with more income. This means not only universal living wages, but the opportunity of obtaining something more than that amount for all who are willing to work hard and faithfully. All the other measures for labor betterment recommended in the preceding pages would likewise contribute directly or indirectly to a more just distribution of wealth in the interest of the laborer.

ABOLITION AND CONTROL OF MONOPOLIES

For the third evil mentioned above, excessive gains by a small minority of privileged capitalists, the main remedies are prevention of monopolistic control of commodities, adequate government regulation of such public service monopolies as will remain under private operation, and heavy taxation of incomes, excess profits and inheritances. The precise methods by which genuine competition may be

restored and maintained among businesses that are naturally competi-
tive, cannot be discussed here; but the principle is clear that human
beings cannot be trusted with the immense opportunities for oppression and extortion that go with the possession of monopoly power.
That the owners of public service monopolies should be restricted
by law to a fair or average return on their actual investment, has
long been a recognized principle of the courts, the legislatures, and
public opinion. It is a principle which should be applied to competi-
tive enterprises likewise, with the qualification that something more
than the average rate of return should be allowed to men who exhibit
exceptional efficiency. However, good public policy, as well as equity,
demands that these exceptional business men share the fruits of their
efficiency with the consumer in the form of lower prices. The man who
utilizes his ability to produce cheaper than his competitors for the
purpose of exacting from the public as high a price for his product as
is necessary for the least efficient business man, is a menace rather
than a benefit to industry and society.

Our immense war debt constitutes a particular reason why incomes
and excess profits should continue to be heavily taxed. In this way
two important ends will be attained: the poor will be relieved of
injurious tax burdens, and the small class of specially privileged capitalists will be compelled to return a part of their unearned gains to
society.

A NEW SPIRIT A VITAL NEED

"Society," said Pope Leo XIII, "can be healed in no other way
than by a return to Christian life and Christian institutions."[11] The
truth of these words is more widely perceived to-day than when they
were written, more thàn twenty-seven years ago. Changes in our
economic and political systems will have only partial and feeble
efficiency if they be not reinforced by the Christian view of work
and wealth. Neither the moderate reforms advocated in this paper,
nor any other program of betterment or reconstruction will prove
reasonably effective without a reform in the spirit of both labor and
capital. The laborer must come to realize that he owes his employer
and society an honest day's work in return for a fair wage, and that
conditions cannot be substantially improved until he roots out the
desire to get a maximum of return for a minimum of service. The
capitalist must likewise get a new viewpoint. He needs to learn the

---

[11] *Rerum Novarum*, May 15, 1891, in John J. Wynne, S.J. (Ed.), *The Great
Encyclical Letters of Pope Leo XIII* (New York, 1903), p. 225.

long-forgotten truth that wealth is stewardship, that profit-making is not the basic justification of business enterprise, and that there are such things as fair profits, fair interest, and fair prices. Above and before all, he must cultivate and strengthen within his mind the truth which many of his class have begun to grasp for the first time during the present war; namely, that the laborer is a human being, not merely an instrument of production; and that the laborer's right to a decent livelihood is the first moral charge upon industry. The employer has a right to get a reasonable living out of his business, but he has no right to interest on his investment until his employees have obtained at least living wages. This is the human and Christian, in contrast to the purely commercial and pagan, ethics of industry.

156. The Founding of the National Catholic Welfare Conference and Its Final Approval by the Holy See, May 1, 1919–July 4, 1922.

ONE of the most significant developments in the Catholic Church of the United States in the twentieth century has been National Catholic Welfare Conference, an organization to which the Holy See has in recent years referred the hierarchies of a number of countries as a model to follow in the co-ordination of their various large-scale activities. At a meeting held at the Catholic University of America on August 11–12, 1917, there was founded the National Catholic War Council with a view to co-ordinating Catholic efforts in World War I. The meeting, which had been brought about largely through the initiative of Father John J. Burke, C.S.P. (1875–1936), editor of the *Catholic World* and founder of the Chaplains' Aid Association, was attended by representatives of sixty-eight dioceses and twenty-seven national Catholic organizations. The National Catholic War Council proved so successful in its manifold enterprises that when the war ended many felt some kind of a peacetime equivalent should be continued to look after the national interests of the Church. This sentiment was shared by a majority of the bishops and at the celebration of Cardinal Gibbons' golden episcopal jubilee in February, 1919, it was decided to seek the approval of the Holy See for such an organization, as well as for an annual meeting of the entire hierarchy. Pope Benedict XV gave his approval to both projects in April, 1919, and at the first annual meeting of the hierarchy held in Washington the following September the National Catholic Welfare Council was set up under the direct management of an administrative committee of bishops. At this meeting, attended by ninety-two of the 101 ordinaries of the United States, Charles E. McDonnell (1854–1921), Bishop of Brooklyn, was the only one who voiced opposition to the idea of the N.C.W.C. on the score that it went beyond what the pope's letter had envisioned and that it would be detrimental to the authority of the bishops in their respective dioceses. But as it turned out, more than McDonnell were opposed to the N.C.W.C. and eventually a request for its dissolution was laid before the Holy See. In Cajetan Cardinal De Lai (1853–1928), Secretary of the Consistorial Congregation, the minority party found a strong ally. De Lai succeeded in convincing Benedict XV that the N.C.W.C. was a risky experiment that carried in it dangerous overtones of a national church in the United States. De Lai, therefore, made out a decree of dissolution but before Benedict XV could sign it he died on January 22, 1922. Pius XI, elected on February 6, found the decree among the unfinished business of his predecessor, gave it his assent, and the decree was fixed on February 23. News of this action did not reach the United States until late March. The Administrative Committee of the N.C.W.C. held an emergency meeting in Cleveland on April 6, cabled asking the Holy See to withhold publication of the decree in the *Acta Sanctae Sedis,* and delegated Bishop Schrembs to go to Rome to present their side of the case. After many anxious weeks Schrembs cabled on June 23: "Fight is won. Keep program Bishops' meeting September. Official notice will be cabled next week. Hard struggle. Complete victory. At farewell audience Pope blesses Bishops and Welfare Council. Sail Olympic Aug. 2nd" (Archives of the Diocese of Rockford, Diary of Bishop Muldoon). The National Catholic Welfare Conference was thus saved from dissolution and on June 22, 1922, a decree of approval was issued by the Consistorial Congregation. The following documents illustrate the initiation of the project and the final approval of the Holy See for the N.C.W.C. and the annual meeting of the American hierarchy. Sources: "The September Meeting of the American Hierarchy," *Ecclesiastical Review,* LXI (July, 1919), 7–9; *The National Catholic Welfare Conference. Its Organization, Departments and Functions* (Washington: Administrative Board, N.C.W.C., 1942) (privately printed), pp. 23–25.

Baltimore
May 1, 1919.

My Dear Archbishop:

After the celebration of my Episcopal Jubilee which was honored by the gracious presence of so many of the Hierarchy, there was a general meeting of all the Prelates who had participated. At this meeting there were present nearly all the Archbishops and Bishops of the country.[1]

On this occasion, the Prelates present unanimously adopted three important resolutions, to which I desire to call your attention.

The first was that we should take extraordinary measures to aid the Holy Father in his present financial straits occasioned by the war.

The second measure adopted by the assembled Prelates was that annually all the Bishops, including Auxiliaries and the Rector of

---

[1] The celebration was held in Washington on February 20, 1919, and drew two cardinals (O'Connell of Boston and Begin of Quebec), twelve archbishops, and fifty-eight bishops.

the University, — if he is a Bishop, — shall be invited to be present in Washington at the annual meeting of the Metropolitans.

The third measure adopted was that the Archbishop of Baltimore name a committee of five Prelates to be known hereafter as "The Committee on General Catholic Interests and Affairs."

These measures were all suggested and urged in an address to the Bishops who attended my Jubilee, by the special Representative of our Holy Father, Most Reverend Archbishop Cerretti.[2]

I assure you that, great as was my joy in being permitted to commemorate my fifty years in the Episcopate, and my gratitude to Almighty God for His many blessings, the pleasure of the celebration was enhanced by knowing that it had been made the occasion for this meeting of the Hierarchy and for the inauguration of these measures which I regard as the most important since the Third Plenary Council of Baltimore.

The appointment of "The Committee on General Catholic Interests and Affairs" is especially gratifying to me. Hitherto, through the courtesy of my Confrères in the Episcopate and largely because the center of our National Government is within the limits of the Baltimore Archdiocese, the burden of the Church's general interests has in great measure rested on me. My experience has made me feel keenly the necessity of such a committee which with adequate authority and the aid of sub-committees could accomplish more than any individual, however able and willing he might be.

It is recognized by all that the Catholic Church in America, partly through defective organization, is not exerting the influence which it ought to exert in proportion to our numbers and the individual prominence of many of our people. Our diocesan units indeed are well organized. But the Church in America as a whole has been suffering from the lack of a unified force that might be directed to the furthering of those general policies which are vital to all. It was the general opinion of the Prelates present that we need a committee of the Hierarchy which shall be representative, authoritative and directive. It should be representative in the sense that it would stand for and express the views of the whole Hierarchy. It should be authoritative in as much as it would possess the confidence and have the support of

---

[2] Bonaventura Cerretti (1872–1933) was at the time Archbishop of Corinth and Secretary of the Congregation for Extraordinary Ecclesiastical Affairs. It was during Cerretti's time as auditor of the Apostolic Delegation in Washington, 1906–1914, that he and Gibbons had become close friends. He was later Apostolic Nuncio to France, 1921–1925.

the whole Hierarchy. Probably, too, it should be empowered to act when any emergency arises for which no provision has been made, but when immediate action is imperative and it would be impossible for lack of time to obtain the views of the individual members of the Hierarchy. Such a committee will unify our forces if entrusted with the powers above outlined.

I was asked by the Prelates who were present at the meeting to appoint the members of this committee, and I have named the committee to act until the next meeting of the Hierarchy. For the permanent and regular method of choosing this committee, however, it will, I think, be more satisfactory to all the Hierarchy, and more authoritative, if the committee be elected by secret ballot by all the members present at our annual meeting. It might be understood that those who are unable to attend the annual meeting should send their votes before the meeting.

The committee so chosen would naturally be composed of Prelates representing as far as possible all the interest of the Church at large, as well as the various sections of our country.

If this plan for organizing the committee is agreeable to you, we shall at our next annual meeting elect in the way I have suggested four Prelates by ballot. In the meantime, as a temporary measure, I have asked the four Prelates of the National Catholic War Council, who were selected, with the consent of the majority of the Hierarchy, to serve on the "Committee on General Catholic Interests and Activities";[3] and as I was Chairman of the War Council I will act as chairman of the new Committee until our next general meeting.

A meeting of the Committee will be held during the month of May.[4] Several very important matters naturally impose themselves for consideration:

The collection for the Holy Father;

The continuation of the activities of the National War Council as far as may be deemed expedient;

Measures to safeguard general Catholic interests in National Legislation;

The vital interests of Catholic education;

---

[3] The members of the committee were: Peter J. Muldoon (1863–1927), Bishop of Rockford, vice-chairman; Joseph Schrembs (1866–1945), Bishop of Toledo; Joseph S. Glass, C.M. (1874–1926), Bishop of Salt Lake; and William T. Russell (1863–1927), Bishop of Charleston.

[4] The meeting was held in New York on May 8, 1919, on the occasion of the conferring of the pallium on Archbishop Hayes.

The awakening of concern about the needs of home and foreign missions.

Suggestions concerning these or any other matters of general Catholic interest will be greatly appreciated by myself and the other members of the Committee.[5]

Faithfully yours in Xto.

J. Card. Gibbons

In a Plenary Session held on the twenty-second day of the month of June, the Sacred Consistorial Congregation, acting on new data, has decided that nothing is to be changed concerning "The National Catholic Welfare Council"; and that, therefore, the Bishops of the United States of North America may meet next September as is their custom, in accordance, however, with the instructions given below.

Given at Rome at the Office of the Sacred Consistorial Congregation on the twenty-second day of June, 1922.

C. Card. De Lai, *Bishop of Sabina,*

Secretary.

A. Sincero, *Assessor.*

These instructions for the meeting of the Bishops, which is to be held in the coming month of September, in accordance with the Decree of the twenty-second day of June, 1922, are issued by order of His Holiness.

1. Whereas, some Bishops for reasons which seem to be weighty, have expressed a wish that these meetings be not held every year, the Bishops should consider whether or not hereafter the meetings should be held at longer intervals.

2. In any case, to dispel misgivings, it must be very well understood that Bishops are not bound to attend these meetings, either in person or by representative.

3. Likewise, as the decisions of the Bishops at these meetings have

---

[5] On May 5, 1919, Gibbons outlined in considerable detail for the four bishops of the committee his ideas concerning the lines along which he thought the organization should be developed. On May 17 in a letter to the entire hierarchy, which enclosed a report of the committee's meeting in New York on May 8, Gibbons likewise included copies of Benedict XV's letter of April 10 which he had just received and which gave the pope's approval to their plans for an annual meeting of all the bishops and for the future N.C.W.C. A week later, May 24, Gibbons and the four bishops of the committee sent a formal notice to all members of the American hierarchy announcing the date of September 24, 1919, as that on which the first annual meeting of the hierarchy would assemble at the Catholic University of America and asking the bishops to send any suggestions they might have for the agenda to Bishop Muldoon who was in charge of details or arrangement. These letters are all printed in the *Ecclesiastical Review*, LXI (July, 1919), 10–19.

nothing in common with conciliar legislation, which is governed by a prescript of the Sacred Canons (Cod. Can. 281, seq.), they will not have force of law since, as from the beginning, it has been clearly understood the meetings are held merely for friendly conference about measures of a common public interest for the safeguarding of the Church's work in the United States.

4. That the Bishops may be in a position to enter into the discussions with proper deliberation, they should be provided in due season by those in charge of the meeting with a summary of the points or questions to be considered. This, however, should not hinder any Bishop from proposing to the meeting any other question of particular interest. Yet all questions should deal with those topics proposed by His Holiness, Pope Benedict XV in the Brief, "Communes," dated the 10th of April, 1919.[6]

5. The Chairman of the meeting will be determined by the prescriptions of canon law.

6. The minutes of the meeting are to be sent to the Holy See so that if need be the Holy See may duly intervene.

7. The Ordinaries of each ecclesiastical province may before the General Meeting meet with their Metropolitan or senior Bishop to confer beforehand upon some point.

8. Whereas the name, the National Catholic Welfare Council, is open to some misunderstandings, and in fact has not been acceptable to all, it may be well for the Bishops to consider whether it would not be wise to choose some other name, as for instance, "The National Catholic Welfare Committee."[7] Meanwhile, all should know that this organization however named, is not to be identified with the Catholic hierarchy itself in the United States.

9. The Bishops in their General Meeting may delegate an individual

---

[6] In his brief *Communes* of April 10, 1919, addressed to Cardinal Gibbons, Benedict XV had stated: "We learn that you have unanimously resolved that a yearly meeting of all the bishops shall be held at an appointed place, in order to adopt the most suitable means of promoting the interests and welfare of the Catholic Church, and that you have appointed from among the bishops two commissions, one of which will deal with social questions, while the other will study educational problems, and both will report to the Episcopal brethren. This is truly a worthy resolve, and with the utmost satisfaction We bestow upon it Our approval." *Ecclesiastical Review*, LXI (July, 1919), 4.

[7] The word "council" in the official title of the organization was changed to "conference" at the annual meeting of the hierarchy on September 27, 1922. The change was made because the former word was believed to involve some delicate and difficult points of both civil and canon law. It was Archbishop Hayes of New York who suggested the word "conference" for the title.

or a committee, to undertake some definite commission during the interval between the meetings. But care must be taken:

(a) That the commission be limited from the beginning, both as to time and method of operation.

(b) That no infringement of canonical authority of any Ordinary in the government of his diocese be made by any agent or committee thus established.

(c) That on due denunciation by a Bishop and proof of interference in the internal management of a diocese by any agent of the Welfare Council, the said agent shall be summarily dismissed from office.

(d) The choice of those who are to be thus employed as agents of the Bishops will be made by the Bishops at their General Meeting, and at their pleasure. Those who are so engaged will hold office meeting to meeting and must make reports especially of their accounts at every meeting. The Bishops, if they so please, may re-elect those agents according to the needs of the work.

Given at Rome at the Office of the Sacred Consistorial Congregation on the fourth day of July, 1922.

C. Card. De Lai, *Bishop of Sabina,*

Secretary.

A. Sincero, *Assessor.*

157. The Supreme Court Affirms the Right of Private Religious Schools, June 1, 1925

THE right of private schools has more than once been questioned in the United States but never, perhaps, more seriously than by an Oregon law of November, 1922, which would have compelled all children in the state between the ages of eight and sixteen to attend the public schools. The constitutionality of the law was challenged by the Sisters of the Holy Names of Jesus and Mary who had many schools in Oregon, an action in which they were joined by the Hill Military Academy as a defendant. The case was ultimately appealed to the Supreme Court of the United States, and in the following unanimous decision in *Pierce* v. *Society of Sisters* handed down by Justice James C. McReynolds (1862–1946) the state was forbidden to deny the right of parents to choose a private school for their children as a violation of the fourteenth amendment. Source: *Pierce* v. *Society of Sisters,* 268 U.S. 510 (pp. 529–536).

These appeals are from decrees, based upon undenied allegations, which granted preliminary orders restraining appellants from threatening or attempting to enforce the Compulsory Education Act adopted November 7, 1922, under the initiative provision of her Constitution by the voters of Oregon. They present the same points of law; there are no controverted questions of fact. Rights said to be guaranteed by the federal Constitution were specially set up, and appropriate prayers asked for their protection.

The challenged Act, effective September 1, 1926, requires every parent . . . of a child between eight and sixteen years to send him "to a public school for the period of time a public school shall be held during the current year" in the district where the child resides; and failure to do so is declared a misdemeanor. . . . The manifest purpose is to compel general attendance at public schools by normal children between eight and sixteen, who have not completed the eighth grade. And without doubt enforcement of the statute would seriously impair, perhaps destroy, the profitable features of appellees' business, and greatly diminish the value of their property.

Appellee, the Society of Sisters,[1] is an Oregon corporation, organized in 1880, with power to care for orphans, educate and instruct the youth, establish and maintain academies or schools, and acquire necessary real and personal property. It has long devoted its property and effort to the secular and religious education and care of children, and has acquired the valuable good will of many parents and guardians. It conducts interdependent primary and high schools and junior colleges, and maintains orphanages for the custody and control of children between eight and sixteen. In its primary schools many children between those ages are taught the subjects usually pursued in Oregon public schools during the first eight years. Systematic religious instruction and moral training according to the tenets of the Roman Catholic Church are also regularly provided. All courses of study, both temporal and religious, contemplate continuity of training under appellee's charge; the primary schools are essential to the system and the most profitable. It owns valuable buildings, especially constructed and equipped for school purposes. The business is remunerative — the annual income from primary schools exceeds thirty thousand dollars — and the successful conduct of this business requires long-time contracts with teachers and parents. The Compulsory Education Act of 1922 has already caused the withdrawal from its schools of children who would otherwise

---

[1] The Sisters of the Holy Names of Jesus and Mary, founded in Canada, first came to Oregon in October, 1859, at the invitation of Francis Norbert Blanchet (1795–1883), first Archbishop of Oregon City. They were the first religious congregation of women to make a permanent settlement in Oregon where they still conduct numerous schools.

continue, and their income has steadily declined. The appellants, public officers, have proclaimed their purpose strictly to enforce the statute.

After setting out the above facts the Society's bill alleges that the enactment conflicts with the right of parents to choose schools where their children will receive appropriate mental and religious training, the right of the child to influence the parents' choice of a school, the right of schools and teachers therein to engage in a useful business or profession, and is accordingly repugnant to the Constitution and void. And, further, that unless enforcement of the measure is enjoined the corporation's business and property will suffer irreparable injury.

No question is raised concerning the power of the State reasonably to regulate all schools, to inspect, supervise and examine them, their teachers and pupils; to require that all children of proper age attend some school, that teachers shall be of good moral character and patriotic disposition, that certain studies plainly essential to good citizenship must be taught, and that nothing be taught which is manifestly inimical to the public welfare.

The inevitable practical result of enforcing the Act under considera-tion would be destruction of appellees' primary schools, and perhaps all other private primary schools for normal children within the State of Oregon. Appellees are engaged in a kind of undertaking not in-herently harmful, but long regarded as useful and meritorious. Certainly there is nothing in the present records to indicate that they have failed to discharge their obligations to patrons, students, or the State. And there are no peculiar circumstances or present emergencies which demand extraordinary measures relative to primary education.

Under the doctrine of *Meyer* v. *Nebraska,* 262 U.S. 390,[2] we think it entirely plain that the Act of 1922 unreasonably interferes with the liberty of parents and guardians to direct the upbringing and education of children under their control. As often heretofore pointed out rights guaranteed by the Constitution may not be abridged by legislation which has no reasonable relation to some purpose within the competency of the State. The fundamental theory of liberty upon which all govern-ments in this Union repose excludes any general power of the State to standardize its children by forcing them to accept instruction from

---

[2] In 1923 the Supreme Court in *Meyer* v. *Nebraska* declared unconstitutional a law forbidding the teaching of any language other than English to any child below the eighth grade by any teacher in a public or private school. The court upheld the right of the plaintiff, an instructor in a Lutheran parochial school, to teach a foreign language, as well as the right of the parents to engage him to instruct their children, both as being within the liberty of the fourteenth amendment.

public teachers only. The child is not the mere creature of the State; those who nurture him and direct his destiny have the right, coupled with the high duty, to recognize and prepare him for additional obligations.

The suits were not premature. The injury to appellees was present and very real, not a mere possibility in the remote future. If no relief had been possible prior to the effective date of the Act, the injury would have become irreparable. Prevention of impending injury by unlawful action is a well recognized function of courts of equity.

The decrees below are

Affirmed.

158. Governor Smith's Answer to the Religious Bigotry of the Presidential Campaign, September 20, 1928

FOLLOWING the decline of the A.P.A. in the late 1890's the American people were not again subjected to an organized outburst of religious and racial bigotry until the revival of the Ku Klux Klan. The second K.K.K. was founded in November, 1915, in Georgia by William J. Simmons and a group of associates for the purpose of opposing Catholics, Negroes, Jews, and the foreign-born. One of its principal targets was Alfred E. Smith (1873–1944), four times Governor of New York. Smith was a strong contender for the presidential nomination in the Democratic conventions of 1920 and 1924, and on June 28, 1928, he was nominated on the first ballot by the convention at Houston. Once the nomination had become an accomplished fact the K.K.K. concentrated all its fire on Smith with the result that his Tammany Hall connections, his opposition to prohibition, but, above all, his Catholic faith were made the objects of the most scurrilous attacks. As the campaign progressed the attacks on his religion became increasingly insidious, and on September 20 at Oklahoma City Smith brought the subject into the open. A recent work states that the hostility at Oklahoma City was so marked that there was "real concern for Smith's personal safety, and his eastern advisers were relieved when the telephone brought word that the Governor had reached his hotel safely after an emotion-packed evening" (Edmund A. Moore, *A Catholic Runs for President. The Campaign of 1928* [New York, 1956], p. 180). The same authority remarks, "At Oklahoma City, Smith neither invented nor introduced the issue. His address there stands beside his 'Reply' to Marshall as a great effort in the arduous struggle to extend freedom in the United States" (*ibid.*, p. 187). Yet his candor and straightforwardness, and his brilliant record as Governor of New York, had little effect on the final result, and on November 6 it was found that he had carried only eight states with an electoral vote of eighty-seven against 444 for his Republican rival. In spite of the abuse to which he had been subjected, Governor Smith spoke to the nation in a postelection address on November 13 with true magnanimity in which he called for the aid and co-operation of all citizens for the president-elect. The measure of the man's greatness was evident in his closing words when he said, "Regardless of the outcome, in a spirit of the deepest appreciation of the opportunities afforded me and of the loyal support given to me by upward of 15,000,000 of my fellow citizens, I pledge my unceasing interest and concern with public affairs and the well-being of the American people" (*op. cit.*, p. 322). Source: *Campaign Addresses of Governor Alfred E. Smith* (Washington: Democratic National Committee, 1929), pp. 43–45, 49, 51, 53–58.

. . . In a presidential campaign there should be but two considerations before the electorate: The platform of the party, and the ability of the candidate to make it effective.

In this campaign an effort has been made to distract the attention of the electorate from these two considerations and to fasten it on malicious and un-American propaganda.

I shall tonight discuss and denounce that wicked attempt. I shall speak openly on the things about which people have been whispering to you. . . .

Twenty-five years ago I began my active public career. I was then elected to the Assembly, representing the neighborhood in New York City where I was born, where my wife was born, where my five children were born and where my father and mother were born. I represented that district continuously for twelve years, until 1915, when I was elected Sheriff of New York county.

Two years later I was elected to the position of President of the Board of Aldermen, which is really that of Vice-Mayor of the City of New York.

In 1918 I was elected by the delegates to the State convention as the candidate of the Democratic Party for Governor and was elected.

Running for re-election in 1920, I was defeated in the Harding landslide. However, while Mr. Harding carried the State of New York by more than 1,100,000 plurality, I was defeated only by some 70,000 votes.

After this defeat I returned to private life, keeping up my interest in public affairs, and accepted appointment to an important State body at the hands of the man who had defeated me.

In 1922 the Democratic Convention, by unanimous vote, renominated me for the third time for Governor. I was elected by the record plurality of 387,000, and this in a State which had been normally Republican.

In 1924, at the earnest solicitation of the Democratic presidential candidate,[1] I accepted nomination. The State of New York was carried by President Coolidge by close to 700,000 plurality, but I was elected Governor. On the morning after election I found myself the only Democrat elected on the State ticket, with both houses of the Legislature overwhelmingly Republican.

Renominated by the unanimous vote of the convention of 1926, I made my fifth State-wide run for the governorship and was again elected the Democratic Governor of a normally Republican State.

Consequently, I am in a position to come before you tonight as the Governor of New York finishing out his fourth term.

The record of accomplishment under my four administrations recommended me to the Democratic Party in the nation, and I was nominated for the presidency at the Houston convention on the first ballot.

To put the picture before you completely, it is necessary for me to refer briefly to this record of accomplishment. . . . [Governor Smith then went into detail concerning the main legislative enactments, appointments, etc., of his administrations.]

One scandal connected with my administration would do more to help out the Republican National Committee in its campaign against me than all the millions of dollars now being spent by them in malicious propaganda. Unfortunately for them, they cannot find it, because the truth is it is not there. I challenge Senator Owen[2] and all his kind to point to one single flaw upon which they can rest their case. But they won't find it. They won't try to find it, because I know what lies behind all this, and I will tell you before I sit down to-night. . . .

I know what lies behind all this and I shall tell you. I specifically refer to the question of my religion. Ordinarily, that word should never be used in a political campaign. The necessity for using it is forced on me by Senator Owen and his kind, and I feel that at least once in this campaign, I, as the candidate of the Democratic Party, owe it to the people of this country to discuss frankly and openly with them this attempt of Senator Owen and the forces behind him to inject bigotry, hatred, intolerance and un-American sectarian division into a campaign which should be an intelligent debate of the important issues which confront the American people. . . .

A recent newspaper account in the City of New York told the story of a woman who called at the Republican National headquarters

[1] John W. Davis (1873–1955) had been nominated on the 103rd ballot after a prolonged fight between the forces of Smith and William G. McAdoo.
[2] Robert L. Owen (1856–1947) had served three terms as United States Senator from Oklahoma, 1907–1925. He left the Democratic Party in 1928 to go over to the Republicans on the score that Smith was the creature of Tammany Hall.

in Washington, seeking some literature to distribute. She made the request that it be of a nature other than political. Those in charge of the Republican Publicity Bureau provided the lady with an automobile and she was driven to the office of a publication notorious throughout the country for its senseless, stupid, foolish attacks upon the Catholic Church and upon Catholics generally.

I can think of no greater disaster to this country than to have the voters of it divide upon religious lines. It is contrary to the spirit, not only of the Declaration of Independence, but of the Constitution itself. During all of our national life we have prided ourselves throughout the world on the declaration of the fundamental American truth that all men are created equal.

Our forefathers, in their wisdom, seeing the danger to the country of a division on religious issues, wrote into the Constitution of the United States in no uncertain words the declaration that no religious test shall ever be applied for public office, and it is a sad thing in 1928, in view of the countless billions of dollars that we have poured into the cause of public education, to see some American citizens proclaiming themselves 100 per cent. American, and in the document that makes that proclamation suggesting that I be defeated for the presidency because of my religious belief.

The Grand Dragon of the Realm of Arkansas, writing to a citizen of that State, urges my defeat because I am a Catholic, and in the letter suggests to the man, who happened to be a delegate to the Democratic convention, that by voting against me he was upholding American ideals and institutions as established by our forefathers.

The Grand Dragon that thus advised a delegate to the national convention to vote against me because of my religion is a member of an order known as the Ku Klux Klan, who had the effrontery to refer to themselves as 100 per cent. Americans.

Yet totally ignorant of the history and tradition of this country and its institutions and, in the name of Americanism, they breathe into the hearts and souls of their members hatred of millions of their fellow countrymen because of their religious belief. . . .

I would have no objection to anybody finding fault with my public record circularizing the whole United States, provided he would tell the truth. But no decent, right-minded, upstanding American citizen can for a moment countenance the shower of lying statements, with no basis in fact, that have been reduced to printed matter and sent broadcast through the mails of this country.

One lie widely circulated, particularly through the southern part of the country, is that during my governorship I appointed practically nobody to office but members of my own church.

What are the facts? On investigation I find that in the cabinet of the Governor sit fourteen men. Three of the fourteen are Catholics, ten Protestants, and one of Jewish faith. In various bureaus and divisions of the Cabinet officers, the Governor appointed twenty-six people. Twelve of them are Catholics and fourteen of them are Protestants. Various other State officials, making up boards and commissions, and appointed by the Governor, make a total of 157 appointments, of which thirty-five were Catholics, 106 were Protestants, twelve were Jewish, and four I could not find out about.

I have appointed a large number of judges of all our courts, as well as a large number of county officers, for the purpose of filling vacancies. They total in number 177, of which sixty-four were Catholics, ninety were Protestants, eleven were Jewish, and twelve of the officials I was unable to find anything about so far as their religion was concerned.

This is a complete answer to the false, misleading and, if I may be permitted the use of the harsher word, lying statements that have found their way through a large part of this country in the form of printed matter.

If the American people are willing to sit silently by and see large amounts of money secretly pour into false and misleading propaganda for political purposes, I repeat that I see in this not only a danger to the party, but a danger to the country. . . . [Here other instances of bigotry in the campaign were cited.]

I have been told that politically it might be expedient foɪ me to remain silent upon this subject, but so far as I am concerned no political expediency will keep me from speaking out in an endeavor to destroy these evil attacks.

There is abundant reason for believing that Republicans high in the councils of the party have countenanced a large part of this form of campaign, if they have not actually promoted it. A sin of omission is some times as grievous as a sin of commission. They may, through official spokesmen, disclaim as much as they please responsibility for dragging into a national campaign the question of religion, something that according to our Constitution, our history and our traditions has no part in any campaign for elective public office. . . .

One of the things, if not the meanest thing, in the campaign is a circular pretending to place someone of my faith in the position of seeking votes for me because of my Catholicism. Like everything of this kind, of course it is unsigned, and it would be impossible to trace its authorship. It reached me through a member of the Masonic order who, in turn, received it in the mail. It is false in its every line. It was designed on its very face to injure me with members of churches other than my own.

I here emphatically declare that I do not wish any member of my faith in any part of the United States to vote for me on any religious grounds. I want them to vote for me only when in their hearts and consciences they become convinced that my election will promote the best interests of our country.

By the same token, I cannot refrain from saying that any person who votes against me simply because of my religion is not, to my way of thinking, a good citizen. . . .

The constitutional guaranty that there should be no religious test for public office is not a mere form of words. It represents the most vital principle that ever was given any people.

I attack those who seek to undermine it, not only because I am a good Christian, but because I am a good American and a product of America and of American institutions. Everything I am, and everything I hope to be, I owe to those institutions.

The absolute separation of State and Church is part of the fundamental basis of our Constitution. I believe in that separation, and in all that it implies. That belief must be a part of the fundamental faith of every true American. . . .

159. Dom Michel Explains the Origins of the Liturgical Movement in the United States, February 24, 1929

ONE of the most serious lacunae in the literature of American Catholicism is that pertaining to the inner life of the Church. Yet every historian must recognize the importance that forms and methods of worship and devotion play in the spiritual life of the people. In that connection. the liturgical movement of the twentieth century has been of special significance. The movement, which has sought through the doctrine of the Mystical Body to bring all Catholics into active participation in the official worship of the Church, is now over a century old in Europe. But it was only in the 1920's that it began to take shape in the United States with the establishment of the Liturgical Press of St. John's Abbey, Collegeville, Minnesota, and its monthly journal, *Orate Fratres* (now called *Worship*), the first number of which appeared in November, 1926. The movement owed its origin to a number of persons scattered throughout the country, as the following document makes clear, but its successful launching was due to none more than to Virgil Michel, O.S.B. (1890–1938), first editor of *Orate Fratres,* and to the active support of his superior, Abbot Alcuin Deutsch (1877–1951). In a letter to a fellow religious Dom Michel fixed the date of the efforts at St. John's when he said, "The first ideas of our plans were penned in February 1923, and by dint of slow correspondence the plans grew until they are now full-fledged" (Archives of St. John's Abbey, Michel to Francis Augustine Walsh, O.S.B., Collegeville, January 25, 1926, copy). The success that has attended the movement in the past thirty years may be measured in part by the fact that, whereas in 1926 use of the daily missal among American Catholics was very limited, there are today nineteen editions in English of the missal in millions of copies for those who assist at Mass and the divine offices of the Church. Moreover, the National Liturgical Week, held annually in various cities since 1940, is drawing a larger and increasingly enthusiastic following each year. Source: "The Apostolate," *Orate Fratres,* III (February 24, 1929), 121–123.

It was only recently we received two fall numbers of the "midweek" section of an excellent Catholic paper. One number contained an article in which St. John's Abbey was spoken of with enthusiasm as the "source of the Liturgical Movement." The unnamed author is evidently a very good friend. In the second number there was an answer to the first article, written by two intimate friends of ours. The second article briefly describes earlier European "sources" of the Liturgical Movement, mentions the fact that the spirit of the movement began to manifest itself "almost simultaneously in various sections of the United States some seven or eight years ago," and that various promoters of it were at work independently and, at first, even unknown to each other, until a number of them were brought together. Their deliberations and plans finally resulted in an organized liturgical apostolate, the founding of the Liturgical Press at St. John's Abbey, and the publishing of *Orate Fratres* by the monks of St. John's with the assistance of fellow editors outside the monastery. In the interest of truth we are glad to add a few facts that happen to come to mind at the present writing, especially since no written record of the beginning of the movement exists.

There were various "sources" of liturgical movement in the United States quite independent of St. John's Abbey, and antedating the public apostolate in which the latter is now engaged. Foremost among these must be mentioned well-known O'Fallon (Mo.), where Father Hellriegel[1] and the late Father Jasper[2] commenced activities that have

---

[1] Martin B. Hellriegel (1890 –), spiritual director of the Sisters of the Most Precious Blood, O'Fallon, Missouri, 1918–1940; pastor of Holy Cross Church, St. Louis, 1940 –.
[2] Anthony Jasper (d. 1925), pastor of Assumption Church, O'Fallon, Missouri.

been a great inspiration to many. From O'Fallon — in part at least, unless we are mistaken — came the spark that grew to a live flame among some of the Jesuit Fathers of St. Louis, at whose University lectures on aspects of the liturgy have been given for some years, and where the recent National Students Spiritual Leadership Convention took place. . . . Over a decade ago the late Dr. Shields,[3] as head of the Education Department of the Catholic University of America, was seeking to imbue a complete program of Catholic primary education with the spirit of the liturgy. More recently, Dr. George Johnson[4] has done excellent work in directing efforts along the same line. It was at least under the encouragement of Dr. Shields that the work of Mrs. Justine B. Ward[5] grew into an extensive program of gregorian revival, and with the co-operation of the Religious of the Sacred Heart resulted in the influential Pius X Institute of Liturgical Music,[6] soon to enter upon its thirteenth flourishing year. At the St. Paul Seminary the Reverend William Bush [*sic*][7] was working quietly but perseveringly for many years, and the results of his inspiration are now showing themselves in the zeal and efforts for a more liturgical formation of the people on the part of many young priests that caught the divine spark from him. His translation of Father Kramp's[8] *Eucharistia* [St. Paul, 1926] antedated *Orate Fratres* by some months, as did also the translation of Father Kramp's *The Sacrifice of the New Law* [St. Louis, 1926] by Rev. Leo F. Miller. The translations of the Latin sacramental texts by the Reverend Richard E. Power, published in our Popular Liturgical Library and known everywhere for their excellent qualities, are the result of years of study engaged upon when The Liturgical Press was not even existing in any human dream-world. There were many other centers of liturgical life carrying on unknown to each other, quietly preparing the way for a more conscious general revival.

Not only were our Associate Editors, among others, so many inde-

---

[3] Thomas E. Shields (1862–1921), professor of education in the Catholic University of America, founder of the Sisters College and the *Catholic Educational Review* in 1911.

[4] George Johnson (1889–1944), associate professor of education in the Catholic University of America and director of the Department of Education of the National Catholic Welfare Conference.

[5] Justine B. Ward (1879 —), writer and promoter of reform in church music.

[6] Pius X School of Liturgical Music at Manhattanville College of the Sacred Heart, New York, was founded in 1916.

[7] William Busch (1882 —), professor of church history in the St. Paul Seminary since 1913.

[8] Joseph Kramp, S.J. (1886 —), a pioneer of the liturgical movement in Germany and contributor to the *Ecclesia Orans* series of the Abbey of Maria Laach edited by Abbot Ildefons Herwegen.

pendent "sources" of liturgical awakening. They have also been co-operators in organizing and developing the work that centers in our abbey; and this, first of all, by their active part in the plans and discussions preceding the launching of our ventures; and then by their continued advice, and their free contribution of efforts — which later assistance is of no mean importance for a new journalistic undertaking, especially in our own day when money rules the day and is all-decisive. Some of our contributors have also helped us in a similar way, notably Miss Ellen Gates Starr,[9] whose articles on the Breviary received special mention from many of our correspondents.

All of these are doing their own part towards what is now consciously a common cause, one which it is also our privilege to promote to the best of our abilities. All of them have their efforts and intentions recorded in the Book of Life and they are not seeking for recognition of this work here below. Yet we have mentioned the above facts here, not so much for their sake — for we know their good will and desires — but for our own sake, lest in any way we should appear willing to receive credit beyond our desert. God forbid! It is from Him and Him alone that all sufficiency comes.

The liturgical apostolate is bigger than any individual, than any abbey, than any order, than any larger group of men, than the entire body of those who are spending their efforts in its promotion throughout the world. For it is in truth a spiritual ferment destined to permeate the entire body mystic of Christ according to the words of its official inaugurator.[10] Its aim is to imbue the members of this body more thoroughly with "the true Christian spirit," and through this renewed vigor to institute also a renewed growth of that mystic body unto an ever greater attainment here on earth of the "fullness of him who is filled all in all."[11]

---

[9] Ellen Gates Starr (1859–1940), best known as a co-founder with Jane Addams of Hull House, Chicago, in 1889, the first settlement house in the United States; a pioneer social worker, converted to Catholicism in 1920, and a promoter of the American liturgical movement in its early years.

[10] St. Pius X (1835–1914) by his *Motu proprio* of November 22, 1903, on the subject of sacred music and his later pronouncements on the reform of the breviary, frequent Communion, etc., is looked upon as the "official inaugurator" of the liturgical movement.

[11] Eph. 1:23.

160. Dorothy Day Describes the Launching of *The Catholic Worker* and the Movement Behind It, May, 1933

THE great depression of the 1930's set on foot numerous projects throughout the United States for the relief of the immense army of unemployed. During this period of severe distress the charitable agencies of the Church were taxed as never before, but there was no more distinctive and inspiring example of Catholic charity than that of the Catholic Worker Movement. Through its houses of hospitality, its organization of farming communes, and its program of discussion groups, study clubs, and publications disseminating the social doctrines of the Church, the Catholic Worker Movement not only gave a new start in life to many of the victims of the depression, but it likewise inspired and trained young Catholic workers and intellectuals who in the years that followed found their way into other enterprises like the Association of Catholic Trade Unionists and the Catholic youth movement. The undertaking was due in the main to Dorothy Day (1898 —) who had been a member of the Socialist Party, the I.W.W., and communist affiliates and who knew, therefore, at first hand what the social philosophy was from the angle of the left. In December, 1927, she became a convert to Catholicism, and when the depression struck she channeled her zeal and love for the poor in a way that proved eminently practical for countless men and women who had been cut adrift from their normal walks of life. In the excerpts from her memoirs that follow she tells of the beginnings of the movement's best known publication, as well as something about how the original house of hospitality was operated in its early days. Source: *The Long Loneliness. The Autobiography of Dorothy Day* (New York: Harper & Bros., 1952), pp. 182–186.

We started publishing *The Catholic Worker* at 436 East Fifteenth Street in May, 1933, with a first issue of 2,500 copies. Within three or four months the circulation bounded to 25,000, and it was cheaper to bring it out as an eight-page tabloid on newsprint rather than the smaller-sized edition on better paper we had started with. By the end of the year we had a circulation of 100,000 and by 1936 it was 150,000. It was certainly a mushroom growth. It was not only that some parishes subscribed for the paper all over the country in bundles of 500 or more. Zealous young people took the paper out in the streets and sold it, and when they could not sell it even at one cent a copy, they gave free copies and left them in streetcar, bus, barber shop and dentist's and doctor's office. We got letters from all parts of the country from people who said they had picked up the paper on trains, in rooming houses. One letter came from the state of Sonora in Mexico and we read with amazement that the reader had tossed in an uncomfortable bed on a hot night until he got up to turn over the mattress and under it found a copy of *The Catholic Worker*. A miner found a copy five miles underground in an old mine that stretched out under the Atlantic Ocean off Nova Scotia. A seminarian said that he had sent out his shoes to be half-soled in Rome and they came back to him wrapped in a copy of *The Catholic Worker*. These letters thrilled and inspired the young people who came to help, sent by Brothers or Sisters who taught in the high schools. We were invited to speak in schools and parishes, and often as a result of our speaking others came in to help us. On May Day, those first few years, the streets were literally lined with papers. Looking back on it, it seemed like a gigantic advertising campaign, entirely unpremeditated. It grew organically, Peter[1] used to say happily, and not through organization. "We are not an organization, we are an organism," he said.

First there was Peter, my brother and I. When John took a job at Dobb's Ferry, a young girl, Dorothy Weston, who had been studying journalism and was a graduate of a Catholic college, came to help. She lived at home and spent her days with us, eating with us and taking only her carfare from the common fund. Peter brought in three young men from Columbus Circle, whom he had met when discussing the affairs of the world there, and of these one became bookkeeper (that was his occupation when he was employed), another circulation manager, and the third married Dorothy Weston. Another girl came to take dictation and help with mailing the paper, and she married the circulation manager. There were quite a number of romances that first year — the paper appealed to youth. Then there were the young intellectuals who formed what they called Campion Committees in other cities as well as New York, who helped to picket the Mexican and German consulates and who distributed literature all over the city. Workers came in to get help on picket lines, to help move dispossessed families and to make demonstrations in front of relief offices. Three men came to sell the paper on the street, and to eat their meals with us. Big Dan had been a truck driver and a policeman. The day he came in to see us he wanted nothing more than to bathe his tired feet. That night at supper Peter indoctrinated him on the dignity of poverty and read some of Father Vincent McNabb's *Nazareth or Social Chaos*.[2] This did not go

---

[1] Peter Maurin (1877–1949), a Frenchman of peasant origin, was co-founder with Dorothy Day of the Catholic Worker Movement.

[2] This particular volume of the many books written by the well-known

over so well, all of us being city people, and Father McNabb advocating a return to the fields, but he made Dan Orr go out with a sense of a mission, not worrying about shabby clothes or the lack of a job. Dan began to sell the paper on the streets and earned enough money to live on. He met others who had found subsistence jobs, carrying sandwich signs or advertising children's furniture by pushing a baby carriage, a woman who told fortunes in a tea shop, a man who sold pretzels, which were threaded on four poles one on each corner of an old baby carriage. He found out their needs, and those of their families, and never left the house in the morning without bundles of clothes as well as his papers.

Dan rented a horse and wagon in which to deliver bundles of the paper each month. (We had tried this before he came but someone had to push the horse while the other led it. We knew nothing about driving a wagon.) Dan loved his horse. He called it Catholic Action, and used to take the blanket off my bed to cover the horse in winter. We rented it from a German Nazi on East Sixteenth Street, and sometimes when we had no money he let us have the use of it free for a few hours. It rejoiced our hearts to move a Jewish family into their new quarters with his equipment.

Dan said it was a pious horse and that when he passed St. Patrick's Cathedral, the horse genuflected. He liked to drive up Fifth Avenue, preferably with students who had volunteered their help, and shout, "Read *The Catholic Worker*" at the top of his lungs. He was anything but dignified and loved to affront the dignity of others.

One time he saw me coming down the street when he was selling the paper in front of Gimbel's and began to yell, "Read *The Catholic Worker!* Romance on every page." A seminarian from St. Louis, now Father Dreisoner [*sic*],[3] took a leaf from Dan's book and began selling the paper on the corner of Times Square and at union meetings. He liked to stand next to a comrade selling *The Daily Worker,* and as the one shouted "Read *The Daily Worker*," he in turn shouted, "Read *The Catholic Worker* daily." Between sales they conversed. . . .

Peter, the "green" revolutionist, had a long-term program which called for hospices, or houses of hospitality, where the works of mercy could be practiced to combat the taking over by the state of all those services which could be built up by mutual aid; and farming communes

---

English Dominican, Vincent NcNabb (1868–1943), was published in London in 1933.

[3] Father John H. Dreisoemer is at present pastor of St. Clement's Church, Bowling Green, Missouri.

to provide land and homes for the unemployed, whom increasing technology was piling up into the millions. In 1933, the unemployed numbered 13,000,000.

The idea of the houses of hospitality caught on quickly enough. The very people that Peter brought in, who made up our staff at first, needed a place to live. Peter was familiar with the old I.W.W.[4] technique of a common flophouse and a pot of mulligan on the stove. To my cost, I too had become well acquainted with this idea.

Besides, we never had any money, and the cheapest, most practical way to take care of people was to rent some apartments and have someone do the cooking for the lot of us. Many a time I was cook and cleaner as well as editor and street seller. When Margaret, a Lithuanian girl from the mining regions of Pennsylvania, came to us and took over the cooking, we were happy indeed. She knew how to make a big pot of mashed potatoes with mushroom sauce which filled everyone up nicely. She was a great soft creature with a little baby, Barbara, who was born a few months after she came to us. Margaret went out on May Day with the baby and sold papers on the street. She loved being propagandist as well as cook. When Big Dan teased her, she threatened to tell the "pasture" of the church around the corner.

To house the women we had an apartment near First Avenue which could hold about ten. When there were arguments among them, Margaret would report them with gusto, giving us a blow-by-blow account. Once when she was telling how one of the women abused her so that she "felt as though the crown of thorns was pressing right down on her head" (she was full of these mystical experiences), Peter paused in his pacing of the office to tell her she needed to scrub the kitchen floor. Not that he was ever harsh, but he was making a point that manual labor was the cure of all such quarreling. Margaret once told Bishop O'Hara of Kansas City[5] that when she kissed his ring, it was just like a blood transfusion — she got faint all over.

Jacques Maritain[6] came to us during these early days and spoke to the group who were reading *Freedom and the Modern World* [sic]

---

[4] The International Workers of the World grew out of the coal strikes of 1904, finding its main recruits among the unskilled laborers. For many years it was the radical left wing of the American labor movement.

[5] Edwin V. O'Hara (1881–1956), Bishop of Kansas City from 1939 to his death. In June, 1954, he was named an archbishop *ad personam* in recognition of his outstanding leadership in social movements and in the Confraternity of Christian Doctrine.

[6] Jacques Maritain (1882 —), the French-born philosopher who has played a leading role in the revival of scholasticism, published his *Freedom in the Modern World* in 1935.

at that time. He gave special attention to the chapter on the purification of means. Margaret was delighted with our distinguished guest, who so evidently loved us all, and made him a box of fudge to take home with him when he sailed for France a few weeks later.

Ah, those early days that everyone likes to think of now since we have grown so much bigger; that early zeal, that early romance, that early companionableness! And how delightful it is to think that the young ones who came into the work now find the same joy in community. It is a permanent revolution, this Catholic Worker Movement. . . .

161. Pope Pius XII's Encyclical *Sertum laetitiae* on the Sesquicentennial of the American Hierarchy, November 1, 1939

IN NOVEMBER, 1939, the American hierarchy celebrated the one hundred and fiftieth anniversary of its establishment. From a single diocese with one bishop in 1789 the Church in the United States had by that time expanded to nineteen ecclesiastical provinces with 115 dioceses and 130 bishops, figures that since 1939 have increased to twenty-six archdioceses, 105 dioceses and 216 bishops. In his greeting on this occasion Pope Pius XII reviewed the progress of the American Church and had words of special commendation for certain distinctively American Catholic institutions. But he also warned against the dangers to good morals in American society by reason of the prevalence of divorce and birth control, the weakening of respect for authority, and a system of education that ignored religious values. The last part of the encyclical was devoted to a summary of moral principles as applied to social and economic problems. Source: *Sertum laetitiae* (New York: Paulist Press, 1939).

TO OUR BELOVED SONS:

WILLIAM O'CONNELL, CARDINAL PRIEST OF THE HOLY ROMAN CHURCH, ARCHBISHOP OF BOSTON.

DENNIS DOUGHERTY, CARDINAL PRIEST OF THE HOLY ROMAN CHURCH, ARCHBISHOP OF PHILADELPHIA.

AND TO ALL THE VENERABLE BRETHREN, THE ARCHBISHOPS, BISHOPS AND ORDINARIES OF THE UNITED STATES OF AMERICA, IN PEACE AND COMMUNION WITH THE APOSTOLIC SEE.

VENERABLE BRETHREN, HEALTH AND APOSTOLIC BENEDICTION:

In Our desire to enrich the crown of your holy joy We cross in spirit the vast spaces of the seas and find Ourselves in your midst as you celebrate, in company with all your faithful people, the one hundred and fiftieth anniversary of the establishment of the ecclesiastical Hierarchy in the United States of America.[1] And this We do with great gladness, because an occasion is thus afforded Us, as gratifying as it is solemn, of giving public testimony of Our esteem and Our affection for the youthfully vigorous and illustrious American people.

To one who turns the pages of your history and reflects upon the causes of what has been accomplished it is apparent that the triumphal progress of divine religion has contributed in no small degree to the glory and prosperity which your country now enjoys. It is indeed true that religion has its laws and institutions for eternal happiness but it is also undeniable that it dowers life here below with so many benefits that it could do no more even if the principal reason for its existence were to make men happy during the brief span of their earthly life.

It is a pleasure for Us to recall the well remembered story.

When Pope Pius VI gave you your first Bishop in the person of the American, John Carroll, and set him over the See of Baltimore, small and of slight importance was the Catholic population of your land. At that time, too, the condition of the United States was so perilous that its structure and its very political unity was threatened by grave crisis. Because of the long and exhausting war the public treasury was burdened with debt, industry languished and the citizenry, wearied by misfortunes was split into contending parties. This ruinous and critical state of affairs was put to rights by the celebrated George Washington, famed for his courage and keen intelligence. He was a close friend of the Bishop of Baltimore. Thus the Father of His Country and the pioneer pastor of the Church in that land so dear to Us, bound together by the ties of friendship and clasping, so to speak, each the other's hand, form a picture for their descendants, a lesson to all future generations, and a proof that reverence for the Faith of Christ is a holy and established principle of the American people, seeing that it is the foundation of morality and decency, consequently the source of prosperity and progress.

Many are the causes to which must be ascribed the flowering of the Catholic Church in your country. One of them We wish to point out as worthy of attention. Numbers of priests, forced to flee to your shores from lands where persecution raged, brought welcome aid to Bishop Carroll and by their active collaboration in the sacred ministry sowed the precious seed which ripened to an abundant harvest

---

[1] The See of Baltimore was formally erected and Carroll named first bishop on November 6, 1789.

of virtues. Some of them later became Bishops and thus had a more glorious share in the progress of the Catholic cause. And thus, as history teaches us again and again, the zeal of the apostle, provided that, nourished by unfeigned faith and sincere charity, it burns within the breast of valiant men, is not quenched by the storms of persecution but is carried farther across the earth.

On the centenary of the event which now fills your hearts with legitimate rejoicing, Pope Leo XIII of happy memory with his letter *Longinqua Oceani*[2] recalled and examined the progress that had been made by the Church in America and he accompanied his review with some admonitions and directions whose wisdom equals their paternal benevolence.

What Our august predecessor then so well wrote is worthy of repeated consideration. During these past fifty years the Church has not faltered in her course but has extended her influence to wider fields and increased her members. For in your country there prevails a thriving life which the grace of the Holy Spirit has brought to flower in the inner sanctuary of your hearts; the faithful throng your churches; around the Sacred Table they gather to receive the Bread of Angels, the Food of the Strong; the spiritual exercises of St. Ignatius are followed with great devotion in your closed retreats; and many heeding the Divine Voice that calls them to the ideals of a higher life receive the priesthood or embrace the religious state.

At the present time there are in the United States 19 ecclesiastical provinces, 115 dioceses, almost 200 seminaries and innumerable houses of worship, elementary and high schools, colleges, hospitals, asylums for the poor and monasteries. It is with good reason then that visitors from other lands admire the organization and system under which your schools of various grades are conducted, the generosity of the faithful upon whom they depend, the vigilant care with which they are watched over by the directors. From these schools there comes forth a host of citizens, strong in heart and mind, who, by reason of their reverence for divine and human laws, are justly considered to be the strength and the flower and the honor of Church and of country.

Missionary associations also, notably the Society for the Propagation of the Faith, are well established and active; they are outstanding examples in assisting, by prayer, almsgiving and other means, the heralds of the Gospel engaged in carrying the standard of the Cross of Salvation into the lands of the infidel. In this connection, We cannot refrain from a public expression of praise for those missionary

[2] January 6, 1895. Cf. No. 140.

enterprises proper to your own nation which devote themselves with zeal and energy to the wider diffusion of the Catholic Faith. They are: The Catholic Church Extension Society, an organization which has gained glorious distinction for its pious benefactions;[3] The Catholic Near East Welfare Association,[4] which furnishes a providential aid to the interests of Christianity in the Orient; The Indian and Negro Missions, an association approved by the Third Council of Baltimore[5] which We confirm and recommend because it is imposed by a very particular charity toward your fellow citizens.

We confess that We feel a special paternal affection, which is certainly inspired by heaven, for the Negro people dwelling among you; for in the field of religion and education We know they need special care and comfort and are very deserving of it. We therefore invoke an abundance of heavenly blessing and We pray fruitful success for those whose generous zeal is devoted. to their welfare.

Moreover, in order to render more fitting thanks to God for the inestimable gift of the true Faith, your countrymen, eager for arduous enterprise, are supplying to the ranks of the missionaries numerous recruits whose capacity for toil, whose indomitable patience and whose energy in noble initiative for the Kingdom of Christ have gained merits which earth admires and which heaven will crown with due reward.

No less vigorous among you are those works of zeal which are organized for the benefit of the children of the Church within the confines of your country: the diocesan charity offices, with their wise and practical organization, by means of the parish priests and through the labors of the religious institutes, bring to the poor, to the needy and to the sick the gifts of Christian mercy and relief from misery. In carrying on this most important ministry the sweet discerning eyes of faith see Christ present in the poor and afflicted who are the mystic suffering members of the most benign Redeemer.

Among the associations of the laity — the list is too long to allow of a complete enumeration — there are those which have won for themselves laurels of unfading glory: Catholic Action, the Marian Congregation, the Confraternity of Christian Doctrine: their fruits are

---

[3] Founded on October 18, 1905.

[4] Established in 1926 to support missions in the Near and Middle East and to aid refugees among the Eastern Rite Catholics.

[5] The Commission for Catholic Missions Among the Colored People and the Indians was established in 1886.

the cause of joy and they bear the promise of still more joyful harvests in the future. Likewise the Holy Name Society,[6] an excellent leader in the promotion of Christian worship and piety.

Over a manifold activity of the laity, carried on in various localities according to the needs of the times, is placed the National Catholic Welfare Conference, an organization which supplies a ready and well-adapted instrument for your episcopal ministry.[7]

The more important of these institutions We were able to view briefly during the month of October, 1936, when We journeyed across the ocean and had the joy of knowing personally you and the field of your activities. The memory of what We then admired with Our own eyes will always remain indelible and a source of joy in Our Heart.

It is proper then that, with sentiments of adoration, We offer with you thanks to God and that We raise to Him a canticle of thanksgiving: "Give glory to the God of Heaven: for His mercy endureth for ever."[8] The Lord Whose goodness knows no limits, having filled your land with the bounty of His gifts, has likewise granted to your churches energy and power and has brought to fruition the results of their tireless labors. Having paid the tribute of Our gratitude to God, from Whom every good thing takes its origin, We recognize, dearly beloved, that this rich harvest which We joyfully admire with you today is due also to the spirit of initiative and to the persistent activity of the pastors and of the faithful. We recognize that it is due also to your clergy who are inclined to decisive action and who execute your orders with zeal; to the members of all the religious Orders and congregations of men who, distinguished in virtue, vie with each other in cultivating the vineyard of the Lord: to the innumerable religious women who, often in silence and unknown to men, consecrate themselves with exemplary devotion to the cause of the Gospel, veritable lilies in the Garden of Christ and delight of the Saints.

We desire, however, that This Our praise be salutary. The consideration of the good which has been done must not lead to slackening which might degenerate into sluggishness; it must not issue in a vainglorious pleasure which flatters the mind; it should stimulate renewed energies so that evils may be avoided and those enterprises which are useful, prudent and worthy of praise may more surely and more

---

[6] The Holy Name Society was organized in the United States in 1909.

[7] The National Catholic Welfare Conference dates from the first annual meeting of the hierarchy in September, 1919. Cf. No. 158.

[8] Ps. 135:26.

solidly mature. The Christian, if he does honor to the name he bears, is always an apostle; it is not permitted to the Soldier of Christ that he quit the battlefield, because only death puts an end to his military service.

You well know where it is necessary that you exercise a more discerning vigilance and what program of action should be marked out for priests and faithful in order that the religion of Christ may overcome the obstacles in its path and be a luminous guide to the minds of men, govern their morals and, for the sole purpose of salvation, permeate the marrow and the arteries of human society. The progress of exterior and material possessions, even though it is to be considered of no little account, because of the manifold and appreciable utility which it gives to life is nonetheless not enough for man who is born for higher and brighter destinies. Created indeed to the image and likeness of God, he seeks God with a yearning that will not be repressed and always groans and weeps if he places the object of his love where Supreme Truth and the Infinite Good cannot be found.

Not with the conquest of material space does one approach to God, separation from Whom is death, conversion to Whom is life, to be established in Whom is glory; but under the guidance of Christ with the fullness of sincere faith, with unsullied conscience and upright will, with holy works, with the achievement and the employment of that genuine liberty whose sacred rules are found proclaimed in the Gospel. If instead, the Commandments of God are spurned, not only is it impossible to attain that happiness which has place beyond the brief span of time which is allotted to earthly existence, but the very basis upon which rests true civilization is shaken and naught is to be expected but ruins over which belated tears must be shed. How, in fact, can the public weal and the glory of civilized life have any guarantee of stability when right is subverted and virtue despised and decried? Is not God the Source and the Giver of law? Is He not the inspiration and the reward of virtue with none like unto Him among lawgivers?[9] This, according to the admission of all reasonable men, is everywhere the bitter and prolific root of evils: the refusal to recognize the Divine Majesty, the neglect of the moral law, the origin of which is from heaven, or that regrettable inconstancy which makes its victims waver between the lawful and the forbidden, between justice and iniquity.

Thence arise immoderate and blind egotism, the thirst for pleasure,

---
9 Job 36:22.

the vice of drunkenness, immodest and costly styles in dress, the prevalence of crime even among minors, the lust for power, neglect of the poor, base craving for ill-gotten wealth, the flight from the land, levity in entering into marriage, divorce, the break-up of the family, the cooling of mutual affection between parents and children, birth control, the enfeeblement of the race, the weakening of respect for authority, or obsequiousness, or rebellion, neglect of duty toward one's country and toward mankind.

We raise Our voice in strong, albeit paternal, complaint that in so many schools of your land Christ often is despised or ignored, the explanation of the universe and mankind is forced within the narrow limits of materialism or of rationalism, and new educational systems are sought after which cannot but produce a sorrowful harvest in the intellectual and moral life of the nation.

Likewise, just as home life, when the law of Christ is observed, flowers in true felicity, so, when the Gospel is cast aside, does it perish miserably and become desolated by vice: "He that seeketh the law shall be filled with it: and he that dealeth deceitfully shall meet with a stumbling block therein."[10] What can there be on earth more serene and joyful than the Christian family? Taking its origin at the Altar of the Lord, where love has been proclaimed a holy and indissoluble bond, the Christian family in the same love nourished by supernal grace is consolidated and receives increase.

There is "marriage honorable in all and the (nuptial) bed undefiled."[11] Tranquil walls resound with no quarreling voices nor do they witness the secret martyrdom which comes when hidden infidelity is laid bare; unquestioning trust turns aside the slings of suspicion; sorrow is assuaged and joy is heightened by mutual affection. Within those sacred precincts children are considered not heavy burdens but sweet pledges of love; no reprehensible motive of convenience, no seeking after sterile pleasure brings about the frustration of the gift of life nor causes to fall into disuse the sweet names of brother and sister. With what solicitude do the parents take care that the children not only grow in physical vigor but also that, following in the footsteps of their forbears whose memory is often recalled to them, they may shine with the light which profession of the pure faith and moral goodness impart to them. Moved by the numerous benefits received, such children consider it their paramount duty to honor their parents, to be attentive to their desires, to be the staff of their

---

[10] Eccl. 32:19.
[11] Heb. 13:4.

old age, to rejoice their gray hairs with an affection which unquenched by death, will be made more glorious and more complete in the mansion of heaven. The members of the Christian family, neither querulous in adversity nor ungrateful in prosperity, are ever filled with confidence in God to Whose sway they yield willing obedience, in Whose will they acquiesce and upon Whose help they wait not in vain.

That the family may be established and maintained according to the wise teachings of the Gospel, therefore, the faithful should be frequently exhorted by those who have the directive and teaching functions in the churches and these are to strive with unremitting care to present to the Lord a perfect people. For the same reason it is also supremely necessary to see to it that the dogma of the unity and indissolubility of Matrimony is known in all its religious importance and sacredly respected by those who are to marry.

That this capital point of Catholic Doctrine is of great value for the solidity of the family structure, for the progress and prosperity of civil society, for the healthy life of the people and for civilization that its light may not be false is a fact recognized even by no small number of men who, though estranged from the Faith, are entitled to respect for their political acumen. Oh! If only your country had come to know from the experience of others rather than from examples at home of the accumulation of ills which derive from the plague of divorce; let reverence for religion, let fidelity toward the great American people counsel energetic action that this disease, alas so widespread, may be cured by extirpation.

The consequences of this evil have been thus described by Pope Leo XIII, in words whose truth is incisive: "Because of divorce, the nuptial contract becomes subject to fickle whim; affection is weakened; pernicious incentives are given to conjugal infidelity; the care and education of offspring are harmed; easy opportunity is afforded for the breaking up of homes; the seeds of discord are sown among families; the dignity of woman is lessened and brought down and she runs the risk of being deserted after she has served her husband as an instrument of pleasure. And since it is true that for the ruination of the family and the undermining of the State nothing is so powerful as the corruption of morals, it is easy to see that divorce is of the greatest harm to the prosperity of families and of states."[12]

With regard to those marriages in which one or the other party does not accept the Catholic teaching or has not been baptized, We

---

[12] *Arcanum divinae*, February 10, 1880, in John J. Wynne, S.J. (Ed.), *The Great Encyclical Letters of Pope Leo XIII* (New York, 1903), pp. 74–75.

are certain that you observe exactly the prescriptions of the Code of Canon Law. Such marriages, in fact, as is clear to you from wide experience, are rarely happy and usually occasion grave loss to the Catholic Church. A very efficacious means for driving out such grave evils is that individual Catholics receive a thorough training in the divine truths and that the people be shown clearly the road which leads to salvation.

Therefore We exhort the priests to provide that their own knowledge of things divine and human be wide and deep; that they be not content with the intellectual knowledge acquired in youth; that they examine with careful scrutiny the Law of the Lord, Whose oracles are purer than silver; that they continually relish and enjoy the chaste charms of Sacred Scripture; that with the passing of the years they study more deeply the history of the Church, its dogmas, its Sacraments, its laws, its precepts, its liturgy, its language, so that they may advance in grace, in culture and wisdom.

Let them cultivate also the study of letters and of the profane sciences, especially those which are more closely connected with religion, in order that they may be able to impart with clarity and eloquence the teaching of grace and salvation which is capable of bending even learned intellects to the light burden and yoke of the Gospel of Christ.

Fortunate the Church, indeed, if thus it will lay its "foundations with sapphires."[13] The needs of our times then require that the laity, too, and especially those who collaborate with the Hierarchy of the Church, procure for themselves a treasure of religious knowledge, not a poor and meager knowledge, but one that will have solidity and richness through the medium of libraries, discussions and study clubs; in this way they will derive great benefit for themselves and at the same time be able to instruct the ignorant, confute stubborn adversaries and be of assistance to good friends.

We have learned with no little joy that your press is a sturdy champion of Catholic principles; that the Marconi Radio — whose voice is heard in an instant round the world — marvelous invention and eloquent image of the Apostolic Faith that embraces all mankind — is frequently and advantageously put to use in order to insure the widest possible promulgation of all that concerns the Church, and We commend the good accomplished. But let those who fulfill this ministry be careful to adhere to the directions of the teaching Church even when they explain and promote what pertains to the social

---

[13] Isa. 54:11.

problem; forgetful of personal gain, despising popularity, impartial, let them speak "as from God, before God, in Christ."[14]

Because of Our constant desire that scientific progress in all its branches be ever more universally affirmed, We gladly take this opportune occasion to signify to you Our cordial interest in the University at Washington. You remember well with what ardent wishes Pope Leo XIII greeted this noble temple of learning when it came into being and on how many occasions testimonies of particular affection were bestowed upon it by Our immediate predecessor. He was intimately persuaded that if this great school, however blessed already with success, should become still stronger and gain even greater renown not only would the growth of the Church be aided but also the civil glory and prosperity of your fellow citizens.[15]

Sharing this hope, We ask you to do your very best, leaving nothing untried, that this University, protected by your benevolence, may overcome its difficulties and, with ever more gratifying increase, abundantly fulfill the high hopes that have been placed in it. We greatly appreciate, too, your desire to erect in Rome a more worthy and suitable building for the Pontifical College which receives for their ecclesiastical education students from the United States.[16]

If it is indeed true that the elite of our youth with profit travel abroad to complete their education, a long and happy experience shows that candidates for the priesthood derive very great profit when they are educated here close to the See of Peter, where the source of faith is purest, where so many monuments of Christian antiquity and so many traces of the Saints incite generous hearts to magnanimous enterprises.

We desire to touch upon another question of weighty importance, the social question, which remaining unsolved, has been agitating States for a long time and sowing amongst the classes the seeds of hatred and mutual hostility. You know full well what aspect it assumes in America, what acrimonies, what disorders it produces. It is not necessary therefore that We dwell on these points. The fundamental point of the social question is this, that the goods created by God for all men should in the same way reach all, justice guiding and charity helping. The history of every age teaches that

---

[14] 2 Cor. 2:17.

[15] Cf. Pope Pius XI's letter of September 21, 1938, to the American hierarchy written in anticipation of the university's golden jubilee, *The Catholic University of America Bulletin,* VII (November, 1938), 2–3.

[16] The new North American College on the Janiculum Hill, Rome, was dedicated on October 14, 1953.

there were always rich and poor; that it will always be so we may gather from the unchanging tenor of human destinies. Worthy of honor are the poor who fear God because theirs is the kingdom of heaven and because they readily abound in spiritual graces. But the rich, if they are upright and honest, are God's dispensers and providers of this world's goods; as ministers of Divine Providence they assist the indigent through whom they often receive gifts for the soul and whose hand — so they may hope — will lead them into the eternal tabernacles.

God, Who provides for all with counsels of supreme bounty, has ordained that for the exercise of virtues and for the testing of one's worth there be in the world rich and poor; but He does not wish that some have exaggerated riches while others are in such straits that they lack the bare necessities of life. But a kindly mother of virtue is honest poverty which gains its living by daily labor in accordance with the scriptural saying: "Give me neither beggary, nor riches: give me only the necessaries of life."[17]

Now if the rich and the prosperous are obliged out of ordinary motives of pity to act generously toward the poor their obligation is all the greater to do them justice. The salaries of the workers, as is just, are to be such that they are sufficient to maintain them and their families. Solemn are the words of Our Predecessor, Pius XI on this question: "Every effort must therefore be made that fathers of families receive a wage sufficient to meet adequately normal domestic needs. If under present circumstances this is not always feasible, social justice demands that reforms be introduced without delay which will guarantee such a wage to every adult working man. In this connection We praise those who have most prudently and usefully attempted various methods by which an increased wage is paid in view of increased family burdens and special provision made for special needs."[18]

May it also be brought about that each and every able bodied man may receive an equal opportunity for work in order to earn the daily bread for himself and his own. We deeply lament the lot of those — and their number in the United States is large indeed — who though robust, capable and willing, cannot have the work for which they are anxiously searching.

May the wisdom of the governing powers, a far-seeing generosity on the part of the employers, together with the speedy re-establish-

---

[17] Prov. 30:8.

[18] *Quadragesimo anno,* May 15, 1931, in *Two Basic Social Encyclicals* (New York, 1943), pp. 133–135.

ment of more favorable conditions, effect the realization of these reasonable hopes to the advantage of all.

Because social relations is one of man's natural requirements and since it is legitimate to promote by common effort decent livelihood, it is not possible without injustice to deny or to limit either to the producers or to the laboring and farming classes the free faculty of uniting in associations by means of which they may defend their proper rights and secure the betterment of the goods of soul and of body, as well as the honest comforts of life. But to unions of this kind, which in past centuries have procured immortal glory for Christianity and for the professions an untarnishable splendor, one cannot everywhere impose an identical discipline and structure which therefore can be varied to meet the different temperament of the people and the diverse circumstances of time.

But let the unions in question draw their vital force from principles of wholesome liberty; let them take their form from the lofty rules of justice and of honesty, and, conforming themselves to those norms, let them act in such a manner that in their care for the interests of their class they violate no one's rights; let them continue to strive for harmony and respect the common weal of civil society.

It is a source of joy to Us to know that the above cited encyclical *Quadragesimo anno,* as well as that of the Sovereign Pontiff Leo XIII, *Rerum novarum,* in which is indicated the solution of the social question in accordance with the postulates of the Gospel and of the eternal philosophy, are the object in the United States of careful and prolonged consideration on the part of some men of keener intellect whose generous wish pushes them on toward social restoration and the strengthening of the bonds of love amongst men, and that some employers themselves have desired to settle the ever-recurring controversies with the working man in accordance with the norms of these encyclicals, respecting always the common good and the dignity of the human person.

What a proud vaunt it will be for the American people, by nature inclined to grandiose undertakings and to liberality, if they untie the knotty and difficult social question by following the sure paths illuminated by the light of the Gospel and thus lay the basis of a happier age! If this is to come to pass power must not be dissipated through disunion but rather strengthened through harmony. To this salutary union of thought and policy, whence flow mighty deeds, in all charity We invite them, too, whom Mother Church laments as separated brethren. Many of these when Our glorious predecessor reposed in the sleep of the just and when We, shortly after his death, through the mysterious disposition of divine mercy ascended the throne of St. Peter; many of these — and this did not escape Our attention — expressed by word of mouth and by letter sentiments full of homage and noble respect. This attitude — We openly confess — has encouraged a hope which time does not take from Us, which a sanguine mind cherishes and which remains a consolation to Us in hard and troublous times.

May the enormity of the labors which it will be necessary fervently to undertake for the glory of the most benign Redeemer and for the salvation of souls not daunt you, Dearly Beloved, but may it rather stimulate you, whose confidence is in the divine help, since great works generate more robust virtues and achieve more resplendent merits.

May the attempts with which the enemies secretly banded together seek to pull down the scepter of Christ be a spur to us to work in union for the establishment and advancement of His reign. No greater fortune can come to individuals, families, and nations than to obey the Author of human salvation, execute His commands, accept His reign, in which we are made free and rich in good works; "A kingdom of truth and life; a kingdom of holiness and grace, a kingdom of justice, love and peace."[19]

Wishing from Our heart that you and the spiritual flock for whose welfare you provide as diligent shepherds may advance always toward better and higher goals and that also from the present solemn celebration you may gather a rich harvest of virtue, We impart to you as a pledge of Our benevolence the Apostolic Benediction.

Given at the Vatican, on the Feast of All Saints, in the Year of Our Lord, 1939, the first of Our Pontificate.

PIUS PP XII.

162. American Catholics and the Intellectual Life, 1956

ONE of the liveliest topics of discussion among educated Catholics during the 1950's centered around their failure to make a contribution to the cultural life of the nation in keeping with their numbers, wealth, and increasingly high percentage of college graduates. The Catholic Commission for Intellectual and Cultural Affairs took up the matter and devoted its annual meeting of 1955 in St. Louis largely to this subject. On May 14 at

[19] Preface of the Mass of Christ the King.

one of the sessions of the C.C.I.C.A., John Tracy Ellis, professor of church history in the Catholic University of America, read a paper entitled "American Catholics and the Intellectual Life" which, in turn, provoked a good deal of discussion. The paper was first published in *Thought* (Autumn, 1955) and appeared in book form the following summer with a preface by the Most Reverend John J. Wright, then Bishop of Worcester and since 1959 Bishop of Pittsburgh. The statement of Bishop Wright is given here as one of the most thoughtful and representative of the contributions to what he has himself called the "great debate." Source: Prefatory Note by John J. Wright to John Tracy Ellis, *American Catholics and the Intellectual Life* (Chicago: Heritage Foundation, Inc., 1956), pp. 5–10.

. . . .

Monsignor Ellis' paper provoked a reaction that is in itself irrefutable evidence of how well timed and accurate are his contentions. A great number of others were emboldened by his statements to lift their own voices on the urgency of a re-evaluation of Catholic intellectual life in the United States, and their witness frequently added proof both that the cause is critical and that it is far from hopeless. The passion with which the few dissenters from Monsignor Ellis' position set forth their indignant reservations proved that he had touched a tender nerve. In an article in *America*,[1] Monsignor Ellis himself summarized some of the reactions to his original piece. He has received several hundred letters. All but four seem to be in agreement with his analysis. The article itself is an important contribution to the documentation on the "great debate," but there is no reason to believe that all the reactions are by any means yet registered. One awaits with mingled sentiments of dread and curiosity this season's commencement addresses, for example!

What we have called the "great debate" raging here in the United States at the moment is doubtless no more than a phase within our own land of an argument that has been going on in Europe for decades. Traditionally, the European intellectual has been acknowledged by his contemporaries, even those who might disagree with him, to have a 'vocation' beyond the limits of his own profession of writing or science or teaching. It is a vocation quite apart from that of the functionary or representative of Church or of State, and it has obvious and grave perils as well as elements of prestige. These perils are as real as ignominy, exile or prison, even death, the frequent destinies of the traditional intellectuals in Europe. And yet, the intellectual has usually enjoyed a veneration in Europe which scarcely has a parallel in the

---

[1] John Tracy Ellis, "No Complacency," *America*, XCV (April 7, 1956), 14–25.

common American attitude toward those who take on the valiant role of questioner, critic, or intellectual trail blazer. The reader will note the "witty extravagance" which Monsignor Ellis recalls as differentiating the attitudes of Europeans and Americans toward intellectuals: in the old world an ordinary mortal on seeing a professor tipped his hat, while in America he taps his head.

Such a suspicious attitude toward the intellectual life is far from being an exclusive Catholic phenomenon in the United States. Indeed, this kink in the American character generally may be due, as an editorial in the Washington *Post and Times Herald* pointed out on December 19, 1955, to specifically non-Catholic sociological and even theological influences on the formation of our national character. For example, the thoroughly practical problems confronting the first settlers on New England's stern and rock-bound coast no doubt intensified the predisposition of their Calvinist theology to emphasize results rather than theories and to reverence achievement rather than abstract speculation. There is a characteristically American esteem for the word "industry," in all its senses, which has never been accorded to the word "intellectual" or any of its variations.

The anti-intellectual attitude, however, is more unbecoming and embarrassing in Catholics because it is so entirely inconsistent with any authentic Catholic position. So many of the heresies which have wounded the Church and despoiled her of whole nations have been voluntarist heresies, anti-intellectual in their roots and pretensions, that it is bitterly ironic when anti-intellectualism threatens to become characteristic of those who have remained faithful to her obedience.

One wonders whether Catholics themselves always appreciate the extent to which the battles of the Church against the modern heresies have been at one and the same time battles against the heresy of anti-intellectualism. Luther's "stat pro ratione voluntas," his voluntaristic *fides fiducialis* with its repudiation of the intellectual elements in the act of faith, and his violent but typical description of the intellect as the "devil's whore," are as much the evidence of his departure from Catholic traditions as any of his theses nailed to the chapel door. The blind fatalism of Calvin, the perverse austerities of Jansenism, the sentimentality and exaltation of instinct or religious emotion which, for all its show of scholarship, characterized Modernism, are all typical of the heresies which have divided the Christian flock in these last four centuries. In defending supernatural revelation against these the Church was at the same time defending the validity of natural reason and the primacy of the intellect over the will, the emotions, the instincts or any of the other faculties to which voluntarism has always appealed, whether in Luther's dogma, the moral theories of Jansenius, the religious psychology of the moderns or the political philosophy of totalitarianism.

We usually think of the Council of Trent, the Vatican Council and the syllabus against Modernism in terms of the defense of revealed dogmas, and such, of course, they were. But he understands them poorly who fails to perceive that they were frequently Catholic affirmations of the validity of reason as well as of the reality of revelation, and that they bore witness to the essential part of rational elements even in the supernatural act of faith, and to the divine origin of the primacy and rights of the intellect in the natural order.

It is, therefore, a problem for the Church when any who might be taken as her representatives in any sense in the world of the campus, the press, or the forum reveal contempt for that "wild living intellect of man" of which Cardinal Newman spoke, or cynicism about the slow, sometimes faltering, but patient, persevering processes by which the intellectual seeks to wrest some measure of order from the chaos about us.

The problem is manifold. Monsignor Ellis' paper and others which followed give good hope that its solution may be in process of realization. First of all, there is a problem of definitions. What precisely do we now mean when we use the word intellectual and when we speak of either the virtues of faults of "intellectualism"? It is this initial problem which has been highlighted by the editor of the Brooklyn *Tablet* in his evaluation of recent writings on the subject.

Then there is a problem which we can best call spiritual or apostolic. What is the vocation of the intellectual in the life of the Church? How can he best bear his specifically intellectual witness, a witness which may involve a living martyrdom, given the temper of the times and the suspicion with which even his own will all too often views his gifts and his works? How shall we persuade intellectuals to find in Christ, the *Logos,* the eternal Word made flesh to dwell among us, a divine prototype of their special vocation and unique dignity, as we have persuaded workers to find their model in the carpenter's Son, Christian youth to find a model in the youthful Christ's obedience to Joseph and Mary at Nazareth, and patriotic citizens to see the exemplar of their proper loyalty in the Christ who paid the coin of tribute and wept tears of predilection over the capital city of His nation? A spirituality of Christian humanism, centered about the concept of Christ the divine Intellectual, is a critical need of our generation if the evidence presented here proves as much as we have good reason to believe it does.

The problem of the apostolic role of the Catholic intellectual cannot be too often emphasized. Father Raymond L. Bruckberger, O.P., our friendly French critic, in an article in *Harper's Magazine* for February, 1956,[2] on the patriotic responsibilities of the American intellectual, makes a point worthy of meditation by Catholic intellectuals who sincerely seek to understand their contemporary religious responsibilities. The American intellectual often tends to say that his country has failed him, that she will not give him the honor which is his due, and that he feels like a spiritual exile. Perhaps, the contrary is more nearly true, and the American intellectual is more deeply missed than is at first apparent. When the intellectual turns his back on his country and confines himself to berating her, his place remains empty, all the while that he complains that he has no place at all. A more valiant generation of European intellectuals accepted it as their destiny to be unappreciated and mocked for false prophets; in this they found a secret consolation and often their abiding glory.

Catholic intellectuals have a point for meditation here. Intellectually gifted Catholics suffer all too often from a "whining" tendency in their attitude toward the Church. They lament that they are not sufficiently appreciated or encouraged. They berate the indifference of their fellow Catholics to their vocation. In a curious paradox on the lips of Christians, particularly Christians with presumably keener powers of insight and understanding than the rest, they protest against being made martyrs. Where in the New Testament, the Church of the Fathers, or the history of the saints from Paul to Thomas More, were the genuinely thoughtful promised any other lot, whether at the hands of the world or at the hands of their uncomprehending brethren, than contradiction and constant testing?

Finally, and urgently, there is an intensely practical problem in this matter of American Catholic intellectual life. It is the problem of how we can increase the proportions of authentic scholars and trained, competent intellectuals among us.

Statistics have been offered recently which point up and analyze the dearth of Catholic lay scholars. These statistics have been challenged by those who resented certain of its implications, although their resentment did not inspire much in the way of effective refutation of the facts. The facts add up to a conclusion which is a primary justifica-

---

[2] Raymond L. Bruckberger, O.P., "Assignment for Intellectuals," *Harper's Magazine,* CCXII (February, 1956), 68–72.

tion for the republication of this present paper, by a man who dearly loves the Faith and is one of those who spare themselves nothing to contribute to the solution of whatever problems impede the freedom and well being of our Holy Mother the Church.

In the early days of the Church in America, humble Catholics struggled to retain the Faith in an anti-Catholic atmosphere. These early pioneers built schools and churches which are responsible for the survival of Catholic America today. These foundations for growth and expansion have been firmly rooted within the American tradition in our soil, but future progress and expansion will come only through a determined effort based upon the development of Catholic scholarship. It is to this problem that Monsignor Ellis addresses himself so effectively, and we recommend a reading and rereading of his provocative message at regular intervals. Both Catholicism and America have need of an intellectual apostolate of distinction.

163. The American Catholic Bishops and Racism, November 14, 1958

IT WOULD be difficult to think of any problem that has done more to disturb the internal peace of the United States than discrimination against various groups on the score of race or nationality. Friction between whites and native Indians and Negroes has been a fairly constant phenomenon in American history, but it has been especially acute in regard to the latter since World War II. That some American Catholics have been influenced by racist doctrines is, unfortunately, true, and had they accepted the Church's teaching on this subject there would probably be more than 675,000 colored people and 125,000 Indians among the American Catholics at the present time (1961). Yet strenuous efforts have not been lacking in recent years on the part of members of the hierarchy to emphasize in a practical way the Church's mission to men of all races and nationalities. And these efforts have produced effective results, even if in certain localities race prejudice has not permitted more progress to be made. For example, Joseph E. Ritter, Archbishop of St. Louis, ordered the integration of the schools of his archdiocese in September, 1947, seven years in advance of the Supreme Court's ruling of May, 1954. Likewise in the autumn of 1948 integration of the Catholic schools of the national capital was begun at the instance of Patrick A. O'Boyle, Archbishop of Washington, and in June, 1954, Vincent S. Waters, Bishop of Raleigh, instituted the same policy in all the churches and diocesan institutions of his southern see. Nationally speaking, however, the situation has yielded — if at all — only after great resistance. It was with that background that the Catholic bishops determined to set forth in detail the Church's doctrine on this controversial question. Source: "Discrimination and the Christian Conscience," New York *Times,* November 14, 1958.

Fifteen years ago, when this nation was devoting its energies to a World War designed to maintain human freedom, the Catholic Bishops of the United States issued a prayerful warning to their fellow citizens. We called for the extension of full freedom within the confines of our beloved country. Specifically, we noted the problems faced by Negroes in obtaining the rights that are theirs as Americans. The statement of 1943 said in part:

"In the Providence of God there are among us millions of fellow citizens of the Negro race. We owe to these fellow citizens, who have contributed so largely to the development of our country, and for whose welfare history imposes on us a special obligation of justice, to see that they have in fact the rights which are given them in our Constitution. This means not only political equality, but also fair economic and educational opportunities, a just share in public welfare projects, good housing without exploitation, and a full chance for the social advancement of their race."

In the intervening years, considerable progress was made in achieving these goals. The Negro race, brought to this country in slavery, continued its quiet but determined march toward the goal of equal rights and equal opportunity. During and after the Second World War, great and even spectacular advances were made in the obtaining of voting rights, good education, better-paying jobs, and adequate housing. Through the efforts of men of good will, of every race and creed and from all parts of the nation, the barriers of prejudice and discrimination were slowly but inevitably eroded.

Because this method of quiet conciliation produced such excellent results, we have preferred the path of action to that of exhortation. Unfortunately, however, it appears that in recent years the issues have become confused and the march toward justice and equality has been slowed if not halted in some areas. The transcendent moral issues involved have become obscured, and possibly forgotten.

Our nation now stands divided by the problem of compulsory segregation of the races and the opposing demand for racial justice. No region of our land is immune from strife and division resulting from this problem. In one area, the key issue may concern the schools. In another it may be conflicts over housing. Job discrimination may be the focal point in still other sectors. But all these issues have one main point in common. They reflect the determination of our Negro people, and we hope the overwhelming majority of our white citizens, to see that our colored citizens obtain their full rights as given to them by God, the Creator of all, and guaranteed by the democratic traditions of our nation.

There are many facets to the problems raised by the quest for racial justice. There are issues of law, of history, of economics, and of sociology. There are questions of procedure and technique. There are conflicts in cultures. Volumes have been written on each of these phases. Their importance we do not deny. But the time has come, in our considered and prayerful judgment, to cut through the maze of secondary or less essential issues and to come to the heart of the problem.

The heart of the race question is moral and religious. It concerns the rights of man and our attitude toward our fellow man. If our attitude is governed by the great Christian law of love of neighbor and respect for his rights, then we can work out harmoniously the techniques for making legal, educational, economic, and social adjustments. But if our hearts are poisoned by hatred, or even by indifference toward the welfare and rights of our fellow men, then our nation faces a grave internal crisis.

No one who bears the name of Christian can deny the universal love of God for all mankind. When Our Lord and Savior, Jesus Christ, "took on the form of man" (Phil. 2, 7) and walked among men, He taught as the first two laws of life the love of God and the love of fellow man. "By this shall all men know that you are my disciples, that you have love, one for the other." (John 13, 35) He offered His life in sacrifice for all mankind. His parting mandate to His followers was to "teach all nations." (Mat. 28, 19)

Our Christian faith is of its nature universal. It knows not the distinctions of race, color, or nationhood. The missionaries of the Church have spread throughout the world, visiting with equal impartiality nations such as China and India, whose ancient cultures antedate the coming of the Savior, and the primitive tribes of the Americas. The love of Christ, and the love of the Christian, knows no bounds. In the words of Pope Pius XII, addressed to American Negro publishers twelve years ago, "All men are brothered in Jesus Christ; for He, though God, became also man, became a member of the human family, a brother of all." (May 27, 1946)

Even those who do not accept our Christian tradition should at least acknowledge that God has implanted in the souls of all men some knowledge of the natural moral law and a respect for its teachings. Reason alone taught philosophers through the ages respect for the sacred dignity of each human being and the fundamental rights of man. Every man has an equal right to life, to justice before the law, to marry and rear a family under human conditions, and to an equitable opportunity to use the goods of this earth for his needs and those of his family.

From these solemn truths, there follow certain conclusions vital for a proper approach to the problems that trouble us today. First, we must repeat the principle — embodied in our Declaration of Independence — that all men are equal in the sight of God. By equal we mean that they are created by God and redeemed by His Divine Son, that they are bound by His Law, and that God desires them as His friends in the eternity of Heaven. This fact confers upon all men human dignity and human rights.

Men are unequal in talent and achievement. They differ in culture and personal characteristics. Some are saintly, some seem to be evil, most are men of good will, though beset with human frailty. On the basis of personal differences we may distinguish among our fellow men, remembering always the admonition: "Let him who is without sin . . . cast the first stone . . ." (Jn., 8, 7) But discrimination based on the accidental fact of race or color, and as such injurious to human rights regardless of personal qualities or achievements, cannot be reconciled with the truth that God has created all men with equal rights and equal dignity.

Secondly, we are bound to love our fellow man. The Christian love we bespeak is not a matter of emotional likes or dislikes. It is a firm purpose to do good to all men, to the extent that ability and opportunity permit.

Among all races and national groups, class distinctions are inevitably made on the basis of like-mindedness or a community of interests. Such distinctions are normal and constitute a universal social phenomenon. They are accidental, however, and are subject to change as conditions change. It is unreasonable and injurious to the rights of others that a factor such as race, by and of itself, should be made a cause of discrimination and a basis for unequal treatment in our mutual relations.

The question then arises: Can enforced segregation be reconciled with the Christian view of our fellow man? In our judgment it cannot, and this for two fundamental reasons.

1) Legal segregation, or any form of compulsory segregation, in itself and by its very nature imposes a stigma of inferiority upon the

segregated people. Even if the now obsolete Court doctrine of "separate but equal" had been carried out to the fullest extent, so that all public and semipublic facilities were in fact equal, there is nonetheless the judgment that an entire race, by the sole fact of race and regardless of individual qualities, is not fit to associate on equal terms with members of another race. We cannot reconcile such a judgment with the Christian view of man's nature and rights. Here again it is appropriate to cite the language of Pope Pius XII. "God did not create a human family made up of segregated, dissociated, mutually independent members. No; He would have them all united by the bond of total love of Him and consequent self-dedication to assisting each other to maintain that bond intact." (September 7, 1956)

2) It is a matter of historical fact that segregation in our country has led to oppressive conditions and the denial of basic human rights for the Negro. This is evident in the fundamental fields of education, job opportunity, and housing. Flowing from these areas of neglect and discrimination are problems of health and the sordid train of evils so often associated with the consequent slum conditions. Surely Pope Pius XII must have had these conditions in mind when he said just two months ago: "It is only too well known, alas, to what excesses pride of race and racial hate can lead. The Church has always been energetically opposed to attempts of genocide or practices arising from what is called the 'color bar.'" (September 5, 1958)

One of the tragedies of racial oppression is that the evils we have cited are being used as excuses to continue the very conditions that so strongly fostered such evils. Today we are told that Negroes, Indians, and also some Spanish-speaking Americans differ too much in culture and achievements to be assimilated in our schools, factories, and neighborhoods. Some decades back the same charge was made against the immigrant, Irish, Jewish, Italian, Polish, Hungarian, German, Russian. In both instances differences were used by some as a basis for discrimination and even for bigoted ill-treatment. The immigrant, fortunately, has achieved his rightful status in the American community. Economic opportunity was wide open and educational equality was not denied to him.

Negro citizens seek these same opportunities. They wish an education that does not carry with it any stigma of inferiority. They wish economic advancement based on merit and skill. They wish their civil rights as American citizens. They wish acceptance based upon proved ability and achievement. No one who truly loves God's children will deny them this opportunity.

To work for this principle amid passions and misunderstandings will not be easy. It will take courage. But quiet and persevering courage has always been the mark of a true follower of Christ. We urge that concrete plans in this field be based on prudence. Prudence may be called a virtue that inclines us to view problems in their proper perspective. It aids us to use the proper means to secure our aim.

The problems we inherit today are rooted in decades, even centuries, of custom and cultural patterns. Changes in deep-rooted attitudes are not made overnight. When we are confronted with complex and far-reaching evils, it is not a sign of weakness or timidity to distinguish among remedies and reforms. Some changes are more necessary than others. Some are relatively easy to achieve. Others seem impossible at this time. What may succeed in one area may fail in another.

It is a sign of wisdom, rather than weakness, to study carefully the problems we face, to prepare for advances, and to by-pass the non-essential if it interferes with essential progress. We may well deplore a gradualism that is merely a cloak for inaction. But we equally deplore rash impetuosity that would sacrifice the achievements of decades in ill-timed and ill-considered ventures. In concrete matters we distinguish between prudence and inaction by asking the question: Are we sincerely and earnestly acting to solve these problems? We distinguish between prudence and rashness by seeking the prayerful and considered judgment of experienced counselors who have achieved success in meeting similar problems.

For this reason we hope and earnestly pray that responsible and sober-minded Americans of all religious faiths, in all areas of our land, will seize the mantle of leadership from the agitator and the racist. It is vital that we act now and act decisively. All must act quietly, courageously, and prayerfully before it is too late.

For the welfare of our nation we call upon all to root out from their hearts bitterness and hatred. The tasks we face are indeed difficult. But hearts inspired by Christian love will surmount these difficulties.

Clearly then, these problems are vital and urgent. May God give this nation the grace to meet the challenge it faces. For the sake of generations of future Americans, and indeed of all humanity, we cannot fail.

Signed by members of the Administrative Board, National Catholic
Welfare Conference, in the name of the Bishops of the United States:

FRANCIS CARDINAL SPELLMAN,
Archbishop of New York.
JAMES FRANCIS CARDINAL MCINTYRE,
Archbishop of Los Angeles.
FRANCIS P. KEOUGH,
Archbishop of Baltimore.
KARL J. ALTER,
Archbishop of Cincinnati.
JOSEPH E. RITTER,
Archbishop of St. Louis.
WILLIAM O. BRADY,
Archbishop of St. Paul.
ALBERT G. MEYER,
Archbishop of Chicago.
PATRICK A. O'BOYLE,
Archbishop of Washington.
LEO BINZ,
Archbishop of Dubuque.
EMMET M. WALSH,
Bishop of Youngstown.
JOSEPH M. GILMORE,
Bishop of Helena.
ALBERT R. ZUROWESTE,
Bishop of Belleville.

164. The Issue of Religious Freedom in a Presidential Campaign, October 5, 1960

THE presidential candidacy of Senator John F. Kennedy of Massachusetts
which ended successfully in the election of November 8, 1960, was pre-
ceded by a campaign in which the Democratic candidate's Catholic faith
became one of the major issues. The candidates of both major parties
sought to bar the question of religion; but as one writer has stated, "the lens
of national reporting was soon to focus attention on this religious im-
ponderable as the central political question of the campaign. . . . Both
candidates were to denounce the prejudice; but neither could erase the
intrusion of religious feeling" (Theodore H. White, *The Making of the
President 1960* [New York, 1961], p. 92). The question of the Catholic
doctrine on religious freedom occupied a foremost position in the debate

and gave rise to statements of the widest variety — and validity — from non-Catholic sources. In an effort to make clear their uncompromising acceptance of the American tradition of separation of Church and State, and what that implied by way of freedom for citizens of all religious faiths and none, on October 5, a month in advance of the election, a group of 166 Catholic laymen issued a statement embodying their views on this subject. Source: *Catholic Mind*, LIX (March-April, 1961), 179–180.

The present controversy about the Catholic Church and the Presidency proves once again that large numbers of our fellow-citizens seriously doubt the commitment of Catholics to the principles of a free society. This fact creates problems which extend far beyond this year's elections and threaten to make permanent, bitter divisions in our national life. Such a result would obviously be tragic from the standpoints both of religious tolerance and of civic peace.

In order to avert this, we ask all Americans to examine (more carefully, perhaps, than they have in the past) the relationship between religious conscience and civil society. We think that, in the present situation, Catholics especially are obliged to make their position clear.

There is much bigotry abroad in the land, some of it masquerading under the name of "freedom." There is also genuine concern. To the extent that many Catholics have failed to make known their devotion to religious liberty for all, to the extent that they at times have appeared to seek sectarian advantage, we must admit that we have contributed to doubts about our intentions. It is our hope that this statement may help to dispel such doubts.

To this end we make the following declarations of our convictions about religion and the free society. We do this with an uncompromised and uncompromising loyalty both to the Catholic Church and to the American Republic.

1. We believe in the freedom of the religious conscience and in the Catholic's obligation to guarantee full freedom of belief and worship as a civil right. This obligation follows from basic Christian convictions about the dignity of the human person and the inviolability of the individual conscience. And we believe that Catholics have a special duty to work for the realization of the principle of freedom of religion in every nation whether they are a minority or a majority of the citizens.

2. We deplore the denial of religious freedom in any land. We especially deplore this denial in countries where Catholics constitute a majority — even an overwhelming majority. In the words of Giacomo Cardinal Lercaro, the present Archbishop of Bologna: "Christian

teaching concerning the presence of God in the human soul and belief in the transcendent value in history of the human person lays the foundation for the use of persuasive methods in matters of religious faith and forbids coercion and violence." The Catholic's commitment to religious liberty, therefore, he says, "is not a concession suggested by prudence and grudgingly made to the spirit of the times." Rather, it is rooted "in the permanent principles of Catholicism."

3. We believe constitutional separation of Church and State offers the best guarantee both of religious freedom and of civic peace. The principle of separation is part of our American heritage, and as citizens who are Catholics we value it as an integral part of our national life. Efforts which tend to undermine the principle of separation, whether they come from Catholics, Protestants or Jews, believers or unbelievers, should be resisted no matter how well-intentioned such efforts might be.

4. We believe that among the fundamentals of religious liberty are the freedom of a church to teach its members and the freedom of its members to accept the teachings of their church. These freedoms should be invulnerable to the pressures of conformity. For civil society to dictate how a citizen forms his conscience would be a gross violation of freedom. Civil society's legitimate interest is limited to the public acts of the believer as they affect the whole community.

5. In his public acts as they affect the whole community the Catholic is bound in conscience to promote the common good and to avoid any seeking of a merely sectarian advantage. He is bound also to recognize the proper scope or independence of the political order. As Jacques Maritain has pointed out, the Church provides Catholics with certain general principles to guide us in our life as citizens. It directs us to the pursuit of justice and the promotion of the common good in our attitudes toward both domestic and international problems. But it is as individual citizens and office holders, not as a religious bloc, that we make the specific application of these principles in political life. Here we function not as "Catholic citizens" but as citizens who are Catholics. It is in this spirit that we submit this statement to our fellow Americans.

165. Federal Aid to Religious Schools, April, 1961

IN THE midst of a controversy in 1890 between Catholics and Protestants regarding parochial schools — a controversy that also involved serious differences between Catholics themselves — Cardinal Gibbons sought to explain the situation to Pope Leo XIII. Speaking of the divisions between American Protestants and Catholics, he said they were caused

"above all by the opposition against the system of national education which is attributed to us, and which, more than any other thing, creates and maintains in the minds of the American people the conviction that the Catholic Church is opposed by principle to the institutions of the country, and that a sincere Catholic cannot be a loyal citizen of the United States" (Gibbons to Leo XIII, Baltimore, December 30, 1890, in John Tracy Ellis, *The Life of James Cardinal Gibbons, Archbishop of Baltimore, 1834–1921* [Milwaukee, 1952], I, 664–665).

The same attitude had prevailed for over a half century before Gibbons wrote, and for many non-Catholic Americans it remains true today. A recent manifestation of it came in connection with a bill submitted to Congress by President John F. Kennedy, which for the first time proposed federal aid on a large scale to public schools, but made no provision for any assistance to private schools. A large and articulate sector of the Catholic community voiced opposition to the measure for its omission of religious schools, although there were likewise Catholics who made it clear that they were not in favor of any kind of government aid to private schools. During the ensuing debate the position of the opponents of the Kennedy Bill was expressed by a committee of twenty-one lawyers of the Archdiocese of Washington, and it is their statement in part that is printed below. Source: "Freedom of Choice in Education," statement of the Washington Archdiocesan Catholic Lawyers' Committee on Equal Educational Rights, *Catholic Standard* (Washington), April 7, 14, 21, 1961.

FREEDOM OF CHOICE IN EDUCATION

The Congress is now considering legislation to authorize a program of Federal assistance for education costing $2,300,000,000 over a three-year period. This proposed legislation, as presently drawn, is supported by the National Administration as a means of bringing about "the maximum development of every young American's capacity." (Statement by President Kennedy.)[1] It would give money grants to public elementary and secondary schools but would deny such grants to private and church-related elementary and secondary schools.

This proposed legislation has engendered national concern and has been the subject of intense debate, as many see in it the possible ultimate doom of parochial and private elementary and secondary education and a frustration of the very purpose attributed to this legislation, namely that of providing "rich dividends in the years ahead — in increased economic growth, in enlightened citizens, in

[1] Text of President Kennedy's special message to Congress on education, New York *Times*, February 21, 1961.

national excellence." (Statement by President Kennedy.)[2] While Catholics have always held steadfastly to the upholding of the Constitution, and still do, nevertheless it is the position of Catholic parents, the Catholic hierarchy and many others that it is contrary to principles of social justice, equal treatment and nondiscrimination to provide money grants to public schools but to withhold such grants from private and parochial schools and that such unjust treatment and discrimination is contrary to the best interests of our national existence.

No criticism is raised to the giving of Federal aid to education. It is the position of Catholics that the granting or withholding of Federal aid is a political and economic decision to be made by the citizens of our country acting within the structure of our representative form of government. But it is further the Catholic position, once Congress decides that Federal aid is necessary, that there should be full equality of treatment with respect to all children whether they be enrolled in public, private or church-related schools. . . .

This is a matter of high principle. The parochial schools of this country are discharging a public service. They provide an educational program which fully satisfies present governmental standards for competence. The state and all the citizens thereof benefit from this educational effort. If massive Federal expenditures are to be made from the tax collections of all the people, this aid should not go only to a select segment, however large, of the population. To the extent that parochial schools provide a recognized and accredited secular education they are entitled to equal treatment.

A child in a parochial school deserves the same opportunity to achieve excellence (the national purpose, as stated by President Kennedy) as his public school neighbor. A physics laboratory, provided by Federal funds, does not teach the tenets of any religious faith. It is equally suitable for instruction whether it be located in a public or parochial school. Any other judgment erroneously assumes that the government may expect to achieve the excellence of its future citizens only in the public schools.

If it is wrong in principle to so discriminate against the private and parochial school children of this country, then any proposed legislation which seeks to effectuate this discrimination would be wrong. It is upon this high ground that Catholic parents and the hierarchy have determined to oppose any aid program which seeks to deprive Catholic children of their opportunities for future intellectual development. . . .

---

[2] *Ibid.*

The principal argument raised against the Catholic position is a constitutional one. Our opponents say it clearly violates the First Amendment and breaches the wall of separation between church and state. The question is largely one of the means to be employed. Catholic lawyers together with distinguished non-Catholic constitutional scholars like Professor Corwin[3] of Princeton and Professor Sutherland[4] of Harvard feel that equitable treatment can be afforded the parents of parochial school children without offending the Constitution.

It is helpful to recall the language of the First Amendment.[5] It does not say that there should be an absolute wall of separation between church and state. It says, in relevant part:

> Congress shall make no law respecting an establishment of religion, or prohibiting the free exercise thereof.

These words had a clearly defined purpose to the framers of the Constitution. The word "establishment" possessed an historical significance now lost to many interpreters of the Constitution. It referred to the practice in England and many European countries of establishing a state religion to which all citizens were required to take an oath of allegiance and to support by contributions or taxes. Many American colonies, notably Virginia and Massachusetts Bay, followed this tradition in their early years. Yet to escape these burdens of conscience many colonists had originally come to America and it was to avoid this practice that the language of the First Amendment was framed. There was to be no national church. Persons were to follow the dictates of their conscience. The language of the First Amendment was framed as a *means* to preserve individual freedom of conscience. The latter was the *end* intended, not the secularization of society.

However, there has been engrafted by the Supreme Court upon the words of the First Amendment a phrase taken from the writings of Thomas Jefferson — "a wall of separation between church and state." That this does not mean a wall, high and impenetrable, is clear from the majority opinion of Mr. Justice Douglas[6] in *Zorach* v. *Clauson*, 343 U.S. 306, 312 (1952):

---

[3] Edward S. Corwin (1878 —) retired in 1946 after holding the McCormick professorship of jurisprudence at Princeton University since 1918.

[4] Arthur E. Sutherland (1902 —) has been professor of law in Harvard University since 1950.

[5] Made applicable to the states by the Fourteenth Amendment. Cf. *Everson* v. *Board of Education*, 330 U.S. 1 (1946).

[6] William O. Douglas (1898 —) has been an associate justice of the United States Supreme Court since 1939.

The First Amendment, however, does not say that in every and all respects there shall be a separation of Church and State. Rather, it studiously defines the manner, the specific ways, in which there shall be no concert or union or dependency one on the other. That is the common sense of the matter. Otherwise the state and religion would be aliens to each other — hostile, suspicious, and even unfriendly.

Mr. Justice Reed[7] in his brilliant dissent in *McCollum* v. *Board of Education,* 333 U.S. 203, 238 (1948) has suggested that the Court should return to the language of the Amendment and interpret that rather than Jefferson's phrase. Whatever the merits of that suggestion, it is clear that the meaning of the metaphor has gotten so confused that many people cannot distinguish the metaphor from the principles involved.

The First Amendment means simply that the Government may not *actively* and *directly* support any religion. Accordingly, any legislation which is intended to favor directly a particular religion is forbidden. The words of emphasis are "actively" and "directly." Legislation which has an incidental and secondary effect upon religious activity is not forbidden. Legislation which accords religious persons the same benefits afforded the public generally is not forbidden.

These principles are clear from the decided cases and from our American traditions. This is what we demand, as Catholic parents, from Government — constitutionally permissible treatment which attempts to equalize our burden with those of our non-Catholic neighbors. . . .

---

[7] Stanley F. Reed (1884 —) retired in 1957 after having served for nineteen years as an associate justice of the United States Supreme Court.

166. The Open Parish, April, 1965

THE Catholic Church, as is true of all churches in the United States, finds itself confronted in the second half of the twentieth century by a situation radically different from that in which she has hitherto sought to fulfill her mission. One of the principal causes arises from the massive urban concentrations, another from the mounting mobility of the American people, it being estimated that one family in five changes its domicile in the course of a calendar year. What this has meant for the traditional parish was highlighted by Dr. Jaroslav Pelikan. He said:

When one considers the mobility of the American people and the stability of the American churches, one gets some idea of why the churches seem to be museum pieces and the system of parishes and dioceses an utter anachronism. We are attempting to apply a stay-put ministry to a nation on wheels. ["The Parish An Anachronism," *The Register* (Denver), July 31, 1966, p. 71.]

More important than question of movement, however, has been the growing number for whom religious belief is altogether irrelevant. Harvey Cox's judgment is, unfortunately, all too true when he says:

As for "the anxiety of doubt" about the God of theism, the closest today's man gets to such a state is a mild curiosity or at most a kind of wistfulness. Urban-secular man came to town after the funeral for the religious world-view was already over. He feels no sense of deprivation and has no interest in mourning. [*The Secular City, Secularization and Urbanization in Theological Perspective.* (New York: Macmillan Co., 1965), p. 80.]

For no American religious group has the implications of this changed situation more relevance than for Catholics whose Church is overwhelmingly an urban one. A century ago the Catholic immigrants crowded into the industrial slums where they often worshipped in churches purchased for their use from the more prosperous native Protestants who had moved to more desirable neighborhoods. At that time the Catholic Church was the church of the immigrant, of the working classes, of the dispossessed. In the 1960's, however, she finds herself in danger of losing that status due to two causes: the increasing number of her own members who are steadily passing over into the affluent society, and, secondly, the great majority of today's dispossessed who are not, ethnically speaking, from Catholic backgrounds. The new situation has given rise to insistent questions to which the Church must find an answer, e.g., how serious is the Church's commitment to charity? Is she willing to take on the burdens of the disestablished even when they are not of her fold? Will today's Catholic Church become yesterday's Protestant Church, identified in the main with the established and prosperous? Will the Church in the United States repeat the error of the Church in Europe in losing the masses? The American Church's answer to these questions lies in the restructuring of the parish in an attempt to make her apostolate relevant to the problems of the present hour. Obviously the ecclesiastical unit most drastically affected will be the parish—especially of the inner city —and a sustained discussion of the parish, in the editorial judgment of *The Commonweal* was one of Vatican Council II's "striking omissions." ["Reforming the Parish," LXXXIV (March 25, 1966), 3.] It is to a solution of these problems that the following document addresses itself. Source: Joseph H. Fichter, S.J., "The Open Parish in the Open Society," *The Catholic World*, CCI (April, 1965), 16-21.

Adaptation of the ancient Church to the needs of contemporary people has become a kind of slogan since the pontificate of Pius XI. Some would date its modern stirrings back to the social encyclicals of Leo XIII. Measured against other cultural changes, it has had a slow beginning; but the post-war period, culminating in the Second Vatican Council, has witnessed an acceleration of the pace of change. New and exciting ideas and practices have been introduced by the Church. It seems only proper, on the centenary of *The Catholic World,* to point out that the Paulist Fathers from their beginning vigorously promoted the adaptation of the Church to the American society. Perhaps, from a European ecclesiastical point of view, they were "ahead of their time," but from an American cultural point of view, they should now be credited with foresights that are finally becoming recognized and confirmed.

The progressive Paulist Fathers of the last century met with opposition of a determined kind, and were honored with the accusation that they were the main instigators of the so-called heresy of "Americanism." This was a phantom heresy. The Americanism of the Paulists was basically an attempt to interpret and present the Church in a way acceptable to Americans; and it is finally being justified by the numerous adaptations, now approved by Rome and presently occurring in the United States. Yet there are still pockets of opposition to such change, even from within the Church. One hears complaints from scattered places, like Philadelphia, New Orleans and Los Angeles, where progress is said to be slow and adaptation only selectively permitted.

It would be a mistake to claim that everywhere in America the Church is moving successfully and progressively. One thing is certain, however, the "outside" opposition to Catholicism, except among the sick and perennial hate-mongers, has significantly diminished. When the Paulists tried to open the closed Church of a century ago, non-Catholic Americans were more antagonistic than curious about it. Now the reverse is the case. Whatever other liberalizing factors are at work in our society, the attitudinal changes on the part of Catholics themselves are a central factor.

Let us reflect here on only one area of adaptation—the parochial system of the American Church. It seems only logical to suggest that the open Church cannot continue to maintain the closed parish, and if this is true there is a need for structural as well as attitudinal reform. The very word, parochial, is often synonymous with terms like local, in-bred, closed-minded, limited and self-centered. Many old-line pastors (and parishioners) seem to feel that you cannot be a good Catholic unless you are first a good parishioner. This is analogous to the notion that you must first be a family man, and then successively become interested in the neighborhood and the larger collectivities until you embrace universal mankind. This is a gross oversimplification of both human personality and human society.

A century ago a significant proportion of American Catholics were immigrants—what we now call "ethnics"—and they lived in separately identifiable national parishes. That this is a natural phenomenon of all immigrant groups, that they cluster together when they first come to a strange country or region (witness the "Appalachian whites" now in Chicago), is a commonplace of demography. The almost inevitable accompaniment to this phenomenon was the fact that urban neighborhoods were fairly stable sub-communities, often identified by the name of the parish church. Unlike many contemporary urban slums, they were often ghettos of hope rather than ghettos of despair. These were "closed" parishes wherever enough people of the same nationality had their own priests and groups, their own language and culture.

While ethnic parishes are still maintained in some of the larger cities (and are so identified in Kenedy's *Catholic Directory*), the trends of population movement are away from ethnic neighborhoods. Such movements will probably increase in the coming decades. Even with these changes and shifts, and often in parishes that are English-speaking with native American parishioners and priests, there persist two sociologically outdated notions: The first is that the parish is, or must be, or should return to, a form of community. The second is that the Catholic's prime loyalty, as a Church member, must be to his parish.

We employed these two concepts as testable hypotheses after the war, when we began a series of intensive sociological research studies of urban parish life. We felt that if these concepts were valid, membership in a parish ought to exhibit some kind of solidarity that could be termed parochial, or at least Roman Catholic, that would distinguish it from membership in other kinds of groups. This quest for proofs of parochial community and solidarity failed in the places where we looked, places that were not ethnic neighborhoods or small villages, but large American cities. In the typical urban parishes we found that the "best" Catholics were often extra-parochial Catholics, and that sharing the same religion was the least effective basis for social solidarity; less a factor than race, school ties and occupational similarity.

Conventional knowledge often remains in men's mental baggage long after the facts of life have discarded it. This is a form of unconscious resistance to change, a retention of outmoded concepts that no longer fit contemporary reality. The basic notion was that a vigorous American Church cannot exist unless it primarily depends on, stems from and is reinforced by a vigorous parish life. There were those who said that the parish is the Church in miniature, and that the Church is simply the parish grown large. If this was ever true (even in some analogous sense) it had to be verified in the small village of a closed society, and even there, for none but the natives whose religious contact and church life were restricted to the local parish.

This old-fashioned interpretation of parochialism can be clarified and better understood side by side with a similar concept of familism. Here the notion is that the family is a miniature society, and the society is simply a large family. The strength of the nation depends upon the strength of its family life. The fact is, of course, that kinship ties and family power flourish in backward areas—witness the rural American Southeast, most of Latin America, Southern Italy, the emerging African nations. The rational organization and functioning of the larger society, with its ultimate benefit and protection of individuals and subgroups, are impeded by this kind of familistic culture. Personal and particularistic relations are important in primary groups, but they can be overemphasized only to the detriment of modern, urban society.

What does this kind of research finding and the reasoning that derives from it, do to the concepts of subsidiarity, of home rule, of local loyalties and responsibilities, whether in the ecclesiastical or political structure? Within the Catholic Church we are supposedly moving toward decentralization, episcopal collegiality and the participation of the laity at the grass roots. This is indeed a movement consonant with the open society and is in no way contradictory to the relative absence of community and solidarity at the parochial level of the Church structure.

In an open Church, as in an open society, loyalties and responsibilities must be multiple, and they must be dependable at every level. The plea for a "States' Rights" type of subsidiarity is sociological fakery precisely because it precludes broader responsibility to either the total society or the neglected individual. There can be no argument about the fact that people are most strongly loyal to those who are closest to themselves, but there are also some sad similarities between the parish-firster and the America-firster.

What is developing here at the parish level is symbolized, at least ideally, in the essence of the liturgical act, as Romano Guardini describes it. The new liturgy has been publicized as an instrument for the restoration of solidarity and Christian love. Close observation of people in the parish suggests that this publicity be reversed. The truly liturgical act is rather a consequence, or expression, of the universal—not merely parochial—love of the Christian believer. What may be expected to happen here—provided that the liturgy becomes more than "good theater"—is precisely the extension of a concerned charity outside the parish limits. The most social-minded Catholics are usually liturgical-minded; but too often those interested in the liturgy do not have a genuine social awareness.

To compound the parochial problem is the fact that Protestants, often rural and Southern, and both white and Negro, have largely replaced the ethnic Catholics in the lower stratum of the urban American society. These are souls to whom religion can be relevant, and to whom the Catholic Church must make itself relevant. By and large, the Church has had a "good press" on race relations, especially the publicity on strong moral stands and episcopal pronouncements. The day-to-day implementation of these principles is quite another matter, not only for pastors and parishioners, but for Catholic hospitals, schools and other groups and organizations.

If one had to rank the problems of the parish in order of importance and severity, he would probably put this question of the inner-city population in first place. The old, closed parish knew how to service and hold Catholic immigrants, but felt no great need to look outside its own immediate functions. The new, open parish still suffers from ignorance of sociological procedures, but enjoys the impetus of the *aggiornamento*, more healthy relations between priests and people, the devices of the liturgy, a more competent laity, the freedom to participate. The open parish system has to be flexible to meet this inner-city challenge, and flexibility here means that it has to be much less parochial than it has been. No urban parish can be an island unto itself.

Catholics who used to huddle in language groups for their own survival in an alien society, are replaced by Catholics who huddle in social class groups to protect themselves in a society they regard possessively. Their closed parishes, with the help of their priests, want to safeguard what they have against the encroachments of others: uncouth whites from the Southern Hills, Negroes from anywhere, Mexicans who are guilty of immigrant ethnic behavior, Puerto Ricans who dare to seek equal job opportunities.

One way to avoid these threats of unwanted human invasions is to escape to the suburbs and there work hard and generously to construct a new closed parish. Here life is comfortable with one's own—real friendly achieving fellow Americans who appreciate the better things of religion and society. No gaudy statues with votive candles on their altars; no dirty people in the pews mumbling the rosary during mass. Human relations are local and involuted, and the suburban parish becomes more closed than the old ethnic city parish ever was. The greatest irony of the "best" of the American Church is this educated, well-fixed, liturgically-expert parish which uses its parochial solidarity as a further fortification of the local community's residential exclusiveness.

An open parish does not just happen, any more than the open character of the American society can be called simply an historical accident. An open parish is one in which everyone has a chance to obtain its benefits and share its burdens. In a sense it is a religious reflection of the cultural ideology of America, the first large society in the world that has deliberately attempted to open its opportunities to all of its citizens. Such a deliberate effort within the Church, based on a modern understanding of the Church's mission, is required for the formation and maintenance of the open parish.

Participation by the laity is more than the liturgy, and it will mean more than echoes of the lay voice in the parish church. We shall undoubtedly see the end of the peculiar "trustee" system, where there are three clerical votes "against" two lay votes. There are already progressive American parishes in which lay committees have a genuine voice in the administration of parochial affairs. This change of structure and administration is not an automatic wonder-worker. It is only as effective as the people involved in it. In spite of wide-scale protests, most lay people are still reluctant to take on responsibilities. Those who do accept nomination and election often show excessive deference to the pastor, so that in the long run the latter's ideas prevail. At any rate, in these situations the lay leadership that has been talked about for more than thirty years will have an opportunity to express itself. Where freedom and democratic procedures in the parish do not succeed, the failure will not always be the fault of the clergy.

Two of the most obvious structural changes among American Catholics concern the reformation of parish societies themselves and the extension of extra-parochial lay groups and activities. Already in the more progressive urban parishes there are only remnants of the old groupings based on sex, age and marital status. Mass organizations of this kind had some meaning when their main function was to promote monthly reception of Holy Communion; but there were always other parochial functions, and these will continue to be performed by people in groups. The large difference is that they will have less direct dependence on the priests of the parish and thus a greater exercise of lay responsibility.

The proportion of active lay Catholics, who do more than attend services at their parish church, will always be relatively small. But the population of young adults will continue to increase, enjoy more educational advantages, exercise more freedom of choice, and is thus likely to augment the numbers of extra-parochial Catholics. It is not that they are interested only in city-wide and diocesan Catholic groups. They are interested also in participating as Catholics in occupational, recreational, civic and other organizations. From this point of view and in the long run, it is probably not the clergy but the laity who will spell out the relevance of Catholicism to American society.

In spite of the pull away from the parish, and of the growth of extra-parochial organizations, it would be rash to say that the territorial parish has lost its usefulness. It fixes pastoral obligations, allows more efficient bookkeeping—if not easier administration—and provides the statistical base of the Catholic population. Parish societies can still raise money, and even the more affluent parishes can do this to help the poorer and struggling parishes of the diocese. Missions, downtown chapels, storefront, second-story apartment locations, etc. supplement the fixed city parish in providing religious and sacramental service to the people.

As long as the territorial parish performs useful functions it is here to stay, and it has to maintain itself in existence in order to fulfill its purpose. This simple remark, however, contains the possibility of two crucial differences of approach. The first is the concept of the closed Church and the closed parish: That it must above all protect its rights; that it must promote its own growth and success; that the defense of the Faith is the first duty of every Catholic. This is a continuation of the Reformation mentality which sees the Church and the parish beleagured in a hostile, secular, immoral American environment. This is as though Christ's people were a completely independent organization, aloof from and irrelevant to the rest of society.

The second approach is that of the open Church and the open parish: This is a concern for performance over mere maintenance in existence. In this view the whole organization is worth maintaining only if it performs its mission as an instrument of sanctification and salvation for individuals and society. This means that parishioners live in the world of men, trying to be the salt of the earth, the leaven for their fellow citizens of whatever religion, race or social status. The open parish is deeply enmeshed in the American culture; it serves God, but only through people. It answers the central question of organized religion: It is relevant to this country in this century.

At the risk of repetition we must emphasize that progress is a good thing, that ecclesiastical and parochial changes are pointed in the direction of progress. The maintenance of the organization undergoes alteration for the purpose of better performance. The prime objective cannot be to enhance the status of parishioners, to weaken the authority of the clergy, to lessen the complications of bureaucracy or to develop greater autonomy for the bishop. These effects may or may not occur, but they are ancillary to the mission of the open parish in the open society.

167. The New Theology of the Era of Vatican Council II, 1965

EVERY age is an age of change for both Church and State, but the 1960's will doubtless be characterized by ecclesiastical historians as more of an age of revolution than the Church has experienced since the Protestant Revolt. While the ecumenical council, convened in October, 1962, accounted for much of the intellectual ferment in Catholic circles, it was not solely the cause. In a quiet way a number of new and original ideas had been circulating among the Church's scholars long before that time. Especially was this true of Pierre Teilhard de Chardin (1881-1955), the famous Jesuit scientist, whose intellectual stature grows apace with each succeeding year. And about no single topic has there been more controversy in Catholic ranks than evolution, a prime concept in all of Teilhard de Chardin's research. To accept evolution is not simply to accept a scientific theory; it is an assent to a Heraclitan approach to reality. Thus it influences the very depths of one's philosophical assumptions which, in turn, influence his psychological thinking. It touches many areas of theological speculation, therefore, e.g., the concept of original sin as was evidenced by the article of Maurizio Flick, S.J., "Peccato originale ed evolution—nismo. Un problem a teologico," in *La Civiltà Cattolica*, II, No. 2783. Anno 117 (4 giugno 1966), 440-447. [*The Tablet* of London published an English translation under the title, "Original Sin and Evolution," CCXXI (September 10, 1966), 1008-1010; (September 17, 1966), 1039-1041.] Likewise the Aristotelian mode of thought in which so much of Catholic theology has been framed, the necessity of accepting change as a mode of existence, and the consequent need of adaptation which permeates all sectors of life, including religion—all are affected. So deep, in fact, are the influences of the evolutionary approach that it cannot help but cause reverberations throughout the entire structure of the Church. The document that follows is a condensation of a book, the title of which indicates a point of view that up to recent years would have been thought dangerous for a Catholic to hold. Source: Condensed from *The Wisdom of Evolution* by Raymond J. Nogar. Copyright © 1963 by Raymond J. Nogar. Reprinted by permission of Doubleday and Company, Inc.

THE WISDOM OF EVOLUTION

After one hundred years of careful research and enlightened discussion, scientific evolution is generally accepted as a fact by the educated person. The days of religious polemic among scientists, philosophers, and theologians are over. As the dust of former battles has settled, the field of controversy has been cleared by mutual understanding. Yet many basic problems remain unresolved, and much work is yet to be done to ensure tranquility among the disciplines upon which evolution touches.

Scientific evolution is definable in general terms as a one-way irreversible process in time, which during its course generates novelty, diversity, and higher levels of organization. Evolution, as an epigenic unfolding of organized matter, is understood to apply to all sectors of the universe, the inanimate, the world of the living, the origin and development of man. In the domain of science, furthermore, evolution is no longer considered an *hypothesis;* it is a *fact,* scientifically established by experts whose empirical evidence and methodological inferences are now recognized as conclusive. Exactly *how* the evolutionary process works in each sector of reality is not known with uniform documentation. But *that* evolution is an historical fact is established as thoroughly and fully as science can establish facts of the past witnessed by no human eye.

It is difficult for some philosophers and theologians to understand that to call evolution an established fact is not to attribute to evolution the status of unqualified *certitude*. Scientists do not use the term "certitude," especially in matters about which only indirect evidence can be had. They are rather looking for a convergence of evidence which is great enough to generate conviction in the mind of the competent and unbiased observer. The philosopher looks for *necessary* relations; the theologian looks for *certain inferences* from revealed truth; the scientist looks for lines of evidence, often circumstantial, which so converge upon and mutually support a single conclusion, that reasonable doubts are practically removed. An analogy to the logic of evolutionary theory can be found in the Warren Committee's investigation of the case of Lee Oswald. There was no direct, incontrovertible witness, no confession. Yet the convergence of disparate lines of evidence (Oswald's writings, his gun, his wife, the Texas Textbook Co., the bus driver, the cabbie, the rooming-house matron, the department-store clerk, the waitress, the police, etc.) yielded such a preponderance of converging weight as to establish guilt beyond a reasonable doubt. It is this kind of inference which establishes the fact of evolution.

It is not easy to grasp the power of evolutionary statements. The reason is that few persons have the competence to weigh the evidence now accumulated. Yet the interdisciplinary problems of science, philosophy, and theology require clear understanding of how inferences are drawn in each field if misrepresentation and useless friction are to be avoided. Evolution touches upon the very nature of the cosmos, upon the meaning of man, upon the Christian revelation. It is of utmost importance to bring these areas into harmony. The first step is to see the *power* of the fact of evolution, even as it applies to man; the second step is to examine the *limits* of scientific theory as it is extended into the philosophical domain; the third is to bring evolution into *harmony with the revelation* itself.

Conversation with the Dead

Among the arguments of converging evidence for the fact of evolution, the most primary and direct evidence in favor of evolution on a large scale is furnished by *paleontology*. If evolution has taken place, the study of fossils deposited in the surface of the earth will reveal its development. In this important area of evidence, the most ingenious refinements in scientific technique have been developed, many of them within the last twenty years. The paleontologist has two extremely difficult tasks: one, to discover ways of reading the record of fossils deposited in the rocks of the earth; two, to discover ways of measuring time in the far distant past.

Fortunately, nature has many built-in time clocks which keep ticking away, and by a systematic cross-checking of many techniques, both absolute and relative chronologies have been set up with increasing reliability. Besides the ordinary methods of geological stratification, physical and chemical analysis, the recently discovered *radioactive* dating methods have brought a new dimension to this difficult area of evolutionary investigation. This method is based upon the uniform rate of disintegration of radioactive isotopes of certain elements found in the fossil deposits. The radio-carbon method and the potassium-argon method are examples of the latest techniques of telling time and interpreting the fossil record.

Piecing together the time scales devised by the various techniques of measurement, scientists place the origin of the earth about 4½ billion years ago, slightly younger than the solar system itself. Continents originated about 3½ billion years ago and the first organisms are probably about 2 billion years old. The first well-marked fossil beds are about 600 million years old. Within this span, the great eras and periods and epochs of geological time are subdivided with the forms of plant and animal life recorded in the fossils discovered in great abundance throughout the world.

What does the fossil record reveal after one hundred years of painstaking research? The paleontologist finds: (1) the presence of very simple forms, few in number, in the early periods of space-time distribution; (2) a progressive multiplication of numbers and kinds of organic forms from simple to complex during the passing of time; (3) the extinction of most of the species of prior ages and their successive replacement by very similar forms in successive periods. From this general picture, documented in detail, not only on the level of the family, but also of the genus and the species, the evolutionist draws the following inference: The only natural explanation of the fossil record is common descent with modification, i.e., evolution.

Logically speaking, what are the alternatives? There are three possibilities. The first is that God created all the forms from the beginning of time. This form of *immediate creationism* was the explanation which Linnaeus (and most theologians) proposed before evolutionary facts began to emerge in the middle of the 19th century. The second possibility is *sequential creationism,* that God created these forms in space and time as they appear in the fossil record. The third possibility is that of *epigenic emergence* of plant and animal forms by some evolutionary process of common descent with modification.

To the scientist, it is obvious only one of these possibilities is a *natural* one. He would not accept the intrusion of any form of creationism unless a natural explanation were not forthcoming. Further, if scientific paleontology is to be retained, it is evident that all known organic species were not created from the beginning. Sequential creationism is equally unacceptable to him, since evolution is a very good natural explanation, supported in detail by extensive evidence. But both philosopher and theologian, true to good method, would have to concur with this judgment. For both theology and philosophy assume that God works in an orderly way through natural causes, and as long as natural explanations are available, direct intervention of God is not invoked. Thus, to all observers—scientist, philosopher, and theologian—evolution is the best explanation if (1) the evidence supports it, and if (2) there are no philosophical or theological contradictions inherent in the explanation.

The Reaper and Immortality

Fossil witness to a sequence of living forms is telling evidence for evolution, but it is not conclusive. The question remains: Could such an evolution, a descent with modification which resulted in the present panorama of over a million and a quarter living species, have taken place by known natural means? Charles Darwin, in his *Origin of Species,* was not primarily concerned with proving the fact of evolution; he wanted to show *how* it happens in nature. To discover the process of evolution is itself a convergent proof for the fact. As in the case of the trial lawyer, if he can find motive, circumstances which make the fact possible or even probable, he has an important contribution to a resolution of the case.

Two of the most important convergent arguments come from *genetics* and *ecology;* more precisely, from the *mutation* of *genes* and from the forces of *natural selection.* Darwin knew that if descent with modification was to take place in organic populations then there must be differential survival in generation and differential selection in the natural environment. It has taken one hundred years to isolate and specify these factors with empirical detail. Two new sciences have grown up since Darwin, *genetics and ecology,* which have brought conclusive force to his theory of natural selection. The laws of genetics establish the continuity of natural species, but a constant influx of mutations brings new materials and potentialities into the populations. The internal and external forces of nature are constantly acting upon the population to bring selective pressure on the favorable varieties. Gradually, novelty is introduced, new sub-species arise, and finally new species emerge—and many old ones become extinct. This natural dynamism makes some kind of evolution necessary and general evolution of the entire biotic community quite plausible. Two more strong convergent arguments for evolution have been added.

Charles Darwin was an expert natural historian with a genius for deep biological insight. One of his most important insights, so simple and evident to us now, became an axiom in evolutionary thinking and the basis for several more convergent arguments. Often puzzled by the close similarities of structure and function in animals and plants and the close relationship between organism and environment, he enunciated the principle: The only known natural cause for close similarity among organisms is *descent from common ancestors.* Let us apply this axiom to the multiple patterns found in nature and studied by various sciences.

In *biogeography,* we find biogeographical realms, discontinuous distribution, and ecological zones. Within the local areas, we find marvelous resemblance and adaptations to the particular environment. For example, we find distinct species of finches on each of the Galapagos Islands, yet belonging to the genera on the mainland of South America. Are we to say that a distinct species was created for each island—or that they originated on the mainland, flew to the islands and the species developed by adaptation to the singular conditions of each ecological niche? The best explanation for the anomalies of biogeography is descent with modification—evolution.

In *taxonomy,* the classification of plants and animals, a marvelously delicate hierarchical relationship is manifested, so that the logical structure of anatomical similarity arranges itself into the shape of a tree or bush. The closer the structural similarity, the more likely the family relationship. Taxonomical arrangement is best explained by common descent with modification—evolution. A similar convergent argument is contributed by the morphological sciences, e.g., *comparative anatomy* and *physiology.* A study of the organ systems of animals manifests a phyletic prototype which is varied from class to class, family to family, etc. For example, the design of the forelimb is *structurally* the same, bone for bone, in the shrew, the mole, the bat, the horse, the deer, the rhinoceros, and man. Yet the *function* of the forelimb varies from digging, to running, to flying, to writing poetry! This structural similarity with diversified function strongly suggests common descent with modification by adaptation to new conditions of life. Thus, the general patterns of living things, studied by biogeography, taxonomy, comparative anatomy, and physiology seem to provide additional convergent evidence for a single natural explanation—evolution.

The same axiom of similarity applies equally well to the functional aspects of living organisms, which have a remarkable unity of cellular organization, chemical composition, metabolism (involving growth, maintenance, repair, reproduction, and decay), and adaptation. Besides the amazing similarities of biochemical and physiological characteristics throughout the biotic community, the more closely related (taxonomic) plants and animals manifest, in direct proportion to their proximity in the scale of classification, more similar basic biochemical and physiological characteristics. Perhaps the most dramatic example of the argument for evolution drawn from functional similarity is put forward by *embryology* and is often called Haeckel's "biogenetic law." If the embryos of a fish, a salamander, a tortoise, a chick, a hog, a calf, a rabbit, and man are compared at different stages of development, an important observation can be made. In the first stage of development, the embryos appear identical; in the next stage, only by little do the embryos begin to diversify; in the last stage, the specific characteristics emerge. The related vertebrates seem to retrace identical embryonic steps. The best explanation, argues the embryologist, is that "ontogeny recapitulates phylogeny," or that each species in its early stages retraces its ancestral evolution.

Disparate arguments from the several sciences of biology could be multiplied by the scores. Taken singly, any one series is established with the use of a scientific methodology which is vulnerable to the stringent rules of demonstrative logic. Yet, in view of the singular nature of the problem of origins and the indirect nature of the evidence, a high degree of convergent probability can be had. If the several lines of argument based upon apparently unrelated data converge on and mutually support the same general conclusion, the probability that this conclusion is correct may appear so high as to carry conviction to the mind of the unbiased observer. This is the force of the evolutionary argument. To the expert and to those who have examined the convergence of evidence in detail, the fact of evolution is established, not with certitude, but beyond a reasonable doubt.

The Birth of Adam

For many observers, it is only when man is introduced into the evolutionary picture that serious problems begin to arise. The chief philosophical and theological problems with evolution touch upon its meaning for man and its influence upon his moral and religious life, and it is no mere anthropomorphism to accede to the factual demands of general evolution and seriously question whether man belongs in this discussion. Man's spirituality, his unique capacity to adapt with choice and intelligence (creativity), make *homo sapiens* a special evolutionary problem, even to the scientist. In 1889, Alfred R. Wallace, co-founder with Charles Darwin of the principle of natural selection, effectively drove a wedge which split the human species off from the other primates in evolutionary discussions. He argued that man's biological nature seemed to place him within the plan of evolution, but his moral and social nature seemed to place him in a plan apart. From that time, it has been customary to divide evolutionary discussions of man into his *biological evolution* and his *psycho-social evolution,* the significance of which cannot be underestimated.

Biologically, man belongs in the taxonomic classification of animals just as properly as does any other species. Although David sings of man in the Psalms as "a little less than the angels," traditional philosophy has always regarded him as an animal with intelligence and choice. Biologically, man belongs in the phylum *chordata,* the sub-phylum *vertebrata,* the class *mammalia,* the order *primates,* the sub-order *anthropoidea,* the family *hominidae,* the genus *homo* and the species *sapiens.* In classifying man thus, the same rules are applied to this species as to any other. The importance of this fact is that when the anthropologist speaks of *Homo sapiens,* he is ascribing the fullness of animality to him, the fullness which relates man to the primates, the mammals, the vertebrates, and the rest of the animal kingdom with a common attribute which is not mere metaphor.

The upshot of this biological relationship is that one would expect the arguments for evolution to apply to this animal species just as fully and properly as they apply to any other. And this is just what the evidence bears out. There is no single piece of convergent evidence drawn from any department of biology and applied to any other animal species which does not state with equal security that man descended biologically from a family of primates by genetic change, natural selection, and the other mechanisms of evolution.

The most dramatic evidence of the biological evolution of *Homo sapiens* is, of course, the fossil record. A classification of skulls and other fossilized parts (based upon several fundamental characteristics, which, taken together, comprise a total morphological pattern distinguishing the anthropoid ape skull from the hominoid type skull) reveals a graduated series rivaling that of the horse family. From *Australopithecus* and *Homo habilis* (800,000-2,000,000 years ago) through *Pithecanthropus* (300,000-800,000) represented by Java and Pekin man, *Pre-Mousterian* (100,000-300,000) represented by Steinheim, Fontechevade, and Swanscombe, *Early Mousterian* (50,000-100,000) represented by Mt. Carmel in Palestine and others in Europe, to *Late Mousterian and Modern Man* (about 50,000) represented by the Neanderthals and Cro-Magnon man, we find surprisingly complete documentation of descent with modification of the human body. Recent excavations of Dr. L. S. B. Leakey reveal that much important evidence is forthcoming. But even without the details we would wish for, no anthropologist today seriously doubts that the human species emerged about a million years ago by the natural process of descent—evolution.

Psychosocial Novelty

However, a fact which is equally affirmed by anthropology is that *Homo sapiens* is a unique animal with a very singular evolutionary process. He has emerged as the only animal which not only adapts to its environment; he creates his own environment. Man, in a real sense, determines his own future, his own evolution. So unique is this capacity in man that anthropology has developed into two directions: *physical* anthropology and *cultural* anthropology. True, man is but one person, but his biological capacities and his psychosocial capacities are irreducible in principle. Over and above his biological functions of metabolism, nourishment, repair, reproduction, and fulfilment of his life-cycle, man conceptualizes, understands, makes a language and speaks, judges, reasons, constructs science, technology, art, is free to choose and set goals of happiness and moral behavior. In a word, he has spiritual capacities which, though in harmony with, are not reducible to and determined by biological evolution. It is in this harmonious duality of human activity that difficulty with evolutionary theory arises. On the one hand a complete Cartesian separation between matter and spirit would be unrealistic. If biological man evolved, the *whole* man evolved. On the other hand, the spiritual capacity of man cannot be reduced to the materials and agents which are found in the emergence of the primates. For this reason, Pope Pius XII, in the name of Christian tradition, proclaimed that God has created the human spirit with a special providence. How to explain this activity of God without unduly intruding into the gradual, natural unfolding of the evolutionary process remains one of the knotty philosophical and theological issues in evolutionary thinking.

The difficulty of the interdisciplinary discussion of this issue among anthropologists, philosophers, and theologians is compounded by the lack of adequate, uniform language. The anthropologist speaks of the uniqueness of psychosocial man, meaning that his physical and social qualities of understanding, creativity, and freedom make him a designer of his future unfolding. The philosopher and theologian speak of the spirit (or soul) of man as the source of his freedom and intelligence. Both are referring to the unique phenomenon, unique capacity and activity. But the world of the spiritual as such does not fall within the terms and methods of anthropological research. Yet the first great step has been taken in understanding. If one admits the extent to which evolutionary theory does apply to man's origin and development and yet does not press the power of evolutionary science to account for *everything* about man, the door is open to harmonious synthesis of fragments of our present understanding of the mystery of man.

Cosmic Evolution

We now begin to see how important it is not only to assess the *power* of evolutionary theory and acknowledge the evidence available but also to draw forth the logical *limits* of application of evolutionary thinking to other than the biological domain. We have already seen that when we speak of cultural origins and evolution, we do not use the term "evolution" in the same sense. How far can the term "evolution" be extended? Is it a fact that life originated from non-life by a natural process of evolution? Did the planets evolve? The stars? The galaxies? The universe? Very often this cosmic extension of the evolutionary concept without determining its precise meaning and the degree to which the facts have been documented leads to needless but serious philosophical and theological difficulties.

For example, when we examine the status of the question of *biogenesis,* the origin of life, two observations must be made: (1) Evolution has taken on an equivocal sense; and (2) the convergence of facts assembled to date do not have the force of eliminating every reasonable doubt. Biopoesis, the natural origin of life from the physicochemical agents and materials of this planet about 2-3 billion years ago, is a valuable hypothesis, but the extreme difficulty of setting up experiments which would test the hypothesis adequately limits the force of inference and extrapolations available today.

When the concept "fact of evolution" is applied to the origin of chemical and physical elements, an even greater degree of equivocation on the term "evolution" is present. Chemists, physicists, and cosmologists are very guarded about the extremely hypothetical nature of our present knowledge about the formation of the elements of our own solar system. How much more tentative and equivocal must be the term "evolution" when it is applied to the origin of the planets, the stars, the galaxies, the quasars. And when cosmologists speculate about the origin and development of the universe, the activity can hardly be called an application of the scientific knowledge of evolution at all. The purpose here is not to minimize the value of various evolutionary hypotheses to scientific inquiry in these important questions of origins and development. The observer must recognize however that, scientifically speaking, there is no known cosmic law of evolution. There is historical change and development in every sector of the cosmos which we have investigated. Space-time contingency belongs to the being of every material thing we know. But there is no universal law of cosmic evolution which can be elevated to the level of a philosophical principle. There are trends, discernible directions of development in some sectors of the material world. But scientific evolution has only the power which can be established by convergence of evidence. It does not apply with identical meaning and equal force in every area of existence.

From Evolution to Evolutionism

The importance of this last observation cannot be overestimated. It is precisely at this point that evolutionary theory provides an illegitimate extrapolation, often quite surreptitious, from a partially documented and very useful model called the "fact of evolution" into the realm of philosophy or ideology. The fact remains that the supposition of a universal, causal, cosmic law of evolution is not a valid inference from any known series of natural facts or laws established by science. It is absolutely necessary to disengage ideologies based upon this false supposition from scientific evolution in order to clear the air of many ambiguities which impede not only the educated person's understanding of evolution, but also the discussions of serious related issues in philosophy and theology. It is often wrongly thought, for instance, that the theological document *Humani Generis* is an unenlightened veto of the biological "fact of evolution." A close reading will show that Pius XII was repudiating, rather, the philosophies of evolutionism, whether they be mechanistic and monistic, dialectical materialism or some exaggerated forms of historicism and existentialism. Without denying a single piece of scientific evidence or a single legitimate inference, and even encouraging the useful research into origins, he was denying that there is a shred of evidence from the natural sciences to prove that evolution is a cosmic law which explains the origin of *all* things, a law which repudiates all that is absolute, firm, and immutable and gives value only to events and their evolutionary history.

Whether the suppositions be monistic materialism, dialectical materialism, humanism, existentialism, or historicism, the first step to evolutionism is the elevation of the "fact of evolution" to the status of law. The next step is to elevate the "law of evolution" to the level of a narrative world-view to which everything else must bow and in the light of which everything else must be understood. The third step is to personalize this new world-view with a rhetoric of conviction. It is the ideology of evolutionism, not the science of evolution, which intrudes into philosophy and theology and in the name of science calls into question the relevance of traditional metaphysics and even the Christian revelation itself.

Toward a Philosophy of Novelty

Although scientific evolution may not warrant the excesses of ideological evolutionisms, this new-found epigenic unfolding of nature in the various sectors of reality demands the close attention of philosophers and theologians, especially those of the Western tradition. Evolution needs a philosophy. It is equally true to say that realistic philosophy (and theology) needs evolution. One of the most serious shortcomings of traditional world-views, based fundamentally upon a Platonic or an Aristotelian approach to reality, is their failure to account for the place of space-time (history) in the understanding of the universe and man. Since the time of Hegel, and especially since the upsurge of the science of origins and development of cosmic entities, the great scandal of traditional metaphysics and Christian theology has been to regard the historical unfolding of nature irrelevant. Preoccupation with the necessary, the eternal, the immutable provided the tradition with an ontological blind spot. It could not see what the contemporary mind with its gaze upon the space-time contingency of existence could see only too well: that the historical unfolding of cosmic being and the life of man belongs, not to the realm of the incidental, but to the very heart of reality. Any philosophy or theology which neglected the timely for the timeless and eternal could not be but illusory.

Thus the philosophies of "essence" have given way today to the philosophies of existence and history. And scientific evolution, with its concentration on origins, development, and epigenic newness of nature is playing its role of focusing attention on the contingency of reality. The old cosmic world-views are dead; determinism on the microscopic, macroscopic, and megaloscopic planes has given way to indeterminism and dynamic transformation. The stability which science studies today is not the static universe of the ancients; it is an ever-changing dynamic stability. There is order, but the order is constantly being replaced by another order, and each is a function of space and time. Even in the human sphere, man may not be *merely* his history, but he is not a man without his history. Nor are his morals, spirituality, and religion untouched by time and space.

This consideration raises an old question. What is the relation between stability and change in nature? The ancients answered by neutralizing time and history—and hence evolution. Species were eternal. But evolutionary science has set the cosmos and the world of man into an essential space-time spin. The universe is not so stable, so orderly as we once thought. Change in space and time touches the very essence of reality. We need a new philosophy of evolution, of epigenic unfolding of nature. But it must avoid the excesses of the past which attended to the timeless to the neglect of the timely, and the excesses of contemporary thought which attends to the timely and neglects the timeless and the eternal.

Beginnings

The problem for any philosophy of evolution is to account for the origins and development of natural species in terms of ultimate natural explanation. Hence the account must be (1) philosophical, (2) evolutionary, (3) natural. In this explanation, both stability and change must be fully accounted for and their roles in the emergence of natural being properly assessed.

In evolution, just as in individual generation and development, two natural tendencies prevail: *constancy* and *variation*. The marks of constancy in nature are three: constancy of regularity, constancy of type, and constancy of unicity. In natural generation, the regularities of physical, chemical, and biological agents and materials are everywhere observed. In a sense, every biological law places restrictions upon evolution, and without the regularity of nature, science would be inoperative. Too, when nature generates, it reproduces a type; the parent is the model of the progeny. The third constancy of unfolding nature is the unique development of each species. On the other hand, evolutionary nature is equally inconstant. That is to say, nature is subject to variation in its developmental activity. This variation is especially marked in the long-term evolutionary picture where the effects of novelty and extinction are dramatic. The ancients thought that constancy was primary (per se) and variation in species was incidental. Today we see them as natural correlatives.

Evolutionary philosophy, then, must stress the historical *contingency* of natural being. Space and time are no longer incidental, and variation of species lies at the heart of natural being. Evolution is the potentiality or virtuality of natural being to change in species. The very metaphysics of the philosophy of evolution will stress the potential and the contingent instead of stressing exclusively the actual and the necessary. The world of evolutionary being is a balanced dualism of stability and change, of the actual and the potential, of the necessary and the contingent. Evolutionary essence must be a space-time existent; the timely and the timeless must be equally acknowledged.

Nature's Freshness

Can the natural philosopher find a fundamental concept of stability and change which expresses this balanced dualism of constancy and novelty? Casting a glance back into the wisdoms of tradition, is there a basic view of the universe which avoids the rigidity of the archetype (Plato) and the fluidity of incomprehensible matter (Heraclitus)? Perhaps Heidegger is not far from this important discovery when he goes back to the Greek concept *phusis* which has entered the Aristotelian tradition and come down to us as *nature* (*natura*). But it would not be an acceptable concept for the evolutionary problem unless it is purified of the later excessive rigidity given to it by a platonizing of the tradition of natural philosophy.

Originally, nature in the sense of *phusis* meant the entire being in process of unfolding from birth until maturity and death. This developmental concept was drawn from the life sciences and was intended to designate the ground of natural being, the intrinsic spring and source of spontaneous, yet characteristic activity. The concept was intended to express both stability and change, type and variety, to the extent that each was found in reality. But because the ancients had very poor instruments of natural science and natural species seemed to be immutable, the concept *nature* came to mean the unchanging *essence* of natural being, thought to be necessary, immutable, and eternal. The change of species could not be observed, nature was viewed as a mathematical species, and the static cosmos with its metaphysics of essence obscured and almost obliterated the dynamic aspect of the original concept of nature.

Many natural philosophers of the Aristotelian tradition attempted to preserve the relativistic, fluid aspect of the concept "nature," St. Thomas among them. But without an empirical knowledge of evolution of natural species, it was difficult to find reason to accent the timely, the contingent, historical unfolding of nature. Most of the resistance of traditional philosophers to evolutionary claims, even today, stems from an excessive typological concept of nature in which fixity and stability are so stressed that time-space contingent history is a secondary, incidental, and even uninteresting philosophical consideration. This excessive rigidity of the concept "nature" is an accretion, however, and if the primitive meaning is maintained, then we do have the possibility of a basic evolutionary concept which can retain both stability and novelty in realistic balance.

Nature's Law and Cosmic Order

Not only would a return to the original concept of nature be useful to evolutionary theory, it would assist greatly in resolving the difficulties of traditional philosophers concerning the laws of nature (and natural law), the hierarchy of natural beings, order in nature, and the role of chance in the evolutionary world-view. In the causal scheme of analysis, a rigid, typological idea of natural species would (and does) register the objection that the higher could not come from the lower. But if the original flexible concept of nature is used and the content of the concept is determined by empirical fact, in this case evolutionary development of species, then the doubt loses its force.

In the evolutionary picture, are there natural laws? Of course. Otherwise there could be no scientific pursuit at all. But we must introduce at every turn what we have learned about the indeterminacy basic to cosmic beings, and the opportunism of the space-time evolution of cosmic entities. Nature is constant and regular, but not so constant and regular as we once thought. Inconstancy, irregularity, novelty, surprise, mystery—all of which are not subject to scientific laws—are as characteristic of nature as regularity. This is evident when we take the large, long, evolutionary view of the history of the cosmos.

The facts reveal that *chance* plays a large role in evolutionary unfolding. Nature generates its like, *ut in pluribus,* but not in a vacuum. The direction of development is dominated by environmental forces like isolation and natural selection which are unpredictable, irrepeatable. Cosmic beings obey laws in an orderly way; but they are also under the command of history which obeys no law. Evolution is not predictable, but neither is it random.

Hence, the old static order of the cosmos has to be replaced by a new, thoroughgoing *dynamic order.* Nature's constancies give a general structure and orientation to the cosmos within which the laws of nature are operative. But even as those laws establish that general orientation, the parts of the cosmos are coming to be and are passing away. New species are arising, many old ones are perishing. Order gives way to new order—in an orderly way, but not entirely orderly, that is, not without the unpredictable play of history, of space and time. The more we grasp the contingent nature of this dynamic order, the more realistically can we ask our philosophical questions. Many of the traditional questions about "species," "higher-lower," "hierarchy of being," etc. are irrelevant today simply because the static world-view in which those notions arose has been shown to be illusory in the face of evolutionary fact.

By far the most serious difficulties which evolution has created for man in the past one hundred years have to do with his religious sensibilities. In the Judeo-Christian tradition, evolution has been seen as a threat to two important religious facts: (1) the philosophical proofs for the existence of God and (2) the revelation of God in the Bible. Through these two avenues, evolutionary thinking appears to some to undermine the whole super-structure of Christian theology. But a close inspection of these problems reveals that evolutionary science enhances rather than undermines Christian theology.

Traditional "proofs" for the existence of God rest upon the contingency of the universe. The motion, the causes, the order of this universe are not self-contained nor self-explanatory. Whatever brings this contingency of cosmic being more forcibly to light enhances, not destroys, the impact of the proofs. Evolutionary science, with its insistence on the role of the indetermined, of a natural selection filled with chance, of extinction and failure, contributes enormously to the revelation of contingency. Time and space dominate the beings of cosmic development, and the reason for this is the contingency of those beings. A necessary being is demanded more by an evolutionary cosmos than for the static, unhistorical one of the tradition. The "proof" from cosmic order, for example, is likewise enhanced and for the same reason. A relatively indetermined dynamic order, shot through with chance, has to replace the static, determined order of classical cosmology. But an Orderer, a Governor, a Provider is more necessary for the unified coordination of a dynamic universe than for a determined, undeveloping one. The intellectual atmosphere of the mid-twentieth century, with its preoccupation on the timely to the neglect of the timeless, may consider the "proofs" irrelevant, but that is not because the "facts" of evolution have robbed them of their pristine force. The rational inference from the cosmos to a transcendent being upon which it depends has been buttressed, not weakened, by evolutionary science.

More serious by far is the charge that evolutionary science threatens Christian teaching by contradicting the Bible account of origins, especially of man. Progress in the cosmic sciences has been accompanied, especially in the last twenty-five years, by an unprecedented progress in biblical exegesis among Catholics, Protestants, and Jews. Since Pope Pius XII's encyclical *Divino Afflante Spiritu,* Catholic biblical scholarship has taken great strides in discovering the literal meaning of the revelation about origins. There are two general principles which must govern any reading of the biblical account: (1) the Bible is a revelation of moral and religious truths, not a manual of science; (2) to discover God's message, you must first discover the message intended by his instrument, the human author. This can only be done by patient research into the author's personality, his times, his language, his audience, his history—in short, the very conditions of his writing the book. Only when the writer's intention is discovered, can you proceed with the analogy of faith to an understanding of the divine message.

Evolutionary science has exerted a healthy pressure upon biblical scholars to apply these canons rigorously to the accounts of origins in the Bible. The literary forms, the imagery used by the writers, have been carefully disengaged from the moral and religious truths to be retained by the Christian believer. Now it becomes abundantly clear that the sacred author had no intention of settling *how* God created, but only the moral and religious intentions of that creation. Physical origins, the place, the time, the conditions must be left to science. The Scriptures tell us of the *meaning* of it all, not the mechanics of development. In a word, the Bible is neutral on the subject of scientific origins, it could not, therefore, be in opposition to evolutionary science.

But what if scientific inferences seem to contradict a moral and religious truth which has been traditionally traced to the biblical account of origins? This question has arisen in the knotty issue of the origin of original sin: *monogenism* vs. *polygenism*. Evolutionary science, dealing only with populations in their accounts of species development, thinks of man's physical origins among the Australopithecines in terms of a group (polygenism). Christian theologians, interpreting Genesis and the account of the Fall through the eyes of St. Paul and the Council of Trent, think instinctively in terms of a single pair, Adam and Eve (monogenism), at the origin of the human species. This issue seems to bring evolutionary science and the Bible into direct confrontation.

But as in every other serious discussion which science and theology have quietly and professionally conducted, a resolution of this problem seems forthcoming. In the first place, it is important to see that science and theology are considering two different problems, each with its own methods. Although Pope Pius XII positively indicated monogenism as the only teaching reconcilable with the teaching of the Council of Trent (*Humani Generis,* 1950), he did not declare this statement irreformable. Since 1950, many biblical scholars have researched the biblical texts, the teaching of St. Paul, and the Council of Trent, and possibilities of reconciling polygenism with the *de fide* teaching of the Church on original sin have been proposed. It may be that the moral and religious teaching of the Bible (and Trent) are neutral on the question of physical numbers and therefore neutral on this evolutionary question too. Patient research and discussion will tell.

It would be gross oversimplification to imply that after one hundred years of polemics and debate over evolutionary conflicts between science and theology there are no important and difficult issues remaining. The tension between concern for the timely and concern for the timeless remains at the heart of contemporary intellectual anxiety. Man's entire world-view is in the process of reformation, just as the Catholic Church is at this moment redefining her relation to the world and its contingencies. But this can be said. By disengaging erroneous ideological interpretations from established scientific facts, one can view evolution as fully in accord with the wisdom of traditional philosophy and the wisdom of revelation. Evolution, then, is not merely a fact or a theory; it is a wisdom of the timely, making luminous the wisdom of the timeless.

168. Declaration on Religious Freedom of Vatican Council II, December 7, 1965

OF the sixteen major and official documents that emanated from the Church's twenty-first ecumenical council (October, 1962-December, 1965), none reflected more closely the experience of the Catholics of the United States than the Declaration on Religious Freedom. From the outset of the Church's history in the new Republic, the father of the Catholic hierarchy, John Carroll, as first bishop and then Archbishop of Baltimore, made clear his adherence to the principles governing relations between Church and State as they were ultimately embodied in the Constitution and the Bill of Rights. Confronted in 1784 with the distasteful duty of replying to a serious attack on the Church, Carroll stated that he did so solely to vindicate the religious faith of those entrusted to his care. Yet even that grave duty would not have induced him to engage in the controversy if, as he said, he could fear that it would disturb

the harmony now subsisting among all Christians in this country, so blessed with civil and religious liberty; which if we have the wisdom and temper to preserve, America may come to exhibit a proof to the world, that general and equal toleration, by giving a free circulation to fair argument, is the most effectual method to bring all denominations of Christians to a unity of faith. [For the text, see No. 47, pp. 146-147 of this volume.]

In the century and a half between the death of Carroll and the close of Vatican Council II, there was no variation from this position on the part of the American bishops, priests, religious, or members of the laity. Thus when the problem arose in the conciliar debates at Rome, the Americans could speak from a long and successful background. The document that follows bore another claim to special favor with the American Catholics insofar as the principal author was the distinguished theologian, John Courtney Murray, S.J. (1904-   ). And during the frequently heated exchanges on this subject the American bishops were heard in the aula of Saint Peter's with a forcefulness and persistence as they were not, perhaps, heard on any other single issue. It would seem appropriate, therefore, that the latest edition of this collection should include this remarkable document with which the American Catholic name has recently been so clearly and honorably identified throughout the Universal Church. Source: *Second Vatican Council.*

Declaration on Religious Freedom, December 7, 1965. (Washington: National Catholic Welfare Conference, 1966.)

---

1. A sense of the dignity of the human person has been impressing itself more and more deeply on the consciousness of contemporary man,[1] and the demand is increasingly made that men should act on their own judgment, enjoying and making use of a responsible freedom, not driven by coercion but motivated by a sense of duty. The demand is likewise made that constitutional limits should be set to the powers of government, in order that there may be no encroachment on the rightful freedom of the person and of associations. This demand for freedom in human society chiefly regards the quest for the values proper to the human spirit. It regards, in the first place, the free exercise of religion in society. This Vatican Council takes careful note of these desires in the minds of men. It proposes to declare them to be greatly in accord with truth and justice. To this end, it searches into the sacred tradition and doctrine of the Church—the treasury out of which the Church continually brings forth new things that are in harmony with the things that are old.

First, the Council professes its belief that God Himself has made known to mankind the way in which men are to serve Him, and thus be saved in Christ and come to blessedness. We believe that this one true religion subsists in the Catholic and Apostolic Church, to which the Lord Jesus committed the duty of spreading it abroad among all men. Thus He spoke to the Apostles: "Go, therefore, and make disciples of all nations, baptizing them in the name of the Father and of the Son and of the Holy Spirit, teaching them to observe all things whatsoever I have enjoined upon you" (Matt. 28:19-20). On their part, all men are bound to seek the truth, especially in what concerns God and His Church, and to embrace the truth they come to know, and to hold fast to it.

This Vatican Council likewise professes its belief that it is upon the human conscience that these obligations fall and exert their binding force. The truth cannot impose itself except by virtue of its own truth, as it makes its entrance into the mind at once quietly and with power.

Religious freedom, in turn, which men demand as necessary to fulfill their duty to worship God, has to do with immunity from coercion in civil society. Therefore it leaves untouched traditional Catholic doc-

---

[1] Cf. John XXIII, Encyclical Letter, *Pacem in Terris,* April 11, 1963: *AAS* 55 (1963), p. 279; *ibid.,* p. 265; Pius XII, Radio Message, Dec. 24, 1944: *AAS* 37 (1945), p. 14.

trine on the moral duty of men and societies toward the true religion and toward the one Church of Christ.

Over and above all this, the Council intends to develop the doctrine of recent popes on the inviolable rights of the human person and the constitutional order of society.

2. This Vatican Council declares that the human person has a right to religious freedom. This freedom means that all men are to be immune from coercion on the part of individuals or of social groups and of any human power, in such wise that no one is to be forced to act in a manner contrary to his own beliefs, nor is anyone to be restrained from acting in accordance with his own beliefs, whether privately or publicly, whether alone or in association with others, within due limits.

The Council further declares that the right to religious freedom has its foundation in the very dignity of the human person as this dignity is known through the revealed Word of God and by reason itself.[2] This right of the human person to religious freedom is to be recognized in the constitutional law whereby society is governed and thus it is to become a civil right.

It is in accordance with their dignity as persons—that is, beings endowed with reason and free will and therefore privileged to bear personal responsibility—that all men should be at once impelled by nature and also bound by a moral obligation to seek the truth, especially religious truth. They are also bound to adhere to the truth, once it is known, and to order their whole lives in accord with the demands of truth. However, men cannot discharge these obligations in a manner in keeping with their own nature unless they enjoy immunity from external coercion as well as psychological freedom. Therefore the right to religious freedom has its foundation not in the subjective disposition of the person, but in his very nature. In consequence, the right to this immunity continues to exist even in those who do not live up to their obligation of seeking the truth and adhering to it and the exercise of this right is not to be impeded, provided that just public order be observed.

3. Further light is shed on the subject if one considers that the highest norm of human life is the divine law—eternal, objective and universal—whereby God orders, directs and governs the entire universe

---

[2] Cf. John XXIII, Encyclical Letter, *Pacem in Terris*, April 11, 1963: *AAS* 55 (1963), pp. 260-261; Pius XII, Radio Message, Dec. 24, 1942: *AAS* 35 (1943), p. 19; Pius XI, Encyclical Epistle, *Mit Brennender Sorge*, March 14, 1937: *AAS* 29 (1937), p. 160; Leo XIII, Encyclical Letter, *Libertas Praestantissimum*, June 20, 1888: *Acts of Leo XIII* 8 (1888), pp. 237-238.

and all the ways of the human community by a plan conceived in wisdom and love. Man has been made by God to participate in this law, with the result that, under the gentle disposition of divine Providence, he can come to perceive ever more fully the truth that is unchanging. Wherefore every man has the duty, and therefore the right, to seek the truth in matters religious in order that he may with prudence form for himself right and true judgments of conscience, under use of all suitable means.

Truth, however, is to be sought after in a manner proper to the dignity of the human person and his social nature. The inquiry is to be free, carried on with the aid of teaching or instruction, communication and dialogue, in the course of which men explain to one another the truth they have discovered, or think they have discovered, in order thus to assist one another in the quest for truth.

Moreover, as the truth is discovered, it is by a personal assent that men are to adhere to it.

On his part, man perceives and acknowledges the imperatives of the divine law through the mediation of conscience. In all his activity a man is bound to follow his conscience in order that he may come to God, the end and purpose of life. It follows that he is not to be forced to act in a manner contrary to his conscience. Nor, on the other hand, is he to be restrained from acting in accordance with his conscience, especially in matters religious. The reason is that the exercise of religion, of its very nature, consists before all else in those internal, voluntary and free acts whereby man sets the course of his life directly toward God. No merely human power can either command or prohibit acts of this kind.[3] The social nature of man, however, itself requires that he should give external expression to his internal acts of religion: that he should share with others in matters religious; that he should profess his religion in community. Injury therefore is done to the human person and to the very order established by God for human life, if the free exercise of religion is denied in society, provided just public order is observed.

There is a further consideration. The religious acts whereby men, in private and in public and out of a sense of personal conviction, direct their lives to God transcend by their very nature the order of terrestrial and temporal affairs. Government therefore ought indeed to take account of the religious life of the citizenry and show it favor, since the

---

[3] Cf. John XXIII, Encyclical Letter, *Pacem in Terris,* April 11, 1963: *AAS* 55 (1963), p. 270; Paul VI, Radio Message, Dec. 22, 1964: *AAS* 57 (1965), pp. 181-182.

function of government is to make provision for the common welfare. However, it would clearly transgress the limits set to its power, were it to presume to command or inhibit acts that are religious.

4. The freedom or immunity from coercion in matters religious which is the endowment of persons as individuals is also to be recognized as their right when they act in community. Religious communities are a requirement of the social nature both of man and of religion itself.

Provided the just demands of public order are observed, religious communities rightfully claim freedom in order that they may govern themselves according to their own norms, honor the Supreme Being in public worship, assist their members in the practice of the religious life, strengthen them by instruction, and promote institutions in which they may join together for the purpose of ordering their own lives in accordance with their religious principles.

Religious communities also have the right not to be hindered, either by legal measures or by administrative action on the part of government, in the selection, training, appointment, and transferral of their own ministers, in communicating with religious authorities and communities abroad, in erecting buildings for religious purposes, and in the acquisition and use of suitable funds or properties.

Religious communities also have the right not to be hindered in their public teaching and witness to their faith, whether by the spoken or by the written word. However, in spreading religious faith and in introducing religious practices everyone ought at all times to refrain from any manner of action which might seem to carry a hint of coercion or of a kind of persuasion that would be dishonorable or unworthy, especially when dealing with poor or uneducated people. Such a manner of action would have to be considered an abuse of one's right and a violation of the right of others.

In addition, it comes within the meaning of religious freedom that religious communities should not be prohibited from freely undertaking to show the special value of their doctrine in what concerns the organization of society and the inspiration of the whole of human activity. Finally, the social nature of man and the very nature of religion afford the foundation of the right of men freely to hold meetings and to establish educational, cultural, charitable and social organizations, under the impulse of their own religious sense.

5. The family, since it is a society in its own original right, has the right freely to live its own domestic religious life under the guidance of parents. Parents, moreover, have the right to determine, in accordance with their own religious beliefs, the kind of religious education that

their children are to receive. Government, in consequence, must acknowledge the right of parents to make a genuinely free choice of schools and of other means of education, and the use of this freedom of choice is not to be made a reason for imposing unjust burdens on parents, whether directly or indirectly. Besides, the rights of parents are violated, if their children are forced to attend lessons or instructions which are not in agreement with their religious beliefs, or if a single system of education, from which all religious formation is excluded, is imposed upon all.

6. Since the common welfare of society consists in the entirety of those conditions of social life under which men enjoy the possibility of achieving their own perfection in a certain fullness of measure and also with some relative ease, it chiefly consists in the protection of the rights, and in the performance of the duties, of the human person.[4] Therefore the care of the right to religious freedom devolves upon the whole citizenry, upon social groups, upon government, and upon the Church and other religious communities, in virtue of the duty of all toward the common welfare, and in the manner proper to each.

The protection and promotion of the inviolable rights of man ranks among the essential duties of government.[5] Therefore government is to assume the safeguard of the religious freedom of all its citizens, in an effective manner, by just laws and by other appropriate means.

Government is also to help create conditions favorable to the fostering of religious life, in order that the people may be truly enabled to exercise their religious rights and to fulfill their religious duties, and also in order that society itself may profit by the moral qualities of justice and peace which have their origin in men's faithfulness to God and to His holy will.[6]

If, in view of peculiar circumstances obtaining among peoples, special civil recognition is given to one religious community in the constitutional order of society, it is at the same time imperative that the right of all citizens and religious communities to religious freedom should be recognized and made effective in practice.

Finally, government is to see to it that the equality of citizens before

---

[4] Cf. John XXIII, Encyclical Letter, *Mater et Magistra,* May 15, 1961: *AAS* 53 (1961), p. 417; idem, Encyclical Letter, *Pacem in Terris,* April 11, 1963: *AAS* 55 (1963), p. 273.
[5] Cf. John XXIII, Encyclical Letter, *Pacem in Terris,* April 11, 1963: *AAS* 55 (1963), pp. 273-274; Pius XII, Radio Message, June 1, 1941: *AAS* 33 (1941), p. 200.
[6] Cf. Leo XII, Encyclical Letter, *Immortale Dei,* Nov. 1, 1885; *AAS* 18 (1885), p. 161.

the law, which is itself an element of the common good, is never violated, whether openly or covertly, for religious reasons. Nor is there to be discrimination among citizens.

It follows that a wrong is done when government imposes upon its people, by force or fear or other means, the profession or repudiation of any religion, or when it hinders men from joining or leaving a religious community. All the more is it a violation of the will of God and of the sacred rights of the person and the family of nations when force is brought to bear in any way in order to destroy or repress religion, either in the whole of mankind or in a particular country or in a definite community.

7. The right to religious freedom is exercised in human society: hence its exercise is subject to certain regulatory norms. In the use of all freedoms the moral principle of personal and social responsibility is to be observed. In the exercise of their rights, individual men and social groups are bound by the moral law to have respect both for the rights of others and for their own duties toward others and for the common welfare of all. Men are to deal with their fellows in justice and civility.

Furthermore, society has the right to defend itself against possible abuses committed on the pretext of freedom of religion. It is the special duty of government to provide this protection. However, government is not to act in an arbitrary fashion or in an unfair spirit of partisanship. Its action is to be controlled by juridical norms which are in conformity with the objective moral order. These norms arise out of the need for the effective safeguard of the rights of all citizens and for the peaceful settlement of conflicts of rights, also out of the need for an adequate care of genuine public peace, which comes about when men live together in good order and in true justice, and finally out of the need for a proper guardianship of public morality.

These matters constitute the basic component of the common welfare: they are what is meant by public order. For the rest, the usages of society are to be the usages of freedom in their full range: that is, the freedom of man is to be respected as far as possible and is not to be curtailed except when and insofar as necessary.

8. Many pressures are brought to bear upon the men of our day, to the point where the danger arises lest they lose the possibility of acting on their own judgment. On the other hand, not a few can be found who seem inclined to use the name of freedom as the pretext for refusing to submit to authority and for making light of the duty of obedience. Wherefore this Vatican Council urges everyone, especially those who are charged with the task of educating others, to do their utmost

to form men who, on the one hand, will respect the moral order and be obedient to lawful authority, and, on the other hand, will be lovers of true freedom—men, in other words, who will come to decisions on their own judgment and in the light of truth, govern their activities with a sense of responsibility, and strive after what is true and right, willing always to join with others in cooperative effort.

Religious freedom therefore ought to have this further purpose and aim, namely, that men may come to act with greater responsibility in fulfilling their duties in community life.

9. The declaration of this Vatican Council on the right of man to religious freedom has its foundation in the dignity of the person, whose exigencies have come to be more fully known to human reason through centuries of experience. What is more, this doctrine of freedom has roots in divine revelation, and for this reason Christians are bound to respect it all the more conscientiously. Revelation does not indeed affirm in so many words the right of man to immunity from external coercion in matters religious. It does, however, disclose the dignity of the human person in its full dimensions. It gives evidence of the respect which Christ showed toward the freedom with which man is to fulfill his duty of belief in the Word of God and it gives us lessons in the spirit which disciples of such a Master ought to adopt and continually follow. Thus further light is cast upon the general principles upon which the doctrine of this declaration on religious freedom is based. In particular, religious freedom in society is entirely consonant with the freedom of the act of Christian faith.

10. It is one of the major tenets of Catholic doctrine that man's response to God in faith must be free: no one therefore is to be forced to embrace the Christian faith against his own will.[7] This doctrine is contained in the Word of God and it was constantly proclaimed by the Fathers of the Church.[8] The act of faith is of its very nature a free act.

---

[7] Cf. CIC, c. 1351; Pius XII, allocution to prelate auditors and other officials and administrators of the tribune of the Holy Roman Rota, Oct. 6, 1946: *AAS* 38 (1946), p. 394; idem. Encyclical Letter, *Mystici Corporis*, June 29, 1943: *AAS* (1943), p. 243.

[8] Cf. Lactantius *Divinarum Institutionum*, Book V, 19: CSEL 19, pp. 463-464, 465: PL 6, 614 and 616 (ch. 20); St. Ambrose, *Epistola ad Valentianum Imp.*, Letter 21: PL 16, 1005; St. Augustine, *Contra Litteras Petiliani*, Book II, ch. 83: CSEL 52, p. 112: PL 43, 315; cf. C. 23, q. 5, c. 33 (ed. Friedberg, col. 939); idem, Letter 23: PL 33, 98; idem, Letter 34: PL 33, 132; idem, Letter 35: PL 33, 135; St. Gregory the Great, *Epistola ad Virgilium et Theodorum Episcopos Massiliae Galliarum*, Register of Letters I, 45: MGH Ep. 1, p. 72: PL 77, 510-511 (Book I, ep. 47); idem, *Epistola ad Johannem Episcopum Constantinopolitanum*, Register of Letters, III, 52: MGH Letter 1, p. 210: PL 77, 649 (Book III,

Man, redeemed by Christ the Saviour and through Christ Jesus called to be God's adopted son,[9] cannot give his adherence to God revealing Himself unless, under the drawing of the Father,[10] he offers to God the reasonable and free submission of faith. It is therefore completely in accord with the nature of faith that in matters religious every manner of coercion on the part of men should be excluded. In consequence, the principle of religious freedom makes no small contribution to the creation of an environment in which men can without hindrance be invited to the Christian faith, embrace it of their own free will, and profess it effectively in their whole manner of life.

11. God calls men to serve Him in spirit and in truth, hence they are bound in conscience but they stand under no compulsion. God has regard for the dignity of the human person whom He Himself created and man is to be guided by his own judgment and he is to enjoy freedom. This truth appears at its height in Christ Jesus, in whom God manifested Himself and His ways with men. Christ is at once our Master and our Lord [11] and also meek and humble of heart.[12] In attracting and inviting His disciples He used patience.[13] He wrought miracles to illuminate His teaching and to establish its truth, but His intention was to rouse faith in His hearers and to confirm them in faith, not to exert coercion upon them.[14] He did indeed denounce the unbelief of some who listened to Him, but He left vengeance to God in expectation of the day of judgment.[15] When He sent His Apostles into the world, He said to them: "He who believes and is baptized will be saved. He who does not believe will be condemned" (Mark 16:16). But He Himself, noting that the cockle had been sown amid the wheat, gave orders that both should be allowed to grow until the harvest time, which will come at the end of the world.[16] He refused to be a political messiah, ruling by force.[17] He preferred to call Himself the Son of

---

Letter 53); cf. D. 45, c. 1 (ed. Friedberg, col. 160); Council of Toledo IV, c. 57; Mansi 10, 633; cf. D. 45, c. 5 (ed. Friedberg, col. 161-162); Clement III: X., V, 6,9 (ed. Friedberg, col. 774); Innocent III, *Epistola ad Arelatensem Archiepiscopum*, X., III, 42,3 (ed. Friedberg, col. 646).

[9] Cf. Eph. 1:5.
[10] Cf. John 6:44.
[11] Cf. John 13:13.
[12] Cf. Matt. 11:29.
[13] Cf. Matt. 11:28-30; John 6:67-68.
[14] Cf. Matt. 9:28-29; Mark 9:23-24; 6:5-6; Paul VI, Encyclical Letter, *Ecclesiam Suam*, Aug. 6, 1964: *AAS* 56 (1964), pp. 642-643.
[15] Cf. Matt. 11:20-24; Rom. 12:19-20; 2 Thes. 1:8.
[16] Cf. Matt. 13:30 and 40-42.
[17] Cf. Matt. 4:8-10; John 6:15.

Man, who came "to serve and to give His life as a ransom for the many" (Mark 10:45). He showed Himself the perfect servant of God,[18] who "does not break the bruised reed nor extinguish the smoking flax" (Matt. 12:20).

He acknowledged the power of government and its rights, when He commanded that tribute be given to Caesar: but He gave clear warning that the higher rights of God are to be kept inviolate: "Render to Caesar the things that are Caesar's and to God the things that are God's" (Matt. 22:21). In the end, when He completed on the Cross the work of redemption whereby He achieved salvation and true freedom for men, He brought His revelation to completion. For He bore witness to the truth,[19] but He refused to impose the truth by force on those who spoke against it. Not by force of blows does His rule assert its claims.[20] It is established by witnessing to the truth and by hearing the truth, and it extends its dominion by the love whereby Christ, lifted up on the Cross, draws all men to Himself.[21]

Taught by the word and example of Christ, the Apostles followed the same way. From the very origins of the Church the disciples of Christ strove to convert men to faith in Christ as the Lord; not, however, by the use of coercion or of devices unworthy of the Gospel, but by the power, above all, of the Word of God.[22] Steadfastly they proclaimed to all the plan of God our Saviour, "who wills that all men should be saved and come to the acknowledgement of the truth" (1 Tim. 2:4). At the same time, however, they showed respect for those of weaker stuff, even though they were in error, and thus they made it plain that "each one of us is to render to God an account of himself" (Rom. 14:12),[23] and for that reason is bound to obey his conscience. Like Christ Himself, the Apostles were unceasingly bent upon bearing witness to the truth of God, and they showed the fullest measure of boldness in "speaking the word with confidence" (Acts 4:31)[24] before the people and their rulers. With a firm faith they held that the Gospel is indeed the power of God unto salvation for all who believe.[25] Therefore they rejected all "carnal weapons":[26] they fol-

---

[18] Cf. Is. 42:1-4.
[19] Cf. John 18:37.
[20] Cf. Matt. 26:51-53; John 18:36.
[21] Cf. John 12:32.
[22] Cf. 1 Cor. 2:3-5; 1 Thes. 2:3-5.
[23] Cf. Rom. 14:1-23; 1 Cor. 8:9-13; 10:23-33.
[24] Cf. Eph. 6:19-20.
[25] Cf. Rom. 1:16.
[26] Cf. 2 Cor. 10:4; 1 Thes. 5:8-9.

lowed the example of the gentleness and respectfulness of Christ and they preached the Word of God in the full confidence that there was resident in this Word itself a divine power able to destroy all the forces arrayed against God [27] and bring men to faith in Christ and to His service.[28] As the Master, so too the Apostles recognized legitimate civil authority. "For there is no power except from God," the Apostle teaches, and thereafter commands: "Let everyone be subject to higher authorities. . . . He who resists authority resists God's ordinance" (Rom. 13:1-5).[29] At the same time, however, they did not hesitate to speak out against governing powers which set themselves in opposition to the holy will of God: "It is necessary to obey God rather than men" (Acts 5:29).[30] This is the way along which the martyrs and other faithful have walked through all ages and over all the earth.

12. In faithfulness therefore to the truth of the Gospel, the Church is following the way of Christ and the Apostles when she recognizes and gives support to the principle of religious freedom as befitting the dignity of man and as being in accord with divine revelation. Throughout the ages the Church has kept safe and handed on the doctrine received from the Master and from the Apostles. In the life of the People of God, as it has made its pilgrim way through the vicissitudes of human history, there has at times appeared a way of acting that was hardly in accord with the spirit of the Gospel or even opposed to it. Nevertheless, the doctrine of the Church that no one is to be coerced into faith has always stood firm.

Thus the leaven of the Gospel has long been about its quiet work in the minds of men, and to it is due in great measure the fact that in the course of time men have come more widely to recognize their dignity as persons, and the conviction has grown stronger that the person in society is to be kept free from all manner of coercion in matters religious.

13. Among the things that concern the good of the Church and indeed the welfare of society here on earth—things therefore that are always and everywhere to be kept secure and defended against all injury—this certainly is preeminent, namely, that the Church should enjoy that full measure of freedom which her care for the salvation of men requires.[31] This is a sacred freedom, because the only-begotten

---

[27] Cf. Eph. 6:11-17.
[28] Cf. 2 Cor. 10:3-5.
[29] Cf. 1 Pet. 2:13-17.
[30] Cf. Acts 4:19-20.
[31] Cf. Leo XIII, Encyclical Epistle, *Officio Sanctissimo,* Dec. 22, 1887: *AAS* 20 (1887), p. 269; idem, letter, *Ex Litteris,* April 7, 1887: *AAS* 19 (1886), p. 465.

Son endowed with it the Church which He purchased with His blood. Indeed it is so much the property of the Church that to act against it is to act against the will of God. The freedom of the Church is the fundamental principle in what concerns the relations between the Church and governments and the whole civil order.

In human society and in the face of government the Church claims freedom for herself in her character as a spiritual authority, established by Christ the Lord, upon which there rests, by divine mandate, the duty of going out into the whole world and preaching the Gospel to every creature.[32] The Church also claims freedom for herself in her character as a society of men who have the right to live in society in accordance with the precepts of Christian faith.[33]

In turn, where the principle of religious freedom is not only proclaimed in words or simply incorporated in law but also given sincere and practical application, there the Church succeeds in achieving a stable situation of right as well as of fact and the independence which is necessary for the fulfillment of her divine mission. This independence is precisely what the authorities of the Church claim in society.[34]

At the same time, the Christian faithful, in common with all other men, possess the civil right not to be hindered in leading their lives in accordance with their consciences. Therefore, a harmony exists between the freedom of the Church and the religious freedom which is to be recognized as the right of all men and communities and sanctioned by constitutional law.

14. In order to be faithful to the divine command, "teach all nations" (Matt. 28:19-20), the Catholic Church must work with all urgency and concern "that the word of God be spread abroad and glorified" (2 Thes. 3:1). Hence the Church earnestly begs of its children that, "first of all, supplications, prayers, petitions, acts of thanksgiving be made for all men. . . . For this is good and agreeable in the sight of God our Saviour, who wills that all men be saved and come to the knowledge of the truth" (1 Tim. 2:1-4). In the formation of their consciences, the Christian faithful ought carefully to attend to the sacred and certain doctrine of the Church.[35] For the Church is, by the will of Christ, the teacher of the truth. It is her duty to give utterance to, and authoritatively to teach, that truth which is Christ

---

[32] Cf. Mark 16:15; Matt. 28:18-20; Pius XII, Encyclical Letter, *Summi Pontificatus*, Oct. 20, 1939: *AAS* 31 (1939), pp. 445-446.

[33] Cf. Pius XI, Encyclical Epistle, *Firmissimam Constantiam*, March 28, 1937: *AAS* 29 (1937), p. 196.

[34] Cf. Pius XII, allocution, *Ci Riesce*, Dec. 6, 1953: *AAS* 45 (1953), p. 802.

[35] Cf. Pius XII, Radio Message, March 23, 1952: *AAS* 44 (1952), pp. 270-278.

Himself, and also to declare and confirm by her authority those principles of the moral order which have their origins in human nature itself. Furthermore, let Christians walk in wisdom in the face of those outside, "in the Holy Spirit, in unaffected love, in the word of truth" (2 Cor. 6:6-7), and let them be about their task of spreading the light of life with all confidence[36] and apostolic courage, even to the shedding of their blood.

The disciple is bound by a grave obligation toward Christ, his Master, ever more fully to understand the truth received from Him, faithfully to proclaim it, and vigorously to defend it, never—be it understood—having recourse to means that are incompatible with the spirit of the Gospel. At the same time, the charity of Christ urges him to love, prudence and patience in his dealings with those who are in error or in ignorance with regard to the faith.[37] All is to be taken into account —the Christian duty to Christ, the life-giving Word which must be proclaimed, the rights of the human person, and the measure of grace granted by God through Christ to men who are invited freely to accept and profess the faith.

15. The fact is that men of the present day want to be able freely to profess their religion in private and in public. Indeed, religious freedom has already been declared to be a civil right in most constitutions, and it is solemnly recognized in international documents.[38] The further fact is that forms of government still exist under which, even though freedom of religious worship receives constitutional recognition, the powers of government are engaged in the effort to deter citizens from the profession of religion and to make life very difficult and dangerous for religious communities.

This Council greets with joy the first of these two facts as among the signs of the times. With sorrow, however, it denounces the other fact, as only to be deplored. The Council exhorts Catholics, and it directs a plea to all men, most carefully to consider how greatly necessary religious freedom is, especially in the present condition of the human family. All nations are coming into ever closer unity. Men of different cultures and religions are being brought together in closer relationships. There is a growing consciousness of the personal responsibility that every man has. All this is evident. Consequently, in order

---

[36] Cf. Acts 4:29.

[37] Cf. John XXIII, Encyclical Letter, *Pacem in Terris*, April 11, 1963: *AAS* 55 (1963), pp. 299-300.

[38] Cf. John XXIII, Encyclical Letter, *Pacem in Terris*, April 11, 1963: *AAS* 55 (1963), pp. 295-296.

that relationships of peace and harmony be established and maintained within the whole of mankind, it is necessary that religious freedom be everywhere provided with an effective constitutional guarantee and that respect be shown for the high duty and right of man freely to lead his religious life in society.

May the God and Father of all grant that the human family, through careful observance of the principle of religious freedom in society, may be brought by the grace of Christ and the power of the Holy Spirit to the sublime and unending and "glorious freedom of the sons of God" (Rom. 8:21).

✠   ✠   ✠   ✠

The entire text and all the individual elements which have been set forth in this Declaration have pleased the Fathers. And by the Apostolic power conferred on us by Christ, we, together with the Venerable Fathers, in the Holy Spirit, approve, decree and enact them; and we order that what has been thus enacted in Council be promulgated, to the glory of God.

Rome, at St. Peter's, 7 December, 1965

I, PAUL, Bishop of the Catholic Church

There follow the signatures of the Fathers.

169. War and Peace. A Pastoral Letter to the Archdiocese of Atlanta, October, 1966

THE plight of the world in the aftermath of World War II and the mounting peril of nuclear warfare, is well illustrated by the opening paragraph of the introduction to a volume of papal documents on peace, published in 1943, which read as follows:

> At some future hour, known now only to God, a group of statesmen will take their places around a conference table and hammer out a treaty designed to settle the staggering problems of a world torn apart by years of bitter war. When that hour strikes, what role will the Pope play in forging that instrument which will decisively determine the character of the post-war world? [Harry C. Koenig (ed.), *Principles for Peace. Selections from Papal Documents, Leo XIII to Pius XII* (Washington: National Catholic Welfare Conference, 1943), p. xv.]

Twenty-three years have passed since Monsignor Koenig wrote those lines and the statesmen have not yet taken their places around the conference table to negotiate a general peace treaty. Meanwhile the "staggering problems" of 1943 have multiplied and deepened in their complexity with the shadow of nuclear conflict. And the answer to the question concerning the role that the Pope will play in a final settlement is as uncertain as it was in 1943. During the early 1940's Pius XII issued a series of striking Christmas messages which, in the judgment of Thomas P. Neill of St. Louis University, constituted "the most profound consideration on the nature and requirements of peace in modern times." Yet, as he said, while most people in the free world received the Pope's words respectfully, they were generally dismissed as "impractical theorizing," whereas had his advice been followed, "the problems confronting statesmen today would not be as difficult as they are." ["The Practicality of 'Idealism,' " *Saint Louis Review,* October 7, 1966, p. 19.] The voice of American Catholics has not been nearly as strong in pursuit of world peace as one might rightly have expected. To remedy the deficiencies on that score, and to awaken the conscience of their co-religionists and of others as well, several bishops of the United States have issued formal statements on this pressing problem, but none with more balance and sound reasoning than that of Archbishop Hallinan and Bishop Bernadin of Atlanta. The following document not only echoes Paul VI's piercing cry, "never war again," but it summons the conscience of American Catholics and all men of good will to serious reflection on this gravest of all problems that now face the world. Source: *War and Peace. A Pastoral Letter to the Archdiocese of Atlanta, October, 1966.* (Distributed in pamphlet form by The Chancery, 2699 Peachtree Road, N.E., Atlanta, Georgia 30305.)

WAR AND PEACE

The slaughter of men and the death of villages are certainly not new to the history of mankind. Yet the passionate desire for true peace has never died in men's hearts. The tension created by the desire for peace and the realities of war has been brought into sharp focus by the current conflict in Viet Nam. But as Pope Paul reminded us in his encyclical two weeks ago,[1] this war is just one of many tragedies which severely threaten the peace and stability of the human family. "For instance," he stated, "there are the increasing race for nuclear weapons, the unscrupulous efforts for the expansion of one's nation, the excessive glorification of one's race, the obsession for revolution, the segregations enforced on citizens, the iniquitous plotting, the murder of the innocent."

1. The Five Questions

The Church cannot remain silent in the face of these grave disorders. True peace will not be brought about solely by military victory; it will

---

[1] *Christi Matri Rosarii,* September 15, 1966, *The Monitor* (San Francisco), September 29, 1966, p. 9.

not be achieved by maintaining a balance of power between enemies. Reflecting the thinking of Pope John XXIII as expressed in *Peace on Earth*, the Second Vatican Council has stated very clearly that, "peace results from the harmony built into human society by its Divine Founder, and actualized by men as they thirst after ever greater justice." All action and all talk about peace will be irrelevant unless it is cast in a moral context.

The Church, then, as the living voice of Christ must speak out. It must give an effective witness to the gospel message which provides a sure framework for universal brotherhood. This must be based on mutual respect and love so essential to the establishment of peace. For this reason, an American Catholic who has lost his moral perspective on war can hardly be considered a true Christian patriot.

As the great debate on war and peace gathers momentum, certain urgent questions demand that we respond:—

1. What are the demands of true patriotism?
2. Is it possible to speak of a "just war" today as we did in the past?
3. On a broader level, should nations try to maintain peace by a "balance of terror"?
4. Does universal disarmament (all sides) differ morally from unilateral disarmament (one side)?
5. What are our obligations in contributing toward a genuinely moral consensus regarding American involvement in Viet Nam?

2. Who Is the Patriot?

The well being of every nation depends on the patriotism of its citizens. The American Catholic—citizen, soldier, pacifist—has held an honorable place in our country's history, side by side with those of other faiths. The Bishops of Vatican II, however, clearly point out that there is a significant difference between *true patriotism* which is "living for God and Christ by following the honorable customs of one's own nation" and *false patriotism* which stems from "a narrowing of mind . . . racial prejudice and bitter nationalism." [2] True patriotism, in other words, does not end at a nation's borders. That American is truly patriotic who, while devoting himself to the legitimate needs and concerns of his country, also seeks "the welfare of the whole human family . . . a universal love for mankind." As Pope John stated in

---

[2] Reference to documents of Vatican Council II are generally to the "Pastoral Constitution on the Church in the Modern World," Walter M. Abbott, S.J., and Joseph Gallagher (Eds.), *Documents of Vatican II* (New York: Guild Press, 1966), pp. 183-316.

his last encyclical, *Peace on Earth*: "Individual countries cannot rightly seek their own interests, and develop in isolation from the rest."

This is not to say, of course, that a country cannot defend itself. While making it clear that all means short of force must first be employed, the Council restates the traditional teaching of the Church regarding the right of self-defense: "As long as the danger of war remains and there is no competent and sufficiently powerful authority at the international level, government cannot be denied the right to legitimate defense . . ." Moreover, the Council Fathers commend those in the military forces who serve as "agents of security and freedom on behalf of their people" as long as they fulfill this role properly.

In the light of our duty to examine the moral position of our country, another question remains: that of the right of a conscientious objector. The Church, after a brief warning that peace cannot exist "unless personal values are safeguarded" states clearly:

> It seems right that laws make humane provisions for the case of those who (for reasons of conscience) refuse to bear arms, provided however, that they accept some other form of service to the human community.

3. Limits and Illusions

If men are to remain human, there must be definite limits to the conduct of any war. The Council clearly defines these limits:

1. Any act of war aimed *indiscriminately at the destruction* of entire cities or of extensive areas along with their population is a crime against God and man himself. It merits univocal and unhesitating condemnation.
2. Those actions designed for the *methodical extermination* of an entire people, nation or ethnic minority must be vehemently condemned as horrendous crimes. . . . Blind obedience cannot excuse those who yield to them.

The Council also considered the massing of arms as a means of avoiding war. It pronounced such a method of deterrence a "treacherous trap for humanity." It is a trap because it is, without question, a dangerous way of maintaining peace. Moreover, the causes of war are actually intensified because the vast sums used for stockpiling weapons make it extremely difficult, if not totally impossible in some cases, to give attention to the human misery which is usually the root cause of war. For this reason the Bishops made an urgent plea for disarmament. But they realized that disarmament is a two-sided coin: it would have little meaning unless all sides agreed on it and unless there were effective means of enforcing it.

What bearing do these general principles have on our involvement in Viet Nam? What implications do they have generally for our efforts to promote world-wide peace?

4. The Only Alternative—?

As in every great human problem, there is no simple solution. American Catholics can put faith in the integrity of our government's aims in Viet Nam. There is surely abundant evidence of it in a number of areas: the recent large vote in South Viet Nam opening the door to local civilian government; the aid we have given to get such projects as the Mekong Delta improvements underway in Southeastern Asia; the support of the United States voiced in Washington last month by President Ferdinand Marcos of the Philippines; the total withdrawal of American troops from the Dominican Republic, leading the way to a constitutional government free of extremists, both left and right.

In the light of events rather than slogans, then, it can be argued that to the present course of action in Viet Nam there may be no visible alternative.

But we cannot stop here. It is the Christian duty to keep looking for *other alternatives.* We must know as much about the factual situation as possible, in order that these alternatives be realistic. To a limited extent our national security requires secrecy. Except for that, however, we must keep insisting that our leaders fully inform us of the facts and issues involved in the Viet Nam war.

We must help to enlarge the new climate of thought, based on Pope John's principle: in an age which prides itself on its atomic energy, it is unreasonable to hold that war is still a suitable way to restore violated rights. We can help by conversation, study, example, discussion groups and lectures.

Christians should advocate what they believe is the best way to bring about disarmament:—mutual agreements, safeguards and inspection; world federalism; the creation of a public authority empowered to negotiate toward peace.

We have the obligation to make sure that our government pursues, vigorously, wholeheartedly and repeatedly every opening which has even the slightest hope of peaceful settlement. Ambassador Arthur Goldberg's recent summary of the present American policy was such an opening. To the United Nations, he stated that we were ready to join in a phased withdrawal of all external forces, and a halt to bombing upon the assurance from North Viet Nam that it would halt its war effort.

As Cardinal Lawrence Shehan of Baltimore recently said in his splendid pastoral:

> Those who argue against restraint and against keeping a nation's war-making acts within moral bounds are likely to win an even greater hearing . . . (But) if our means become immoral, our cause will have been betrayed.[3]

We must protest, therefore, whenever there is danger that our conduct of the war will exceed moral limits. A Christian simply cannot approve indiscriminate bombing, methodical extermination of people, nuclear arms designed for "overkill" or disregard for noncombatants.

In short, our dedication to the cause of peace must become so evident, so intense, so convincing that the old balance of mutual terror will be phased out to make way for a new balance of mutual trust. In Christian confidence, we can hope that if many nations come to trust each other, those who instead rely on war will reevaluate their own positions.

On a broader level, we must give our leaders a mandate to pursue the problem of disarmament. While no Catholic teaching demands that a nation disarm by itself, the whole Catholic momentum today is toward a disarmament that is complete, thorough and internal, resting on mutual agreement and workable safeguards. We cannot stand aside because such a solution is hard to visualize or difficult to achieve.

Moreover, we must never cease to do everything in our power to help make it possible for the poorer nations of the world to give their people what they need—educationally, culturally, materially, and socially—to live in a way that squares with their God-given human dignity. We must be strong for the working out of the social and economic programs that will heal, not inflame, the causes of war.

5. "Never War Again!"

Mankind longs for peace, and has tragically sought it through the inhuman process of war. The Church calls us all—especially parents, teachers and those who form public opinion—to make known "fresh sentiments of peace." Pope Paul, speaking of the purpose of his recent encyclical, asked, "What is the use of it?" and answered that all Christians should "speak out and pray."

We must speak out; we cannot remain silent. In his novel, *War and Peace*, Tolstoy asks how men can ignore the continued disasters in which "Christians, professing the law of love, murder one another."

---

[3] *The Catholic Review* (Baltimore), July 1, 1966, p. 2.

Christian consciences and voices must be raised against the savagery and terror of war. We must speak out—for justice, for truth, for freedom and for peace.

And we must pray with Christian minds and hearts until hope replaces anxiety, and love crowds out hatred. On October 11, we observe the Motherhood of Our Lady, mother of the Son of God and of all His brothers. Do we love them as brothers? The month ends with the Feast of Christ the King, patron of our Cathedral. The preface of that feast describes a world not stained with the blood of men, but marked by the blood of Christ, the Lamb of God—"a Kingdom of truth and life, of holiness and grace, a Kingdom of justice, of love and peace."

Through the courage and the prayers of each of us, may our country and every other sovereign state "beat their swords into plowshares, and their spears into pruning hooks. One nation shall not raise the sword against another, nor shall they train for war again." (Is. 2,4)

As people of God, let us reaffirm what Paul VI, His vicar on earth said a year ago to the United Nations:—"never war again!"

✠ Paul J. Hallinan
Archbishop of Atlanta
✠ Joseph L. Bernardin
Auxiliary Bishop of Atlanta

Index

Abbelen, Peter M.
and German Catholic immigrants, 438n, 439n, 476n
and neglect of the immigrant, 480
Acadians, in Massachusetts, 120-124
"An Act Concerning Religion," 112-114
Adams, Henry, influence of LaFarge, noted, 39n
Adams, John, impressions of a Catholic service, 132-133
Adams, John Quincy, and Bishop England's speech (1826), 229-231
Alexander VI, Pope, *Inter caetera* (bull), 1-3
Allen, George, and conversion of Eliza Starr, noted, 306
Allouez, Claude, S.J., and Sault Ste. Marie ceremony, 60-63
Altham, John, S.J., English missionary in Maryland, 100-108
American College
in Louvain, appeal by Kindekens for, 315-317
in Rome, O'Connor's appeal for, 335-339
Americanism
controversy, 494-498
Paulist Fathers' association with, 660
Testem benevolentiae on, 537-547
American Protective Association
and the Catholic Church, 499
growth and activities, 483-485
oath of, 483-485
on Satolli's appointment as apostolic delegate, 513
American Protestant Association, constitution, 263-265
American Review of History and Politics, prospectus for, 190-197
Annual Letter
on Catholicism in Maryland (1638), 108-110
persecution of Catholics in Maryland (1656), 115-116
Anti-Catholicism, *see* Nativism; Persecution, religious
"Antillon," 128
Antonelli, Lorenzo, Cardinal, Carroll named superior of American missions, 142-144
Apostolic Delegation, established, 505n
Architecture, church, 19th century, 412-415
Arizona, missions, 24-27
Articles of Confederation, and religious freedom, 140
"The Ascension" (painting), John LaFarge, 441-444
Authorities, civil, Carroll's prayer for, 174-175

Ayguacen (archdiocese), suppressed, 5n-6n

Badin, Stephen Theodore, description of Catholicism in Kentucky, 179-184
Baltimore (archdiocese)
Catholicism in, 19th century, 202-220
Eccleston on state of (1838), 246-251
erected, 163-167
Baraga, Frederic, Bp., Slovenian missionary in United States, 366n
Barron, Edward, Bp., and Savannah cholera epidemic (1854), 310
Bayunen (Bayuna) (see), suppressed, 5n-6n
Becker, Thomas A., Bp., and Catholic University of America, 464
Bedini, Gaetano, Abp., tour of United States (1853-1854), noted, 329
Benavides, Alonso de, Fray, description of New Mexico missions, 15-17
Benedictines
and the German Catholic Brotherhood, 265
need of, in United States, stressed by Wimmer, 279-288
Bennett, James Gordon, on Bishop Lynch and slavery issue, 348
Bergier, Jean, report on Illinois missions, 81-83
Bernardin, Joseph L., pastoral letter on war and peace, 696-702
Bigotry
in Smith presidential campaign (1928), 616-621
in Kennedy campaign (1960), 652-654
Bishop(s)
appointment of first American, 163-167
need for colonies, 125-128
number in United States (1939), 629
The Bishops and the Catholic Press, 387-389
Bishops' Program of Social Reconstruction, 589-607
Bladensburg, Maryland, defeat of Americans at, mentioned, 239n
Blaine, James G., and school issue (1875), 395-397
Blaine Amendment, *see* Blaine, James G.
Blatchford, Richard M., American diplomatic relations with Papal States, 386-388
Bonaparte, Charles J., and Church-State relations, 470-473
Bosque, Fernando del, account of the first high Mass in Texas (1675), 23-24
Boston *Pilot*, editorial on western Catholic colonization (1856), 311-314
Bougainville, Louis Antoine de, founder of Falkland Island colony, noted, 123n
Bouquillon, Thomas

Index

Index

Index

Disfranchisement, of Catholics, in Maryland, 114-115

Divino Afflante Spiritu (encyclical), *see* Pius XII

Divorce, Edward Douglass White on, 565-567

Dominicans
and California missions, 398
in Florida, 11-12
and Franciscan concordat concerning California missions, 31-33

Dongan, Thomas, furthers religious toleration, 116-118

Dooley, Mr.
The Church Fair, 534-535
1924 (Democratic National Convention), 535-537
The Philippine Peace, 531-534

Doyle, John T., and Pious Fund, 403n

Draft, Edward Douglass White on 1918 draft law, 565, 567-568

Dred Scott Decision, noted regarding slavery, 322

Drexel, Mother Katharine, founder, Sisters of the Blessed Sacrament for Indians and Colored People, 574-576

Drexel and Company, noted, 574

Dubois, Jean, Bp., mentioned as missionary in Maryland, 182n

Dubuque (Iowa), editorial on Buffalo convention, 311-314

Dulany, Daniel, debate with Carroll, 128-130

Dunne, Finley Peter, excerpts from Mr. Dooley, 531-537

Early, James M., and papal infallibility, 390-395

Eccleston, Samuel, S.S., and Society for the Propagation of the Faith, 246-251

Echo d'Italia, noted regarding American liberty and the Holy See, 331n

Education, Catholic, *see* Catholic Church, education

Education, freedom of choice in, 655-658

Education, religious, *see* Religious education

Education: To Whom Does It Belong?, noted, 475n

Egan, Maurice Francis, and purchase of Danish West Indies, 586-588.

Elder, William Henry, Bp., on the apostolate to the Negro slaves, 325-329

Elliott, Walter, C.S.P., *The Life of Father Hecker*, and Americanism, 339, 537

Ellis, John Tracy, *American Catholics and the Intellectual Life*, 641-646

England, John, Bp.
account of speech before Congress (1826), 228-231
United States Catholic Miscellany, 227-228

England, literary trends in (1811), 190-197

England, Louise Imogen Guiney on, 568-574

Equitable Life Assurance Society, and Thomas Fortune Ryan, 580-586

Evolution
ancestral, 671
biological, 673, 674
cosmic, 674, 675
fossil witness for, 668, 669, 673
historical fact of, 667, 668, 670, 672, 676, 677, 683
philosophy of, 676-678
process of, 670
scientific, 666, 667, 675, 676

Ex hac apostolicae (brief), 163-167

Extension Magazine, 560

Faith, Congregation of the Propagation of the, *see* Congregatio de Propaganda Fide

Farmer, Ferdinand, S.J., on the missionaries' reasons for not wanting a bishop, 125-128

Fenwick, Edward D., O.P., death noted, 231

Figaro, Le, newspaper, noted, 462n

Filicchi, Filippo, friend of Mother Seton, 188n

Finance, Thomas Fortune Ryan and the Equitable Life Assurance Company, 580-586

"First Citizen," 128

FitzSimons, Thomas, and ratification of the Constitution, 154-156

Flaget, Benedict Joseph, S.S., impressions of his Middle West bishopric, 187-199

Florida
conquest of, by Spain, 12-14
Dominican missions in, 11-12
missions, report of Bishop Calderón, 18-23
withdrawal of Jesuits from, 14-15

France, neutrality of, during Civil War, 370-373

Francis Borgia, St., withdrawal of Jesuits from Florida, 14-15

Franciscans
and California missions, 398
and Dominican concordat concerning California missions, 31-33
missions, 9-10
in New Mexico, 15-17

Franciscans, French, *see* Récollets

Freeman's Journal (New York), editor noted, 342

Freemasons, condemnation noted, 418

Gallagher, Simon Felix, mentioned regarding trusteeism, 211n

Index

Galvéz, Don José de, noted as helper to Serra, 35n

Gartland, Francis X., Bp., description of cholera epidemic in Savannah (1854), 310-311

Gaston, William
first student in Georgetown Academy, 168
plea for religious freedom, 242-246

George, Henry, and opposition of condemnation by Gibbons, 457-460

Georgetown Academy, first Catholic college, 167-169, 530

German Catholic Brotherhood, colonization project, 265-269

Gervase, Thomas, S.J., English missionary in Maryland, 100-108

Gibault, Pierre, and the American cause, 141-142

Gibbons, James, Cardinal
on Americanism, 538
Church and State in United States, 460-463
and condemnation of Henry George, 457-460
defense of Knights of Labor, 444-457
and friendship with Keane, 437-441
and Ireland's stand on school controversy, 473-480
and N.C.W.C., noted, 611n

Godefroy, Maximilien, architect, noted, 408

Grant, Ulysses S., and school issue (1875), 395-397

Guilday, Peter, on Shea, 422

Guiney, Louise Imogen, on living in England, 568-574

Guiney, Patrick Robert, noted, 568

Guy Fawkes Day, banned by Washington, 136

Haddock v. Haddock, 585-587

Hallinan, Paul J., Abp., pastoral letter on war and peace, 696-702

Healy, George P. A., American portrait painter, 485-488

Heath, Sister Angela, nursing sisters in Civil War, 368-370

Hecker, Isaac Thomas, C.S.P.
Catholic University of America, 464
founder of Catholic Publication Society, 389
plans for the Paulists, 339-342

Heim, Ambrose J., and Society of St. Vincent de Paul, 289

Heiss, Michael, report on Wisconsin Catholicism (1861), 357-367

Helbron, John Charles (Capuchin), pastor of Holy Trinity Church (Philadelphia), 160

Hennepin, Louis (Récollet), work with Indians, 75-81

Henni, John Martin, Bp., report to Ludwig-Missionsverein on Catholicism in Wisconsin, 274-277

Hérésie fantôme, l'Américanisme, Une, 550

Hierarchy, *see* Clergy

History of the Catholic Clergy in the United States, 422-432

Holy See, *see* Vatican

Holy Trinity Church (Philadelphia), first national parish in United States, 160-162

Homestead Strike (1892), noted, 489

Hopkins, John Henry, *The Church of Rome in her Primitive Purity Compared to the Church of Rome at the Present Day*, 251

Hospitality, houses of, 625-629

"How Father Jogues was Taken by the Hiroquois and What He Suffered on His First Entrance into Their Country," 52-60

Hughes, John, Abp.
on American liberty and the Holy See, 329, 335
and Civil War, 347-356
and French neutrality during Civil War, 370-373
and North American College at Rome, 335
opposition to Western Catholic colonization, 317-321
pastoral letter on the Catholic Press, 387

Humani Generis (encyclical), *see* Pius XII

Hungarians
in United States, parish life, 555-560
population (1910), 555

Huret, Jules, interview with Archbishop Ireland, 489-494

Hutchinson, Thomas, on Acadians, 121-124

Illinois
Catholic Church on frontier of, 141-142
missions in, 81-84

Immigrants
Catholic
neglect of, protested, 480-483
number entering United States (1840's), 300
plan for Western colonization (1856), 311-314, 317-321
German
aided by Ludwig-Missionsverein, 274-288
number of Catholics in Pennsylvania (1757), 160
and trusteeism, 160-162
Hungarians, parish life in United States, 555-560

Index

Index

Lamy, John Baptist, Abp.
account of trip across the plains, 303-304
impressions of the Southwest, 301-303

Lancaster, John, prominent Catholic in Kentucky, mentioned, 182n

Laval, François de Montmorency, first Bishop of Quebec, 82

Leakage, from Catholic Church noted, 481n

Leclerc, Maximilien on American Catholicism, 494-498

LeClercq, Maxim (Récollet), death noted, 72

Legislation, civil, in a democracy, Keane's views on, 511-513

Leo XIII, Pope
on the Church in the United States, 547-549
Longinqua oceani, on American society, 499-511
plea for Italian immigrants in the United States, 466-470
Testem benevolentiae, on Americanism, 537-547

Leopoldinen-Stiftung of Vienna, aid to German Catholic missions noted, 275n

Letter to the Roman Catholics of the City of Worcester, 145

Liberty, American, and the Holy See, Hughes on (1858), 329-335

Life of Father Hecker, The, 537

Lincoln, Abraham, criticism of administration by McMaster, 342-347

Linton, William S., and the American Protective Association, 484

Linnaeus, 669

Literary and Religious Magazine, beginning of, noted, 249n

Liturgical Movement, in United States, 621-624

Liturgical Press of St. John's Abbey, 621

Longinqua oceani (encyclical), on American society, 499-511

Loras, Mathias, Bp.
and Buffalo convention (1856), 311-314
description of cholera epidemic (1832), 231-233, 233n

Lotbinière, Louis E., Canadian chaplain, 376

Louisiana
ecclesiastical jurisdiction of (1722), 84-86
ecclesiastical state of (1806), 185-188
religious conditions in (1795), 177-179

Ludwig-Missionsverein
founding noted, 287n
report on Catholicism in Wisconsin, 274-277

Lynch, Dominik, leading Catholic layman, mentioned, 171n

Lynch, Patrick N., Bp., and Civil War, 347-356

McClellan, George B., noted as commander of the Department of the Ohio, 344n

McDonnell, Charles E., Bp., and the National Catholic Welfare Council, 607

McGee, Thomas D'Arcy, noted as an organizer of Buffalo convention, 319n

McGlynn, Edward
and advocacy of Henry George's theories, 457
excommunication, 432, 436

McMahon Hall, Catholic University of America, dedication noted, 503n

McMaster, James A.
criticism of the Lincoln administration, 342-347
and slavery, 379

McQuaid, Bernard J., Bp.
Abbé Klein's impressions of, 550-555
and papal infallibility, 389-395

Madison, James, Secretary of State, on a bishop for Louisiana, 185-188

Magnien, Alphonse L., S.S., noted as Director of Society for the Propagation of the Faith, 561n

Maguen (Magua) (see), suppressed, 5n-6n

Magyars, first parish in United States, 558n

Man, brotherhood of, 7-9

Maréchal, Ambrose, S.S., Abp.
report on American Catholicism (1818), 202-220
report on trusteeism, 220-227

Martinelli, Sebastiano, O.S.A., appointed apostolic delegate, 513

Maryknoll, see Catholic Foreign Mission Society of America

Maryland
Act of Religious Toleration, 112-114
Catholicism in (1638), 108-110
charter (1632), 95-98
colonists in, 98-100
Declaration of Rights (1776) and religious freedom, 137
missions, 100-108, 124-125
persecution of Catholics (1656), 115-116
ratification of Constitution urged in, 157-159

Mason, Stephen C., president of the N.A.M., on *Bishops' Program of Social Reconstruction*, 589

Masons (secret order), see Freemasons

Mass, high, first time celebrated in Texas (1675), 23-24

Massachusetts
Acadians in, 120-124
anti-priest laws in
(1647), 111-112
(1700), 118-120

Index

Constitution (1780) and religious freedom, 139-140

Mathew, Theobald (Capuchin), temperance work noted, 272

Maurin, Peter, and Catholic Worker Movement, noted, 626n

Mazzuchelli, Samuel Charles, O.P., 365n
on Catholic temperance societies, 272-274

Membré, Zénobe (Récollet), missioner in Illinois, 72-74

Menéndez de Avilés, Pedro, and conquest of Florida, 12-14

Merton, Thomas, quoted on contemplative monasteries, 294

Metropolitan Record, started by Hughes, 342

Mexico, and Pious Fund, 398-404

Meyer v. Nebraska, 615n

Michel, Virgil, O.S.B., and the liturgical movement, 621-624

Michigan Essay or Impartial Observer, 202

Middle West, Flaget's impressions of, 197-199

Military training, Edward Douglass White on draft law, 565, 567-568

Missionary Sisters of the Sacred Heart of St. Francesca Cabrini, founding noted, 469n, 516n

Missions
Indian, 49-51
Oblate, 296-300

Mississippi Valley, Catholic Church in, 81-84

Mobile, Church of the Immaculate Conception, first French parish in the West, 82

Mott, Frank Luther, quoted on attacks on government (1861), 343

Moylan, Stephen, patriotism noted, 169

Mulkern, M. B., resolutions of Buffalo convention, 311-314

Mullaly, John, and slavery, 379

Mullanphy, Bryan, mentioned as Mayor of St. Louis (1847), 290n

Mullanphy, John, St. Louis philanthropist, noted, 290n

Mulledy, Thomas F., S.J., and slavery issue, 383n

Murray, John Courtney, principal author of Declaration on Religious Freedom of Vatican Council II, 683

Nagot, François Charles, S.S., first superior of Sulpicians in United States, 176n

Napoleon III (France), on effect of Civil War and French commercial interests, 371n

National Catholic War Council
Bishops' Program of Social Reconstruction, 589-607

see also National Catholic Welfare Conference

National Catholic Welfare Conference founding, 607-613

National Liturgical Week, noted, 622

National Municipal League, founder noted, 470

National War Labor Board, appointment noted, 597n

Nativism, American, beginning of, 263-265

Neale, Francis, S.J., president of Georgetown College, mentioned, 183n

Negroes
and John Boyle O'Reilly's campaign for, 432-436
Bishops on discrimination against, 646-652
see also Sisters of the Blessed Sacrament for Indian and Colored People; Slavery; Xavier University

New Mexico
impressions of Lamy (1851), 301-303
missions, 15-17

New Orleans, Satolli's visit, 513-530

New Theology of the Era of Vatican Council II, 666-683

New York
Constitution (1777) and religious freedom, 138-139
grant of religious toleration (1683), 116-118
lay trusteeism in (1786), 150-154

New York Committee of State Senate, on *Bishops' Program of Social Reconstruction*, 589

New York *Freeman's Journal*, editor noted, 342

Nogar, Raymond J., author of *Wisdom of Evolution*, book condensation appears on 666-683

North American College at Rome, appeal for, 335-339

North Carolina, Gaston's plea for religious freedom in, 242-246

Notre Dame, University of, broadside on, 291-294

Nuclear warfare, 696

Nugent, Andrew (Capuchin), and lay trusteeism, 151-154

Nursing, sisterhoods in Civil War, 368-370

Oblates of Mary Immaculate, Northwest mission life described, 296-300

O'Brien, William Smith, a leader of Young Irelanders, 332n

O'Brien, William V., O.P., and lay trusteeism, 151

O'Callaghan, Edmund B., noted, 422

O'Callaghan, Eugene M., *see* "Jus"

O'Connell, Eugene, on the Church in San Francisco (1853), 304-306

Index

O'Connor, James, on school issue (1875), 395

O'Connor, Michael, Bp., appeal for North American College at Rome (1858), 335-339

Odin, Jean Marie, Bp., on missions in Texas, 253-258

O'Keefe, Sister Camilla, 368

Olive Branch, writing of, 236-242

Ollivier, Emile, and papal infallibility, 407n

Open Church, 660, 662, 665

The Open Parish, 658-666

Orate Fratres, 621

Orban, Alexis, S.S., and Satolli, 513-530

Oregon and right of private schools, 613-616

O'Reilly, John Boyle
and campaign against racism, 432-436
and Dr. McGlynn, 432, 436

Origin of Species, see Charles Darwin

Our Lady of Gethsemani Abbey (Kentucky), founding, 294-296

Ozanam, Frédéric and Society of St. Vincent de Paul, 288

Padilla, Juan de, O.F.M., murder of, 9-10

Painters
Healy, George P.A., 485-488
LaFarge, John, 441-444

Papacy
relation to temporal affairs explained by Kenrick, 251-253
see also Popes

Papal infallibility, *see* Popes, infallibility

Papal States
and United States diplomatic relations, 374-376
see also Vatican

Parish
"closed," 660, 661, 663, 665
inner city, 659, 663
"open," 663, 664, 665, 666
territorial, 665
traditional, 658
urban, 661, 663, 664

Parish life, in United States, 575-579

Paul III, Pope, *Sublimis Deus* (bull), 7-8

Paul VI, Pope, at the U.N., 697, 702

Paulist Fathers, Hecker's plans for, 339-342

Peace on Earth, see John XXIII

Pelikan, Jaroslav, 658-659

Peñaalver y Cardenas, Luis Ignacio Maria de, on religious conditions in Louisiana (1795), 177-179

Pennsylvania
Declaration of Rights (1776) and religious freedom, 137
missions, 125-128
St. Mary's colonization project, 265-269

Persecution, religious
in Maryland (1654), 114-115
in Maryland (1656), 115-116
in Massachusetts (1647), 111-112
in Massachusetts (1700), 118-120
in Virginia, 110-111

Philadelphia, Holy Trinity Church, first national parish in United States, 160-162

Philip II (Spain), and conquest of Florida, 12-14

Pierce v. Society of Sisters, 613-616

Pilot (Boston), editorial on western Catholic colonization (1856), 311-314

Pious Fund (1875), 398-404

Pius VI, Pope, *Ex Hac apostolicae* (brief), 163-167

Pius IX, Pope, portrait of, by Healy, 485-488

Pius X, Pope
and liturgical movement noted, 624n
Sapienti consilio, missionary status of United States, 576

Pius XII, Pope
Divino Afflante Spiritu, beginning of improvement in Catholic biblical scholarship, 681
Humani Generis, repudiated philosophies of evolutionism, 676; upheld Council of Trent's teaching on monogenism, 682
Sertum laetitiae, on sesquicentennial of the American hierarchy, 629-641

Plenary Council, Baltimore, 1st and 2nd, and necessity of Catholic education, 405, 407n, 408n

Plenary Council, Baltimore, 3d, and forbidden societies, 418-421

Plessis, Joseph Octave, Bp., impressions of Richard, 200-202

Politics, and religion, 616-621

Polk, James Knox, U.S. diplomatic relations with Papal States, 578

Popes, infallibility, 389-395

Portuguese, right of patronage in India, noted, 222n

Poughkeepsie Plan, 479n

Powderly, Terence V., Knights of Labor, noted, 447n

Price, Thomas Frederick, M.M., Catholic Foreign Mission Society of America, 576-580

Propagation of the Faith, *see* Congregatio de Propaganda Fide

Protestant revivalism, impressions of Spalding on, 269-272

Pugin, Augustus Welby, architect, noted, 413

Pullman Company, strike (1894), noted, 489

Purcell, Edward, stand on slavery, 378-383

Index

Index

Schrembs, Joseph, Bp., and the National Catholic Welfare Council, 608
Scott, Winfield, loyalty to the Union noted, 344n
Secession, and the South (1861), 347-356
Second Plenary Council of Baltimore, 387
Secret societies, *see* Societies, secret
Sedella, Antonio de (Capuchin), and Louisiana bishopric, 185
Segale, Sister Blandina, and Colorado missionary activities, 409-412
Selective Draft Law (1918), Edward Douglass White on, 565, 567-568
Semmes, Thomas J., American Bar Association president, noted, 518n
Serra, Junipero, O.F.M.
  departure for California missions, 27-31
  report on San Carlos de Monterey mission, 34-47
Sertum laetitiae (encyclical), on sesquicentennial of American hierarchy, 629-641
Seton, Elizabeth, Blessed, letter planning her religious community, 188-190
Seward, William H.
  American diplomatic relations with Papal States, 374-376
  and French neutrality during Civil War, 370-373
Shea, John Gilmary
  History of the Catholic Church in the United States, 422, 432
  Laetare Medal recipient, noted, 413n
  Prize instituted, 422
Simmons, William J. and the Ku Klux Klan, 616
Sisterhoods, contributions in United States, 409-412
Sisters of the Blessed Sacrament for Indians and Colored People, constitution, 574-576
Sisters of the Good Shepherd (New Orleans), arrival in United States, 519n
Sisters of the Holy Family, founding noted, 528n
Sisters of the Holy Names of Jesus and Mary, and Oregon school law, 613-616
Slavery
  and the Catholic Church, 325-329, 378-383
  controversy (1861), 347-356
  in Mississippi (1858), 325-329
  Taney's views on, 322-325
Smarius, Cornelius, S.J., *Points of Controversy*, 360n
Smith, Alfred E., and religious bigotry of the 1928 campaign, 616-621
Socialism, Abp. Ireland on, 489-494
Social justice, John A. Ryan on, 589-607

Social reform, programs in United States (1919), 589-607
Societies, secret
  and Knights of Labor, 444-457
  and Third Plenary Council of Baltimore, 418-421
  see also American Protective Association; Freemasons
Society, American, *Longinqua oceani*, 499-511
Society of Jesus, *see* Jesuits
Society of St. Vincent de Paul, first conference in the United States, minutes, 288-290
Sorin, Edward, C.S.C., broadside on University of Notre Dame, 291-294
South, and secession (1861), 347-356
Spain
  and Catholic Church in New World, 4-6
  colonization of Florida, 11-12
  and conquest of Florida, 12-14
  territorial claims (1493), 1-3
Spalding, John Lancaster, Bp.
  and Catholic intellectual leadership, 415-417
  and Catholic University of America, 464-466
  noted as one of the founders of Irish Catholic Colonization Association, 317
Spalding, Martin John, Abp.
  and American College, Louvain, 315-317
  impressions of Protestant revivalism, 269-272
Sparks, Jared, noted, 426
Stanley, David S., conversion noted, 376
Starr, Eliza Allen, conversion to Catholicism, 306-310
Starr, Ellen Gates, and liturgical movement noted, 624n
Students, college life (1847), 291-294
Sublimis Deus (bull), 7-8
Suffolk Resolves, 133-136
Sulpicians, in United States, nineteenth century, 175-176, 202-220

Tablet, The (London), *The Vatican: A Weekly Record of the Council*, 408n
Taney, Roger Brooke
  as Chief Justice, noted, 565
  letter on slavery (1857), 322-325
Tax, single, Henry George on, 457-460
Tegahkouita, Catharine, 63-71
Temperance
  in America, Mazzuchelli on, 272-274
  societies in United States (1844), 272-274
Testem benevolentiae (encyclical), on Americanism, 537-547
Texas, Catholic Church in (1841), 253-258
"Things in Dubuque," editorial, 311-314

Index

Thornton, Sir Edward, and Pious Fund, 398

Timon, John, C.M., and Society of St. Vincent de Paul, 289

Tocqueville, Alexis de, on American Catholicism and democracy, 233-236

Toleration, religious
in 1842, 263-265
in 1843, 265-269
in Maryland, 95-98, 112-114
in New York (1683), 116-118

Tordesillas, Treaty of, 3-4

Trappists, in United States, 294-296

Treaty of Ryswick, mentioned, 118

Treaty of Tordesillas, 3-4

Tracy, Jeremiah F., promoter of western Catholic colonization, 313n

Trent, Council of, upheld position of monogenism, 682

Trusteeism, 220-227
in first national parish in United States, 160-162
in New York (1786), 150-154

Ubeda, Luis de, O.F.M., missionary to Indians, 9-10

United States
and papal diplomatic relations, 374-376
world mission of, Brownson on, 383-385

United States, Civil War
and neutrality of France, 370-373
nursing sisters and, 368-370
and slavery, 347-356

United States, Constitution
ratification of
urged by Carroll, 157-159
urged by FitzSimons, 154-156
religious freedom and, 140

United States history, national period, 163-654

United States, Supreme Court and private religious schools (1925), 613-616

United States Catholic Historical Society of New York, founding noted, 428n

United States Catholic Miscellany, prospectus, 227-228

Universal brotherhood, 698

Universalis ecclesiae (bull), 4-6

University of Notre Dame, *see* Notre Dame, University of

Ursulines, Jefferson's reassurance on their future in United States, 184-185

Van de Velde, James, S.J., on conditions in Diocese of Chicago (1849), 300-301

Van Dyke, Henry, quoted on Maurice Egan, 586

Vassar College, charter of, noted, 549

Vatican, American liberty and, Hughes on, 329-335

Vatican: A Weekly Record of the Council, The, 392n

Vatican Council (1870) and papal infallibility, 389-395

Vatican Council II
Declaration on Religious Freedom, 683-696
on world peace, 698

Vay, Peter, Hungarian parish life (1905), 556-560

Velasco, Lúis de, and Florida missions, 11-12

Vietnam, 697, 700

Villeneuve, Alphonse, on Catholic leakage, 481n

Vincennes, Gibault's part in attack on, 141-142

Virginia
laws against Catholics (1642), 110-111
trusteeism in, 220-227

Waldeck-Rousseau, René, and the French Church, 547

Wallace, Alfred R., co-founder of the principle of natural selection, 672

Walmesley, Charles, O.S.B., consecreation of Carroll as bishop, 172

Walsh, James Anthony, Bp., Catholic Foreign Mission Society of America, 576, 580

Walsh, Robert
on literary trends in England (1811), 190-197
prospectus for *American Review of History and Politics*, 190-197

Wappeler, William, S.J., 160

War and Peace: A Pastoral Letter to the Archdiocese of Atlanta, 696-702

Washington, George
bans Guy Fawkes Day, 136
Catholics' congratulations to (1790), 169-172

Watrin, François Philibert, S.J., on banishment of Jesuits from Louisiana, 86-93

Webb, James W., noted as editor of New York *Courier and Enquirer*, 346n

"Webster Replying to Hayne," painting by Healy, 485

Weninger, Francis X., S.J., missionary among German Catholics, 359n

Wharton, Charles H., attack on Catholic faith, 145-147

Whelan, Charles (Capuchin), and lay trusteeism, 151-154

White, Andrew, S.J., on the missions of Maryland, 100-108

White, Edward Douglass
decision regarding divorce, 565-567
decision on selective draft law (1918), 565, 567-568

Whitty, Sister Eulalia, 409n

Index